Publisher's note:
This modern version has been updated from the original text. Words, expressions, and sentence structure have been revised for clarity and readability.

All rights are reserved. No part of this revised text may be reproduced or distributed without the publisher's explicit written consent.

AbidingInk.org

Version: 2025-08-10

THE DOCTRINE OF JUSTIFICATION BY FAITH

JOHN OWEN (1677)
REVISED TO MODERN ENGLISH (2025)

Originally titled:
THE DOCTRINE OF JUSTIFICATION BY FAITH, THROUGH THE IMPUTATION OF THE RIGHTEOUSNESS OF CHRIST; EXPLAINED, CONFIRMED, AND VINDICATED

Preface		1
1.	General Considerations	7
2.	Justification Comes Through Faith	85
3.	Defining Justifying Faith	115
4.	Faith's Role and Object in Justification	135
5.	The Biblical Meaning of Justify	155
6.	Justification as One Complete Act	174
7.	Personal Righteousness and the Final Judgment	195
8.	Imputation of Christ's Righteousness	208
9.	Our Sins Imputed to Christ, Our Surety	229
10.	The Righteousness by Which We Are Justified	270
11.	Our Own Righteousness Cannot Justify	295
12.	God's Requirement of Perfect Obedience	319
13.	Christ's Obedience Imputed to Believers	333
14.	Justification and the Two Covenants	365
15.	No Works Contribute to Justification	370
16.	Justification by Faith Alone	389
17.	Biblical Testimony	396
18.	Gospel Testimonies on Justification	402
19.	Paul's Doctrine of Justification	414
20.	Imputed Righteousness and Holy Living	509
21.	James on Faith and Works: Consistent With Paul	525

Preface

I need not detain the reader with an account of the nature and significance of the doctrine that is the subject of this discourse. Although various persons, even among ourselves, hold different understandings of it, all agree that knowledge of its truth is of the utmost importance to the souls of men. Indeed, anyone who sees themselves as a sinner—and therefore under God's judgment—will long for some understanding of it, since it reveals the only way of deliverance from the evil state and condition in which they find themselves.

I acknowledge that multitudes, though they cannot wholly escape a general conviction of sin and its consequences, fortify their minds against accepting the practical conclusions that follow. Such people, deceiving themselves with empty hopes and imaginations, do not seriously inquire about the means by which they might obtain peace with God and acceptance before Him. They prize the immediate enjoyment of sinful pleasures far more. It is therefore fruitless to recommend the doctrine of justification to those who neither desire nor strive to be justified.

But those who are truly conscious of their estrangement from God, of the evil of their nature and life, and of the dreadful consequences — namely, the wrath of God and eternal punishment due to sin — have nothing more pressing than to learn the divine way of deliverance from this condition. Such persons need no long arguments to convince them of the doctrine's importance; their own plight is sufficient.

I assure them that throughout this discourse my sole intention has been to explore diligently the divine revelation of that way, and the means and causes by which the conscience of a distressed sinner may attain assured peace with God through our Lord Jesus Christ. I value the steady guidance of one soul in this inquiry more highly than the refutation of twenty contentious or fiery disputants.

Having stated the question at the start of our discourse, it is necessary to explain the doctrine itself and the terms commonly used to express it. Yet the main weight of the work lies in interpreting scriptural testimonies and applying them to the experience of believers and to the state of those who seek salvation through Jesus Christ. There are, therefore, a few points I would have the reader consider so they may gain from what follows. At least, if it is not their own fault, they may be freed from prejudices against the doctrine or from a vain opposition to it.

Though many debates currently surround the doctrine of justification and many books oppose it, this discourse was not written to engage any one particular opinion. Some passages may seem to take that direction, but they are of a kind every fair-minded reader will find necessary. I have not attributed views to specific persons, nor misrepresented anyone's words, nor assailed their character, nor taken advantage of presumed biases. I have not distorted opinions, imagined intentions that their words do not express, or sought the empty satisfaction of seeming to triumph over them. Such weaknesses of mind and disorder of affections fuel many recent controversial writings. My aim has been to declare and defend the truth for the instruction and edification of those who sincerely love it, to help them through difficulties that some seek to impose on gospel mysteries, to guide the consciences of those who desire lasting peace with God, and to strengthen believers' faith. This labor is fit to my place in the church, which God has graciously assigned to me.

I have written only what I judge to be true and useful for promoting gospel obedience. The reader should not expect a compilation of others' ideas or a collection of their arguments dressed up in elaborate reasoning or stylish language. This is a plain inquiry into the subjects treated, as revealed in Scripture and proven in their power and efficacy in the minds of believers. The focus is on practical guidance for those coming to God through Jesus Christ for deliverance from the curse of a fallen state and for peace with Him, and on the effect of this approach in producing universal gospel obedience. Anyone who would discuss this appropriately must carefully consider everything they assert from their own mind and experience, and must not set forth to others what they do not hold in their deepest thoughts—especially in their closest encounters with God: in times of danger, in deep afflictions, in preparation for death, and in humble reflections on the infinite distance between God and themselves. Other discussions and debates about justification, lacking these elements, however polished their language, are ultimately insipid and unprofitable, soon dissolving into a fruitless dispute over words.

I am aware that many charge the doctrine I advocate with denying the necessity of personal holiness, good works, and gospel obedience, even asserting that it altogether sets them aside. This was the charge when the apostle Paul first formulated the doctrine clearly; he meets it repeatedly. Yet he sufficiently shows that the doctrine is the chief principle and incentive for all obedience acceptable to God through Jesus Christ, as we shall later demonstrate.

It is conceded that the objective grace of the gospel, as set forth in its doctrine, may be abused where there is no subjective grace in the heart, and the ways in which it acts on the life of a person are often beyond carnal reason. This criticism was raised by the Papists at the Reformation and is still urged today.

Yet, just as it sparked the Reformation itself, it also freed many souls from bondage to superstitious fears and practices that were inconsistent with true gospel obedience. It directed them toward peace with God through Jesus Christ and resulted in genuine holiness and the abundant fruits of the life of God—fruits that were rarely seen among their adversaries.

This same accusation was raised by the Socinians and continues to be leveled against us. I believe, however, that wise and impartial people will give little weight to those charges until the accusers can show better outcomes and fruits from the beliefs they advance in opposition.

The character of those who first formulated the religious system they now follow is well known. One man, who was familiar with them and inclined toward their Antitrinitarian views, asked Socinus and his followers a pointed question: "If this," he said, "is the truth you advocate, how is it that it is only proclaimed by individuals 'without any commendation of piety, without any praised examples of prior lives; indeed, as we often see, by vagabonds and people filled with carnal zeal for contention, and others from camps, courts, and taverns?'"

The harshest criticisms from such people—those who denounce any doctrine they oppose as incompatible with the motives required for godliness—only serve to recommend those doctrines to thoughtful minds.

There is no surer way to undermine religion than to denounce the doctrine of justification by faith alone and other truths about the grace of our Lord Jesus Christ as if they removed the necessity of moral duties, good works, and gospel obedience. Especially damaging is when those who reject these truths give no evidence of the gospel's power or grace in their own hearts and lives.

Therefore, since the entire gospel is the truth that leads to godliness — declaring and exhibiting the grace of God that teaches us that, "denying ungodliness and worldly lusts, we should live soberly, righteously, and godly in the present age," — I recognize that we have fallen into times when fierce disputes over notions, opinions, and practices in religion have brought about a terrible decline in true gospel purity and holiness among the general populace. While holding to the only standard of truth, I readily concede that a secondary evaluation of proposed and contested doctrines should be made according to the lives, conduct, and conversations of those who profess them.

I acknowledge that the doctrine defended in the following discourse can be abused and twisted into licentiousness by corrupt minds — just as any doctrine of God's grace through Jesus Christ may be misused. The way it produces obedience and holiness often lies beyond mere carnal reasoning, and its power may not be apparent to those entirely without a principle of spiritual life. If, when properly understood and received, it cannot demonstrate a beneficial tendency toward godliness and prove necessary for all who truly believe, then I will accept its rejection.

I have learned that several people thought it useful to publish objections to a few passages I wrote years ago on this subject. I am somewhat apprehensive that those same people, or others of a similar disposition, may try to oppose what is set forth here. If they choose to pick at expressions, misinterpret my words, draw unwarranted inferences I do not endorse, attack my character, or seize on incidental remarks and non-essential parts of the discourse to parade a pretence of success and reputation—without Christian moderation, fairness, or integrity—I will treat their writings as no more than trivial nonsense. The same applies to any similar opposition to my other works; I have more important matters than to spend the remainder of my life on such controversial writing, which good people lament and wise men mock. The primary purpose of this discourse is to set forth the doctrine of justification from Scripture and to support it with its testimonies. I will not consider it refuted unless our interpretation of those testimonies and their application to the present argument are disproved by sound rules of interpretation and a better meaning is convincingly established. I have included and explained all other matters I judge necessary for the proper understanding and application of the truth I advocate. These are the few points I wished to remind the reader of.

J. O. From my study, May 30, 1677.

1. General Considerations

To treat the doctrine of justification usefully for its intended purposes—namely, the glory of God in Christ and the peace and advancement of believers' obedience—certain considerations must be kept in view throughout our discourse. Among other relevant points, the following should not be overlooked:

The first duty in this matter is to seek proper relief for the conscience of a sinner who is troubled and distressed by a sense of guilt. Justification is the means by which such a person obtains acceptance before God and a right and title to a heavenly inheritance.

Only what can be spoken to the conscience of a person in that state, or to another's conscience when they are anxious about this issue, is relevant. Therefore, the individual in question—the one to be justified—is, in themselves, ungodly (Romans 4:5) and guilty before God (Romans 3:19). They are subject to the righteous judgment of God, which declares that "those who practice such things are deserving of death" (Romans 1:32). Consequently, such a person is under the curse (Galatians 3:10), and the wrath of God remains on them (John 3:18, 36). In this condition they are without excuse (anapologētos) and have no plea for their own relief; "every mouth may be stopped" (Romans 3:19).

In God's judgment, Scripture says we are "confined all under sin" (Galatians 3:22).

Many evils afflict individuals in this condition, which can be traced back to the two errors of our first parents: first, they foolishly attempted to hide from God, and then, even more foolishly, they blamed Him for their sin. Such are the natural thoughts of those under conviction. But whoever is the subject of the justification we are discussing is brought to the point of crying out, "Sirs, what must I do to be saved?"

In relation to this state and condition of individuals, the inquiry must be made: on what basis does God pardon all their sins, receive them into His favor, pronounce them righteous and acquitted from all guilt, remove the curse, and turn away all His wrath from them, granting them the right and title to eternal life? This is the sole concern of the consciences of sinners in this state. They do not ask about anything other than what they can use to answer or satisfy the justice of God in the commands and curse of the law, and what they can rely on for acceptance with Him unto life and salvation.

The apostle addresses this matter in the third and fourth chapters of the Epistle to the Romans, where he declares the nature of justification and all its causes; this will be shown later. We will also show that the apostle James, in the second chapter of his epistle, does not address this inquiry or provide an answer to it; he speaks of justification in a different sense and for a different purpose.

Since we cannot safely or usefully discuss this doctrine without considering the same ends for which it is declared and to which it is applied in Scripture, we should not be diverted from focusing on this case and its resolution. Our duty is to provide direction, satisfaction, and peace for consciences, rather than indulge the curiosity of notions or the subtlety of disputes. I will therefore avoid philosophical terms and distinctions that only complicate, rather than clarify, this evangelical doctrine. The steady guidance of a believer's mind and conscience, genuinely concerned about the foundation of their peace and acceptance with God, is far more important than refuting ten quarreling disputants.

The inquiry into the basis on which a person may be acquitted of sin and accepted by God leads us to ask whether it rests on something within ourselves—such as our faith and repentance, the renewal of our natures, inherent habits of grace, or the actual works of righteousness we have done or may do—or whether it rests on the obedience, righteousness, satisfaction, and merit of the Son of God, our mediator and surety of the covenant, which is imputed to us. It must be one of these: either something properly our own, however influenced by God's grace, or something not our own, not inherent in us nor wrought by us, yet imputed to us for the forgiveness of our sins and the acceptance of our persons. These two categories cannot be mixed or combined (Romans 11:6). The crux of our inquiry is which of these a convinced sinner should rely upon when appearing before God.

How sinners may seek relief, assuming it is through the righteousness of Christ, and how they can partake in what is not inherently their own to the same benefit as if it were their own, is a distinct consideration. Scripture clearly addresses this, and it is acknowledged in the experience of all who truly believe. We should not be overly concerned with the opinions or arguments of those who have never been thoroughly convinced of sin, or who have never personally "fled for refuge to lay hold of the hope set before us."

These matters must always be kept in view in our exploration of the nature of evangelical justification. Without constant regard for them, we may quickly stray into curious and perplexing questions that do not concern the consciences of guilty sinners. Such questions do not pertain to the substance or truth of this doctrine and should not be mixed with it. Our inquiry is solely focused on the relief of those who are guilty before God and liable to His judgment. This relief is not found in anything within themselves; it is provided outside of them, established in infinite wisdom and grace through the mediation of Christ, His obedience, and His death. This truth is secured in Scripture against all contradiction, as stated in Matthew 11:28.

It is acknowledged that several aspects are necessary to clarify the truth and order of God's grace in this matter. These include the nature of justifying faith, its role and use in justification, the causes of the new covenant, and the true understanding of Christ's mediation and suretyship. All these will be examined. However, we must not be easily drawn into discussions that do not directly guide minds and satisfy souls seeking a stable foundation for acceptance with God. We must avoid losing the comfort and benefit of this crucial evangelical truth in needless and unproductive disputes. Among the many pitfalls encountered in these discussions, this is one to be especially avoided.

The doctrine of justification is essential for guiding Christian practice. No other evangelical truth bears more directly on our obedience. The foundation, reasons, and motives for all our duties toward God are contained in it. Therefore, it should be taught so that people understand it.

Our chief aim in learning this doctrine is to know how to obtain and keep peace with God and to live in a way that is acceptable to Him. It should satisfy minds and consciences. To complicate it with speculative notions and fine distinctions only harms the church's faith.

Mixing evangelical revelation with philosophical categories has historically corrupted religion. The pretense of precision and scholastic skill often handles sacred matters badly. That method confines the spiritual depth of divine truth to low, philosophical terms and produces endless divisions and disputes.

When controversies are pursued through metaphysical considerations and technical terms, the truth that is vital for souls is lost amid senseless words. As a result, those who may agree on justification as Scripture presents it and as believers experience it can be driven into irreconcilable conflict by philosophical definitions and distinctions. People invent interpretations to defend themselves against objections, and even the clearest propositions become confused.

As a result, there appears to be a multitude of opinions among Protestants regarding justification, as charged by Bellarmine and Vasquez, and others on the Roman side, citing Osiander. Yet the faith of these people remains fundamentally the same.

When men enter the realm of disputation, overgrown with thorns of subtlety, perplexing notions, and technicalities, they often aim to entrap others rather than to find truth. In such contests they forget the essential question: how may a guilty sinner obtain favor and acceptance with God? I fear they sometimes dispute in ways they cannot reconcile with their own reflections on their standing before God.

I place little value on the judgments of those who argue from their imagined position before God, especially when their lives and hearts show inconsistency with the grace and truth of this doctrine.

We upset the faith of Christians and disturb the peace of the true church when we quarrel over expressions, terms, and notions that are unnecessary to state the doctrine. The essence of what is revealed can be declared and believed without those disputes.

A careful attention to Scripture together with an honest examination of our own experience is all that is required to understand this truth. Every true believer, taught by God, knows to place full trust in Christ alone and in God's grace through Him for mercy, righteousness, and glory. Such believers are not burdened by the thorns of definitions, distinctions, and exotic philosophical terms that some insist upon.

The Holy Spirit uses many metaphorical expressions when He sets forth the chief parts of our justification, especially the act by which we are justified. Today some regard such language as rude, undisciplined, or even ridiculous. On what ground? Those who deny that such expressions convey more spiritual sense and experience to repentant hearts than the most precise philosophical terms are ignorant of the truth in this matter.

The appropriateness of certain expressions belongs to natural science; but spiritual truths should be taught "which things we also speak, not in words which man's wisdom teaches but which the Holy Spirit teaches, comparing spiritual things with spiritual." God is wiser than man, and the Holy Spirit knows best how to enlighten our minds with the knowledge of evangelical truths we must understand and attain. Any further knowledge or rhetorical skill beyond our duty is not to be prized.

It is therefore pointless to approach the mysteries of the gospel as if we must summon Hilcot and Bricot, Thomas and Gabriel, and the Sententiaries, Summists, and Quodlibetarians of the old Roman peripatetic school to guide us. They would do us no good in the doctrine of justification.

Those scholastics adhered stubbornly to Aristotle's philosophy, which admitted no righteousness except as an inherent habit in ourselves and its acts. They forced the doctrine of justification into that mold. Pighius himself lamented that scholastics, by their thorny questions and definitions, have often obscured this foundational Christian truth rather than illuminating it.

Secondly, a proper consideration of God, the Judge of all, is necessary for stating and understanding the doctrine of justification. Romans 8:33; Isaiah 43:25; 45:25; Psalm 143:2; Romans 3:20 — what thoughts arise in men when they reflect on these passages? Isaiah 33:14; Micah 6:6, 7; Isaiah 6:5 — the plea of Job against his friends and before God is different. Job 40:3-5; 43:4-6 — directions for visiting the sick given long ago — testimonies of Jerome and Ambrose — the sense of men in their prayers, Daniel 9:7, 18; Psalm 143:2; 130:3, 4 — a paraphrase of Augustine on that passage — the prayer of Pelagius — public liturgies.

Secondly, a right consideration of Him with whom we have to do is necessary for forming correct thoughts about justification. Scripture makes this plain: "Who shall bring a charge against God's elect? It is God who justifies" (Romans 8:33). He claims the prerogative to do what belongs to Him.

"I, even I, am He who blots out your transgressions for My own sake; And I will not remember your sins" (Isaiah 43:25). It is hard to imagine any other ground for the pardon of our sins, since He has taken it upon Himself to blot them out for His own sake—"for the Lord's sake" (Daniel 9:17). In Him, "In the Lord all the descendants of Israel shall be justified, and shall glory" (Isaiah 45:25).

Before His tribunal men are either justified or condemned. "Do not enter into judgment with Your servant, for in Your sight no one living is righteous" (Psalm 143:2). The whole work of justification and everything related to it is presented as a legal proceeding before God's court, as we shall see later. "Therefore by the deeds of the law no flesh will be justified in His sight, for by the law is the knowledge of sin" (Romans 3:20). Whatever a man may be before men or angels by his own obedience or by the deeds of the law, in God's sight none can be justified by them.

Anyone who is to stand trial, and whose case has great consequence for them, must consider the judge before whom they appear and by whom their case will finally be decided. If we discuss justification without keeping before our minds the One who will judge or acquit us, we will not know what our plea should be.

Therefore the greatness, majesty, holiness, and sovereign authority of God must always be present in our thinking when we ask how we may be justified before Him.

Yet it is hard to see how some are moved by these considerations when they fiercely defend the role of their own works in justification: "By prayers or price, let them cling to something." Scripture, however, shows what thoughts both sinners and saints have had and will have when they truly apprehend God and His greatness.

A sense of the guilt of sin filled our first parents with shame and fear and drove them to hide from Him. Their descendants show little wisdom under such convictions unless a promise is revealed that offers relief. Those who are secure and do not fear the coming trial are indifferent to whatever doctrine of justification is taught. They prefer the version that flatters their reasoning, shaped by self-conceit and corrupt affections. Whatever they cannot achieve themselves, they assume Christ will somehow supply; that misuse or misunderstanding of Christ's role is one of the greatest sources of sin next to our depravity.

When God reveals His glory to sinners, all their pretensions and contrivances bring dreadful horror and distress. "The sinners in Zion are afraid; Fearfulness has seized the hypocrites: 'Who among us shall dwell with the devouring fire? Who among us shall dwell with everlasting burnings?'" (Isaiah 33:14). This is not peculiar to one class of sinner; these thoughts will rise in every guilty person at some point. Those who now hide from such torment by sensuality, security, or superstition will face it when terror becomes unbearable.

We are warned that "For our God is a consuming fire" (Hebrews 12:29). Men will one day see how vain it is to array their briars and thorns against Him in battle. Under any true view of God's majesty and holiness, convinced sinners will resort to extravagant contrivances. "With what shall I come before the Lord, And bow myself before the High God? Shall I come before Him with burnt offerings, With calves a year old? Will the Lord be pleased with thousands of rams, Ten thousand rivers of oil? Shall I give my firstborn for my transgression, The fruit of my body for the sin of my soul?" (Micah 6:6-7). I do not reckon those who ignore or despise these matters fit to contend about the doctrine of justification.

This is the proper effect of conviction of sin intensified by an awareness of the terror of the Lord who will judge it. In the Papacy this conviction spawned countless superstitious inventions meant to appease troubled consciences. People quickly learn that nothing in their own obedience will justify them before the high and holy God. So they seek refuge in devices He has not commanded, trying to deceive their consciences and find relief by diversions.

This is not only the case with profligate sinners under conviction. Even the best of men, when they have had close and convincing representations of the greatness, holiness, and glory of God, have been cast into the deepest self-abasement. They have seriously renounced all trust and confidence in themselves.

The prophet Isaiah, upon his vision of the glory of the Holy One, cried out, "Woe is me, for I am undone! Because I am a man of unclean lips," (Isaiah 6:5). He was not relieved until he received evidence of the free pardon of sin (verse 7).

Similarly, holy Job, in all his disputes with his friends — who accused him of hypocrisy and held him up as a uniquely guilty sinner —

confidently and persistently vindicated his sincerity, faith, and trust in God against their charges. He insisted so fully in his own integrity that he not only defended his vindication at length but frequently appealed to God Himself regarding the truth of his plea.

Job followed the counsel the apostle James later gave to believers. James's doctrine is shown in Job as clearly as anywhere in Scripture: Job proved his faith by his works and pleaded his justification through them. Just as Job justified himself and was justified by his works, so many think it is the duty of every believer to do the same. His plea for justification by works, in the sense some understand it, was a noble plea, and no controversy has ever been managed on a greater occasion.

At last, Job is called into the immediate presence of God to plead his own case. The dispute is no longer the one between him and his friends—whether he was a hypocrite, or whether his faith and trust in God were sincere—but the matter is stated between God and Job. It appears Job may have assumed too much on his own behalf. The question is reduced to this: on what grounds might he be justified in the sight of God?

To prepare him for a proper judgment in this matter, God reveals His glory and instructs him in the greatness of His majesty and power. He does this repeatedly, because we are often slow to accept right conceptions of God when we are under temptation.

The holy man quickly acknowledged that the state of the case had utterly changed. All his previous pleas—his faith, hope, trust in God, and his claims to sincerity in obedience—were utterly set aside. He saw they were not valid pleas at the tribunal before which he now stood. In deepest self-abasement and abhorrence he turned to sovereign grace and mercy.

Job answered the Lord, saying, "Behold, I am vile; What shall I answer You? I lay my hand over my mouth. Once I have spoken, but I will not answer; Yes, twice, but I will proceed no further." (Job 40:3-5). Again he said, "Listen, please, and let me speak; You said, 'I will question you, and you shall answer Me.' I have heard of You by the hearing of the ear, But now my eye sees You. Therefore I abhor myself, And repent in dust and ashes." (Job 42:4-6).

Let any man place himself in the condition Job was in — face to face with God — and consider what God truly speaks to him in His Word. Think what one would answer to the charge He brings, and what the best plea would be before His tribunal, if one seeks to be justified.

I do not believe any living person had better grounds to plead for an interest in his own faith and obedience in justification before God than Job had. Though he may have lacked the scholastic skill to argue with the Jesuits' subtle distinctions, I fear that, however well equipped we may be with clever arguments, we shall not safely venture farther before God than he dared.

There was an ancient direction for the visitation of the sick, attributed to Anselm and published by Casparus Ulenbergius, which expresses a clearer understanding of these matters than some now possess. The question to the sick man runs: "Do you believe that you cannot be saved except through the death of Christ?" He answers, "Yes."

Then he is told: "Therefore, while your soul remains in you, place all your confidence in this death alone; trust in nothing else; commit yourself entirely to this death; cover yourself entirely with this alone; immerse yourself wholly in this death. And if the Lord wishes to judge you, say, 'Lord, I place the death of our Lord Jesus Christ between me and Your judgment; otherwise, I will not contend with You.' And if He says to you that you are a sinner, say, 'I place the death of our Lord Jesus Christ between me and my sins.' If He says that you deserve damnation, say, 'Lord, I place the death of our Lord Jesus Christ between You and my evil merits; I offer His merits for the merit that I should have but do not.' If He says that He is angry with you, say, 'Lord, I place the death of our Lord Jesus Christ between me and Your anger.'"

Those who provided these directions understood what it is to appear before the tribunal of God. They knew how unsafe it is for us to insist on anything in ourselves.

Hence Anselm's words in his Meditations: "My conscience has deserved damnation, and my repentance is not sufficient for satisfaction; but it is certain that Your mercy surpasses all offense." I prefer that to some more recent directions in the Roman church.

For example, Johan Polandus suggested to a sick man this prayer: "Lord Jesus, I beseech You to join my obedience with all that You have done and suffered out of perfect love and obedience, and with the riches of satisfaction and merits of love, offer it to the eternal Father." Another author advised: "You, O roseate throng of martyrs, offer for me now and at the hour of my death the merits, faithfulness, constancy, and precious blood, shed for the salvation of all."

Jerome, long before Anselm, spoke to the same purpose: "When the day of judgment or death comes, all hands will be dissolved; to which it is said in another place, 'Strengthen the weak hands, And make firm the feeble knees.' But all hands will be melted down because no work will be found worthy of God's justice, and no flesh will be justified in His sight. Whence the prophet says in the psalm, 'If You, O Lord, should mark iniquities, O Lord, who could stand?'"

And Ambrose, to the same purpose, urged: "Let no man arrogate anything to himself, let no man glory in his merits, let no man boast of his power; let us all hope to find mercy through our Lord Jesus, for we shall all stand before His judgment seat. From Him will I seek pardon; from Him will I ask for indulgence. What other hope is there for sinners?"

Therefore, if men are diverted from a continual regard to the greatness, holiness, and majesty of God by their inventions in the heat of disputation; if they forget to reverentially consider what will become of them and what they may turn to when they stand before His tribunal, they may engage in such notions as they dare not uphold in their own personal trials. "How shall man be just with God?" It has been observed that the schoolmen themselves, in their meditations and devotional writings, where they had immediate thoughts of God, spoke quite differently about justification before God than they did in their fiery, philosophical disputes regarding it. I would prefer to learn what some individuals truly believe about their own justification from their prayers rather than their writings. I do not recall ever hearing a good man in his prayers use any expressions about justification, pardon of sin, and righteousness before God that included any plea based on anything in themselves. The prayer of Daniel has been the substance of their supplications: "O Lord, righteousness belongs to You, but to us shame of face. We do not present our supplications before You for our righteousnesses, but for Your great mercies. O Lord, hear; O Lord, forgive; for Your own sake, O my God" (Daniel 9:7, 18, 19).

Or the psalmist's cry: "Do not enter into judgment with Your servant, For in Your sight no one living is righteous." (Psalm 143:2) Or again: "If You, O Lord, should mark iniquities, O Lord, who could stand? But there is forgiveness with You, That You may be feared." (Psalm 130:3-4).

Augustine's exposition on these words is remarkable. He speaks of David and applies the words to himself: David cries out under the weight of his iniquities. He examined his life and found it everywhere covered with sin. Wherever he turned, he found nothing good in himself. Seeing so many and such great sins, he exclaimed, "If You, O Lord, should mark iniquities, O Lord, who could stand?" He perceived that nearly the whole of human life is surrounded by sins; consciences are accused by their own thoughts; no pure heart can presume upon its own righteousness. Since none can be found righteous, every heart should rely on the mercy of the Lord God and say to Him, "If You, O Lord, should mark iniquities, O Lord, who could stand?" For with You there is forgiveness.

While we may and ought to represent to God in our supplications our faith or what we believe on this matter, I greatly question whether some can find it in their hearts to pray and plead before Him all the arguments and distinctions by which they assert a role for our works and obedience in our justification. Few would be content to "enter into judgment" with God on the basis of those conclusions.

Nor will many be satisfied with the prayer Pelagius taught the widow, which was objected to him at the Diospolitan Synod: "You know, O Lord, how holy, how innocent, how pure from all deceit and rapine are the hands I stretch forth to You; how just, how unspotted with evil, how free from lying are the lips with which I pour forth prayers to You, that You would have mercy on me."

Yet, even though he taught her to plead her own purity, innocence, and righteousness before God, he did so not as the basis for absolute justification but merely as the condition for obtaining mercy. I have not observed any public liturgies — except the mass-book, which frequently refers to the merits and intercession of the saints — that guide individuals in their prayers before God to plead anything for their acceptance with Him, or as the means or condition of acceptance, except grace, mercy, and the righteousness and blood of Christ alone.

Therefore, I cannot help but conclude that it is best (others may think differently) for those who wish to teach or learn the doctrine of justification to place their consciences in the presence of God and their persons before His tribunal. After carefully considering His greatness, power, majesty, righteousness, holiness, and the terror of His glory and sovereign authority, they should inquire what Scripture and their own condition direct them to as their relief and refuge, and what plea they ought to make for themselves. Secret thoughts of God and ourselves, quiet meditations, the spirit's conduct in humble supplications, and preparations for death to appear before God speak of different things than many contend for.

Thirdly, a proper understanding of our apostasy from God, the corruption of our nature as a result, the power and guilt of sin, and the holiness of the law is necessary for a correct view of the doctrine of justification. The apostle's method in this regard is outlined in Romans chapters 1, 2, and 3. The foundations of both ancient and modern Pelagianism lie in the denial of these truths. We see this denial show itself in the boasting of perfection on the same grounds.

A clear understanding of the seriousness of our apostasy from God, the corruption of our nature, the power and guilt of sin, and the holiness and severity of the law is essential for grasping the doctrine of justification. Hence the apostle begins with a comprehensive discourse to convince those seeking justification of these realities, as seen in Romans chapters 1, 2, and 3. He provides rules, prescribes a method, and outlines the intended outcomes, stating generally that "the righteousness of God is revealed from faith to faith," and that "The just shall live by faith" (Romans 1:17). However, he does not specify the causes, nature, and means of our justification until he has thoroughly demonstrated that all men are confined under sin and shown how dire their condition is. Ignorance or denial of these truths lays the groundwork for all misconceptions about God's grace.

Pelagianism, in its original form and in all its current branches, arises from failing to recognize the gravity of our original apostasy from God and its consequences in the universal corruption of our nature. Its adherents deny any need for Christ's satisfaction or the efficacy of divine grace for our recovery or restoration. Consequently, they reject the primary purposes of the missions of both the Son of God and the Holy Spirit, leading in practice to a denial of the deity of the former and the personality of the latter. They treat the fall as minor and its consequences as easily remedied. They see little evil in the unavoidable aspects of our nature and therefore think it unnecessary to be freed or justified by mere favor apart from their own efforts; they also deny God's efficacious grace in sanctification and obedience.

When such notions are accepted, they divert people's minds from a proper apprehension of the state and guilt of sin. Consciences are prevented from feeling the terror of the Lord and the curse of the law. Justification then becomes a concept to be treated lightly or altered as circumstances permit. This leads to the present differences about it — differences that are sometimes genuine and not merely variations in how learned men express their thoughts.

Some outright deny the imputation of the actual apostasy and transgression of Adam, the head of our nature, by which his sin became the sin of the world. This denial undermines the very grounds the apostle uses to demonstrate the necessity of our justification — being made righteous by the obedience of another — and all the arguments in support of that doctrine found in the fifth chapter of his Epistle to the Romans. Socinus, in De Servatore, part IV, chapter 6, admits that this passage strongly supports the doctrine of justification by the imputation of Christ's righteousness. Therefore he employs various tactics to oppose the imputation of Adam's sin to his natural descendants, knowing that acceptance of that truth would inevitably lead to the imputation of Christ's righteousness to His spiritual offspring, as the apostle's argument implies.

Some deny the corruption and depravity of our nature that resulted from our apostasy from God and the loss of His image. If they do not wholly deny it, they downplay its significance and treat it as a minor concern. They may allow for some disorder of the soul arising from the misdirection of our affections, which produces the vicious habits and customs of the world. They claim the guilt associated with this disorder is minimal and thus the danger is not great. Many of them hold that any spiritual filth or stain in our nature has been entirely washed away by baptism.

The deformity of the soul that resulted from losing the image of God — its harmony and beauty when all faculties acted toward their intended end; the enmity toward God that arose in our minds; the darkness that clouded and blinded our understanding; the spiritual death that affected the whole soul; the total alienation from the life of God; the impotence toward good; the inclination toward evil; the deceitfulness of sin; and the influence of corrupt desires — are all dismissed by such people as empty notions or fables. It is unsurprising that they regard imputed righteousness as a mere illusion, since they treat the very things that demonstrate its necessity as fanciful. There is little hope of convincing these men to value Christ's righteousness as imputed to them while they remain ignorant of their own inherent unrighteousness. Until they gain a truer understanding of themselves, they will care very little to know Christ at all.

Against such men, the doctrine of justification must be defended, for we are obliged to contend for the faith once delivered to the saints and to silence the mouths of those who oppose it. But to seek to satisfy them while they are under the influence of such misconceptions is a futile task. As our Savior said to those to whom He had declared the necessity of regeneration, "If I have told you earthly things and you do not believe, how will you believe if I tell you heavenly things?" (John 3:12). Likewise, if men will not believe those things that are evident and known to them, how can they be expected to accept the heavenly mysteries that depend on acknowledging truths within themselves which they refuse to recognize?

Some are so far removed from any concern for a perfect righteousness to be imputed to them that they boast of a perfection in themselves. The Pelagians of old claimed a sinless perfection before God, even while acknowledging their sinful failures in the sight of men, as Jerome notes in *Dialogues*, book II, and Augustine records in *Against Julian*, book II, chapter 8.

Such individuals are not "subjecta capacia auditionis evangelicae" (subjects capable of hearing the gospel).

While people lack a sense, in their hearts and consciences, of the spiritual disorder of their souls and of the secret, ongoing operations of sin that deceive and injure them, they fail to see how these workings obstruct what is good and promote what is evil. These hidden motions defile all they do by the flesh's lust against the Spirit—even if no outward acts of sin or obvious omissions follow.

Those who do not engage in a continual, watchful conflict against the first movements of sin, who do not find these stirrings to be their greatest burden and sorrow in this life, and who do not cry out for deliverance, will confidently reject and condemn the teaching that we are justified by the obedience and righteousness of Christ imputed to us. No one will seek a righteousness that is not their own when they believe they already possess a righteousness of their own.

Ignorance of these truths deceives people into thinking they can be justified before God by their personal righteousness. Were they aware of these realities, they would quickly see the imperfections in their best actions, the frequency of sinful irregularities in their thoughts, and the disorders in their affections. They would perceive how unsuitable all they are and do is — internally and outwardly — when measured against the greatness and holiness of God, and their confidence in their own righteousness for justification would be diminished.

Through these and similar presumptuous ideas held by unenlightened minds, consciences are kept from feeling a proper sense of sin or from seriously considering how to gain acceptance before God.

Neither the holiness or terror of the Lord, nor the severity of the law — which demands a righteousness according to its commands — nor the promise of the gospel, which offers a righteousness from God in response, can move those whose thoughts are clouded by trivial notions of sin. Nor can the uncertainty of their minds in trials and surprises, since they lack a stable foundation for peace, nor the constant inward agitation of their consciences — unless seared or hardened by the deceitfulness of sin — persuade them to seek the only hope set before them or to engage truly with the sole way of deliverance and salvation.

Therefore, to teach or learn the doctrine of justification properly, we must grasp the magnitude of our rebellion against God, have a true sense of the guilt of sin, and a profound experience of its power in relation to God's holiness and law. We have no business with those who, through pride, have lost sight of their own miserable condition.

As Augustine said, "Nature is so corrupted that it is a greater fault not to see it." Those who are well have no need of a physician, but those who are sick. Those who are pierced to the heart by their sin and cry out, "Sirs, what must I do to be saved?" will understand what we say. Against others, we must stand and defend the truth as God enables us.

It can be shown that, as people elevate views that minimize sin, they lessen their regard for the grace of our Lord Jesus Christ. Conversely, as unbelief produces contempt for the person and righteousness of

Christ, people inevitably seek to justify themselves by minimizing sin. Thus minds are subtly diverted from Christ and led to trust in themselves. They may have a vague notion of Him as a relief they do not fully grasp, yet they live in a false confidence of human wisdom. This is what the better philosophers teach: "The only good is to trust in oneself for the sake of a blessed life," as Seneca wrote in his thirty-first letter.

Consequently, the inward sanctifying grace of God is often disregarded along with the imputation of Christ's righteousness. The essence of their faith and the arguments that support it can be summarized by the learned Roman orator: "No one has ever attributed virtue to God; indeed, rightly so. For we are justly praised for virtue, and we rightly glory in virtue, which would not happen if we did not possess it as a gift from God, but from ourselves," as Cicero states in *On the Nature of the Gods*.

Fourthly, the opposition between works and grace concerning justification requires careful attention. The apostle's method in the Epistle to the Romans brings this opposition into view. There are alternative schemes that contradict this teaching, and we must weigh the testimonies that support this opposition.

We should also note the distinctions some make to evade the issue, the uselessness of those distinctions, and the resolution of the matter as presented by Bellarmine, who appeals to Daniel 9:18 and Luke 17:10.

The opposition Scripture establishes between grace and works, especially regarding our justification, is important. This opposition does not concern the essence, nature, or coherence of grace and works in the broader scope of salvation, nor does it deny our duty of obedience. Rather, it is specifically about the way justification is accounted before God.

At this point, I do not intend to present specific scriptural testimonies about their precise meanings or the mind of the Holy Spirit, which will be treated more fully later. For now, I aim to observe how Scripture directs our understanding and how our own experience corresponds with that guidance.

The primary foundation of this doctrine, as all will agree, is found in Paul's Epistles to the Romans and Galatians, with Hebrews also contributing. It is most clearly expressed in Romans, where the apostle treats it extensively — doctrinally and in controversy with opponents. It is worth considering the order he follows in unfolding this doctrine and the principles on which his arguments rest.

He begins by laying down a foundational principle or general thesis that sums up what he will explain and prove: that in the gospel, "For in it the righteousness of God is revealed from faith to faith; as it is written, 'The just shall live by faith'" (Romans 1:17). All who have any knowledge of God and themselves, as they must, seek righteousness to varying degrees. They view righteousness as the sole means of establishing a right relationship with God.

The common assumption is that this righteousness must be their own — internal and performed by them — as Romans 10:3 expresses. This reflects the tone of natural conscience and the law and aligns with all philosophical notions about righteousness. Though the law and the prophets testify to a "righteousness of God apart from the law" (Romans 3:21), that testimony remains hidden to ordinary understanding.

Since righteousness is what everyone seeks, it is futile to expect the law, natural conscience, or philosophy to point to any righteousness other than the habits and works inherent to us. Neither law, conscience, nor reason recognizes any other kind. Against this self-sought righteousness, necessitated by the law and presumed by conscience and reason, the apostle proclaims that the gospel reveals another righteousness—the righteousness of another, the righteousness of God—and that it is disclosed "from faith to faith." Not only is this righteousness distinct from the others, but the way we participate in it—its communication to us "from faith to faith" (God's unfolding in revelation and our faith in accepting it)—is itself a remarkable disclosure.

Where the Papists would expect righteousness to proceed from works to works—from the internal work of grace to external acts of obedience—the apostle answers, "No; it is from faith to faith."

This is the general thesis the apostle proposes for confirmation. He seems to exclude from justification everything except the righteousness of God and the faith of believers.

To establish this, he reviews every person who might claim righteousness or seek it, and every means by which they hope to obtain it. He declares the failure of all individuals and the insufficiency of all means to produce a righteousness of our own before God.

He begins with the Gentiles. He considers their conceptions of God, their religious practices, and the conduct that flows from those views. From these observations he concludes that they neither were nor could be justified before God, and that they all, most deservedly, stand condemned to death.

Any claim that someone can be justified and saved without the revelation of the righteousness of God in the gospel "from faith to faith" contradicts his whole argument in Romans 1—from verse 19 to the end.

He then turns to the Jews, who had the written law and special privileges—especially circumcision, the outward seal of God's covenant. He argues, on many grounds, that they too are excluded from justification before God by their privileges or by their observance of them.

In Romans 2 he clearly excludes both Jews and Gentiles from any claim to righteousness before God. Both groups failed by their own standards: the Gentiles against the light of nature, the Jews against the law. Therefore neither could attain the righteousness their standards prescribed.

He then extends the argument to all people, showing the universal corruption of human nature and the dreadful effects of that corruption in men's hearts and lives, as he sets out in Romans 3. He demonstrates that if all are guilty, it follows necessarily that all are under sin and fall short of righteousness.

Having shown this for persons, he turns to the means by which men imagine they might be made righteous. Since the law is God's rule for our obedience, and the works of the law are what it requires, some might hope the law and its works can ground justification. He therefore examines the nature, purpose, and use of the law, and shows its complete inadequacy as a means of justification before God, as he declares in Romans 3:19–20.

An objection may be raised: perhaps the law and its works fail only when obeyed by unregenerate people in their natural state, without the promised grace. But what of those who are regenerate and believe— whose faith and works God accepts? To meet this, the apostle brings forward two of the most eminent believers of the Old Testament, Abraham and David, and shows that all works were excluded from their justification, as he explains in Romans 4.

From these premises and this order of argument he concludes decisively that, so far as anything within ourselves is concerned—

anything we can do, or anything that can be wrought in us—we are guilty before God, deserving of death, confined under sin, and have our mouths stopped so that we have no excuse.

We have no righteousness to offer before God, and all the means by which we hope to obtain it are utterly inadequate.

He then asks how anyone can be delivered from this condition and be justified in God's sight. He mentions nothing of our own merits. He points only to faith, by which we receive atonement.

He says we are justified by "even the righteousness of God, through faith in Jesus Christ," and that we are "justified freely by His grace through the redemption that is in Christ Jesus" (Romans 3:22-24). Not content with this statement about how guilty, convicted sinners may be justified—namely, that it is by "the righteousness of God is revealed from faith to faith; being justified freely by His grace through the redemption that is in Christ Jesus," and by Him whom God set forth "as a propitiation by His blood"—the apostle goes on at once to exclude anything in us that could claim a part in it. Such a claim would contradict the righteousness of God as revealed in the gospel and testified by the law and the prophets.

How contrary to the apostle's design are those who maintain that before the law men were justified by obedience to the light of nature or by certain particular revelations, and that after the law they were justified by obedience to its commands! They even hold that the heathen might obtain like benefits by following reason—an assertion no impartial reader can defend without contention.

The apostle's declaration, as the Holy Spirit intended it, fits the whole tenor of Scripture. God's grace, the promise of mercy, the free pardon of sin, the blood of Christ, His obedience, and the righteousness of God in Him—all received through faith—are consistently presented as the cause and means of our justification.

This stands opposed to any claim we might make about ourselves, even our best obedience or the highest degree of personal righteousness. Whenever duties, obedience, or personal righteousness are mentioned in relation to justification, they are renounced as grounds, and the emphasis shifts entirely to sovereign grace and mercy. Many passages could be cited to confirm this.

The foundation of the whole matter is set in the first promise, which shows the overthrow of the devil's work by the suffering of the woman's Seed as the only remedy for sinners and the sole way to recover God's favor: "He shall bruise your head, And you shall bruise His heel" (Genesis 3:15).

"And [Abraham] believed in the Lord, and He accounted it to him for righteousness" (Genesis 15:6). "Aaron shall lay both his hands on the head of the live goat, and confess over it all the iniquities of the children of Israel, and all their transgressions, concerning all their sins, putting them on the head of the goat; and the goat shall bear on itself all their iniquities to an uninhabited land; and he shall release the goat in the wilderness" (Leviticus 16:21–22).

"I will go in the strength of the Lord God; I will make mention of Your righteousness, of Yours only" (Psalm 71:16). "If You, Lord, should mark iniquities, O Lord, who could stand? But there is forgiveness with You, That You may be feared" (Psalm 130:3–4). "Do not enter into judgment with Your servant, For in Your sight no one living is righteous" (Psalm 143:2).

"Behold, He puts no trust in His angels; He charges His angels with folly; how much less those who dwell in houses of clay, whose foundation is in the dust?" (Job 4:18-19). "Fury is not in Me. Who would set thorns and briers against Me in battle? I would go through them; I would burn them together. Or let him take hold of My strength, that he may make peace with Me, and he shall make peace with Me" (Isaiah 27:4-5).

"'Surely in the Lord I have righteousness and strength. To Him men shall come, And all shall be ashamed Who are incensed against Him. In the Lord all the descendants of Israel Shall be justified, and shall glory.'" (Isaiah 45:24-25). "All we like sheep have gone astray; We have turned, every one, to his own way; And the Lord has laid on Him the iniquity of us all. By His knowledge My righteous Servant shall justify many, For He shall bear their iniquities." (Isaiah 53:6, 11)

"Now this is His name by which He will be called: THE LORD OUR RIGHTEOUSNESS." (Jeremiah 23:6). "But we are all like an unclean thing, And all our righteousnesses are like filthy rags;" (Isaiah 64:6). "To finish the transgression, To make an end of sins, To make reconciliation for iniquity, To bring in everlasting righteousness," (Daniel 9:24)

"But as many as received Him, to them He gave the right to become children of God, to those who believe in His name:" (John 1:12). "And as Moses lifted up the serpent in the wilderness, even so must the Son of Man be lifted up, that whoever believes in Him should not perish but have eternal life." (John 3:14-15)

"Therefore let it be known to you, brethren, that through this Man is preached to you the forgiveness of sins; and by Him everyone who believes is justified from all things from which you could not be justified by the law of Moses." (Acts 13:38-39). "that they may receive forgiveness of sins and an inheritance among those who are sanctified by faith in Me." (Acts 26:18)

"being justified freely by His grace through the redemption that is in Christ Jesus, whom God set forth as a propitiation by His blood, through faith, to demonstrate His righteousness, because in His forbearance God had passed over the sins that were previously committed, to demonstrate at the present time His righteousness, that He might be just and the justifier of the one who has faith in Jesus. Where is boasting then? It is excluded. By what law? Of works? No, but by the law of faith. Therefore we conclude that a man is justified by faith apart from the deeds of the law." (Romans 3:24-28)

"For if Abraham was justified by works, he has something to boast about, but not before God. For what does the Scripture say? 'Abraham believed God, and it was accounted to him for righteousness.' Now to him who works, the wages are not counted as grace but as debt. But to him who does not work but believes on Him who justifies the ungodly, his faith is accounted for righteousness. Just as David also describes the blessedness of the man to whom God imputes righteousness apart from works, saying, 'Blessed are those whose lawless deeds are forgiven, And whose sins are covered; Blessed is the man to whom the Lord shall not impute sin.'" (Romans 4:2-8)

"But the free gift is not like the offense. For if by the one man's offense many died, much more the grace of God and the gift by the grace of the one Man, Jesus Christ, abounded to many. And the gift is not like that which came through the one who sinned. For the judgment which came from one offense resulted in condemnation, but the free gift which came from many offenses resulted in justification. For if by the one man's offense death reigned through the one, much more those who receive abundance of grace and of the gift of righteousness will reign in life through the one, Jesus Christ. Therefore, as through one man's offense judgment came to all men, resulting in condemnation, even so through one Man's righteous act the free gift came to all men, resulting in justification of life. For as by one man's disobedience many were made sinners, so also by one Man's obedience many will be made righteous." (Romans 5:15-19)

"There is therefore now no condemnation to those who are in Christ Jesus, who do not walk according to the flesh, but according to the Spirit. For the law of the Spirit of life in Christ Jesus has made me free from the law of sin and death. For what the law could not do in that it was weak through the flesh, God did by sending His own Son in the likeness of sinful flesh, on account of sin: He condemned sin in the flesh, that the righteous requirement of the law might be fulfilled in us who do not walk according to the flesh but according to the Spirit." (Romans 8:1-4)

"For Christ is the end of the law for righteousness to everyone who believes." (Romans 10:4). "And if by grace, then it is no longer of works; otherwise grace is no longer grace. But if it is of works, it is no longer grace; otherwise work is no longer work." (Romans 11:6)

"But of Him you are in Christ Jesus, who became for us wisdom from God—and righteousness and sanctification and redemption" (1 Corinthians 1:30). "For He made Him who knew no sin to be sin for us, that we might become the righteousness of God in Him." (2 Corinthians 5:21)

"knowing that a man is not justified by the works of the law but by faith in Jesus Christ, even we have believed in Christ Jesus, that we might be justified by faith in Christ and not by the works of the law; for by the works of the law no flesh shall be justified" (Galatians 2:16).

"But that no one is justified by the law in the sight of God is evident, for 'the just shall live by faith.' Yet the law is not of faith, but 'the man who does them shall live by them.' Christ has redeemed us from the curse of the law, having become a curse for us (for it is written, 'Cursed is everyone who hangs on a tree')" (Galatians 3:11-13).

"For by grace you have been saved through faith, and that not of yourselves; it is the gift of God, not of works, lest anyone should boast.

For we are His workmanship, created in Christ Jesus for good works, which God prepared beforehand that we should walk in them" (Ephesians 2:8-10).

"Yet indeed I also count all things loss for the excellence of the knowledge of Christ Jesus my Lord, for whom I have suffered the loss of all things, and count them as rubbish, that I may gain Christ and be found in Him, not having my own righteousness, which is from the law, but that which is through faith in Christ, the righteousness which is from God by faith" (Philippians 3:8-9).

"who has saved us and called us with a holy calling, not according to our works, but according to His own purpose and grace which was given to us in Christ Jesus before time began" (2 Timothy 1:9).

"that having been justified by His grace we should become heirs according to the hope of eternal life" (Titus 3:7).

"Once at the end of the ages He has appeared to put away sin" (Hebrews 9:26, 28). "When He had by Himself purged our sins, sat down at the right hand of the Majesty on high" (Hebrews 1:3). "For by one offering He has perfected forever those who are being sanctified" (Hebrews 10:14).

"The blood of Jesus Christ His Son cleanses us from all sin" (1 John 1:7). Therefore, "To Him who loved us and washed us from our sins in His own blood, and has made us kings and priests to His God and Father, to Him be glory and dominion forever and ever. Amen" (Revelation 1:5-6).

These are some of the passages that come to mind where Scripture sets forth the grounds, causes, and reasons for our acceptance with God. The specific meaning of many of these verses, and the truth they convey, will be examined later. For now we will take a general overview.

Everything in and of ourselves, under any consideration, appears to be excluded from our justification before God, with the exception of faith, by which we receive His grace and atonement. Conversely, our whole acceptance with Him seems attributed to grace, mercy, the obedience and blood of Christ, in opposition to our own worth, righteousness, or works. I cannot help but think that a convinced sinner, if not biased by prejudice, will rarely be mistaken about which of these opposing ideas he should look to for justification.

However, it is argued that these statements should not be taken absolutely or without qualification. Various distinctions are necessary to discern the mind of the Holy Spirit and the meaning of Scripture regarding the ascriptions to grace and the exclusions of the law, our own works, and our righteousness from justification. For example:

The law can be categorized as either moral or ceremonial. The ceremonial is excluded from any role in our justification; the moral is not.

Works required by the law can be performed either before faith, without the aid of grace, or after believing, with the help of the Holy Spirit. The former are excluded from our justification, but not the latter.

Works of obedience performed after receiving grace may be sincere or absolutely perfect, according to what was originally required in the covenant of works. The latter are excluded from any role in our justification, but not the former.

There are two kinds of justification before God in this life—a first and a second—and we must carefully consider which of these justifications Scripture is referring to.

Justification may be considered in terms of its beginning or its continuation, and thus it has different causes under these different respects.

Works may be considered either as meritorious ex condigno, meaning their merit arises from their own intrinsic worth, or ex congruo, in relation to the covenant and promise of God. The former are excluded, at least from the first justification; the latter may apply to both the first and the second.

Moral causes can be various: preparatory, dispositive, meritorious, conditionally efficient, or merely sine quibus non. We must carefully investigate in what sense, and under what notion of cause or causes, our works are excluded from our justification, and under what notions they are necessary.

Each of these distinctions requires further elaboration, and learned men have indeed made use of them. Such arguments can be presented so artfully that few can discern their true substance or decide on which side the truth lies.

But someone who is genuinely convicted of sin and conscious of what it means to stand before the holy God—seeking to know how to be accepted by Him—will likely answer these distinctions, "You have done well, but I am much more uncertain than before." My inquiry is: How shall I come before the Lord and bow myself before the Most High God? How shall I escape the wrath to come? What shall I plead in judgment before God to be absolved, acquitted, justified? Where shall I find a righteousness that will endure the trial of His presence? If I were burdened with a thousand of these distinctions, I fear they would become thorns and briars that He would pass through and consume.

The inquiry, therefore, is whether, considering the state of the person to be justified as previously described, and the proposals for relief in our justification, it is wiser and safer for such a person seeking justification before God to place their entire trust and confidence in sovereign grace and the mediation of Christ, or to retain some confidence in their own graces, duties, works, and obedience.

To resolve this significant difference, we will refer to one of our most learned adversaries. He states his determination clearly: "Due to the uncertainty of our own righteousness and the danger of vain glory, it is the safest course to place our entire trust in the mercy and kindness of God alone" (Bellarmin, On Justification, Book V, Chapter 7, Proposition 3).

He supports this conclusion with two testimonies from Scripture, which he could have supplemented with many more. The first is from Daniel 9:18: "for we do not present our supplications before You because of our righteous deeds, but because of Your great mercies." The second is from our Savior in Luke 17:10: "When you have done all those things which you are commanded, say, 'We are unprofitable servants.'"

After confirming his resolution with various testimonies from the church fathers, he concludes with this dilemma: "Either a man has true merits, or he does not. If he does not, he is dangerously deceived if he trusts in anything but the mercy of God alone, and he leads himself astray by relying on false merits. If he does have merits, he loses nothing by not looking to them but trusting in God alone. Therefore, whether a man has good works or not, regarding his justification before God, it is best and safest for him not to regard them or place any trust in them."

If this is the case, he might have spared himself the effort he spent writing his convoluted books on justification, whose main purpose is to mislead people into a contrary opinion. Likewise, those who vigorously argue for some form of interest in our own duties and obedience regarding our justification before God may also find their efforts unnecessary, for it will ultimately be revealed that they place their entire trust and confidence in the grace of God through Jesus Christ alone. What is the purpose of laboring and striving with endless disputes, arguments, and distinctions to elevate our duties and obedience to some role in our justification before God, if, when all is said and done, we find it safest to abhor ourselves, like Job, in the presence of God, and to turn to sovereign grace and mercy, like the publican, placing all our confidence in them through the obedience and blood of Christ?

Thus died the great emperor, Charles V, as Thuanus recounts in his Novissima. He reasoned with himself: "I am indeed unworthy to obtain the kingdom of heaven by my own merits; but my Lord God, who possesses it by two rights—by the inheritance of the Father and the merit of His passion—has chosen to be satisfied with one right for Himself and to freely grant me the other. By His gift, I lay claim to it, and in this confidence, I shall not be confounded; for the oil of mercy is poured only into the vessel of faith. This trust is that of a man who is despairing in himself and relying on his Lord; otherwise, to trust in one's own works or merits is not faith but treachery. Sins are blotted out by the mercy of God; therefore, we ought to believe that our sins can only be pardoned by Him alone, against whom we have sinned, in whom there is no sin, and by whom alone sins are forgiven."

This reflects the faith of those who approach death and of those who face temptations in life. Some grow hard in sin and try to leave this world without thinking of the next. Others live in blissful ignorance, neither knowing nor considering what it means to stand before God and be judged by Him.

But those who truly know God and themselves, who reflect on their past and on the eternity they must meet at God's judgment seat, will ultimately renounce all they have been and are. They will turn to Christ alone for righteousness and salvation.

In the following discourse, I will avoid getting entangled in intricate scholastic disputes. The point I press is simple: men should renounce all confidence in themselves and anything that could support such confidence. They should look to the grace of God in Christ alone for righteousness and salvation. This is God's design in the gospel (1 Corinthians 1:29-31). Despite difficulties in explaining some technical terms about justification, I am confident that those who truly understand God and themselves will agree.

Scripture teaches a commutation, by imputation, between Christ and believers concerning sin and righteousness. This is represented by the ordinance of the scapegoat (Leviticus 16:21-22), by the nature of expiatory sacrifices (Leviticus 4:29, etc.), and by the provision for an uncertain murder (Deuteronomy 21:1-9).

That commutation is attested in Isaiah 53:5-6; 2 Corinthians 5:21; Romans 8:3-4; Galatians 3:13-14; 1 Peter 2:24; and Deuteronomy 21:23. Fathers and teachers such as Justin Martyr, Gregory of Nyssa, Augustine, Chrysostom, Bernard, Taulerus, and Pighius have also borne witness to it.

The proper acts of faith that correspond to this truth are found in Romans 5:11; Matthew 11:28; Psalm 38:4; Genesis 4:13; Isaiah 53:11; Galatians 3:1; Isaiah 45:22; and John 3:14-15. A bold calumny is answered. Scripture does represent a commutation between Christ and believers in which their sins are imputed to Him and His righteousness is imputed to them. Understanding and applying this truth is a central part of the life and exercise of faith.

This was taught to the church of God in the offering of the scapegoat: "Aaron shall lay both his hands on the head of the live goat, confess over it all the iniquities of the children of Israel, and all their transgressions, concerning all their sins, putting them on the head of the goat. The goat shall bear on itself all their iniquities" (Leviticus 16:21-22).

Whether this goat, sent away with that burden upon him, lived and so served as a type of Christ's rising after death, or whether he perished in the wilderness by being cast down a precipice by the man who led him away, as some Jews suppose, it is universally acknowledged that what was done to the goat represented what was accomplished in the person of Jesus Christ.

Aaron did not merely confess the people's sins over the goat; he placed them all on its head — ונתן אותם על־ראש השָׂעִיר — putting them on the head of the goat. In consequence it is said that the goat bore them all upon him. This was done by divine institution, which ratified the act. The priest did not transfuse sin from one subject to another; he transferred the guilt from the people to the sacrifice. To show this transfer, he "put and fixed both his hands on his head."

From this practice the Jews conclude that "all Israel was as innocent on the Day of Atonement as they were on the day of creation," as verse 30 states. Yet the apostle shows that they fell short of final perfection or consummation (see Hebrews 10). This is the language of every expiatory sacrifice: Quod in ejus caput sit — "Let the guilt be on him." Hence the sacrifice itself was called חַטָּאת and אָשָׁם — "sin" and "guilt" (Leviticus 4:29; 7:2; 10:17).

So, when an uncertain murder occurred and the murderer could not be found, the elders of the city nearest the slain man were to bring a heifer that had not been worked and had not pulled with a yoke, and they were to break the heifer's neck in a valley with flowing water to remove the guilt from the land (Deuteronomy 21:1-9). Since no culprit was identified, this was only a moral representation of the punishment due to guilt. The men who killed the heifer did not place their hands on it to transfer their own guilt, but washed their hands over it to declare their personal innocence.

By these means, as by all the expiatory sacrifices, God instructed His people in the transfer of sin's guilt to Him who would bear all their iniquities, and in their discharge and justification through that bearing.

So, "And the Lord has laid on Him the iniquity of us all," and "And by His stripes we are healed" (Isaiah 53:5-6). Our iniquity was laid on Him, and He bore it (see verse 11); through His bearing of it, we are freed. His stripes are our healing. Our sin was imputed to Him; His merit is imputed to us.

"He made Him who knew no sin to be sin for us, that we might become the righteousness of God in Him." (2 Corinthians 5:21) This is the commutation I mentioned: He made Him who knew no sin to be sin for us; we are made the righteousness of God in Him.

God does not impute sin to us (verse 19), but imputes righteousness to us on the sole ground that He made Him to be sin for us. If by His being made sin only His being made a sacrifice for sin is intended, it serves the same purpose. The formal reason for anything being made an expiatory sacrifice was the imputation of sin to it by divine institution. The same is expressed by the same apostle in Romans 8:3-4: "God did by sending His own Son in the likeness of sinful flesh, on account of sin: He condemned sin in the flesh, that the righteous requirement of the law might be fulfilled in us."

The sin was made His; He answered for it, and the righteousness which God requires by the law is made ours. The righteousness of the law is fulfilled in us, not by our doing it, but by His. This is the blessed change and commutation wherein alone the soul of a convinced sinner can find rest and peace.

Thus, "Christ has redeemed us from the curse of the law, having become a curse for us (for it is written, 'Cursed is everyone who hangs on a tree'), that the blessing of Abraham might come upon the Gentiles in Christ Jesus, that we might receive the promise of the Spirit through faith."

The curse of the law contained all that was due to sin. This belonged to us, but it was transferred to Him. He was made a curse; His hanging on a tree was the sign and token of this. Hence, He is said to "who Himself bore our sins in His own body on the tree," because His hanging on the tree was the token of His bearing the curse: "for he who is hanged is accursed of God." In the blessing of faithful Abraham all righteousness and acceptance with God is included; "And he believed in the Lord, and He accounted it to him for righteousness."

However, because some individuals — who, for reasons best known to themselves, take every opportunity to object to my writings — have raised an irrelevant clamor about something I previously delivered on this subject, I shall state my complete judgment here in the words of those whom, to my knowledge, they cannot reasonably dispute.

The excellent words of Justin Martyr deserve the first place: "He gave His Son a ransom for us; the holy for transgressors; the innocent for the guilty; the just for the unjust; the incorruptible for the corrupt; the immortal for mortals. For what else could hide or cover our sins but His righteousness? In whom else could we wicked and ungodly ones be justified, or esteemed righteous, but in the Son of God alone? O sweet permutation, or change! O unsearchable work, or curious operation! O blessed beneficence, exceeding all expectations that the iniquity of many should be hidden in one just one, and the righteousness of one should justify many transgressors."

Gregory Nyssen speaks to the same purpose: "He has transferred unto Himself the filth of my sins, and communicated unto me His purity, and made me partaker of His beauty." Augustine also states: "He was sin, that we might be righteousness; not our own, but the righteousness of God; not in ourselves, but in Him; as He was sin, not His own, but ours, — not in Himself, but in us."

The old Latin translation renders those words from Psalm 22:1 "Verba delictorum meorum." He comments on the place: "How says he, 'Of my sins?' Because he prays for our sins; He made our sins to be His, that He might make His righteousness to be ours. O sweet commutation and change!" Chrysostom, on those words of the apostle, "that we might become the righteousness of God in Him," states: "What word, what speech is this? What mind can comprehend or express it? For he says, 'He made Him who was righteous to be made a sinner, that He might make sinners righteous.'"

"What word, what speech is this? What mind can comprehend or express it? For he says, 'For He made Him who knew no sin to be sin for us, that we might become the righteousness of God in Him.' Nor does he merely say so, but expresses the quality itself. For he does not say, he made Him a sinner, but sin; that we might be made, not merely righteous, but righteousness, and that the righteousness of God, when we are justified not by works (for if we should, there must be no spot found in them), but by grace, whereby all sin is blotted out."

So Bernard also states: "Indeed, the man who ought to pay; the man who pays. For 'that if One died for all, then all died,' so that the satisfaction of one may be imputed to all, just as one bore the sins of all: nor can another be found who has sinned, nor another who has satisfied; because Christ is one head and one body."

Many more speak to the same purpose. Hence, Luther, before he engaged in the work of reformation, in a letter to one George Spenlein, a monk, was not afraid to write in this manner: "My sweet brother, learn Christ and Him crucified, learn to sing to Him, and, despairing of yourself, say to Him: 'You, Lord Jesus, are my righteousness, but I am Your sin; You have assumed what You were not, and have given me what I am not. He has received you and made your sins His, and has made His righteousness yours; cursed is he who does not believe this!'"

If those who now appear so contentious about nearly every word spoken concerning Christ and His righteousness had ever been troubled in their consciences about the guilt of sin, as this man was, they would find it no strange matter to speak and write as he did. Indeed, there are some who have lived and died within the communion of the Roman Church itself, who have given their testimony to this truth.

Taulerus speaks to this in his "Meditations on the Life of Christ," chapter seven: "Christ took upon Himself all the sins of the world, and willingly underwent that grief of heart for them, as if He Himself had committed them." He goes on, speaking in the person of Christ: "Since the great sin of Adam cannot go away, I beseech You, heavenly Father, punish it in me. For I take all his sins upon myself. If this tempest of anger has arisen because of me, cast me into the sea of my most bitter passion."

See, in the justification of these expressions, Hebrews 10:5-10. The discourse of Albertus Pighius on this subject, although often cited and urged, shall be repeated once again—both for its worth and truth and to show how some have foolishly pleased themselves in reflecting on certain expressions of mine, as if I had been singular in them. His words are, after others to the same purpose: "For the apostle says, 'that is, that God was in Christ reconciling the world to Himself, not imputing their trespasses to them, and has committed to us the word of reconciliation.'" Therefore, in Him we are justified before God—not in ourselves, not by our own works, but by His righteousness, which is imputed to us and communicated to us in union with Him. Lacking righteousness of our own, we are taught to seek righteousness outside ourselves, in Him.

As He says, "For He made Him who knew no sin to be sin for us" (that is, an expiatory sacrifice for sin), "that we might become the righteousness of God in Him." We are made righteous in Christ, not with our own righteousness, but with the righteousness of God. By what right? By the right of friendship, which makes all things common among friends, according to the ancient and celebrated proverb. Being grafted into Christ—fastened and united to Him—He makes His things ours. He communicates His riches to us, interposes His righteousness between the judgment of God and our unrighteousness, and under that, as under a shield and buckler, hides us from the divine wrath we have deserved. He defends and protects us therewith, communicating it to us and making it ours, so that, being covered and adorned with it, we may boldly and securely present ourselves before the divine tribunal. Thus we not only appear righteous but truly are.

For as the apostle affirms that by one man's fault we were all made sinners, so the righteousness of Christ alone is effective in the justification of us all: "For as by one man's disobedience many were made sinners, so also by one Man's obedience many will be made righteous." This is the righteousness of Christ—His obedience whereby He fulfilled the will of His Father in all things; on the other hand, our unrighteousness is our disobedience and transgression of God's commands.

That our righteousness is placed in the obedience of Christ is because, being incorporated into Him, it is accounted to us as if it were ours. Thus, with it we are deemed righteous. Just as Jacob of old—though not the firstborn—was hidden under the garment of his brother and clothed with his robe, which breathed a sweet fragrance, and so presented himself to his father to receive the blessing of the birthright in another's person, so it is necessary that we lie hidden under the precious purity of our Firstborn and elder Brother. We must be fragrant with His sweet aroma and have our sins buried and covered with His perfections, so that we may present ourselves before our most holy Father to obtain from Him the blessing of righteousness.

God, therefore, justifies us by His free grace and goodness. He embraces us in Christ Jesus and clothes us with His innocence and righteousness as we are grafted into Him. For only that which is true and perfect can endure in the sight of God; only that ought to be presented and pleaded for us before the divine tribunal, as our advocate and plea in our cause. Resting on this, we obtain daily pardon for our sins. With that purity covering us, the filth and uncleanness of our imperfections are not imputed to us but are covered, as if buried, so that they do not come into the judgment of God. Thus, with the old man destroyed and slain in us, divine goodness receives us into peace with the second Adam.

Thus far he expresses the power that the influence of divine truth had on his mind—contrary to the interest of the cause in which he was engaged, and to the loss of his reputation with those for whom he was one of the fiercest champions. Some among the Roman Church, who cannot bear the assertion of an exchange by imputation between Christ and believers, just as some among ourselves cannot, yet affirm the same concerning the righteousness of other men: "The Apostle seems to teach us a kind of exchange. You abound in money, and are in want of righteousness; on the contrary, they abound in righteousness and are in want of money; let there be some exchange: give to the pious who are in need of the money that you have in abundance, and they will in turn communicate their righteousness to you." Hosius, "De Expresso Dei Verbo," vol. 2, p. 21.

But I have mentioned these testimonies primarily to enlighten some individuals' ignorance, who are quick to speak ill of what they do not understand.

This blessed exchange regarding sin and righteousness is presented to us in Scripture as a central object of our faith, the foundation of our peace with God. Although both the imputation of sin to Christ and the imputation of righteousness to us are acts of God and not of ours, we are called by faith to exemplify them in our own souls and to genuinely perform what is required on our part for their application to us, through which we receive "the reconciliation" (Romans 5:11).

Christ invites all who "labor and are heavy laden" (Matthew 11:28) to come to Him. The weight upon men's consciences — the burden that so oppresses them — is the burden of sin. The psalmist laments, "Like a heavy burden they are too heavy for me" (Psalm 38:4). Such was Cain's perception of his guilt (Genesis 4:13). This burden Christ bore when it was laid upon Him by divine estimation, as it is said, "For He shall bear their iniquities" (Isaiah 53:11). He did this when God laid upon Him "the iniquity of us all" (Isaiah 53:6).

In applying this to our own souls, we must first recognize the weight and burden of our sins and how they exceed our ability to bear them. The Lord Christ calls us to Himself with this burden so that we may find relief. He does this through the preaching of the gospel, where He is "clearly portrayed among you as crucified" (Galatians 3:1).

When faith contemplates Christ crucified — for faith is a "Look to Me," (Isaiah 45:22; 65:1) and is like the Israelites looking to the serpent lifted up in the wilderness when they were bitten by the serpents (John 3:14-15) — and when it answers His invitation (for faith is our coming to Him at His call), a believer grasps that God has laid all our iniquities upon Him. This understanding becomes a special object of faith: faith in His blood.

Here the soul approves and embraces the righteousness and grace of God, together with the infinite condescension and love of Christ Himself. It consents that what God has done is fitting for His infinite wisdom and grace, and there it finds rest. Such a person no longer seeks to establish their own righteousness. Instead, they submit to the righteousness of God. By faith they leave that burden on Christ — the burden He called them to bring — and align themselves with God's wisdom and righteousness in placing it on Him. In doing so they receive the everlasting righteousness the Lord Christ secured when He ended sin and provided reconciliation for transgressors.

The reader should note that I am not treating these matters in the formal, argumentative style of a scholastic disputation; that will be done later as I deem necessary. Rather, I am doing something more practical and, I believe, more important — namely, declaring the experience of faith in the language of Scripture and in expressions analogous to it.

I would rather help bring light and understanding to the humblest believer than achieve rhetorical victories over prejudiced disputants. Therefore, by faith acting in this way we are justified and have peace with God. No other foundation in this matter can be laid that will endure the test.

We should not be swayed by those who are unfamiliar with these truths and who dismiss the work of faith as mere fancy or imagination. The preaching of the cross is foolishness to the wisdom of the world; only by the Spirit of God can one truly understand it. Those who know the terror of the Lord — who have been genuinely convicted of their apostasy from God and made aware of their actual sins — and who see how fearful it is to fall into the hands of the living God, seek a solid foundation on which they may be accepted by Him.

Many think of these matters differently and find believing to be something quite unlike what others suppose. It is not mere fancy for a person to abhor and deny themselves, to agree with the righteousness of God in declaring that death is due for their sins, to renounce all hope in any righteousness of their own, and to unite the word and promise of God concerning Christ and righteousness through faith so as to receive the atonement and commit to universal obedience to God.

As for those who, through pride and self-conceit on the one hand, or ignorance on the other, treat these truths as mere imagination, we have no quarrel with them. For those to whom these truths are merely the work of fancy, the gospel appears a fable.

I have already written on this subject in a practical discourse called "Communion with God." Some of lesser standing have found it useful to strengthen their dependence on superiors or to satisfy their own inclination to criticize my writings and revile their author. That book has been singled out for such scrutiny. Recently, one Mr. Hotchkis has taken this course in a book about justification, where he harshly criticizes the doctrine I am presenting here, particularly on page 81.

Were it not for my hope that he might be somewhat benefited by a warning about his improprieties in that discourse, I would not have noticed his other irrelevant remarks. The good man seems capable of becoming angry with people he has never met and about matters he cannot or will not understand, to the point of reviling them in the most opprobrious language.

For my part, though I have never intentionally written on this subject or on the doctrine of justification until now, he could not fail to see, from what was occasionally mentioned in that discourse, that I hold no doctrine other than the common faith of the most learned in all Protestant churches. The reasons I am singled out for his petulance are obvious and need no repetition.

Still, I will tell him what he may not know: I regard it no small honor that the reproaches cast upon the doctrine he opposes have fallen upon me. I say the same of all the reviling and contemptuous language that fills his subsequent pages.

Concerning the present occasion, I ask his pardon if I do not believe him when he claims that reading the passages he cites from my book filled him with "horror and indignation," as he asserts.

He admits that my words may have a meaning he approves of (which then must be good and sound). What honest, sober person would not prefer to take them in that sense rather than twist them into another and so subject himself to the torment of a fit of horrible indignation?

I suppose it was in such a fit, if indeed one did come upon him (for one evil often begets another), that he thought to insinuate something about my denying the necessity of our own personal repentance and obedience.

No one who had read that book, or any of my writings, could, with any regard for conscience or honesty, make such a charge unless his mind were greatly disturbed by an unexpected fit of horror.

Such is his treatment of me from beginning to end. I cannot find a single instance where his objections against me escape that supposed fit and return to honest, sincere thought — which I hope is what primarily engages him.

Although I cannot justify this charge by pointing to any specific reflection of his, I will address what he insists upon most and fills his discourse with the vilest expressions. This appears on page 164 of his book and the pages that follow, where he vehemently attacks me for making it an improper end of our service to God — namely, that we may flee from the wrath to come.

Who would not regard that as an inexpiable crime, especially from a man who has written extensively on the nature and use of threats under the gospel and on the fear that should be placed in men's hearts, as I have?

Thus this supposed crime becomes the target of all his revilings, which he seems to think not only excusable but justified.

But what if all this is a willful misrepresentation, unbecoming of a good man, much less a minister of the gospel? My words, as he reports and transcribes them, are these: "Some serve the house of God as if it were the drudgery of their lives; the principle upon which they yield obedience is a spirit of bondage to fear; the rule they follow is the law in its dread and rigor, demanding the utmost without mercy or mitigation; the end for which they do it is to flee from the wrath to come, to pacify their consciences, and to seek righteousness as if it were by the works of the law."

What follows on the same subject he omits, and what he adds as my words are not mine but his own. Where is the shame? Where is the integrity?

That which I affirmed to be part of an evil end, when it is mixed with various other things expressly mentioned, is singled out as if I had denied that it could be part of a good end in our obedience. I never thought or said that. In fact, I have spoken and written much to the contrary.

Yet, to justify his disingenuous approach, and alongside many other untrue reflections, he adds that I insinuate those I describe are Christians seeking righteousness by faith in Christ.

I must inform him that I believe such works will have no influence on justification. I do not intend to answer his objections to the truth or to myself at length because they are trite and obsolete; whatever force they seem to have will be found in other authors from whom he derives them.

I wish to avoid continually pointing out how forgetful he has been of all rules of integrity, even of common honesty, in his dealings with me. The occasion for this unpleasant digression is simply the substance of my belief — that our sins were imputed to Christ and that His righteousness is imputed to us. This is the faith in which I am assured I shall live and die, even if he were to write twenty learned books against it, as he has already published. The sense in which I believe these things will be declared later.

Although I do not judge men by the phrases that arise in polemical writings, where they often contradict their own experiences and prayers, I will boldly state that for those who do not understand that blessed exchange of sins and righteousness, as to its substance, which I have advocated for, "if our gospel is veiled, it is veiled to those who are perishing."

We can never properly align our thoughts on this matter unless we clearly understand and are satisfied with the introduction of grace by Jesus Christ into our whole relationship with God, and with its relevance to every part of our obedience. There was nothing of that nature in the original constitution of our relationship and obedience as established by the law of our creation.

We were created in immediate relationship with God as our Creator, Preserver, and Rewarder. There was no mystery of grace in the covenant of works. All that was required for the consummation of that state was what was given to us in our creation, enabling us to obey in a manner worthy of reward. "do this and you will live" was the sole rule of our relationship with God.

Originally, there was nothing in religion of what the gospel celebrates under the name of grace, kindness, and love of God—those things from which all our favorable relations with God now proceed and into which they are resolved. There was nothing of the interposition of a mediator regarding our righteousness before God and our acceptance with Him—now the life and soul of religion, the substance of the gospel, and the center of all the truths revealed in it.

The introduction of these elements is what makes our religion a mystery, indeed a "great mystery," if the apostle is to be believed (1 Timothy 3:16). All religion was at first suited to and commensurate with reason. Now that it has become a mystery, most people are very unwilling to accept it. Yet it must be this way: unless we are restored to our original righteousness, a religion suited to the principles of our reason (of which it has none except what corresponds to that original state) will not suffice for our needs.

Therefore, concerning the introduction of Christ and of grace in Him into our relationship with God, there were no notions in the natural conceptions of our minds, nor can they be known by natural reason at its best (1 Corinthians 2:14). Before our understanding was darkened and our reason corrupted by the fall, no such things were revealed or proposed to us.

Indeed, their very supposition contradicts the whole state and condition in which we were to live for God, since they all presuppose the entrance of sin.

It is unlikely that our reason, now corrupted, would willingly embrace what it knew nothing of in its best condition and which contradicts the way of attaining happiness that was perfectly fitted to it. Reason has no faculty or power now except what it derived from that original state.

To suppose that it is now, of itself, fitted and ready to receive such heavenly mysteries of truth and grace—mysteries of which it had no notion and could have had none in innocence—is to assume that by the fall our eyes were opened to know good and evil like the serpent's deception of our first parents. Since our reason was given as our guide in the original constitution of our natures, it is naturally unprepared to receive what is above it; and, being corrupted, it has enmity toward it.

Hence, when this mystery was first openly proposed—namely, the love and grace of God in Christ, the introduction of a mediator, and his righteousness into our standing with God as designed in God's infinite wisdom—the whole scheme was regarded by the greater part of the wise and rational in the world as sheer folly, as the apostle explains in 1 Corinthians 1. Moreover, the faith of such men was never rightly accepted in the world without an act of the Spirit of God renewing the mind.

Those who think nothing more is needed for the human mind to receive the mysteries of the gospel than an outward presentation of its doctrine not only deny the corruption of our nature by the fall but thereby reject the grace by which we are to be restored. Therefore, reason—as has been shown—acting on its own native principles and capacities derived from its original state, and as it is now corrupted, is enmity against the entire introduction of grace by Christ into our relationship with God (Romans 8:7).

To attempt to reduce the doctrine of the gospel—or what it declares concerning the hidden mystery of God's grace in Christ—to the principles and inclinations of men's minds, or to reason as it remains in us after sin, is to debase and corrupt it. This is particularly true when one appeals to those notions and conceptions of religion that reason retains from its original state. In what follows we shall see many instances of such debasement, which pave the way for the gospel's rejection.

Consequently, it is very difficult, both doctrinally and practically, to keep people at the reality and spiritual height of this mystery. Men naturally neither understand nor delight in it. So every attempt to accommodate it to the principles and ingrained notions of corrupt reason proves attractive to many, indeed to most.

Those adaptations are easily grasped. They require no exercise of faith, no earnest seeking in prayer, and no supernatural illumination. That is why they gain so much acceptance.

However, a declaration of the mysteries of the gospel can gain no acceptance in men's minds except by the working of the Spirit of God (Ephesians 1:17-19). The truth appears difficult, perplexing, and unintelligible. Even among many who cannot contradict it, there is no delight in it.

This gives advantage to those who now strive to corrupt the doctrine of the gospel, in whole or in part, by accommodating it to the common notions of corrupted reason. In their confidence they not only oppose the truths themselves but dismiss their declaration as mere enthusiastic nonsense. They gain ground by pretending to reduce everything to reason and by scorning what they cannot understand as unintelligible fanaticism.

I am more convinced than ever that the judgments of such men are not a valid standard of spiritual truth. Despite their scorn and the supposed advantage they claim from exposing certain harsh expressions in some writings, those expressions may simply be unsuited to their own understanding and capacity in these matters. We should not be ashamed of the gospel of Christ, for it is the power of God to salvation for everyone who believes.

This opposition to the mystery of the wisdom and grace of God in Christ—and to the foundation of its whole economy in the distinct operations of the persons of the Holy Trinity—consists of two branches.

First, the attempt to reduce the whole of it to the private reason of men and their weak, imperfect management of it. This is the design of the Socinians. On that ground they deny, challenge, and mock the doctrine of the Trinity. They argue that it is incomprehensible by reason, since the doctrine declares things that are infinite and eternal and cannot be exemplified in or accommodated to the finite and temporal.

This gives apparent force to all their objections. Yet, under the pretence of exercising reason, they embrace the most absurd and irrational principles. Unless one grants them that what is above their reason is thereby contrary to true reason; that the infinite and eternal must be perfectly comprehensible in all its parts; or that what cannot exist in finite things cannot exist in infinite things—along with other such irrational imaginations—their arguments against the Trinity fall away like chaff before the wind.

Consequently, they must deny distinct operations of persons in the Godhead in the dispensation of the mystery of grace; and if there are no such distinct persons, there can be no distinct operations. Once those things are denied, no article of faith can be rightly understood, nor can any duty of obedience be performed acceptably to God. In particular, the doctrine of justification by the imputation of the righteousness of Christ cannot stand.

On the same principles, the incarnation of the Son of God is rejected as the most absurd conception that ever entered human mind. It is useless to argue with those who hold such views of justification. I will freely acknowledge that all we believe about it is no better than old wives' tales if the incarnation of the Son of God is thus set aside.

For I can as easily understand how a mere man, however exalted and glorified, could exercise a spiritual rule over all hearts, consciences, and thoughts — being equally and constantly present to them all — as I can understand how the righteousness and obedience of one should be reckoned the righteousness of all who believe if that one is no more than a man and not acknowledged to be the incarnate Son of God.

While people's minds are occupied with such prejudices, and unless they firmly accept the truths in these foundational matters, you cannot convince them of the truth and necessity of a sinner's justification as revealed in the gospel. If one confines the Lord Christ to nothing more than what they imagine him to be, I will concede there can be no other way of justification than the one they propose — though I cannot believe any sinner would truly be justified that way. These are the consequences of an obstinate refusal to admit the mystery of God and His grace into the way of salvation and our relationship with Him.

For an example of how inventively men object to heavenly mysteries — especially to vindicate the sovereignty of their own reason over God — look to the writings that attack the Trinity and the incarnation of the eternal Word. Their basic rule in divine matters is this: if something in Scripture seems to contradict our reason or exceed our understanding, we must not accept it as saying what it appears to say. In short, if Scripture seems contrary to their reason, they conclude Scripture cannot mean it, whatever the words appear to state.

"Therefore, because Scripture affirms both these things" (the efficacy of God's grace and the freedom of our wills), "we cannot conclude from this that they are not contradictory; but because these things are contradictory, we must determine that one of them is not stated in Scripture," they insist, whatever the text says. This is their convenient way of exalting their reason above Scripture, and it reeks of presumption.

Socinus himself, speaking of the satisfaction of Christ, says plainly: "For my part, if this doctrine were found and written in the holy Scripture, not once, but often, I would not therefore believe it to be so as you do; for where it cannot possibly be so (whatever the Scripture says), I would, as I do with others in other places, employ some less inconvenient interpretation, whereby I would extract a sense from the words that would be consistent with itself." He adds the Latin, "Sacra verba in alium sensum, quam verba sonant, per inusitatos etiam tropos quandoque explicantur." In other words, he would force the words to mean something other than they say, using odd tropes. Indeed, he applies such devices to distort every divine testimony about our redemption, reconciliation, and justification by the blood of Christ.

Once they make this their rule—always preferring their reason to the plain words of Scripture, which must then be twisted to fit—it is endless to catalogue their objections to the holy mysteries. All such objections reduce to one principle: their reason cannot comprehend or approve these truths. For a concrete example of this evasive cunning, read the Jewish rabbis' comments on Isaiah 53 and the Socinians' notes on the opening of the Gospel of John.

The second branch of this opposition comes from failing to grasp the harmony within the mystery of grace and among its parts. That grasp is primarily the fruit of the wisdom the Holy Spirit teaches believers. Understanding God's wisdom in a mystery is not merely an art or a science—neither purely speculative nor merely practical—but a spiritual wisdom. This spiritual wisdom apprehends things not only as notions but in their power, reality, and effectiveness toward their intended ends.

Therefore, although very few — unless they are learned, discerning, and diligent — attain this understanding clearly and distinctly in doctrinal terms, all true believers, even the least, are guided and enabled by the Holy Spirit in their practice and duty to act according to a sense of this harmony, in keeping with the promise that "And they shall all be taught by God." What appears contradictory to others — forcing them to distort Scripture or their experience by rejecting one truth — becomes reconciled in believers' minds and mutually beneficial in their whole obedience. These matters will, however, need further discussion.

Such harmony pervades the whole mystery of God. It is the most intricate effect and product of divine wisdom, and the fact that human reason cannot fully discern it does not undermine its truth. No creature can fully comprehend it in this world. Only by the contemplation of faith can we reach an understanding and admiration that enables us to glorify God and to use all its parts in practice as needed. Concerning this, the holy man mentioned earlier cried, "O unsearchable contrivance and operations!" And the apostle expresses the same truth as a depth of wisdom: "Oh, the depth of the riches both of the wisdom and knowledge of God! How unsearchable are His judgments and His ways past finding out!" (Romans 11:33–36). See also Ephesians 3:8–10 for the same purpose.

There is a harmony, a suitability of one thing to another, in all the works of creation. Yet it is not perfectly or absolutely discoverable even to the wisest and most diligent of men. Consider how far they are from agreement about the order and motions of the heavenly bodies, or about the sympathies and qualities of various things below, in terms of causality and efficiency. New discoveries about any of these only show how distant humanity is from a just and perfect comprehension of them.

Nonetheless, such a universal harmony exists in all parts of nature and its operations that nothing in its proper station and activity is destructively contrary to the whole. Rather, everything contributes to the preservation and utility of the universe. Although this harmony is not absolutely comprehensible to anyone, all living creatures that follow the guidance or instinct of nature make use of it and thrive. Without it, neither their existence nor their operations could be sustained.

In the mystery of God and His grace, the harmony and suitability of one thing to another—and their common tendency toward the same end—are incomparably more excellent and glorious than what we observe in nature. God created all things originally in wisdom, and the new creation of all things through Jesus Christ is especially attributed to the riches and treasures of that infinite wisdom. Yet this harmony can only be discerned by those taught by God; it is understood spiritually. Still, the wisdom in it is often dismissed by the most despised. Some think there is little wisdom in it; others believe no significant wisdom is needed to comprehend it. Few will invest the time in prayer, meditation, self-denial, mortification, and holy obedience—doing Christ's will—to gain a right understanding of the mystery of godliness, as many devote themselves to diligent study and experiment in the natural and mathematical sciences.

Therefore, three things are evident here:

1. There is a harmony throughout every part of the mystery of God, in which all the blessed attributes of the divine nature are glorified.

2. In every case, our duty is directed and put into action, and our salvation through obedience is secured.

3. Christ, as the ultimate end of all, is exalted.

Thus, we must not only consider and understand the several parts of spiritual doctrine but also their relations to one another, their consistency in practice, and their mutual support toward a common end.

A disorder in our understanding of any part of that which owes its beauty and usefulness to harmony can produce confusion about the whole.

To understand this harmony rightly, it is essential that we be taught by God. Without that teaching we can never attain the wisdom required to comprehend the mystery of His grace.

Therefore, seeking God's instruction should be the chief aim of our diligence in pursuing the truths of the gospel.

All who are taught by God to know His will — unless their minds are disturbed by prejudices, false opinions, or temptations — find in themselves, and in their practical obedience, the consistency of all parts of the mystery of God's grace and truth in Christ. They perceive its spiritual harmony and its common tendency toward the same end.

The introduction of Christ's grace into our standing before God does not create confusion or disorder in their minds, even when natural reason conflicts with our original condition and with the renewing grace we receive.

A failure to apprehend this divine harmony fills people's minds with notions of inconsistency between the most important parts of the gospel mystery, and this gives rise to much of the confusion now found in Christian religion.

For instance, the Socinians see no consistency between the grace or love of God and the satisfaction of Christ. They hold that if one is accepted, the other must be excluded from our faith. Consequently, they chiefly oppose the latter while pretending to assert and defend the former.

When these truths are explicitly joined in the same statement of faith — as in the assertion that "being justified freely by His grace through the redemption that is in Christ Jesus, whom God set forth as a propitiation by His blood" (Romans 3:24-25) — they will distort common sense and reason rather than admit a harmony they cannot grasp. Although it is plainly stated that redemption comes through His blood, that He is a propitiation, and that His blood serves as the ransom or price of redemption, they insist it is merely metaphorical — a simple deliverance by power, like the Israelites' deliverance under Moses.

Yet these things are clearly taught in the gospel; they are not only consistent but mutually dependent. There is no hint of any special love or grace of God toward sinners that is not related to Christ's satisfaction as the means by which its effects are conveyed to them. See John 3:16; Romans 3:23-25; 8:30-33; 2 Corinthians 5:19-21; Ephesians 1:7, etc.

Similarly, they see no consistency between Christ's satisfaction and the necessity of holiness or obedience for believers. They repeatedly argue that our doctrine of Christ's mediation removes every obligation to live a holy life. By their sophistical reasoning they deceive many, especially those who lack spiritual experience to test their claims.

But Scripture directly contradicts them, and those who truly believe and experience the power of the truth know how impossible it is to render any acceptable obedience without that truth; this knowledge keeps them from the Socinians' snares.

These and similar errors spring from a reluctance to accept the introduction of the mystery of grace into our standing before God. If we were to appear before God only under the original covenant of creation, which natural reason can grasp, these things would seem inconsistent. Yet the mystery of God's wisdom and grace in Christ cannot be separated from either.

Likewise, God's efficacious grace in converting sinners and the use of their minds in fulfilling duties are treated as contradictory. Although Scripture repeatedly and plainly affirms both, these critics insist they conflict with reason and therefore deny that Scripture truly affirms one of them. The root is the same: in their wisdom they cannot see how the mystery of God's grace fits into our relationship with and obedience to God. Consequently, many ages of the church — especially the most recent — have been filled with endless disputes, either opposing the grace of God or trying to force its truths into the shape of corrupted human reason.

There is no clearer example than the present controversy. Free justification by the imputation of Christ's righteousness is fiercely attacked as inconsistent with the necessity of personal holiness and obedience. Because the Socinians chiefly press this objection, I will examine it at length separately and judge the holiness they, and those who follow them, claim by the unerring standard.

I wish to stress that in defending this doctrine we do so as an essential part of introducing grace into our whole standing before God. We confess it is alien — and to unenlightened, unsanctified reason, absurd; some even call it childish. This, I believe, is the chief cause of the opposition and the troubles the church endures. Men's minds are thus ready soil for sophistical arguments against it, quick to load it with apparent absurdities and to reject it as incompatible with their extraordinary notions of reason. No objection, however trivial, fails to find applause among those who regard the mystery of grace, which surpasses their natural understanding, as unintelligible folly.

The relation between justification by the imputation of Christ's righteousness and the necessity of our personal obedience cannot be clearly apprehended without the exercise of faith's wisdom. We acknowledge this, and anyone may avail themselves of the admission.

True faith has a spiritual light that receives this truth and leads the soul into obedience. I will reserve a fuller treatment for its proper place. For now, I say generally that this relation is evident to the spiritual wisdom which enables us, both doctrinally and practically, to perceive the harmony of God's mystery and the consistency of all its parts.

Scripture plainly affirms both justification by the imputation of Christ's righteousness and the necessity of our personal obedience. We reject the Socinian assertion that because these truths seem inconsistent to their reason one must be excluded from Scripture. What appears inconsistent to them does not carry the same weight for us; we have as much reason to trust our faculties. Yet we do not rely on reason alone — we rely on the authority of God as revealed in Scripture, and we rejoice that our experience confirms His declarations.

This is evident in the gracious guidance of believers' minds under the Spirit of truth and grace, and in the tendencies of the new divine life within them. Though temptations and the remains of sin may arise and sometimes lead to relapse, their minds are formed by the doctrine of grace and by the grace of that doctrine. Thus the abundance of grace becomes the chief spring of their growth in holiness, as we shall show later.

We maintain that these objections from the opponents continually seek to entangle the doctrine. For example:

1. They say that if Christ's passive righteousness — His death and sufferings — is imputed to us, then His active righteousness — the obedience of His life — need not be imputed; conversely, if the active is imputed, the passive is unnecessary. They argue the two cannot coexist.

2. They contend that if all sin is pardoned, righteousness becomes needless; and conversely, if Christ's righteousness is imputed to us, there is no need for the pardon of sin.

3. They hold that if we believe our sins are pardoned, then either they were pardoned before we believed, or we are required to believe something that is not true.

4. If Christ's righteousness is imputed to us, then we are regarded as having done and suffered what we in fact have not. If we are treated as though we have done it, the very idea of imputation is undermined.

5. If Christ's righteousness is imputed to us, then we are as righteous as Christ Himself.

6. If our sins are imputed to Christ, then He is thought to have sinned and to be, in Himself, a sinner.

7. If good works are excluded from any part in our justification before God, then they have no value for our salvation.

8. It is absurd to say that where there is no sin there is still not all the righteousness that could be required.

9. The righteousness imputed to us is said to be merely putative or imaginary, and so on.

Although all these objections—however subtly presented (as Socinus boasts he has employed extraordinary subtlety in this matter)—can be answered plainly, I will not refuse to examine any of them. For now, I will only say that the shadows they cast over people's minds disappear before the light of explicit Scripture testimonies and the experience of believers, where there is any reasonable understanding of the mystery of grace.

There are general prejudices against the imputation of the righteousness of Christ:

It is often claimed that this concept is not explicitly mentioned in Scripture. This was the first objection raised by Bellarmine. He states, "Up to this point, they have been unable to find any passage where it is read that the righteousness of Christ is imputed to us for justification, or that we are justified by the righteousness of Christ imputed to us" (De Justificat., book II, chapter 7). This objection is, without a doubt, unreasonably and immodestly presented by those of this persuasion. They not only profess their entire faith in terms and expressions nowhere found in Scripture, but they also assert many things, as they claim with divine faith, which are neither revealed nor contained in Scripture but are extracted from the traditions of the church.

Therefore, I cannot see how such people can modestly present this as an objection to any doctrine merely because the precise phrases some use are not found in Scripture in those exact words. Applied strictly, this rule could be taken far enough to exclude the principal doctrines of their own church from Christianity.

Furthermore, I see little fairness in those who harshly call the expression "the imputation of the righteousness of Christ" unscriptural, as if anyone who uses it has committed a grave offense. They do this even though, in giving their own judgments, they employ terms, distinctions, and expressions so far removed from Scripture that they likely would not have arisen except under the influence of Aristotle or the schools that sprang from him.

Although a sufficient answer has often been given to Bellarmine's objection, one of our contemporaries has recently translated it into English and made it the substance of the first chapter of a book on justification. He need not have shown so early to whom he owes most of his subsequent discourse, unless his purpose was to disparage others. Remove from him what is not his own, and also the irrelevant criticisms of others' words and expressions and the false accusations he levels at some, and his entire book would disappear.

He asserts that none of the Protestant writers who discuss the imputation of Christ's righteousness—who, until recently, were all of them—have strictly kept to the form of wholesome words and instead have drifted from the language of Scripture. He will excuse them from open error if by their language they mean no more than that we partake in the benefits of Christ's righteousness. But if they mean that Christ's own righteousness is imputed to us—that it stands as our righteousness before God, by which we are pardoned, accepted, forgiven, and given a right to the heavenly inheritance—then he charges them with an error that makes us think we have done what Christ did, and vice versa.

But these charges are mistaken. If we are said to have done anything in our own persons, that cannot be imputed to us as having been done for us by another, as will be shown later. The great and holy persons meant here are no more affected by the accusations or defenses of certain writers than those writers are versed in the learning, wisdom, and judgment in which these saints excelled—qualities clearly evident in all their writings.

The judgment of most Protestants is not only candidly expressed but is, in another place, approved even by Bellarmine. He says, "It would not be absurd if someone were to say that the righteousness and merits of Christ are imputed to us when they are given and applied to us, as if we ourselves had satisfied God" (De Justif., book II, chapter 10). He supports this with a saying from Bernard: "For if one died for all, then all died," indicating that the satisfaction of one is imputed to all, just as one bore the sins of all.

Those who acknowledge no more than a participation, in some way, of the benefits of Christ's obedience and righteousness—the Socinians among them—would do well, in my view, to deny outright any imputation of His righteousness to us. The benefits of His righteousness cannot properly be said to be imputed to us, whatever way we partake in them. To claim that the righteousness of Christ is imputed to us as regards its benefits, when neither the righteousness itself nor its benefits are imputed to us, as we will show later, only provokes unnecessary disputes. I see no reason why people should defend this doctrine under a phrase they themselves call unscriptural, if their meaning is clearly understood. Truth requires no subterfuge.

The Socinians chiefly press this objection. They note that the whole church uses various expressions to state the most important truths of the gospel that are not literally contained in Scripture, and they hope to gain advantage from this in opposing those truths. Such terms include Trinity, incarnation, satisfaction, merit of Christ, and the imputation of His righteousness. Their lack of success in the other cases has been shown sufficiently by those who have answered them.

On the point specifically about the imputation of Christ's righteousness to believers, those who affirm it insist they are only defending a single doctrine. If that doctrine cannot be found plainly taught and confirmed in Scripture, they say they will abandon the phrase. But if they can show that the truth they mean by that phrase is a divine truth sufficiently attested in Scripture and is clearly understood, then the phrase becomes an appropriate scriptural shorthand and the truth it expresses is a divine verity. To deny this would render the whole work of interpreting Scripture and the ministry of the church pointless. This is therefore the matter to be examined.

They contend that Scripture teaches the same thing in equivalent terms. For it says that "by one Man's obedience" (that is, Christ), "many will be made righteous" (Romans 5:19), and that we are made righteous by the imputation of righteousness to us: "just as David also describes the blessedness of the man to whom God imputes righteousness apart from works:" (Romans 4:6). If we are made righteous by the imputation of righteousness, then the obedience or righteousness by which we are made righteous is that which God imputes to us. They are satisfied with stating the doctrine in this way: the obedience of Christ, by which we are made righteous, is the righteousness God imputes to us. So this objection does not overthrow the truth we defend.

Socinus specifically attacks the doctrine of justification by the imputation of Christ's righteousness and satisfaction, claiming that the Gospels do not speak of it—neither in Christ's public sermons to the people nor in his private conversations with the disciples. He vehemently denies that sin is expiated by Christ's death (De Servator., part IV, chapter 9). Worse things can be added to bad inventions; this error is not only used and stressed by someone among ourselves, but is also dangerously compared to the evangelists' writings and the other New Testament writings. To support his case, Socinus asserts that the Gospel accounts—those recording Christ's sermons—do not mention the imputation of Christ's righteousness, nor his satisfaction, merit, atonement for sin, or redemption through his death. He praises our Savior's sermons as superior to the apostles' writings, though the apostles were inspired, and from this he draws many dangerous insinuations and reflections on St. Paul's writings, contrary to the church's faith and understanding through the ages. See pages 240-241.

However, this boldness is not only unwarranted; it should be abhorred. What Scripture, ecclesiastical tradition, precedent from any sober Christian writer, or sound theological reasoning would justify comparing the evangelists with the apostles in the way Socinus does, and drawing such conclusions from that comparison? Such juvenile presumption, together with a profound misunderstanding of divine inspiration and of the order and purpose of the New Testament writings, should give the reader pause.

To answer this pretense, we must note that what the Lord Christ taught his disciples during his earthly ministry was suited to the church's economy that existed before his death and resurrection. He withheld nothing necessary for their faith, obedience, or comfort in that state. He taught them much from Scripture, made new revelations, and occasionally corrected their judgments. But he did not then make a distinct, full disclosure of the sacred mysteries unique to the New Testament faith—truths that could only be fully understood after his death and resurrection.

What the Lord later revealed by his Spirit to the apostles was no less directly from himself than what he spoke to them while on earth. To think otherwise is destructive to the Christian faith. The apostles' epistles are no less Christ's sermons than his teachings on the mount. There is no advantage in either the matter or the manner of delivery. The things written in the epistles come from the same wisdom, grace, and love as those he spoke earlier, and they carry the same divine truth, authority, and efficacy. To distinguish between them on any such grounds is intolerable folly.

The evangelists' writings do not contain every instruction the Lord gave his disciples while on earth. He appeared to them for forty days after his resurrection and spoke of "the things pertaining to the kingdom of God" (Acts 1:3), yet most of this is not recorded, except in a few brief remarks. He had not, before his death, given them a clear and distinct understanding of the things concerning his death and resurrection as they are shown in the Old Testament (see Luke 24:25-27). That fuller understanding was not necessary for them in their earlier state.

Therefore, in the extent of divine revelation, what was given by his Spirit to the apostles after his ascension was greater than what is recorded in the evangelists' narratives. He plainly told them shortly before his death that he had many things to say to them that "you cannot bear them now" (John 16:12). He directed them to the coming of the Spirit for the revelation of these truths, saying, "However, when He, the Spirit of truth, has come, He will guide you into all truth; for He will not speak on His own authority, but whatever He hears He will speak; and He will tell you things to come. He will glorify Me, for He will take of what is Mine and declare it to you" (John 16:13-14). He had previously told them that it was to their advantage that he should go away so the Helper would come, whom he would send from the Father (John 16:7). This refers to the full and clear manifestation of the mysteries of the gospel. Thus the insinuations of Socinus and his followers are both false and dangerous.

The evangelists' writings fulfill their proper ends. Their aim is to record the genealogy, conception, birth, acts, miracles, and teachings of our Savior, to demonstrate that he is the promised Messiah. The author of the last Gospel testifies, "And truly Jesus did many other signs in the presence of His disciples, which are not written in this book; but these are written that you may believe that Jesus is the Christ, the Son of God, and that believing you may have life in His name" (John 20:30-31). Everything recorded by them is necessary to generate and establish faith. In light of this testimony, all that the Old Testament declared concerning him—what was taught in types and sacrifices—became the object of faith as these things were interpreted in their fulfillment. The doctrine had previously been revealed, as will be shown later. Therefore it is not surprising that some of the most important matters are declared more fully in other New Testament writings than in the evangelists.

The assertion is entirely false; there are as many clear testimonies to this truth in one evangelist as in any other New Testament book—namely, in the Gospel of John. I will refer to some of these where they belong: John 1:12, 17; 3:14-18, 36; 5:24.

We may set this aside as one of those inventions over which Socinus boasts in his letter to Michael Vajoditus, claiming that his writings were esteemed for their novelty.

The differences among Protestant writers on this doctrine have been used to discredit it. Osiander, early in the Reformation, erred by teaching that we are made righteous by an essential righteousness of God communicated to us in Christ. When he was vigorously opposed by many learned men, he cried that there were twenty different opinions among Protestants about the formal cause of justification. Roman controversialists seized on this as evidence against our doctrine—see Bellarmine, Vasquez, and others. Yet Osiander's folly has been exposed. Bellarmine himself could identify only four apparently differing opinions, counting Osiander's as one (De Justificat., book II, chapter 1). He knew that Osiander's view was rejected by all, and the other three are simply different aspects of the same doctrine.

Until recently, it could be truthfully said that Protestants agreed overall on this matter. Though they differed in expression and many individuals sought hair-splitting definitions under the guise of logical precision—creating an appearance of contradiction—they generally agreed that it is Christ's righteousness, not our own, by which we receive forgiveness, acceptance with God, a declaration of righteousness in the gospel, and a right to the heavenly inheritance. In this they were united—first against the Papists, later against the Socinians—and where that is acknowledged I shall not contend with anyone about mere verbal expression.

We also have the witness of the early church fathers on this point. Some, notably Augustine, following the Latin etymology of *justificare*, sometimes spoke of justification as making us righteous internally by personal righteousness. Yet they did not teach that we are pardoned and accepted by God on any ground other than the righteousness of

Christ. In controversies with the Pelagians, especially after that heresy arose, the fathers argued strongly that we are made righteous by God's grace, which changes our hearts and natures and creates in us a principle of spiritual life and holiness—not by our own will or by works done in our strength. Their words have sometimes been misapplied contrary to their original intent.

We fully agree with those who affirm that we are made personally righteous and holy by God's efficient grace, apart from any merit of our own works or will. Our sanctification is as truly a matter of grace as our justification. The Roman Church, however, often calls the inward making of us righteous by grace "justification" in a way we cannot accept. That equivocation is used by Roman controversialists who oppose our view of how we are made righteous.

When we speak of our justification before God, we mean the righteousness by which our sins are pardoned and by which we are accepted as righteous in His sight. It is hard to find anyone who attributes this justification to causes other than those acknowledged by Protestants. Thus, while they aim to prove their point, we are in substantial agreement with them. Yet the way they argue is often taken up by the Papists and used for a purpose they did not intend.

Among Protestants there has always been variety in how this doctrine is expressed. That will likely continue, since people's capacities for understanding spiritual matters differ greatly. Lately, some have exaggerated these differences and treated them as if they outweighed the common substance. As a result, whole books have been written full of irrelevant criticisms of other men's words and expressions. This behavior springs from the weaknesses and bad habits of certain individuals and does not concern the doctrine itself. Those who delight in such disputes will continue until they are tired of them.

Moreover, the flood of questions and the intricate disputations that have grown up around this doctrine—where practical directions should have been emphasized—have added little to the truth itself, even when they have not openly opposed it.

The real differences among those who agree in substance may be grouped under a few heads:

There is disagreement about the nature of the faith that justifies us, about its proper object, and about the part it plays in justification. This illustrates both our limited understanding of spiritual things and the lingering confusion in our minds. Indeed, we know in part and we prophesy in part in this life. Faith is an act of the mind directed toward God, yet many who sincerely exercise it do not agree about its nature or its proper object. Still, those who differ usually express their thoughts without prejudice, describing their own experience as best they can.

Despite these differences, all such believers please God by exercising faith as their duty, and they fix their faith on its proper object, which secures their justification and salvation. If we cannot tolerate one another's differing expressions and opinions on these points, it betrays a contentious spirit and weak foundations. I would rather be among those who truly believe in their hearts for righteousness, even if they cannot give a neat definition for others, than among those who can argue with apparent precision but neglect faith's practical duty. I will therefore state my own views briefly, without intending to contradict or oppose others.

A controversy has arisen among some learned theologians of the Reformed churches about the righteousness of Christ that is said to be imputed to us. Some maintain that this imputation relates only to His suffering and the satisfaction rendered by His death; others include the obedience of His life as well. The origin and progress of this dispute, the men concerned, the writings produced, and attempts at accommodation are well known to students of the subject. I do not seek controversy; I will freely give my judgment, since the consideration of Christ's righteousness is inseparable from the truth I defend.

There has also been debate over whether the imputed righteousness of Christ should be called the formal cause of our justification before God. Learned men have expressed this differently in controversies with the Papists. The root of these differences lies in the Roman Church's assertion that the righteousness by which we are reckoned righteous is our own inherent righteousness, not Christ's imputed righteousness. They frame the whole question under the phrase "formal cause of justification," as Bellarmine discusses in his second book on justification.

By contrast, some Protestants insist that the righteousness by which we are accepted by God is Christ's imputed righteousness, not our imperfect own. They have asked what constitutes the formal cause of our justification. Some call it the imputation of Christ's righteousness; others simply call it the righteousness of Christ imputed. But their aim is not to resolve a scholastic controversy. Their intent is to show that what truly belongs to Christ's righteousness in our justification has been wrongly attributed to our own by the Papists. They acknowledge a habitual, infused grace that is the formal cause of our personal righteousness, yet they deny that God pardons or justifies sinners on the ground of this inherent righteousness. Indeed, they maintain there can be no inherent formal cause in the justification of a sinner. By "formal cause" in justification they mean only that which designates the subject—just as the imputation of Christ's righteousness designates the justified person.

Despite differences in expression among some individuals, the substance of the doctrine in the Reformed churches remains the same. They all agree that God does not justify any sinner—does not remove guilt or declare righteousness — except in relation to a true and perfect righteousness. They also agree that this righteousness truly belongs to the person who is justified and that it becomes theirs by God's free grace and gift. The way we are made partakers of this righteousness is by faith alone, and this righteousness is the perfect obedience or righteousness of Christ imputed to us. These points, which I will expand later, comprise the whole truth this discourse aims to explain and confirm.

Because recent challengers of this doctrine borrow more from the Socinians than from the Papists and largely follow their principles, I will focus mainly on the original authors whose ideas these men have adopted and whose arguments they use in their defense.

In closing those discussions, we must recognize how central the doctrine of justification was to the first Reformation and how deeply it shaped the whole movement. People may later alter their views on various doctrines, but no one can rightly call themselves a Protestant who does not hold the first Reformation in high esteem. This is especially true of those whose present temporal advantages stem from it. Those who believe God was specially present and guiding the reformers will see that their conviction on this point and the importance they attached to it merit careful attention.

It is well known that the doctrine of justification was the catalyst for the whole Reformation and the foundation on which it rested. The reformers called it "the article by which the church stands or falls," arguing that vindicating this doctrine alone justified the Reformation's entire effort. Even if people do not fully acknowledge or understand it, that doctrine has profoundly changed the world.

Overall, the Reformation brought significant benefits to the world, even for many who now reject it, despite what critics claim. When evils followed, opponents often blamed the corrupt passions and interests of its defenders. Meanwhile, the enlightenment, freedoms, and benefits that followed are sometimes credited to other causes. Among these outcomes, the doctrine of justification—and the reasons for its discovery and defense—stands out. The first reformers found their own and others' consciences mired in darkness—burdened by fears and anxieties about sin and without any reliable way to find peace with God. They therefore sought the truth diligently, knowing it was essential to their deliverance.

In those days, people were either held captive by endless fears and anxieties about sin; or they sought relief through indulgences, priestly pardons, penances, pilgrimages, and satisfactory works—either their own or others'; or they remained shackled in darkness, awaiting purgatory until the final day. It is impossible to compare past and present without recognizing these profound changes, even within the papal church. Before the Reformation, when the light of the gospel—especially concerning justification—began to shine on people, religion was largely confined to those practices, even among those who did not comprehend or accept the gospel. To encourage diligence in observing these rituals, people were filled with traditions and tales of visions, apparitions, frightful spirits, and other notions that fed their fears and restless anxieties.

"Dreams, magical terrors, miracles, nocturnal spirits, and Thessalian portents,"

[Hor., Ep. ii. 2, 209.] were the primary elements of their creed and the topics of their religious discourse. Compared with the pre-Reformation era, the church is now freer from these fears, although enough of those elements remain to blind people to the need for and truth of the evangelical doctrine of justification.

This development resembles the early spread of Christianity. A sudden burst of gospel light and truth reached people's minds, even while the message faced opposition and persecution. As a result, the common people gained a better grasp of God and his attributes, and of the origin and order of the universe, than they had in the depths of pagan ignorance.

Learned men, too, were influenced by the gospel's truth. They reformed and improved upon the old philosophy, casting off many false and irrelevant ideas that had weighed it down. Yet even after this reform, they still defended their views on the basis of older philosophical principles. Their opposition to the gospel thus became more plausible and more defensible than before. Having rejected the crude popular notions about divine nature and government, they tried to blend Christian truth with their philosophy, mounting a vigorous effort to bolster paganism against the gospel's core message.

We see the same pattern in the Reformation. The light of truth freed even ordinary people from the childish fears that had bound them. At the same time, learned men reshaped their church's beliefs and practices into more defensible positions, making their resistance to the gospel's truths seem more credible. Indeed, a doctrine once so dreadful in its teaching and effects that it drove many from communion is now presented with new representations and artificial coverings, and this presentation is used as an argument for returning to full communion with that doctrine.

To eradicate the superstitions mentioned and to impart the knowledge of the righteousness of God, which is revealed from faith to faith, the first reformers labored diligently in declaring and defending the evangelical doctrine of justification. Their aim was to deliver people from bondage, fear, and distress, and to guide convinced sinners to the only path to true peace with God. We should consider carefully whether we ought to part easily with this doctrine of truth — the doctrine in which they found peace for their own souls and by which they helped countless others attain liberty and peace with God. These labors produced visible effects: holiness and fruitful works of righteousness, all to the praise of God through Jesus Christ.

We must be cautious about dismissing the insights of those who were not taught, employed, or tested in the same way as the first reformers were. This is especially true when their writings lack the wisdom, sound judgment, and deep experience that characterized the reformers' work.

In my opinion, Luther spoke the truth when he said, "Amisso articulo justificationis, simul amissa est tota doctrina Christiana." I wish he had not proved to be a true prophet in predicting that, in future ages, the doctrine of justification would again be obscured. I have explored the reasons for that prediction elsewhere.

Some recent Protestant writers have tried to present the controversy over justification with the Papists as less significant than is commonly perceived. Eliminating unnecessary points of debate and differences in religion is a worthy aim, provided we do not compromise essential truths. The approach here is to acknowledge certain concessions by the more moderate Papists concerning grace and the merit of Christ on one side, and the Protestants' expressed views on the necessity of good works for those who are justified on the other.

Moreover, it often appears that, despite different expressions, both parties frequently mean the same things. Among those who have worked in this area, Ludovicus le Blanc stands out for clarity, moderation, and a lack of contentious spirit. Yet I must say I have not seen the hoped-for results from such efforts. When each side interprets its own concessions — which they may rightly claim — they do so in a way that fits their understanding of the core doctrine where the main differences lie. Thus the divide remains as wide as ever. There is no basis for peace won by concessions or compromises in this matter. Unless we wholly align with the decrees and canons of the Council of

Trent, which anathematizes the doctrines of the Old and New Testaments, any compliance will only serve to amplify our differences.

I mention this not to discourage anyone from granting whatever they can to the Papists without compromising the substance of the truths professed in the Protestant churches, but merely to emphasize the futility of such concessions for achieving peace and agreement with them — especially when they have a Procrustean bed to impose upon us, from which they will not budge.

In the past one hundred and thirty years, only a few individuals within the Roman communion have acknowledged our doctrine of justification in its essence. Albertus Pighius and the Antitagma Coloniense are cited as examples, as Bellarmine himself admits. What he says about Pighius is indeed accurate, as we shall see later; however, I have not encountered the latter work. Cardinal Contarinus, in a treatise on justification written before and published around the beginning of the Council of Trent, expressed support for this doctrine. It is said that he was poisoned shortly after his work was recognized, though I must admit I do not know the source of that claim.

While we strive for peace — which is essential — it cannot be denied that the doctrine of justification, as it operates within the Roman church, is the foundation for many serious errors in belief and practice. I concede that these errors do not now show the same visible dominance and fervor as they once did, nor are the majority of people in such oppressive bondage as formerly. Yet remnants of these problems still flow from that corrupt source and continue to pose a dangerous threat to souls.

Practices such as sacrificial masses for the living and the dead; the necessity of confession with authoritative absolution; penances; pilgrimages; sacramentals; indulgences and commutations; satisfactory and supererogatory works; the merit and intercession of departed saints; particular devotions to certain saints or angels; purgatory; and, in effect, the whole system of monastic devotion—all depend on this doctrine. These practices are merely attempts to soothe consciences or distract people from the charges laid against them by God's law. They serve as inadequate substitutes for a righteousness of their own for those who do not know how to submit to the righteousness of God.

If the doctrine of free justification by the blood of Christ were to be rejected or corrupted until it became unintelligible, people would inevitably revert to those practices. What now seems absurd or foolish to some would then become a refuge. If people are diverted from trusting solely in the righteousness of Christ and the grace of God, they will seize on anything that offers even the slightest appearance of relief when they first feel the weight of their sin. While they are at ease in their own minds, lacking a genuine sense of sin or righteousness, they will argue and dispute and may mock those who lack their false security. But when they are awakened to a truer understanding, they will be compelled to make new resolutions. It is futile to debate justification with those not yet convinced of their sinful condition and guilt, for such people neither understand what they are discussing nor the matters about which they dogmatize.

Therefore, we have the same reasons as the first reformers to be vigilant in preserving the doctrine of the gospel in its pure and complete form. We should not expect the same measure of success they enjoyed. The general mindset of people today is quite different from that of those who engaged with the reformers.

While many then were under the influence of ignorance and superstition, a large number still felt their guilt and sin. By contrast, many today have only a superficial understanding and lack a real sense of sin. That leads them to disregard this doctrine and, indeed, the whole mystery of the gospel.

We have seen the fruits of the faith we advocate in this nation for many years, even centuries. Those who have been most steadfast in upholding the doctrine of justification through the imputation of Christ's righteousness have generally shown the most exemplary holy living, especially in earlier times.

If this doctrine becomes more corrupted, diminished, or forgotten among us, we will quickly slip into one of the extremes pressing upon us from either side. Although the Roman church's remedies for the conscience are now largely scorned and even despised, people who lose the ability to trust wholly in Christ's righteousness and God's grace will not remain uncertain about their own efforts for long. They will turn to whatever offers certain peace and security, even if it now seems foolish to them.

I have no doubt that some, through ignorance of God's righteousness — either from lack of teaching or indifference — have, with some integrity of conscience, sought refuge in the false rest offered by the Roman church. Troubled by their sins, they choose to rely on the many means the Roman church provides to ease consciences rather than remain without any semblance of relief.

They may find temporary comfort. But if they are ever truly confronted with the reality of their sin, they will be driven to look beyond themselves for peace and satisfaction — or be left without it for eternity.

The principles and methods adopted by others who reject this doctrine, though they may appear more attractive, are not genuinely beneficial for souls when compared with those of the Roman church they dismiss as outdated. All these approaches arise from, or lead to, a failure to grasp the true nature and guilt of sin and the holiness and righteousness of God in relation to it.

When such principles gain hold in people's minds, they soon grow careless, negligent, and secure in their sins. That moral indifference often ends in atheism or a deep apathy toward religion and its duties.

2. Justification Comes Through Faith

The assertion that we are justified by faith is frequently and plainly affirmed in Scripture; it is undeniable. Some, biased by controversy, will argue that our justification is often ascribed to other things—such as graces or duties—rather than to faith. That argument can be set aside.

However, certain explanations of that concession—that "justified by faith"—can undermine the assertion just as surely as outright denial. It would be better to reject those misleading explanations at once, instead of letting people wander into a maze of words and distinctions, as with both Romanists and Socinians. For now we accept the proposition and will examine its true sense and meaning.

The first thing to consider is faith itself. We must look at two aspects: the nature of faith and the role faith plays in our justification.

Regarding the nature of faith in general, and the specific character of justifying faith—how it differs from what is called faith but is not justifying—much has already been written. Many of those discussions come from sound judgment and solid experience.

It is unnecessary to rehearse those debates at length here. What is essential is that we clarify what we mean by the faith to which we attribute our justification, and what its role is in that process.

I will put aside the usual distinctions about faith as a term of many meanings. Those distinctions are obvious and well known, and they do not bear directly on our present argument.

What matters is that Scripture speaks of a twofold faith by which people believe the gospel.

There is a faith by which we are justified, and whoever possesses this faith will certainly be saved; it purifies the heart and works through love. Conversely, there is a kind of belief that does none of those things. Those who possess only that kind of belief are not justified and cannot be saved. Therefore, not every faith by which people are said to believe is a justifying faith.

For instance, it is said of Simon the magician that he "believed" (Acts 8:13), yet he remained in the gall of bitterness and bond of iniquity. Thus he did not have that faith which, as Acts 15:9 says, was "purifying their hearts by faith." Many "believed in His name" when they saw the signs which He did, but Jesus did not commit Himself to them, because He knew all men (John 2:23-24). They did not believe in His name as those do to whom, John 1:12 says, "to them He gave the right to become children of God." Some are described, in Luke 8:13, as "when they hear, receive the word with joy; and these have no root, who believe for a while," and so they fall away. Faith without a root in the heart will not justify anyone, for, as Romans 10:10 says, "with the heart one believes unto righteousness." The same is true of those who will cry, "Lord, Lord," on the last day, claiming, "have we not prophesied in Your name," while they are "you who practice lawlessness" (Matthew 7:22-23).

This type of faith is commonly called historical faith. The term does not come from the object of faith, as if it were confined to the historical events of Scripture. Rather, it embraces the whole truth of the Word — the promises of the gospel and other revealed truths. It is called historical faith because it consists of the kind of assent we give to historical facts that are credibly testified to us.

This faith has various differences or degrees, both in its grounds and in its effects. Concerning its grounds or reasons, all faith is an assent based on testimony; divine faith is an assent based on divine testimony. How that testimony is received produces differences in faith.

Some people receive it on the basis of human motives and the credibility of reason alone. Their assent is merely a natural act of understanding and represents the lowest degree of historical faith. Others are spiritually enlightened and perceive the evidence of divine truth; their assent is firmer and more operative than that of the former group.

Moreover, faith also exhibits differences or degrees with respect to its effects. For some, it has little or no influence on the will or affections and brings about no real change in life. This is true of those who profess belief in the gospel yet live in every kind of sin.

In this degree, it is referred to by the apostle James — "Thus also faith by itself, if it does not have works, is dead" — which he compares to a lifeless carcass, devoid of life or motion. This type of faith is like the faith even demons possess and is widespread in the world.

In contrast, for others faith has a significant impact on the affections and produces various effects in life, as the different soils show where the seed of the word is sown. In its highest expression this faith is called temporary faith, because it does not endure against all opposition and will not bring anyone to eternal rest.

That name is taken from our Savior's description of those who have this sort of faith: "yet he has no root in himself, but endures only for a while" (Matthew 13:21).

I acknowledge that this faith is genuine in its own kind and not merely equivocally so called; it is not "pistis pseudōnumos." It corresponds to the general nature of faith, but it is not of the same special nature as justifying faith. Justifying faith is not merely a higher degree of this faith; it is of a different kind or nature.

Accordingly, several observations can be made about this faith, especially in its highest expression as it relates to our present discussion.

This faith, along with all its effects, can exist without justification; and if one does not possess a faith of another kind, they cannot be justified. Justification is never attributed to this faith, and the apostle James affirms that none can be justified by it.

This faith can produce notable changes in people's minds, affections, and conduct, although none of these effects are unique to justifying faith. Still, those in whom these effects appear may — and, on charitable grounds, should — be regarded as true believers in the judgment of charity.

This is the sort of faith that may stand alone in its own sphere. We say that we are justified by faith alone, but we do not mean by that that we are justified by this sort of faith which can stand alone.

The word "alone" refers to faith's role in justification, not to its nature or existence. We deny that one can be justified by a faith that exists independently of a principle of spiritual life and universal obedience, which duty requires.

I note these points solely to meet the slander and reproach some attach to the doctrine of justification by faith alone, through Christ's mediation. Those who hold this doctrine are often called Solifidians, Antinomians, and other names that imply they deny the necessity of universal obedience or good works. Most who use such language know in their own consciences that the charges are unfounded.

This tactic is common in controversies: people will assert anything that seems to serve their cause, to the great detriment of religion.

If by "Solifidians" they mean those who believe that faith alone is the instrument, means, or condition of our justification (a point to be discussed later), then all the prophets and apostles were such, and they were taught so by Jesus Christ, as will be shown. If, however, they mean those who claim that the faith by which we are justified is separate from, or separable from, a principle and the fruit of holy obedience, they must produce such persons; we know of none.

We do not recognize as justifying any faith that does not inherently include a living principle of obedience and good works — just as effect is found in the cause and fruit in the root, operating in every particular duty as rule and circumstance require. We will not accept any faith as justifying, or of the same nature as justifying faith, that is not itself a spiritually vital principle of obedience and good works. If this does not deter some from using disgraceful slanders to gain advantage, it should at least relieve others of concern about them.

Regarding the special nature of justifying faith, the evidence for it can be grouped under four main points:

1. The causes of it, from God's perspective.

2. What is required of us beforehand.

3. The proper object of this faith.

4. Its specific acts and effects.

I will address these points as they are needed for our present discussion. The doctrine concerning the causes of faith — particularly its origin in the divine will and the manner in which it is communicated to us — is broad. It is closely tied to the operation of efficacious grace in conversion, a topic I have examined elsewhere. I will not expand on it here. It cannot be adequately treated in a few words, and a full examination would divert us from our main argument.

I will only say that it can be clearly shown that the faith by which we are justified is of a peculiar kind, distinct from any other faith that is not inseparably joined to justification.

Our first inquiry concerns what duty is required of us prior to justifying faith. In other words, what must be present in us before we can believe for the justification of life?

I maintain that, in those who possess this faith, there is an essential work of the law that convinces them of sin. This conviction of sin is a necessary precursor to justifying faith. Many have debated what this conviction entails and what effects it produces in the mind as it prepares the soul to receive the gospel promise. Because there are varied views about the attendant feelings — such as compunction, humiliation, self-judgment, and sorrow for sin — I will touch on them only insofar as they relate to the conviction I am asserting.

First, I will consider the conviction itself and what is essential to it, and then its effects together with the temporary faith mentioned earlier. I do this not to investigate their nature, which I assume to be known, but only in relation to our justification.

First, the work of conviction in general is necessary for justifying faith. This work enables a person to understand the nature of sin, its guilt, and the punishment it deserves. It makes them aware of their own participation in these matters—both original and actual sin—and of their complete inability to escape the condition in which they find themselves because of these faults. This understanding is essential to justifying faith, especially in adults, for whom the Word serves as the external means and instrument of justification.

A convinced sinner is merely a "subject capable of justification." This does not mean every person who is convinced will necessarily be justified. There is no disposition or preparation from this conviction that guarantees justification, as the Papists claim, nor does justifying grace inevitably follow. Likewise, no such preparation ensures, by divine promise, that a convinced person will be pardoned and justified.

While a person may possess any kind of non-justifying faith—such as the kind mentioned earlier—this conviction is typically necessary for the faith that leads to the justification of life. The purpose of this conviction is not that it guarantees justification, but that without it one cannot attain justification.

This conviction is required in the person to be justified as a prerequisite to the faith by which we are justified. I will support this with the following arguments:

1. Without an understanding of this conviction, the true nature of faith cannot be grasped. As noted above, justification is God's means of delivering the convinced sinner—one whose mouth is stopped, who stands guilty before God, bound by the law, and trapped in sin. An awareness of this state and all that belongs to it is therefore essential for believing.

Le Blanc, who has diligently explored these matters, praises Mestrezat's definition of faith as "the flight of a penitent sinner to the mercy of God in Christ." This definition makes more sense and carries more truth than many definitions that may seem more precise. Yet without the conviction already described, one cannot grasp this definition of faith. It is that conviction which drives the soul to seek refuge in the mercy of God in Christ, aiming to be saved from impending wrath. Hebrews 6:18 states, "who have fled for refuge to lay hold of the hope set before us."

2. The order, relation, and purpose of the law and the gospel show the necessity of this conviction before believing. The first reality a person must confront about their eternal condition—both by nature and by God's design—is the law. The law is presented to the soul with its terms of righteousness and life, and with its curse for failure. Without this understanding, the gospel cannot be properly comprehended or its grace rightly valued. The gospel reveals God's way of rescuing souls from the law's sentence and curse (Romans 1:17).

This was the intent and end of the first promise and of all God's grace revealed in subsequent promises—that is, the whole gospel. Therefore the faith under discussion, being evangelical in nature, requires the gospel as its principle, rule, and object. It cannot operate without the prior work and effect of the law in convincing of sin—giving knowledge of sin, a sense of guilt, and an understanding of the sinner's state. We absolutely deny that any faith lacking this context is the faith by which we are justified (Galatians 3:22-24; Romans 10:4).

3. Our Savior teaches this plainly in the gospel. He calls only those who are weary and burdened, saying, "Those who are well have no need of a physician, but those who are sick," and, "I have not come to call the righteous, but sinners to repentance." In this context He does not mean persons who are truly righteous—since all men are sinners—but those who are conscious of their sin, burdened by it, and seeking deliverance.

Similarly, when Peter set before them the promise of the gospel and the pardon of sin as the object of gospel faith, they were "cut to the heart" and cried out, "Men and brethren, what shall we do?" (Acts 2:37-39). The jailer to whom Paul offered salvation through Christ was in a similar state; he was instructed on what to believe for his deliverance (Acts 16:30-31).

4. The state of Adam and God's dealings with him are the best illustration of the order and method here. After the fall he was utterly lost by sin and became aware of the nature of his sin and its consequences through the law's work upon his mind — what is referred to as the "opening of his eyes." This was the law's communication to his conscience, giving a sense of sin's nature, guilt, effects, and consequences — something the law could teach him only after the fall.

This awareness filled him with shame and fear. To cover the shame he used fig leaves, and to cope with the fear he hid among the trees of the garden. No human contrivance for escaping sin can be wiser or more likely to succeed than God's method. In this lost, hopeless condition God directly addressed the matter. He intensified the conviction by testifying to its truth and by placing Adam under the law's curse through a formal declaration. In that desperate state God also offered the promise of redemption through Christ to him, which became the object of the faith by which he was to be justified.

Although these concepts may not be distinctly expressed in the minds and consciences of everyone called to believe the gospel, their essence — particularly the necessity of conviction of sin before faith — is present in all who sincerely believe.

These matters are generally known and agreed upon in substance. Yet, when examined carefully, they expose the shortcomings and errors in many definitions of faith offered to us. Any definition or description that does not explicitly, or at least implicitly, address this issue is misleading. It fails to reflect the experience of those who truly believe. This includes definitions that reduce faith to mere assent to divine revelation, regardless of the nature of that assent or the effects ascribed to it. Such assent can exist without any acknowledgment of the law's work.

I place little weight on precise arguments about the nature and act of justifying faith from those who have never experienced the law's work in convicting and condemning them for sin. Nor do I give them much weight from those who neglect to consider their own experience—where what they truly believe is often better expressed than in their arguments. The faith by which we are justified is essentially the soul's acting toward God as He reveals Himself in the gospel, seeking deliverance from our state and condition or from the curse of the law pressed on the conscience, according to His will and by the means He has appointed. I do not offer this as a strict definition of faith, but as an account of what necessarily influences it, from which its nature may be discerned.

We may briefly examine the effects of this conviction as they relate to our justification—whether real or pretended. While this conviction is solely a work of the law, it should not be considered in isolation but together with the temporary gospel faith already described. These two elements—temporary gospel faith and legal conviction—are the foundation of all religious duties or actions that precede justification. We must deny that they have any causal power in producing justification. Still, it is acknowledged that many internal and external acts will follow genuine conviction.

The internal acts can be categorized into three main areas:

1. Displeasure and sorrow over our sins. No one can be truly convinced of sin in the manner described without disliking sin, feeling shame for

having sinned, and sorrowing over it. A person whose mind is not affected in this way—whatever their profession or confession—cannot be said to be genuinely convinced of sin (Jeremiah 36:24).

2. Fear of the punishment due for sin. Conviction does not only concern the instructive and preceptive aspects of the law, which reveal the existence and nature of sin, but also its sentence and curse, which judge and condemn it (Genesis 4:13-14). Therefore, if fear of the threatened punishment does not arise, that person is not genuinely convinced of sin, and the law has not fulfilled its proper role toward them, which must precede the administration of the gospel. Since we "flee from the wrath to come" by faith, a sense that that wrath is justly due to us is essential to true belief.

3. A desire for deliverance from the condition in which a convinced sinner finds himself is unavoidable. Often this desire is the first effect of conviction, showing itself in varying degrees of concern, fear, anxiety, and restlessness. These responses have been confirmed by experience and Scripture to the benefit of the church, though others have ridiculed them.

Furthermore, these internal acts lead to various external duties, which themselves may be divided into two categories:

1. Abstaining from known sin as best one can. Those who begin to see how grievous and bitter it is to have sinned against God will strive to avoid future sin. This effort is shaped by the internal acts already described, especially the desire to be delivered from their present state. They often believe that such abstinence is the best means of obtaining deliverance, or at least necessary for it. In this effort they frequently make promises and vows, and they feel renewed sorrow when they fall into sin.

2. Engaging in religious duties: prayer, attentive hearing of the Word, and diligent use of the church's ordinances. They know that without these practices no deliverance can be expected. The reformation of life and conduct partly consists in these actions and partly follows from them. These patterns are typical where convictions are genuine and lasting.

However, these elements are neither individually nor collectively necessary dispositions, preparations, merits, nor conditions for our justification.

1. They are not conditions of justification. If one thing is a condition for another, the latter must follow the fulfillment of that condition; otherwise it is not a condition. Yet these elements can be present without justification occurring. Therefore there is no covenant, promise, or divine constitution that makes them conditions of justification, even if they serve some purpose with respect to what is required of us. They do not have an infallible connection to justification like faith does. No other conditions should be accepted except those established by divine promise; otherwise conditions could be multiplied without end, covering all things, natural and moral. For example, the food we eat could be treated as a condition for justification. Faith and justification are inseparable, but justification does not have the same necessary connection with the elements we are discussing, as experience shows.

2. Justification can occur even when the outward acts and duties arising from temporary convictions and faith are absent. Adam was justified without them, as were the converts at Pentecost (Acts 2:37). The same is true of the jailer (Acts 16:30-31) and of many who truly believe. Therefore these elements cannot be conditions; a condition suspends the outcome until it is met.

3. They are not formal dispositions toward justification, because justification does not introduce any new form or inherent quality into the soul, as has been partly explained and will be further shown.

4. They are not moral preparations for justification. Since they precede evangelical faith, the only intention tied to them is often to "seek righteousness through the works of the law," which does not prepare one for justification. All true apprehensions of God's righteousness and the soul's adherence to it belong to faith alone. There is a repentance that accompanies faith and is included in its nature, at least in a foundational way, and this is necessary for our justification. But the legal repentance that occurs before gospel faith—and that exists without it—is neither a disposition, a preparation, nor a condition for our justification.

In summary, the order of these matters can be seen in God's dealings with Adam, as noted earlier. There are three stages in this process:

1. The opening of the sinner's eyes to see the filth and guilt of sin as the sentence and curse of the law are applied to the conscience (Romans 7:9–10). This awareness drives the sinner to perform all the duties that result from it. At first, those who are convinced usually view their state as evil and dangerous, and they think it their duty to improve it and that they can do so if they apply themselves. But all such efforts to shield or deliver themselves from the law's sentence are no better than fig leaves and hiding.

2. Often, by providence or the preaching of the Word, God gives life and power to the work of the law in a special way, answering Adam's attempt to hide. This brings the sinner to silence, making them fully aware of their guilt before God and showing that no relief can be found in the sorrow or duties they have attempted.

3. In this state, the sinner is called to believe in the promise for justification solely by sovereign grace, independent of the preceding elements. This is God's order; what precedes His call to faith does not cause that call.

The next matter to consider is the proper object of justifying faith, or true faith, with respect to its role, work, and duty in our justification. We must first examine what cannot be readily accepted. Two opinions stand out as extremes: one in excess and the other in deficiency. The first is that of the Roman church and those aligned with it.

The Roman church asserts that the object of justifying faith, as such, includes all divine truth and revelation — whether found in Scripture or conveyed through tradition under the authority of the church. We need not address the latter part here. They hold that the whole of Scripture, with all its parts and truths, serves equally as objects of faith for justification. Consequently, they cannot allow faith to be anything other than a mere assent of the mind.

They argue that since the whole Scripture — including laws, precepts, promises, threats, narratives, and prophecies — constitutes the object of faith, and these are not seen as containing good or evil for us but merely as divinely revealed, no other mental act beyond assent is required. They are so confident in this position that Bellarmine, opposing Calvin (who included knowledge in his definition of justifying faith), claimed it would be better defined by ignorance than by knowledge.

This description of justifying faith and its object has been thoroughly debated and, on clear grounds of Scripture and reason, rejected by Protestant writers of every kind. It need not be dwelt on at length. Still, I will note certain aspects that display both the truth and the failings in their assertions.

I will address not only those from the Roman church who demand nothing more than a bare assent of the mind to divine revelations, but also those who define faith wholly as a firm assent that issues in obedience to all divine commands. While both aspects belong to faith, more is required to define its specific nature. As justifying faith, it is neither a mere assent nor merely a firm degree of assent that yields such effects.

All faith in general is an act of the soul's power that enables us to assent firmly to truth presented on testimony where sense or reason do not furnish evidence. It is "the evidence of things not seen." All divine faith, in general, is an assent to the truth proposed to us on divine testimony. Thus, as commonly agreed, it is distinguished from mere opinion and moral certainty on one side, and from science or demonstration on the other.

Therefore, in justifying faith there is an assent to all divine revelation grounded on God's testimony as the Revealer. We cannot be justified by any other act of mind that does not include or imply this assent — not because that act could not be justifying, but because it would not be faith. This assent, I maintain, is included in justifying faith.

Consequently, we often find it referenced in Scripture (examples compiled by Bellarmine and others) with respect to various matters, not limited to the specific promise of grace in Christ, which they contest. In most such instances, however, the proper object of faith as justifying is included and eventually referred to, even when expressed differently through some of its causes or attendant aspects. It is acknowledged that we believe all divine truth by the very faith by which we are justified, allowing other matters to be rightly attributed to it.

On these concessions, we assert two points:

1. The whole nature of justifying faith does not consist merely in an assent of the mind, however firm and steadfast, nor in whatever obedient effects it may produce.

2. In its role and function in justification—which gives it the specific designation we are explaining—it does not regard all divine revelation equally, but has a particular object presented to it in Scripture. Both points will be demonstrated clearly in our description of the proper object and nature of faith. For now, I will offer a few arguments against the opposing description that are sufficient to show how far it departs from the truth.

First, that mere assent is only an act of the understanding—an act of the mind concerning a truth evidenced to it, regardless of the truth's nature. Thus, we can believe the worst things, which may be grievous to us, just as we believe the best and most beneficial.

But believing is an act of the heart, which Scripture often uses to denote the whole principle of moral and spiritual duties. "With the heart one believes unto righteousness" (Romans 10:10). It is also described as an act of the will, though not solely that. Without an act of the will, no one can believe as they ought. We come to Christ by an act of the will, and "Whoever desires, let him take the water of life freely." To be willing is synonymous with believing (Psalm 110:3), and unbelief is equated with disobedience (Hebrews 3:18-19).

Secondly, not every piece of divine truth is equally the object of this assent. The assent does not treat the specific nature or use of every truth the same; it only concerns divine revelation in general. If it did, the fact that Judas was a traitor would matter for our justification as much as the truth that Christ died for our sins. That is plainly at odds with Scripture, the analogy of faith, and the common experience of believers, and needs no further proof.

Thirdly, such an assent to all divine revelation may be genuine and sincere even without any prior work of the law or conviction of sin. Many who assent to revealed truth lack those prior experiences. But, as we have shown, those are necessary for evangelical, justifying faith. To deny that order and relation between law and gospel is to undermine their respective purposes in God's plan for the salvation of sinners.

Fourthly, this mere assent is not a means of relief for a sinner who is already convinced and silenced by guilt before God. Only such persons are suitable subjects for justification and can properly seek it. Mere intellectual assent is poorly suited to relieve them, because the knowledge of sin is brought home by the law. Faith, by contrast, is a distinctive act of the soul aimed at deliverance.

Fifthly, this assent is no more than what even the devils possess, as the apostle James indicates. Their belief in one God shows they accept whatever that first and fundamental truth implies. Such belief can coexist with every kind of wickedness and without any obedience, and so can be used to make God out to be a liar (1 John 5:10). It is therefore unsurprising that those who know no faith beyond this deny that we are justified by faith.

Sixthly, the description of faith as mere assent does not match the ways Scripture speaks of justifying faith. In regard to justification, we are said to "receive" Christ (John 1:12; Colossians 2:6), and to receive the promise, the word, the grace of God, and the atonement (James 1:21; John 3:33; Acts 2:41; 11:1; Romans 5:11; Hebrews 11:17). The Old Testament also speaks of faith as trust and hope. None of these actions are exhausted by an intellectual assent; they involve movements of the soul beyond understanding alone.

Seventhly, the doctrine must accord with the experience of those who truly believe. Our inquiry aims to determine what real believers do to obtain justification and life. It is not primarily about the abstract notions people may hold or how defensible those notions are in debate. Rather, it concerns what we ourselves do when we truly believe.

Because believers are imperfect, they will sometimes disagree about how to describe their own acts of faith. That, however, should breed mutual tenderness and forbearance, not contention. If people paid more attention to their own experience in seeking God's pardon and righteousness—rather than to disputable notions shaped by occasions or preconceptions—many needless controversies about the nature of justifying faith would fade. I therefore contend that a general assent to revealed truth, however firm, and whatever its outward effects in duty or obedience, does not correspond to the experience of any true believer. It fails to include the full action of the soul toward God for pardon and justification.

Eighthly, only that faith is properly called justifying which is accompanied by actual justification; the name derives from the effect. To suppose a person has justifying faith but is not justified is contradictory. We are concerned with the kind of faith by which a believer is actually justified, not with other kinds of faith. Many who possess mere assent are not thereby justified, and those who defend mere assent generally do not claim that assent alone immediately justifies anyone. Thus, something more than real assent to all divine revelation is required for justifying faith—though that assent is indeed included in the faith by which we are justified.

Some maintain the opposite error: they restrict the object of justifying faith too narrowly, treating that limitation as the essence of faith and thereby excluding other scriptural statements about it. They argue that the special object of justifying faith is the forgiveness of our sins. On that view, faith is a full assurance that our sins are forgiven through Christ's mediation, or that Christ's work as mediator was specifically for us. They make the particular appropriation of special mercy to our own souls and consciences the very essence of faith. Consequently, anyone who lacks a firm assurance of their own forgiveness would be said to lack saving faith.

I cannot accept that account. If anyone has held it, they have either overlooked their own experience or failed to recognize that the other acts of faith are contained within the assurance they emphasize. We will examine this further below. I readily admit that faith rightly directed will ordinarily aim at and come to that assurance in true believers who cultivate and grow in it.

Many eminent Reformation theologians—Lutherans included—identified the mercy of God in Christ, and therefore the forgiveness of sins, as the proper object of justifying faith. They described faith as a trusting reliance on the grace of God revealed in the promises, with a steady application of those promises to oneself. I maintain that those who do not strive for this understanding either misunderstand the nature of believing or are neglectful of both God's grace and their own peace.

The reason those devout and learned men framed the essence of faith in its highest expression, while still presupposing its other acts, was pastoral. They addressed consciences that were deeply burdened. The controversy with the Roman Church concerned how a convinced sinner could find rest and peace with God. At that time, people were taught to seek peace by their own works and by strict observance of many traditions—sacramental sacrifices, absolutions, penances, pilgrimages—practices to which extraordinary efficacy was ascribed. These teachings kept consciences in perpetual turmoil, fear, and bondage, and excluded the rest, assurance, and peace with God that the gospel promises through Christ's blood.

When their opponents realized such means could not secure rest or any true assurance of forgiveness, they condemned the belief in forgiveness and in God's love in Christ as false and pernicious. Given that their procedures could not attain those ends, what else could they do? Thus the central dispute was whether rest and assured peace with God could be experienced in this life under the gospel. Using every argument derivable from the nature, use, and purpose of the gospel, and from God's grace and design in Christ and in His atoning and interceding work, the Reformers set those things before souls as the special object of justifying faith. They urged people to seek peace with God, forgiveness, and a rightful claim to eternal life by placing full trust in God's mercy through Christ alone.

I have never read that any of them claimed every sincere believer always has full assurance of God's special love in Christ or of the forgiveness of their own sins. Rather, they taught that Scripture requires believers to pursue such assurance as a duty and that Christians should strive to attain it.

I will leave these matters as I find them, for the benefit of the church. I do not intend to argue over the manner of expressing the truth so long as the substance is preserved. The aim in these discussions is to magnify and glorify God's grace in Christ and to guide souls toward rest and peace with Him.

Where this is genuinely sought or attained, a variety of expressions and ways of speaking about the same things can serve the useful exercise of faith and the edification of the church. Therefore, without opposing what others have written on this subject, I will set down my own thoughts. I hope they may clarify the issue and help reconcile differences among learned and holy men.

Thus I affirm that the Lord Jesus Christ Himself, as God's ordinance in His mediatorial work for the recovery and salvation of lost sinners, is the proper object of justifying faith or saving faith in relation to our justification.

I define the object of justifying faith in this way because it comprehends all that Scripture attributes to faith and meets its requirements. What belongs to faith in general is assumed, and what is specific to justifying faith is set forth plainly.

A few brief points will clarify this thesis; they will be confirmed in later discussion.

That the Lord Jesus Christ is the proper object of justifying faith is evident in the many passages that speak of believing in Him, believing in His name, receiving Him, or looking to Him, with the promise of justification and eternal life attached. See John 1:12; 3:16, 36; 6:29, 47; 7:38; 14:12; Acts 10:43; 13:38, 39; 16:31; 26:18, etc.

He is not proposed as the object of our faith in an absolute, abstract sense, but as God's ordained provision specifically for that purpose. Hence He is the immediate object of justifying faith, in the respects we will shortly explain.

Justification is frequently ascribed to faith specifically directed toward Him, as in John 5:24: "He who believes in Him who sent Me has everlasting life, and shall not come into judgment, but has passed from death into life." This includes God's grace, love, and favor, which are the chief cause of our justification (Romans 3:23, 24).

John 6:29 likewise completes the object of faith: "This is the work of God, that you believe in Him whom He sent." God the Father, as the Sender, and the Son, as the Sent One—Jesus Christ in His mediatorial office for the recovery and salvation of lost sinners—together constitute the object of our faith. See 1 Peter 1:21.

For Him to be the object of our faith, He is set before us in the promises of the gospel. I therefore include those promises as part of the full object of faith. But I do not mean to make the promises merely the formal object, as if faith were only assent to a set of propositions.

Rather, the promises contain, propose, and present Christ as God's ordinance and the benefits of His mediation to believers. There is a particular assent to the gospel promises, and some have treated that assent as the essence of justifying faith. It is undeniable that specific assent to the promises occurs in the exercise of justifying faith. But that intellectual assent neither exhausts faith's nature nor accomplishes its whole work.

Thus, insofar as the promises contribute to faith's object, they do so materially: they present Christ to believers. Scripture often speaks of the promises as the object of faith for justification. See Acts 2:39; 26:6; Romans 4:16, 20; 15:8; Galatians 3:16, 18; Hebrews 4:1; 6:13; 8:6; 10:36.

The end for which the Lord Christ is God's ordinance in the promises — the recovery and salvation of lost sinners — belongs to the object of justifying faith. Therefore, forgiveness of sins and eternal life are set before us in Scripture as things to be believed for justification, or as proper objects of our faith. See Matthew 9:2; Acts 2:38, 39; 5:31; 26:18; Romans 3:25; 4:7, 8; Colossians 2:13; Titus 1:2.

It is true that "the just shall live by faith," and that each person must apply what he believes to himself. Some have argued that believing specifically for the pardon of our own sins and for our own salvation is the proper object of faith. That appropriation belongs to faith when, in God's order and under the gospel, it is attainable, as appears in 1 Corinthians 15:3, 4; Galatians 2:20; Ephesians 1:6, 7.

Therefore, when I say the Lord Jesus Christ in His mediatorial work is the object of faith for justification, I mean to include together the grace of God, which is the cause; the pardon of sin, which is the effect; and the promises of the gospel, which are the means by which Christ and the benefits of His mediation are offered to us.

These elements are so united and mutually related in God's purpose and in the gospel's declaration that to believe any one of them virtually includes belief in the others. Conversely, to disbelieve any one of them undermines and nullifies the rest, and so destroys faith itself.

A proper grasp of these points clears up many difficulties about the nature and object of faith, whether those difficulties arise from Scripture or from believers' experiences. Scripture names many things that are to be believed for justification; but two observations are immediately plain:

1. None of these can be regarded as the complete and adequate object of our faith.

2. None of them are absolute in themselves; they stand in relation to the Lord Christ as God's ordinance for our justification and salvation.

This accords with the experience of all who truly believe. Because these elements are united and inseparable in God's design, each one virtually includes the others.

1. Some concentrate their faith primarily on God's grace, love, and mercy, especially under the Old Testament before Christ's mediation was plainly revealed. The psalmist (Psalm 130:3-4; 33:18-19) and the publican (Luke 18:13) illustrate this. Scripture often presents these attributes as the causes of our justification (Romans 3:24; Ephesians 2:4-8; Titus 3:5-7).

However, such belief is never absolute. It always stands in relation to Christ's work—what Scripture calls the "redemption through His blood," as the means by which grace, love, and mercy are communicated to us (see Daniel 9:17; Romans 3:24-25; Ephesians 1:6-8). These are the cause, the means, and the way by which that grace, love, and mercy reach us.

2. Others place their faith chiefly in the Lord Christ—His mediation and the benefits of it. The apostle Paul often exemplifies this in his own experience (Galatians 2:20; Philippians 3:8-10). Yet that trust is never isolated. It is always related to God's grace and love, from which these benefits proceed, as Scripture indicates (Romans 8:32; John 3:16; Ephesians 1:6-8).

3. Some especially fix their faith on the promises. Abraham's case shows this (Genesis 15:6; Romans 4:20). Scripture also presents the promises themselves as objects of faith (Acts 2:39; Romans 4:16; Hebrews 4:1-2; 6:12-13).

But this faith in the promises is not merely because they are divine revelations. It is because the promises contain and present the Lord Christ and the benefits of His mediation, which flow from God's grace, love, and mercy. Paul argues at length in Galatians that if justification came by any other way than the promise, God's grace and Christ's death would be nullified. The promise is simply the means by which these truths are communicated to us.

4. Some fix their faith on the very things they seek—namely, the pardon of sin and eternal life. Scripture presents these as things to be believed for justification (Psalm 130:4; Acts 26:18; Titus 1:2).

Yet this must be done in the proper order, especially regarding the application to our own souls. We are not required to believe that these blessings belong to us personally except insofar as they are effects of God's grace and love, applied through Christ and His mediation and proposed in the gospel promises. Therefore believing the pardon of sins and eternal life apart from faith in their causes is, in the order of nature, antecedent to true faith and amounts to presumption.

I have therefore presented the whole object of faith as it concerns justification, in agreement with Scripture's testimonies and the experience of believers.

Acknowledging the proper place of the promises and the resulting pardon and eternal life leads me to affirm that the Lord Christ, in His mediatorial work, is the proper and sufficient object of justifying faith. The true nature of evangelical faith consists in the heart's regard for God's love, grace, and wisdom, together with the mediation of Christ — His obedience, sacrifice, satisfaction, and atonement by His blood.

Some impiously oppose these truths as if they were inconsistent. Socinianism, for example, treats God's grace and Christ's satisfaction as mutually exclusive, as though accepting one requires rejecting the other. But Scripture presents them together. Without accepting both, neither can truly be believed.

Thus faith that sees Christ's mediation as subordinate to God's grace rests on the Lord Christ as God's appointed ordinance: the redemption in His blood is the effect of God's wisdom, grace, and love. Faith finds rest in both and in nothing else.

I need not labor the point. The truth is abundantly declared in Scripture and forms a principal part of the gospel's design and substance. I will therefore cite only several passages where it is taught or well attested.

The whole is summed up in the passage where justification is most clearly taught, Romans 3:24-25: "being justified freely by His grace through the redemption that is in Christ Jesus, whom God set forth as a propitiation by His blood, through faith, to demonstrate His righteousness, because in His forbearance God had passed over the sins that were previously committed."

Consider also Ephesians 1:6–7: "to the praise of the glory of His grace, by which He made us accepted in the Beloved. In Him we have redemption through His blood, the forgiveness of sins, according to the riches of His grace."

What justifies us is the specific object of our faith for justification. That object is the Lord Christ in His mediatorial work. We are justified by the redemption that is in Jesus Christ; in Him we have redemption through His blood, even the forgiveness of sins. Christ, as propitiation, is both the cause of our justification and the object of our faith; we receive justification by faith in His blood.

This is so formally considered because He is God's ordinance for this purpose—appointed, given, proposed, and set forth by God's wisdom, grace, and love. God "made to abound toward us in all wisdom and prudence" (Ephesians 1:8). Therefore the gospel presents Christ as the special object of our faith for justification and life.

We can also confirm the various parts of this assertion distinctly. The Lord Jesus Christ, as presented in the promise of the gospel, is the unique object of faith for justification. Three types of testimonies support this:

1. Those that positively assert this, such as Acts 10:43: "To Him all the prophets witness that, through His name, whoever believes in Him will receive remission of sins." Believing in Christ as the means and cause of the remission of sins is what all the prophets testify.

Acts 16:31 says, "So they said, 'Believe on the Lord Jesus Christ, and you will be saved, you and your household.'" This is the apostle's response to the jailer's inquiry, "Sirs, what must I do to be saved?" His duty in believing, and the object of that belief, is the Lord Jesus Christ.

Acts 4:12 declares, "Nor is there salvation in any other, for there is no other name under heaven given among men by which we must be saved." What is proposed to us as the only way and means of our justification and salvation — exclusive of all other ways — is the object of faith for our justification; and this is Christ alone. Moses and the prophets testify this; the entire design of Scripture directs the faith of the church to the Lord Christ alone for life and salvation, as seen in Luke 24:25-27.

2. All those passages affirming that justifying faith is our belief in Him, or belief in His name, are numerous. John 1:12 states, "To them He gave the right to become children of God, to those who believe in His name:" John 3:16 declares, "For God so loved the world that He gave His only begotten Son, that whoever believes in Him should not perish but have everlasting life." Verse 36 states, "He who believes in the Son has everlasting life;" John 6:29 says, "This is the work of God, that you believe in Him whom He sent." Verse 47 states, "Most assuredly, I say to you, he who believes in Me has everlasting life." John 7:38 adds, "He who believes in Me, as the Scripture has said, out of his heart will flow rivers of living water." Other references include John 9:35-37; 11:25; Acts 26:18, "that they may receive forgiveness of sins and an inheritance among those who are sanctified by faith in Me." 1 Peter 2:6-7.

In all these passages, and in many others, we are not only directed to place our faith in Him, but the effect of justification is ascribed to that faith. This is explicitly stated in Acts 13:38-39, which is what we aim to prove.

3. Those passages that describe the acts of faith, showing Him to be the direct and proper object. Such passages refer to faith as a "receiving" of Him. John 1:12 says, "But as many as received Him," and Colossians 2:6

reads, "As you therefore have received Christ Jesus the Lord, so walk in Him." What we receive by faith is the proper object of that faith.

The image of looking to the brazen serpent when it was lifted up applies here, as in John 3:14-15 and John 12:32. Faith is the act of the soul whereby convinced sinners, otherwise ready to perish, look to Christ—who was made a propitiation for their sins—and those who do so "shall not perish, but have everlasting life." Therefore, He is indeed the object of our faith.

He is indeed the ordinance of God for this purpose. This consideration cannot be separated from our faith in Him. Several types of testimonies confirm this:

1. All those that present the love and grace of God as the sole cause of giving Jesus Christ as the way and means of our recovery and salvation. Therefore, they become, or God in them becomes, the supreme efficient cause of our justification. John 3:16 states, "For God so loved the world that He gave His only begotten Son, that whoever believes in Him should not perish but have everlasting life." This truth is also affirmed in Romans 5:8 and 1 John 4:9-10, and in Romans 3:24: "being justified freely by His grace through the redemption that is in Christ Jesus," and in Ephesians 1:6-8. The Lord Christ continually directs our faith toward Himself, referring all to the One who sent Him and whose will He came to fulfill, as noted in Hebrews 10:5.

2. All those passages where God is said to set forth Christ to be for us what He is for the justification of life. Romans 3:25 states, "Whom God set forth as a propitiation." 1 Corinthians 1:30 declares, "Who became for us wisdom from God, and righteousness and sanctification and redemption." 2 Corinthians 5:21 explains, "For He made Him who knew no sin to be sin for us, that we might become the righteousness of God in Him." Acts 13:38-39 also supports this.

Therefore, when we exercise faith in Christ for justification, we must regard Him solely as the ordinance of God for that purpose. He brings nothing to us, and does nothing for us, except what God appointed, designed, and made Him to do. It is essential to understand that by our faith in the blood, the sacrifice, and the satisfaction of Christ, we do not detract from the free grace, favor, and love of God.

3. Passages that reveal the wisdom of God in devising this way of justification and salvation. Ephesians 1:7-8 states, "In Him we have redemption through His blood, the forgiveness of sins, according to the riches of His grace, which He made to abound toward us in all wisdom and prudence." This wisdom is also declared in Ephesians 3:10-11 and in 1 Corinthians 1:24.

The entirety of this is encapsulated in the apostle's words: "God was in Christ reconciling the world to Himself, not imputing their trespasses to them" (2 Corinthians 5:19). Everything done in our reconciliation to God—concerning the pardon of our sins and acceptance with Him unto life—was accomplished by the presence of God, in His grace, wisdom, and power, through Christ, who designed and effected it.

Therefore, the Lord Christ, presented in the promise of the gospel as the object of our faith for justification unto life, is regarded as the ordinance of God for that purpose. Thus the love, grace, and wisdom of God in sending and giving Him are included in that object. Not only do the actions of God in Christ toward us belong to this, but also all His actions toward Christ Himself for the same end.

Concerning His death, Romans 3:25 says, "whom God set forth as a propitiation," and Romans 8:32 declares, "He who did not spare His own Son, but delivered Him up for us all." Isaiah 53:6 states that the Lord "has laid on Him the iniquity of us all." Romans 4:25 tells us He "was raised because of our justification." Our faith is in God — "that God has raised Him from the dead," as Romans 10:9 says — and in His exaltation (Acts 5:31). These elements complete "the testimony that God has given of His Son," as 1 John 5:10-12 records.

The entirety of this is confirmed by the exercise of faith in prayer, which is the soul's application to God for the participation of the benefits of Christ's mediation. It is referred to as our "through Him we both have access by one Spirit to the Father" (Ephesians 2:18); our coming through Him "Let us therefore come boldly to the throne of grace, that we may obtain mercy and find grace to help in time of need" (Hebrews 4:15-16); and through Him as "having a High Priest over the house of God," according to Hebrews 10:19-22. Thus, we "For this reason I bow my knees to the Father of our Lord Jesus Christ" (Ephesians 3:14). This aligns with the experience of all who understand what it means to pray. We approach in the name of Christ, by Him, through His mediation, to God, even the Father, to receive, through His grace, love, and mercy, what He has promised to communicate to poor sinners through Him. This represents the complete object of our faith.

A proper consideration of these matters will reconcile and harmonize everything Scripture says about the object of justifying faith — that is, what we are said to believe. While Scripture affirms various things distinctly, none of them alone constitutes the entire, adequate object of faith. When considered together in relation to Christ, each element has its proper place: the grace of God as the cause; the pardon of sin as the effect; and the promises of the gospel as the means by which the Lord Christ and the benefits of His mediation are communicated to us.

The reader should note that I not only neglect but also reject recent attempts by some to reduce the person and mediation of Christ to matters outside the doctrine of the gospel. Such attempts are objectionable and impious. They also lack substantial proof, learning, argument, or sobriety.

3. Defining Justifying Faith

What we will now inquire into is the nature of justifying faith — the faith by which we are justified, or upon which justification, according to God's ordination and promise, ensues. The reader should keep in mind the assumptions we have already made regarding sincere faith in general, and what is required before considering its special nature, work, and duty in our justification.

We deny that, according to God's ordinary method of dealing with us as declared in Scripture and by the rule of our duty, anyone can truly believe with faith unto justification without first having undergone the work of conviction described earlier. Definitions of faith that ignore this prior work are vain speculations. Some who offer such definitions appear never to have truly considered what they are doing when they believe on Jesus Christ for life and salvation.

The nature of justifying faith, in respect to the exercise by which we are justified, consists in the heart's approval of the way of justification and salvation of sinners by Jesus Christ as proposed in the gospel. This way proceeds from the grace, wisdom, and love of God. Justifying faith includes the heart's acquiescence to that way with regard to its own concerns and conditions.

To explain this account of faith, we only need to refer to what has already been established about its object. Any perceived deficiencies will be addressed in the subsequent confirmation. The Lord Christ and His mediation—God's ordained means for the recovery, life, and salvation of sinners—are the object of this faith. All aspects of Christ's person and work are understood as effects of God's wisdom, grace, authority, and love, and of God's actions toward Christ in His assuming and fulfilling His office.

At times Scripture emphasizes God's grace, love, or special mercy; at other times it emphasizes God's actions toward the Lord Christ—such as sending Him, giving Him up to death, and raising Him from the dead. But these are always presented in relation to Christ's obedience and the atonement He made for sin. They are not treated in isolation, but as set forth in the promises of the gospel. A sincere assent to the divine truthfulness of those promises is included in this approving faith.

The confirmation of this description of faith can be organized under four main points:

1. The declaration of its contrary—the nature of privative unbelief in response to the gospel. These concepts mutually illustrate one another.

2. The declaration of God's design and purpose in and through the gospel.

3. The nature of faith's compliance with that design, that is, the actions by which faith relates to it.

4. The order, method, and manner of believing, as declared in Scripture:

The gospel reveals the way of justification and salvation for sinners through Jesus Christ—God's ordained provision, founded in His infinite wisdom, love, and grace. When sinners accept this way, it is accompanied by commands to obey and promises of reward.

Paul summarizes the gospel's effect: "For in it the righteousness of God is revealed from faith to faith;" (Romans 1:17). Scripture likewise testifies to the gift of life: "that God has given us eternal life, and this life is in His Son," (1 John 5:11). The preaching of the gospel calls men to proclaim "all the words of this life," (Acts 5:20) and never to shrink from "the whole counsel of God," (Acts 20:27).

Therefore, in preaching the gospel the way of salvation is set before sinners as the great outcome of divine wisdom and grace.

Unbelief, by contrast, is a rejection, neglect, non-acceptance, or disapproval of the gospel as it is proposed—rejection measured against the terms and purposes for which it is offered.

The unbelief of the Pharisees in response to John's preparatory preaching is described in Scripture as having "rejected the counsel of God for themselves," (Luke 7:30). Proverbs expresses the same idea: "They would none of my counsel," (Proverbs 1:30). Hebrews warns against "neglect so great a salvation," (Hebrews 2:3).

To disapprove of Christ—the stone the builders rejected (1 Peter 2:7)—is to disapprove of the way of salvation through Him, as if it were not suited to God's wisdom or purposes. Such refusal, non-reception, and disapproval all point to the same condition of heart.

The point will become clearer as we consider how the gospel was proposed in its first preaching and how it continues to be proposed today, and how that proposal has produced unbelief.

Most who reject the gospel do so because they think the way of salvation it proposes is not in keeping with God's goodness and power,

Defining Justifying Faith

and therefore not trustworthy. Paul sets this out clearly: "but we preach Christ crucified, to the Jews a stumbling block and to the Greeks foolishness, but to those who are called, both Jews and Greeks, Christ the power of God and the wisdom of God." (1 Corinthians 1:23-24).

What the apostolic preaching declared was this central fact: "that Christ died for our sins according to the Scriptures," (1 Corinthians 15:3). In that declaration Christ is presented as God's appointed means – the great manifestation of His wisdom and power for the salvation of sinners. Those who persist in unbelief reject this as weakness and folly. Their failure to see the glory of God in this way of salvation is the unbelief that ruins souls (2 Corinthians 4:3-4).

This holds for all who remain unbelievers despite the gospel's proclamation. Some may mentally assent to its truth and may not feel compelled to deny it. They may even show a temporary faith and perform many religious duties. Yet such behavior proves they are not sincere believers. They do not believe with the heart unto righteousness, as is shown by numerous signs incompatible with justifying faith.

The question, then, is to determine the specific nature of the unbelief that leads to perdition and to identify its formal character. It is not merely a failure to assent to the gospel's doctrines; Scripture often describes such persons as holding an intellectual assent. That assent may be so firmly fixed in their minds that they will even suffer bodily harm or death for it, as people sometimes do in defense of false opinions.

Nor is this unbelief simply the absence of a particular fiduciary application of the promises to one's own pardon and personal interest. That specific application is not always the first thing offered in initial preaching. One may believe unto righteousness without yet making such a personal appropriation (see Isaiah 50:10). The absence of that personal application may indicate a defect in faith, but it is not the formal nature of the unbelief that leads to destruction.

Nor is it merely a lack of obedience to gospel precepts concerning holiness and righteousness. Those commands, as formally given in the gospel, properly pertain only to those who truly believe and are justified.

What is required for evangelical faith, and what constitutes its nature as the root of all future obedience, is the heart's cordial approval of the way of life and salvation through Jesus Christ. This way is presented in the gospel as the effect of God's infinite wisdom, love, grace, and goodness, and as suitable to the needs and overall design of guilty, convinced sinners.

It is this heartfelt, sincere approval of the gospel way that these persons lack. That deficiency defines the formal nature of their unbelief. Without such approval, the gospel cannot truly move a person to forsake sin or encourage obedient living, whatever other motives they may have. Where this sincere approval of salvation by Christ exists, it will inevitably lead to repentance and to obedience.

If the mind and heart of a convinced sinner (for we are speaking only of such individuals) can spiritually discern the wisdom, love, and grace of God in this way of salvation, and if they are under the influence of that persuasion, then they have the gospel's foundation for repentance and obedience. The act of receiving Christ mentioned in Scripture — the expression of faith in its exercise — refers to that part of the description about the soul's acquiescence in God through the proposed way.

Moreover, there were some at first, and there are still those now, who did not absolutely reject this way in itself but rejected it comparatively when it was applied in practice; thus they perished in their unbelief. They regarded their own righteousness as superior and therefore more reliable—a way they could trust more safely and which they thought better suited to God's mind and glory. This was the general mindset of the Jews, as the apostle illustrates in Romans 10:3-4. Many of them assented to the gospel's doctrine in general as true, yet they did not accept in their hearts that it was the best way of justification and salvation; instead they sought these through the works of the law.

Accordingly, unbelief, in its formal nature, is the lack of spiritual discernment and approval of the way of salvation through Jesus Christ as the demonstration of God's infinite wisdom, goodness, and love. When these qualities are rightly perceived, a convinced sinner cannot help but embrace and cling to that way. For such persons, any real acquiescence in this way, together with trust and confidence in committing the soul to it—or to God through it—is impossible; they lack the necessary foundation. This makes plain the nature of true evangelical faith.

The design of God in and through the gospel, and the role of faith in relation to it, further confirm this description. God's ultimate purpose in all His plans is His own glory. He acts for Himself, and, being infinite, He cannot do otherwise. This is especially true in the way of salvation through Jesus Christ.

Particularly, God designed to display the glory of His righteousness: "whom God set forth as a propitiation by His blood, through faith, to demonstrate His righteousness" (Romans 3:25); the glory of His love: "God so loved the world" (John 3:16); "By this we know love, because He laid down His life for us" (1 John 3:16); the glory of His grace: "to the praise of the glory of His grace" (Ephesians 1:5-6); the glory of His wisdom: "Christ the power of God and the wisdom of God" (1 Corinthians 1:24); "the manifold wisdom of God might be made known by the church" (Ephesians 3:10); the glory of His power: "it is the power of God to salvation" (Romans 1:16); and, in a related sense, the glory of His faithfulness (Romans 4:16).

God designed not only the recovery of all the glory obscured by sin's entrance, but also a further exaltation and a more eminent manifestation of it—bringing into view degrees of glory and particular instances that had been previously concealed (Ephesians 3:9). All this is spoken of as "the glory of God in the face of Jesus Christ," which faith beholds (2 Corinthians 4:6).

Since this is the primary design of God in the gospel's way of justification and salvation, what is required of us for participation in its benefits is that we ascribe to God the glory He intends to exalt. We must acknowledge all these glorious attributes of the divine nature as they are shown in the provision and proposal of this way of life, righteousness, and salvation, and approve the way itself as the effect of those attributes. This is faith or believing: "was strengthened in faith, giving glory to God" (Romans 4:20). Even the weakest degree of sincere faith has this essence. No other grace, work, or duty properly meets this requirement, except as a consequence and expression of gratitude.

I cannot fully agree with those who say that faith in Paul's epistles is merely a "magnificent estimation of God's power, justice, goodness, and whatever He has promised," because that definition is too general and not limited to the way of salvation in Christ—the elect in whom He will be glorified. Nevertheless, that description contains much of faith's character. From it we can learn both the nature of faith and why faith alone is required for our justification. Faith is the only grace or duty by which we can give God the glory He intends to manifest and exalt in and by Jesus Christ. That is what faith is suited for, and that is what it means to believe.

Faith, in the sense under consideration, is the heart's approval of and consent to the way of life and salvation for sinners through Jesus Christ, as the means in which the glory of God's righteousness, wisdom, grace, love, and mercy is exalted. It ascribes praise to Him and rests in this way for its ends—namely, justification, life, and salvation. It is to give "giving glory to God" (Romans 4:20); to "beholding as in a mirror the glory of the Lord"—that is, the gospel in which it is represented to us (2 Corinthians 3:18); and to have in our hearts "the light of the knowledge of the glory of God in the face of Jesus Christ" (2 Corinthians 4:6). The opposite attitude makes God out to be a liar and robs Him of the glory of those holy attributes He intended to manifest in this way (1 John 5:10).

If I am not mistaken, this is what the experience of true believers, when they are free from contentious disputes, will testify.

To understand the nature of justifying faith correctly — that is, the act and exercise of saving faith as it relates to our justification — we must consider its proper order. First, we should examine the things that are necessarily prior to faith. Then we must consider what it means to believe with respect to those things.

The state of a convinced sinner is the only "subjectum capax justificationis" (a person capable of receiving justification). This has already been discussed. The necessity of its precedence for the orderly proposal and acceptance of evangelical righteousness for justification has been demonstrated. If we disregard this, we lose our best guide to understanding the nature of faith.

Let no one think they can understand the gospel who knows nothing of the law. God's constitution and the nature of things give the law precedence with respect to sinners: "for by the law is the knowledge of sin." Gospel faith is the soul's action, in line with God's purpose, for deliverance from the state and condition imposed by the law. All those descriptions of faith found in learned writings that do not at least include a virtual regard for this state or for the law's work on the conscience of sinners are mere vain speculations. I insist on the necessity of the convictions mentioned as prior to true believing;

without them not one line of the doctrine can be understood, and people only beat the air in their contentions about it (see Romans 3:21-24).

We assume here a sincere assent to all divine revelation, of which the promises of grace and mercy through Christ are a special part. This is what Paul assumed of Agrippa when he sought to win him to faith in Christ Jesus: "King Agrippa, do you believe the prophets? I know that you believe." (Acts 26:27)

This assent pertains to the promises of the gospel — not merely as they contain, propose, and exhibit the Lord Christ and the benefits of His mediation, but as divine revelations of infallible truth. In its kind it is true and sincere, like what we earlier called temporary faith. However, because it does not go further and does not include an act of the will or heart, it is not the faith by which we are justified.

Nevertheless, this assent is required and is included in justifying faith.

The proposal of the gospel, according to the mind of God, is assumed here — that is, it must be preached according to God's appointment. Not only the gospel itself but also the dispensation or preaching of it in the ministry of the church is ordinarily necessary for believing. The apostle asserts this and proves its necessity at length (Romans 10:11-17).

In this preaching, the Lord Christ and His mediation with God — the only way and means for the justification and salvation of lost, convinced sinners, and the effect of divine wisdom, love, grace, and righteousness — are revealed, declared, proposed, and offered to such sinners: "For in it the righteousness of God is revealed from faith to faith;" (Romans 1:17). The glory of God is represented "as in a mirror" (2 Corinthians 3:18), and is "brought life and immortality to light through the gospel" (2 Timothy 1:10; Hebrews 2:3).

Therefore, those required to believe — and whose immediate duty it is to believe — are persons who, in their own consciences, are brought to the inquiries Scripture records: What shall we do? What shall we do to be saved? How shall we escape the wrath to come? How shall we appear before God? How shall we answer what is laid against us? Or, more broadly, those who, aware of the guilt of sin, seek for righteousness in the sight of God (Acts 2:37-38; 16:30-31; Micah 6:6-7; Isaiah 35:4; Hebrews 6:18).

On those assumptions, the command and direction given to men is, "Believe on the Lord Jesus Christ, and you will be saved." The question then is: what is the act or work of faith by which we obtain a real interest in the promises of the gospel and in the things declared there for our justification before God?

It is evident from what has been discussed that faith does not consist in, nor can it be fully expressed by, any single habit or act of the mind or will. Scripture offers many descriptions of faith, proposes varied objects for it, and records the experiences of all who sincerely believe. No single act of the mind or will can encompass it.

Nor can an exact sequence of the soul's concurrent acts be prescribed. Only what is essential to faith is clear.

What seems to have precedence in the order of nature is the assent of the mind to what the psalmist first turns to for relief under a sense of sin and trouble: "If You, Lord, should mark iniquities, O Lord, who could stand?" (Psalm 130:3-4). The sentence of the law and the judgment of conscience lie against him concerning any acceptance with God. Therefore, he despairs of standing in judgment or being acquitted before Him.

In this state, the soul first fixes its attention on the fact that "there is forgiveness with You." This, as declared in the gospel, means that God, in His love and grace, will pardon and justify guilty sinners through the blood and mediation of Christ, as proposed in Romans 3:23-24. The assent of the mind to this promise of the gospel is the root of faith and the foundation of all that the soul does in believing; there is no evangelical faith without it.

However, when considered abstractly as a mere act of the mind, the essence and nature of justifying faith do not consist solely in this assent, although it cannot exist without it.

This assent is accompanied, in sincere believing, by an approval of the way of deliverance and salvation proposed as an effect of divine grace, wisdom, and love. The heart rests on that way and applies itself according to the mind of God. This is the faith by which we are justified.

I will further demonstrate this by showing what is included in faith and inseparable from it. It includes a sincere renunciation of all other ways and means for attaining righteousness, life, and salvation. This is essential to faith (Acts 4:12; Hosea 14:2-3; Jeremiah 3:23; Psalm 71:16): "I will make mention of Your righteousness, of Yours only."

When a person is in the condition described (and such alone are called immediately to believe, Matthew 9:13; 11:28; 1 Timothy 1:15), many things will present themselves as potential relief—particularly one's own righteousness (Romans 10:3). A renunciation of these, as to any hope or expectation of relief from them, is part of sincere believing (Isaiah 50:10-11).

The will's consent is where the soul sincerely and wholeheartedly places its hope for forgiveness of sin and righteousness before God in the way of salvation presented in the gospel. This is what is meant by "coming to Christ" and "receiving Him," phrases the Scripture often uses to describe true justifying faith. It is also specifically described as "believing in Him" or "believing on His name." Jesus said, "I am the way, the truth, and the life. No one comes to the Father except through Me." (John 14:6)

There is a heart's acquiescence in God as the author and primary cause of the salvation prepared, acting through sovereign grace and mercy toward sinners: "who through Him believe in God, who raised Him from the dead and gave Him glory, so that your faith and hope are in God" (1 Peter 1:21). In this, a sinner's heart gives glory to God for all the holy attributes of His nature that He intended to reveal through Jesus Christ.

This acquiescence in God is the immediate root of the waiting, patience, long-suffering, and hope that are the proper acts and effects of justifying faith (Hebrews 6:12, 15, 18, 19).

Trust in God, or in the grace and mercy of God through the Lord Christ, presented as a propitiation through faith in His blood, is essential to this faith. The person called to believe is, first, convinced of sin and exposed to wrath; second, has nothing else to rely on for help and relief; and third, actually renounces all other means that present themselves for that purpose.

Therefore, without some act of trust, the soul must remain in actual despair, which is entirely inconsistent with faith and the acceptance of the way of salvation just described.

The most common declaration of the nature of faith in Scripture, especially in the Old Testament, is through this trust. It is the act that composes the soul and leads it to all other attainments it can achieve. All our rest in this world comes from trust in God.

The specific object of this trust, as it pertains to the nature of the faith by which we are justified, is "God was in Christ reconciling the world to Himself." This is reflected in His goodness, mercy, grace, name, faithfulness, and power, which are the immediate grounds of our reliance. They are not the objects of our trust except as grounded in the covenant confirmed and ratified by the blood of Christ alone.

Whether this trust or confidence should be considered the essence of faith, or as something that arises from its initial fruits and workings, need not be definitively settled here. I regard it as belonging to justifying faith and as inseparable from it.

If everything previously discussed about faith can be summarized under the notion of a firm assent and persuasion, that summary is incomplete if any such assent can be conceived without this trust.

This trust is what many theologians say is the specific mercy that becomes the unique object of faith, including the pardon of our own sins. Their opponents fiercely deny this. They argue that such assurance cannot be attained in this life and that, if it were attainable, it would lead to security and negligence in duty. That objection betrays ignorance of the subject.

Special mercy may be understood in two ways. First, in itself, as opposed to common mercy; and second, with respect to the believer.

In the first sense, special mercy is the object of justifying faith. It is God's grace setting forth Christ as a propitiation through faith in His blood (Romans 3:23-24). Faith in this special mercy is what the apostle describes as our receiving the reconciliation (Romans 5:11) — our approval of it and adherence to it as the great effect of divine wisdom, goodness, faithfulness, love, and grace, which will not fail those who trust in it.

In the second sense, special mercy is the pardon of our own sins—the particular mercy of God toward our souls. I deny that belief in this particular pardon is the specific object a person is required to believe in order to be justified. I know of no clear testimony or safe experience that proves this requirement.

To deny that a true, undeceiving belief in the pardon of our own sins and in the special love of God in Christ can be attained in this life, or that it is our duty to believe it as the gospel outlines, shows a misunderstanding of the gospel's design, the efficacy of Christ's sacrifice, the nature and work of faith, and the duty and experience of believers recorded in Scripture (see Romans 5:1-5; Hebrews 10:2, 10, 19-22; Psalm 46:1-2; 138:7-8, etc.).

Still, it should be acknowledged that these things often appear as fruits or effects of faith as it is exercised and developed, rather than as the essence of faith itself, which is the instrument of our justification.

Bernard expresses this trust well. He says he considers three things in which his whole hope consists: the love of adoption, the truth of the promise, and the power of redemption. Let foolish thoughts murmur—asking, Who are you? What glory is that? By what merits do you hope for it? He answers confidently: I know whom I have believed. I am sure that He has adopted me in His great love, that He is true to His promise, and that He is powerful in His provision; for He can do whatever He wills.

This, he says, is the threefold cord not easily broken. He prays we hold it firmly. It has been sent from our homeland to this prison to lift us up, draw us, and carry us to the sight of the glory of the great God, who is blessed forever. Amen.

Many maintain that obedience is included within faith, though they describe the relationship differently.

Socinus and his followers assert that obedience is the essential form of faith; Episcopius denies this. The Romanists (Papists) distinguish between an intellectual faith and a faith formed by charity, and they conclude that evangelical faith—what the gospel requires and accepts—may exist without charity or obedience, making it ineffectual.

Socinians do not say obedience is the essence of faith absolutely; rather, they argue that it justifies. They cite the Scripture: "Thus also faith by itself, if it does not have works, is dead." From that they infer that a faith without works can still be the faith required by the gospel as our duty. That notion is monstrous.

Others say that obedience, charity, and love of God belong to the nature of faith, though they do not call obedience the form of faith. They regard these as part of faith's perfection in justification. They do not insist a continuous course of works is necessary for our initial justification, only a sincere, active purpose to obey. They often reproach those who think otherwise.

According to those who hold to justification by faith alone, it is impossible that justifying faith exists without a sincere purpose of heart to obey God in all things.

First, they hold that faith is "not of ourselves; it is the gift of God," a grace wrought in the hearts of men by the exceeding greatness of His power. To suppose this grace to be dead, inactive, unfruitful, and not operative toward the glory of God and the transformation of the souls that receive it reflects poorly on God's wisdom, goodness, and love.

Second, this grace is a principle of spiritual life. As it dwells in the heart, it cannot be truly separated from the other graces by which we live to God. Therefore, it is impossible for the habitual evangelical faith we are considering to exist without a habit of the other graces.

Third, there can be no exercise of this faith unto justification unless the mind is prepared, disposed, and determined toward universal obedience. It is denied, then, that any faith, trust, or confidence can be imagined that is absolutely separable from, and consistent with, the absence of all other graces. Such a supposed faith is not the special gift of God nor what the gospel requires of us.

Some have claimed that men may believe and place firm trust in Christ for life and salvation, and yet not be justified. That position is destructive to the gospel and scandalous to pious minds. It amounts to denying the witness God has given concerning His Son Jesus Christ. I am amazed that any sober, learned person could be led to such a belief.

They may point to many who profess a firm faith and confidence in Christ yet are not justified. True enough, but none of those are justified in the sight and judgment of God — the place where this matter must be assessed. By the light and rule of the gospel, it is not hard to expose the folly and falsehood of such professions, even to their own consciences, if they would attend to instruction.

Therefore, we assert that the faith by which we are justified is found only in those who have received the Holy Spirit and are united to Christ. In them the nature is renewed; there is a principle of all grace and a purpose of obedience.

We also assert that no other grace — such as charity — or any obedience gives life and form to this faith. Rather, it is faith that gives life and efficacy to all other graces and shapes all evangelical obedience.

Nothing in this implies that our adversaries are right to claim all those graces, at least in root and principle, are present in everyone to be justified and exercise the same influence on justification as faith. We maintain that we are justified by faith alone. In reply to Romanist reproaches, we add that we are justified by faith alone, but not by a faith that is alone; by "faith" we include all the graces and obedience that accompany true faith.

Moreover, no other grace can perform the role assigned to faith in justification, nor can any other grace operate alongside faith to do what faith alone does—namely, receive Christ and the promises of life through Him and give glory to God on that account. If anyone can produce a scriptural testimony assigning our justification to another grace, or to all graces together, or to all their fruits, in the same way Scripture assigns it to faith, we will hear them.

This is particularly important with respect to repentance. Many strongly argue that repentance is as necessary for justification as faith. They appeal to numerous scriptures that call all men to repent in order to be saved, especially Acts 2:38-39 and Acts 3:19.

What they must prove, however, is not simply that repentance is necessary for those to be justified, but that it serves the same role in justification as faith does. In Acts 2:38-39, baptism is joined with faith as much as repentance is; in other places repentance is placed in the same condition. Consequently, many ancient writers concluded that repentance is no less necessary for salvation than faith. Yet none of them assigned to repentance the same role in justification that Scripture assigns to faith.

They argue that whatever is a necessary condition of the new covenant must also be a necessary condition of justification. Otherwise, a person could be justified and yet remain in that justified state without being saved because that necessary condition was absent. By a necessary condition of the new covenant they mean whatever is essential for salvation. Repentance, they say, is of this nature and therefore is equally a condition of our justification. The ambiguity of the term "condition" creates much confusion in the present discussion.

Setting that aside for the moment, I assert that final perseverance is a necessary condition of the new covenant; and by their reasoning it would therefore be a condition of justification as well. They distinguish things that are conditions absolutely — such as faith, repentance, and a purpose of obedience — from those that are conditions only on the supposition that a person continues to live in this world — such as a course of obedience, good works, and perseverance to the end. Thus, on the assumption that a person lives in this world, they say perseverance to the end is a necessary condition of his justification. If that is true, then no one can be justified while in this life; for a condition suspends the existence of the thing conditioned until the condition is fulfilled. It would follow that there is no point in continuing the debate about justification if no one is, or can be, justified in this life. How contrary this is to Scripture and to experience is well known.

If one says that final perseverance — clearly a condition of salvation in the new covenant — is not the condition of our initial justification but only the condition for the continuation of our justification, then they abandon their main argument that whatever is a necessary condition of the new covenant is also a necessary condition of justification. Our present discussion concerns only what they mean by first or initial justification. I will later show that the continuation of our justification depends on the same causes as our justification itself. But it has not been proven, nor can it be proven, that everything required of those who are to be justified is a condition upon which their justification immediately depends. We accept as a condition only that which has a causal influence on justification, even if it operates merely as the causality of an instrument.

We ascribe this to faith alone. Because we do so, it is insisted that we ascribe more to ourselves in our justification than those we oppose. They say we attribute the efficacy of an instrument to our own faith, while they view it only as a condition or causa sine qua non of our justification. Yet wise and serious men should not defend a position while being well aware of the contrary. Having given the attractive name of a condition and a causa sine qua non to faith, they at once include all other graces and works of obedience in the same category and use them in justification. After this seemingly valuable gold has been put through the fire of debate, what emerges is the calf of a personal, inherent righteousness by which men are justified before God—virtute fœderis evangelici. As for the righteousness of Christ being imputed to us, they treat it as if it has ascended into heaven and they do not know what has become of it.

Having given a brief account of the nature of justifying faith and its acts—which I judge sufficient for my present purpose—I will not burden myself with a precise definition. My remarks will be better understood from what has been said than from any exact definition I could produce. Learned men have multiplied definitions of justifying faith, producing great variety and manifest inconsistency. Those definitions have not helped the truth; they have created fresh controversies and divisions, as everyone strives to defend the correctness of his own formula. A true believer may find little in these definitions that accords with his own experience; for this reason I hold most of them in low regard.

I know of no one who has labored more diligently on this subject than Dr. Jackson; yet after all his work he offers a definition of justifying faith with which few would wholly agree. Still, in its main scope it is both pious and sound. He states, "Here at length, we may define the faith by which the just live, to be a firm and constant adherence to the mercies and loving-kindness of the Lord; or, generally, to the spiritual food presented in His sacred word, as much better than this life itself and all the pleasures it can offer; grounded on a taste or relish of their sweetness, wrought in the soul or heart of a man by the Spirit of Christ." He adds, "The terms for the most part are the prophet David's; not metaphorical, as some may fancy, much less equivocal, but proper and homogenous to the subject defined" (Tom. i. book iv. chap. 9). The lively scriptural expressions of faith — receiving Christ, leaning on Him, rolling ourselves or our burdens upon Him, tasting how gracious the Lord is — have of late been criticized, even blasphemed, by many. I may have occasion later to show that these expressions convey a clearer apprehension of the nature, work, and object of justifying faith to spiritually enlightened minds than many of the most exact definitions men boast, some of which are destructive and exclusive.

4. Faith's Role and Object in Justification

The description just given of justifying faith sufficiently demonstrates its use in justification, and I will add little more than what appears from that account. Still, because this use has been expressed in many ways and several inconsistent assertions have been made about it, those must be considered here. I will be as brief as possible, for these matters do not touch the central controversy about the nature of justification but only relate to other concepts connected with it.

Once people have settled their view of the principal matters in controversy, they state what concerns the use of faith in light of that view. If the nature of justification they assert is accepted, then the use of faith must be as they claim. Were what is peculiar to any aspect of the doctrine disproved, their account of the use of faith would fall with it. This holds for all who maintain that faith is the instrument, the condition, the causa sine qua non, the preparation and disposition of the subject, or even a meritorious cause in our justification. All these notions about the use of faith are shaped to fit particular opinions about the nature and chief causes of justification.

No judgment can be formed about the truth or propriety of those positions until the causes and the whole nature of justification itself are first examined. It would therefore be endless and vain to argue every collateral point while the principal matter remains undecided. I shall briefly notice the several senses in which men talk of the use of faith in justification, not to debate their truth at length, but to clarify what is intended by each; their truth depends on the substance of the main controversy itself.

Protestant theologians, until recently, have almost unanimously affirmed that faith is the instrumental cause of our justification. This is the language of many public confessions of their churches. At first, the Roman church opposed this view. Later the Socinians also rejected it as false or inappropriate. More recently, some within our own ranks—following Episcopius, Curcellæus, and others—have abandoned the expression. Those who are sober and moderate commonly avoid the term, not always because they deem it false but because they judge it inapt.

Our safest course in these cases is to focus on the matter intended. If that is agreed upon, the person who puts truth first deserves praise for setting aside disputes over the propriety of expressions until after engaging the substance of the issue. Tenacious arguments over terminology lead to endless contention; anyone can find a semblance of probability to support their claims. If our aim in teaching is the same as Scripture's—to inform believers' minds and convey the knowledge of God in Christ—then at times we must use expressions that will not withstand rigorous scrutiny under the arbitrary rules and distinctions of notional and artificial sciences.

Those who flatly reject the idea that faith is instrumental in our justification as unscriptural, as if they could easily dismiss the reasoning of many learned defenders of it, should reconsider the grounds of their confidence. The real question is what is meant by the term. It is not enough to say the word "instrument" does not occur in Scripture for this use. By that logic one could also reject the doctrine of three persons in the divine essence, without which many passages of Scripture cannot be rightly understood.

Those who maintain that faith is the instrumental cause of our justification do so with two aims in view. First, they seek to explain the meaning of those scriptural expressions that say we are justified by faith, which must denote either an instrument, a form, or a manner of action.

For instance, in Romans 3:28 it states, "Therefore we conclude that a man is justified by faith apart from the deeds of the law." Similarly, in other verses we find "through faith" (Romans 3:30), "by faith" (Galatians 3:8), and "For by grace you have been saved through faith" (Ephesians 2:8).

The inquiry is about the most proper, clear, and fitting way to express the meaning of these phrases. The majority of Protestants believe this is best understood as an instrumental cause — some form of causality is plainly implied, the simplest being that of an instrument. These phrases refer to faith in our justification before God, not to any other grace or duty.

Therefore, by this understanding the proper role of faith in our justification is intended. The Greek dia is rarely used with a genitive in the New Testament (or in other reputable authors) without implying at least an instrumental efficiency. Even in the divine works of the Trinity, the operation of the second Person, a principal efficient, is sometimes expressed this way; it may indicate a certain order of operation corresponding to the order of subsistence. For example, Paul says, "For of Him and through Him and to Him are all things, to whom be glory forever. Amen." (Romans 11:36).

Moreover, when Scripture says a man is not justified by the works of the law, all agree that this excludes any efficiency from those works in our justification. Therefore, if we are said to be justified by faith, an instrumental efficiency is intended. Still, I do not want to make this a controversy about whether faith is properly called an instrument or the instrumental cause of our justification. I am not inclined to enter into hair-splitting debates about the kinds of instruments and instrumental causes, which are often obscured by technical terms and fine distinctions.

What I maintain is that, of the common notions used to explain the scriptural phrases—such as "by faith," "from faith," and "through faith"—none fits better than that of an instrument or instrumental cause. These phrases plainly include a notion of causality, and they exclude other kinds of causal relation.

One may object that, if faith is the instrumental cause of justification, it is either the instrument of God or the instrument of believers. It cannot be the instrument of God if it is a duty prescribed to us; faith is an act we perform—we are the ones who believe, not God. No act of ours can be the instrument of His work. If it were our instrument and credited with efficiency, then in some sense we would be the efficient cause of our own justification, implying we justify ourselves and undermining the grace of God and the blood of Christ.

I do not give much weight to these objections. Scripture repeatedly affirms the point: for example, "Therefore we conclude that a man is justified by faith apart from the deeds of the law." It also says "since there is one God who will justify the circumcised by faith and the uncircumcised through faith" (Romans 3:30), and "And the Scripture, foreseeing that God would justify the Gentiles by faith, preached the gospel to Abraham beforehand, saying, 'In you all the nations shall be blessed.'" (Galatians 3:8). As the apostles show, God "made no distinction between us and them, purifying their hearts by faith" (Acts 15:9). And, "For by grace you have been saved through faith, and that not of yourselves; it is the gift of God" (Ephesians 2:8). Given these passages, faith may, in one sense, be regarded as an instrument of God in our justification: it is the way ordained and appointed by Him on our part, and He gives and works it in us for that purpose, so that we may be justified. If someone therefore argues that, with respect to divine ordination and operation, faith is rightly described as an instrument of God in its place and manner—just as the gospel is (see Romans 1:16), the ministers of the gospel (2 Corinthians 5:18; 1 Timothy 4:6), and the sacraments in their roles (Romans 4:11; Titus 3:5)—they may be helping to clarify God's work in this matter, as much as those who deny that formulation.

What is primarily intended, however, is that faith serves as the instrument for those who believe. Believers are not said to justify themselves. Faith does not produce justification by any physical or meritorious action; justification is a sovereign act of God. Faith is not meritorious in itself, nor does it prepare the subject for the introduction of some inherent formal cause of justification, for no such inherent cause exists. The only connection between faith and justification is what God has constituted and appointed. Thus there is no sound reason to attribute the effect of justification to anything other than the principal efficient cause, which is God alone, from whom justification proceeds as an act of free and sovereign grace, who orders things and their relations as He wills.

As stated in Romans 3:24, "being justified freely by His grace," and in verse 25, "by His blood, through faith," it is clear that God has ordained our duty to be justified freely by His grace, with faith functioning as an instrument toward that end. Thus, those who deny faith as the instrumental cause of our justification contribute nothing to a true understanding of this truth—especially if they assert it to be merely a condition of justification without showing that this interpretation is more natural than the expressions used in Scripture, such as "by faith," "from faith," and "through faith." Our aim is to seek a correct understanding of the scriptural propositions and expressions, not to wander in a maze of uncertain conjectures.

Secondly, they aim to clarify the use of faith in justification, which Scripture expresses as the act of apprehending and receiving Christ, His righteousness, and the remission of sins. The Greek terms used to describe this use of faith include lambanō, paralambanō, and katalambanō. In Scripture these words consistently mean to take or receive what is offered, given, or granted to us, or to grasp and make something our own. For example, epilambanomai is used in the same sense in Hebrews 2:16.

By faith we are said to "received Him" (John 1:12; Colossians 2:6), the "abundance of grace and of the gift of righteousness" (Romans 5:17), "his word" (Acts 2:41), "the word of God" (Acts 8:14; 1 Thessalonians 1:6; 2:13), "received the reconciliation" (Romans 5:11), "remission of sins" (Acts 10:43; 26:18), "the promise of the Spirit" (Galatians 3:14), and "the promise" (Hebrews 9:15). Therefore, nothing contributes to our justification except that we receive it by faith. Unbelief is described in the New Testament as not receiving—refusing what is offered (see John 1:11; 3:11; 12:48; 14:17).

Thus, the object of faith in our justification—that by which we are justified—is offered, granted, and given to us by God. Faith's role is to grasp it, receive it, and make it our own. Just as our hands receive outward things given to us and thereby serve as instruments of reception, faith is the instrument by which we apprehend and lay hold of what is given. Other members of the body may serve different functions, but faith uniquely serves to receive and appropriate what is offered.

Since the righteousness by which we are justified is a gift from God, presented in the promise of the gospel, faith's role is to receive, grasp, or lay hold of this righteousness. I cannot think of a better way to express this than by calling faith an instrument, because that term conveys the idea plainly and effectively.

Some may suggest alternative notions to express faith's role, but the present inquiry focuses on how faith receives Christ, the atonement, and the gift of righteousness—its sole use in our justification. Anyone who can explain this better than by describing faith as an instrument ordained by God for that purpose will have made a significant contribution.

Those who place the formal cause of our justification in ourselves or in an inherent righteousness, thereby denying the imputation of Christ's righteousness, cannot accept faith as an instrument in this work. They will not acknowledge that we receive a righteousness that is not our own as a gift, and so they cannot accept any instrument by which it should be received. They treat such righteousness as putative or imaginary, without real attributes.

Therefore, as noted earlier, whether it is proper to call faith an instrumental cause depends on the substance of the doctrine itself—on what the principal causes of justification are. If we are justified through the imputation of Christ's righteousness, which faith alone apprehends and receives, then faith is rightly called the instrumental cause of our justification. If, instead, we are justified by an inherent evangelical righteousness of our own, faith might serve as a condition for its imputation or a disposition for its introduction, but it could not be the instrument. For now, the instrumental view has two advantages: first, it most appropriately matches what Scripture affirms about faith's use in justification, as the examples above show; second, no other notion can be understood without placing it before justification—a position justifying faith itself cannot occupy unless one is a true believer with justifying faith and yet not justified.

Some argue that faith is simply the condition of our justification and that it cannot be conceived otherwise. As I have said, I will not quarrel over words or labels as long as we agree on the meaning. There is a clear sense in which faith can be called the condition of our justification: it signifies the duty God requires of us for justification, and this is supported by the whole testimony of Scripture. But that does not negate the fact that, in its use, faith may also be the instrument by which we apprehend and receive Christ and His righteousness.

To assert that faith is the condition of our justification—that we are justified by it as the condition of the new covenant—while denying its role as the instrumental cause in justification, is hard to accept. Such an assertion implies a change in the substance of the doctrine itself.

The term is not used in Scripture in this technical sense, as I shall argue further, so we lack a definitive rule to measure its meaning. It cannot be introduced with arbitrary senses and then used as an argument for other purposes. For example, some elevate faith to a subordinate righteousness, imputed to us before the imputation of Christ's righteousness and made its condition. Others, trying to diminish its significance in our justification, call it merely a causa sine qua non. Neither approach clarifies the matter; both leave us uncertain about the nature and efficacy of the supposed condition.

If we introduce words into religion that are not used in Scripture—as we sometimes must in order to clarify and convey truth—we should not import arbitrary, preconceived meanings from lawyers or philosophers. The usage of these terms in the best authors of the language, together with their common understanding among us, should determine their sense. The confusion caused by bringing terms into ecclesiastical doctrine without an agreed rule for their significance is well known.

For example, the word "merit" was introduced by some ancient writers to mean impetration or acquisition "by any means." But since there is no compelling reason to restrict the word to that single meaning, its use has contributed to significant corruption within Christian doctrine. We must therefore employ the best available means to understand the intended sense of such terms before accepting them in this context.

The term "conditio" in the best Latin writers is used in various ways. It corresponds to several Greek words—katastasis, tuchē, axia, aitia, and suntēkē—which cover meanings like status, fortune, dignity, cause, and agreement. Determining which of these senses applies here is not straightforward. In ordinary usage it sometimes refers to the state and quality of persons (katastasis and axia). At other times it denotes a valuable consideration for actions to be taken (aitia or suntēkē).

In some contexts a condition expresses the principal procuring cause—for example, when money is lent on the condition of repayment with interest. In other cases it denotes additional requisites attached to the principal cause, where the operation depends on them—such as a bequest that requires the recipient to perform some act to claim it. The variety of meanings tied to "condition" is therefore extensive. We cannot fix a single, definitive understanding of the term without a specific statement about which sense is intended in each case. That does not exclude using the word in explaining how we are justified by faith, but it prevents us from imposing any precise meaning beyond what the subject matter itself supplies. Without that clarity everything remains ambiguous and uncertain in application.

For example, it is often said that faith and new obedience are the conditions of the new covenant. Yet, because the word "condition" is so ambiguous and used in different senses, we cannot clearly understand what is meant by that claim. If the meaning is that God, under the new covenant, requires these things of us—namely, a renewed conscience toward God through Christ's resurrection, for His glory and for our full enjoyment of the benefits—then this is undeniably true.

But if the claim is that these conditions must be fulfilled by us before we can partake of any grace, mercy, or covenantal privilege—so that they become the procuring causes of such benefits—then that is false. It contradicts explicit Scripture and undermines the very nature of the covenant. On the other hand, it is true that these things, though promised in the covenant and worked in us by God's grace, are duties required for participating in the covenant's final glory. Yet if one says that faith and new obedience—meaning the works of righteousness we perform—are conditions of the covenant such that whatever God ordains as a means to justification is thereby ordained for the same end with the same efficacy, this contradicts the apostle's purpose and the overall scope of his argument.

Some will argue that a condition, when faith is called a condition of our justification, simply means a causa sine qua non. That idea is easy to state but does not clarify the issue, because these causæ sine quibus non may be understood broadly or strictly. Scholars commonly distinguish between the two senses. In the broader sense are causes that, though subordinate to principal causes, would produce no effect without them; yet, together with them, they have a real effective influence—either physical or moral—on the outcome.

If we take a condition as a causa sine qua non in that broader sense, we remain uncertain about its role, effectiveness, or merit in relation to justification. If the term is understood more strictly—as something that must be present but has no causal role at all, not even as a receptive instrument—then I cannot see how it could be an ordinance of God. Everything God appoints for a moral or spiritual end must, by that appointment, have either symbolic instructive efficacy, active efficiency, or a rewardable appropriateness toward that end. Other factors may be necessary in a general, natural order—like the air we breathe, which is required for preaching the word—but such things are not divine ordinances and so lack any moral or spiritual causality for that purpose.

Every element appointed by God for a specific spiritual end has some efficacy or operation. Such elements either cooperate with the principal cause in its internal efficiency or operate externally to remove obstacles that hinder the principal cause. This excludes strictly defined sine quibus non causes from any role among divine ordinances. God appoints nothing for an end that will accomplish nothing. His sacraments are not mere symbols; by virtue of His institution they convey the grace they do not in themselves contain. The preaching of the word possesses genuine effectiveness for its intended purposes. Likewise, by His appointment, all the graces and duties He works in us and requires of us contribute to their intended effect; by them God "has qualified us to be partakers of the inheritance of the saints in the light." Our entire obedience, through His gracious appointment, has a rewardable appropriateness with respect to eternal life. Therefore, while faith may be called a condition of our justification in the sense that it signifies what God requires of us for justification, restricting its role solely to being a condition—especially when no precise meaning of that term is agreed upon—only fuels unproductive strife and contention.

To conclude these discussions about faith and its role in our justification, a few additional points must be made about its specific object. What I have already said about faith's nature and general object is sufficient to establish its specific object in many respects. Still, there has been inquiry and debate about the matter under particular terms and in a particular context that merits brief consideration.

The question is whether justifying faith, in our justification or in its role therein, relates to Christ as king and prophet, as well as priest, and to the satisfaction He made for us in those offices—and whether that relation is in the same manner and for the same ends in each case. I will be brief here, for this is a relatively recent controversy and perhaps of more curiosity than of real edification. Moreover, since to my knowledge these precise terms do not appear in any public Reformed confessions, men are at liberty to state their views on the matter.

On this point I affirm that the faith by which we are justified, in receiving Christ, primarily concerns His person insofar as He is the ordinance of God for every purpose for which He was appointed. Faith does not, in its formal act, simply regard Christ absolutely; rather, its formal object is the truth proposed by God—the promise. Thus faith receives and rests upon Christ as He is presented in the promise, and the promise itself is the formal object of its assent.

We cannot receive Christ in the promise without acknowledging any of His offices. Likewise, we cannot view Him at any time without recognizing all His offices. To conceive of receiving Christ as priest but not as king or prophet is not faith but unbelief; it is not receiving Him but rejecting Him.

When we receive Christ for justification, our explicit aim is simply to be justified through Him. To be justified is to be freed from the guilt of sin, to have all our sins pardoned, to possess a righteousness that enables us to stand accepted before God, and to have a right to the heavenly inheritance.

Believers may also desire the renewal of their nature, personal sanctification, and the ability to live in holy obedience. Those concerns are legitimate. But when one approaches Christ or receives Him for justification, the primary focus is the aims I have outlined.

Therefore, justifying faith, in the act by which we are justified, specifically regards Christ in His priestly office as the surety of the covenant and all that He accomplished in fulfilling it. Consideration of

His other offices is not excluded, but they are not the formal object of faith as it relates to justification.

When we say that the priestly office of Christ, or the blood of Christ, or Christ's satisfaction is the sole focus of faith in justification, we do not exclude anything necessary for making them effective. Rather, we include everything required for their efficacy in our justification.

First, we include the free grace and favor of God in giving Christ for us, which Scripture frequently mentions as the basis of our justification (Romans 3:24; Ephesians 2:8; Titus 3:7). We also include God's wisdom, love, righteousness, and power in this consideration.

Secondly, we include whatever was necessary in Christ Himself before He fulfilled that office, whatever was a consequence of it, and whatever accompanied it. That embraces His incarnation, the whole of His obedience, His resurrection, ascension, exaltation, and intercession. Considering all these aspects is inseparable from the exercise of His priestly office.

Thus justification is either explicitly or implicitly ascribed to them as well (Genesis 3:15; 1 John 3:8; Hebrews 2:14–16; Romans 4:25; Acts 5:31; Hebrews 7:27; Romans 8:34). Whenever our justification is attributed to these elements, they are considered not in isolation but in relation to His sacrifice and satisfaction.

Thirdly, we include all the means by which the sacrifice and righteousness of the Lord Christ are applied to us. This includes the primary efficient cause, which is the Holy Spirit; hence we are said to be "justified in the name of the Lord Jesus and by the Spirit of our God" (1 Corinthians 6:11). It also includes the instrumental cause on God's part, which is the promise of the gospel (Romans 1:17; Galatians 3:22, 23).

It would therefore be incorrect to say that this assertion narrows the object of justifying faith. On the contrary, it encompasses the whole of Christ's mediatorial office. It does not exclude His kingly and prophetic roles; it only prevents us from introducing more of ourselves into our justification. This position is supported by the experience of all who are justified or who seek justification according to the gospel.

In seeking justification or righteousness, people universally consider themselves to have become guilty before God and subject to His wrath under the curse of the law, as Romans 3:19 teaches. They recognize their condition to be the same as Adam's after the fall, to whom God offered relief through the incarnation and suffering of Christ (Genesis 3:15). Seeking justification is therefore seeking deliverance from this awful state.

Such seekers may also desire the renewal of their nature and the sanctification of their person so they may live in holy obedience. But regarding the guilt of sin and the need for righteousness before God, their primary concern is justification.

In this respect they look to Christ "whom God set forth as a propitiation by His blood" for their acceptance. For their sanctification they consider His kingly and prophetic offices; but for freedom from guilt and acceptance with God it is Christ crucified, lifted up as the "bronze serpent" in the wilderness, whose blood, propitiation, and atonement they fix their faith upon.

If anyone experiences justification differently, I am not aware of it. I do not claim that conviction of sin is the sole prerequisite for actual justification; however, conviction does make a sinner capable of justification. No one should be considered for justification who is not truly under the conviction of sin, with all its necessary consequences.

Suppose a sinner finds themselves in this condition, as described by the apostle in Romans 3 — "become guilty before God," with "every mouth may be stopped" regarding any pleas or excuses. If they seek relief and deliverance from this state — namely, to be justified according to the gospel — they cannot wisely pursue any other course than what the apostle directs in verses 20-25:

"Therefore by the deeds of the law no flesh will be justified in His sight, for by the law is the knowledge of sin. But now the righteousness of God apart from the law is revealed, being witnessed by the Law and the Prophets, even the righteousness of God, through faith in Jesus Christ, to all and on all who believe. For there is no difference; for all have sinned and fall short of the glory of God, being justified freely by His grace, through the redemption that is in Christ Jesus, whom God set forth as a propitiation by His blood, through faith, to demonstrate His righteousness, because in His forbearance God had passed over the sins that were previously committed."

From this, I argue that what a guilty, condemned sinner — finding no hope or relief in the law of God — turns to by faith for deliverance or justification is the particular object of faith in justification. That object is God's grace alone, given through the redemption that is in Christ; or Christ presented as a propitiation through faith in His blood.

If this is not so, then the apostle does not rightly guide the souls and consciences of men in the condition he describes. It is the blood of Christ alone that he directs the faith of all who would be justified before God. Grace, redemption, propitiation — all through the blood of Christ — are what faith especially regards and rests upon. Those who have carefully observed their own experience of faith in justification will confirm this.

The Scripture plainly shows that justifying faith is directed to the priestly office and actions of Christ. In the old representative rite for the justification of the people—when their sins were expiated and they were accepted by God—the act of faith was confined to placing all their sins upon the head of the sacrifice by the high priest (Leviticus 16).

"By His knowledge My righteous Servant shall justify many; For He shall bear their iniquities" (Isaiah 53:11). The aspect of Christ that faith fixes on for the justification of sinners is His bearing their iniquities. Guilty, convinced sinners look to Him by faith just as those who were stung by "fiery serpents" looked to the "serpent in the wilderness" (John 3:14-15)—that is, as He was lifted up on the cross.

This is how He expressed the nature and action of faith in our justification. Romans 3:24-25 states, "being justified freely by His grace through the redemption that is in Christ Jesus, whom God set forth as a propitiation by His blood."

As He is a propitiation and shed His blood for us, and as we have redemption through Him, He is the specific object of our faith concerning our justification. This is reinforced in Romans 5:9, 10; Ephesians 1:7; Colossians 1:14; Ephesians 2:13-16; and Romans 8:3, 4. "He made Him who knew no sin to be sin for us, that we might become the righteousness of God in Him" (2 Corinthians 5:21).

What we seek in justification is participation in the righteousness of God—to be reckoned the righteousness of God, not by anything in ourselves, but in another, namely Christ Jesus. The only means and cause proposed to our faith for this is His being made sin for us, His sacrifice for sin, whereby all the guilt of our sins was laid upon Him and He bore our iniquities. Therefore, this is the specific object of faith in justification.

Whenever Scripture directs us to seek forgiveness through the blood of Christ, to receive atonement, or to be justified through faith in Him as crucified, the object of justifying faith is clearly defined.

However, one may object that none of these testimonies asserts we are justified by faith in the blood of Christ to the exclusion of considering Christ's other offices and their actions as objects of faith in the same manner and for the same purposes as His priestly work.

This objection reflects a common challenge to the doctrine of justification by faith alone: the word "alone" does not appear in Scripture or in the testimonies cited for justification by faith. Still, it is plain that, though the exact word is not used, equivalent expressions implying exclusivity do occur, as will be shown later.

In this instance — where our justification is explicitly ascribed to faith in the blood of Christ as the propitiation for our sins and to faith in Him as crucified for us — these expressions effectively exclude the latter considerations. I do not mean to say that the kingly and prophetic offices of Christ are altogether excluded from our thinking about justification in the way that works are excluded in opposition to faith and grace. Rather, they are excluded in the sense that they have no part to play in procuring or completing our justification: we must reject any notion that they contribute to our being declared righteous.

But when we regard these offices of Christ as the object of justifying faith, our claim is only that they are not included in that object. To suppose we are justified by His blood while denying a proper place to His other offices is to mistake the nature of justifying faith.

Neither the consideration of these offices nor any of their specific actions can give the relief that convinced sinners seek in justification. We must keep in view the condition of the person to be justified and what they seek: the pardon of sin and righteousness before God alone. Therefore, anything that does not give or offer this relief cannot be the object of the faith by which they are justified.

This relief is found in Christ alone. But under what consideration? The sinner's aim is to be accepted by God, to be at peace with Him, and to have His wrath turned away by a propitiation or atonement. That can only be achieved through the actions of someone acting to God on the sinner's behalf — actions that turn away God's anger and secure acceptance with Him.

It is by the blood of Christ that we "have been brought near" — we who "once were far off" (Ephesians 2:13). By the blood of Christ, we are reconciled; we who were enemies (verse 16). By the blood of Christ, we have redemption (Romans 3:24, 25; Ephesians 1:7, etc.). Therefore, this is the object of faith.

All the actions of Christ's kingly and prophetic offices proceed from God; they are done in God's name and by His authority toward us. None of these actions are directed to God on our behalf in a way that would ground our expectation of acceptance with Him. They are good, blessed, and holy in themselves, and they greatly contribute to God's glory in our salvation. They are no less necessary to our salvation, to the praise of God's grace, than the atonement for sin and the satisfaction He provided.

Through all His offices the Lord Christ pardons and justifies sinners. Yet He did not establish the law of justification as a king; that law was given in the first promise, and He came to fulfill it (John 3:16). By virtue of His atonement and the righteousness imputed to them, He pardons and justifies. Still, it is the acts of His priestly office alone that concern God on our behalf. Everything He did on earth before God for the church — His obedience, His sufferings, His offering of Himself — and everything He does in heaven by interceding and appearing before God for us belongs entirely to His priestly office.

In these priestly actions alone the soul of a convinced sinner finds relief when seeking deliverance from sin and acceptance with God. Therefore the specific object of their faith, which will bring rest and peace, must be found within these considerations. This point suffices to make the distinction clear.

Various objections have been raised against this claim, which I will not examine fully here, since the main issues will arise elsewhere and can be addressed more appropriately in those contexts. In general it may be argued that justifying faith is the same as saving faith; we are not said to be justified by this or that part of faith, but by faith in general — understood as the whole grace of faith.

In that sense there is regard for Christ in all His offices, and obedience itself is included, as many passages of Scripture show. Hence, some conclude there is no reason to restrict the object of faith to Christ acting in His priestly office and its effects and fruits.

1. Saving faith and justifying faith in any believer are the same grace; the labels "saving" and "justifying" only mark different operations and effects. Yet saving faith acts in a distinct way and serves a particular purpose in justification that it does not serve under other considerations.

2. Although saving faith, in general, always includes obedience — not as its form or essence but as a necessary effect, like fruit in the juice — and is frequently mentioned in connection with all gospel duties and ends, this does not prove that it has any other object assigned to it in the act of justification.

This does not mean we are justified by a part of faith rather than by faith considered as a whole. We are justified by the whole grace of faith, although it acts in a particular way in justification, as others have observed.

We need not probe this issue at great length. The real question is not which aspect of Christ must be excluded from the object of justifying faith, but what in ourselves—under the guise of receiving Christ as Lord and King—may be admitted as having any efficiency or conditionality in that work.

It is acknowledged that justifying faith is the receiving of Christ. Anything that pertains to Christ's person, His offices, or acts performed in those offices that could be seen as a cause of our justification—whether meritorious, procuring, material, formal, or manifesting—should be freely included within the object of justifying faith.

I will not argue over that unhelpful framing of the question—what of Christ is or is not the object of justifying faith. The crucial issue is whether our own obedience, either distinct from faith or included within it, is the condition for our justification before God. That will be the focus of the examination and nothing else.

5. The Biblical Meaning of Justify

To understand justification properly, we must examine the meaning of the terms justify and justification. Until we agree on those meanings, our discussion will be unclear. Words taken in different senses can make opposing statements appear true about the same matter. This confusion has indeed occurred here, as we will show.

Some have given the terms one sense and others another, producing conflicting doctrines of justification. Many writers, however, have already clarified the proper meaning. Getting this issue right is crucial to resolving the main controversies about the doctrine. I will therefore present my observations on the matter with care.

The Latin formation "justificatio" has led some scholastic writers to think it denotes an internal change from unrighteousness to righteousness—a physical infusion of a principle or habit of grace. Terms like sanctification, mortification, and vivification are similarly taken to indicate an internal work on the subject. In the Roman school, justification is often described as making a person inherently righteous by an infused habit of grace. If that is the proper meaning, we cannot meaningfully argue with them about the cause and nature of the justification taught in Scripture.

This apparent sense of the term may have caused some early theologians, Augustine among them, to describe gratuitous sanctification—without reference to our works—under the name of justification. Neither he nor others in that tradition conceived of a justification before God that consists merely in the forgiveness of sins and the acceptance of persons as righteous without any inherent grace infused into them by God.

Therefore, we must determine the subject from the scriptural use of the terms before speaking plainly about the doctrine. If to justify in Scripture meant to make men subjectively and inherently righteous, our teaching would be mistaken about its nature and causes. If it does not mean that, then the arguments for justification as an infusion of grace collapse. Thus all Protestants (and even many Socinians) maintain that the use of these terms is forensic—an act of jurisdiction. Only the Socinians and a few others insist it consists solely in the forgiveness of sin, a sense the term does not properly bear. The true meaning is to acquit, declare, and pronounce righteous upon trial; forgiveness of sin accompanies this in the economy of salvation.

The words "justificatio" and "justifico" are not originally Latin in the sense claimed by the scholastics; no reputable ancient author used them to mean making a person inherently righteous if he was not so before. These words were coined to express particular ideas, and we must determine their meaning by the nature of what they were intended to convey.

They derive from jus and justum, and thus pertain to an act of jurisdiction rather than a physical operation. To justificari is to be esteemed, accounted, or adjudged righteous. For example, a man is made a "justus filius" in adoption by the one who adopts him. Budæus explains in his treatise on adoption that "justum" does not mean truly righteous in an inherent sense, but one who stands in the place and rights of a legitimate child. Adoption does not create an internal change in the adopted person; it makes him regarded and adjudged a true son, with all the privileges of a legitimate child.

Thus, in meaning, justification and gratuitous adoption are the same grace in substance, differing only in how we name the subsequent effects or privileges, as indicated in John 1:12.

The true sense of these words must be drawn from the original biblical languages. In Hebrew the term is צָדַק (tzadaq). The Septuagint renders it Dikaion apophainō in Job 27:5; Dikaios anaphainomai in Job 13:18; and Dikaion krinō in Proverbs 17:15 — terms that mean to show or declare one righteous, to appear righteous, or to judge someone as righteous.

The meaning is evident from these uses, as in Job 13:18, where it states, "See now, I have prepared my case, I know that I shall be vindicated." The ordering of his cause — or his presenting of his case — was his preparation for a sentence of absolution or condemnation. His confidence that he would be justified meant that he expected to be absolved, acquitted, and pronounced righteous. This sense is equally clear in the other passages. The common Greek equivalent is dikaioō, which I will discuss further.

In its proper sense the term denotes an action directed toward another only in the Hiphil form; in the Hithpael form it indicates a reciprocal action of a person on himself, as in הִצְטַדֵּק (hitztaq). This distinction alone determines the true meaning of these words. I insist that in no instance, in no conjugation, is it used to denote an action toward another except in the senses of absolving, acquitting, esteeming, declaring, pronouncing righteous, or imputing righteousness.

That is the forensic meaning we maintain. It is the term's consistent use and significance. It never signifies making someone inherently righteous, and it does not mean forgiving or pardoning. The notion that justification consists solely in the forgiveness of sin is unfounded; the word does not bear that sense in Scripture. In nearly all cases this usage is indisputable. There is only one possible exception, and that rests on such weak grounds that it cannot overturn the term's consistent meaning elsewhere.

Therefore, whatever may be meant by an infusion of inherent grace, justification cannot be that—because the word itself does not mean it. Consequently, those in the Roman Church do not merely oppose justification by faith through the imputation of Christ's righteousness; they in effect deny that justification, as we understand it, exists at all. What they call a "first justification," an infusion of an inherent principle of grace, is not justification. Their "second justification," which they ascribe to the merit of works, excludes absolution or the forgiveness of sin and is incompatible with evangelical justification, as I will show later.

Thus, whether the act is of God toward men, of men toward God, or of men among themselves, the term is always used in a forensic sense and does not indicate a physical operation, transfusion, or transformation.

For example, in 2 Samuel 15:4 it states, "everyone who has any suit or cause would come to me," and the Hebrew term וְהִצְדַּקְתִּיו means "and I will do him justice;" that is, "I will justify him, judge in his cause, and pronounce for him."

In Deuteronomy 25:1 it says, "If there is a dispute between men, and they come to court, that the judges may judge them," and the term וְהִצְדִּיקוּ אֶת־הַצַּדִּיק means "they shall justify the righteous;" pronouncing judgment in his favor, as opposed to וְהִרְשִׁיעוּ אֶת־הָרָשָׁע, "and they shall condemn the wicked," which means to declare him wicked, as the word signifies. Thus, he becomes wicked judicially and in the eyes of the law, just as the other is made righteous by declaration and acquittal. The text does not say, "This shall pardon the righteous," for that would undermine both the contrast and the purpose of the passage. The term הִרְשִׁיעַ signifies no more to infuse wickedness into a person than הִצְדִּיק does to infuse a principle of grace or righteousness into him.

The same contrast appears in Proverbs 17:15: "He who justifies the wicked, and he who condemns the just," — it is not that he makes the wicked inherently righteous or changes him from unrighteousness to righteousness; rather, he unjustly acquits him in judgment or declares him to be righteous, which is an abomination to the Lord.

Although this is stated regarding human judgment, God's judgment also adheres to this truth. While He justifies the ungodly — those who are ungodly in themselves — He does so based on the perfect righteousness that is imputed to them. Moreover, by another act of His grace He genuinely and inherently transforms them from unrighteousness to holiness by renewing their natures. These actions of God are unique and cannot be compared to human actions. The imputation of Christ's righteousness to an ungodly person, so that the person is acquitted, absolved, and declared righteous, rests on principles of righteousness, wisdom, and sovereignty that have no parallel among men.

Furthermore, when God justifies the ungodly by imputing righteousness to them, He simultaneously makes them inherently and subjectively righteous or holy by His grace — something humans cannot do for one another. Therefore, whereas man's justification of the wicked merely affirms them and leads them further into evil, God's justification of the ungodly is accompanied by their transformation from personal unrighteousness and unholiness into righteousness and holiness.

The same concept is expressed in Isaiah 5:23, "Who justify the wicked for a bribe," and in Isaiah 50:8-9, where it states, "He is near who justifies Me; Who will contend with Me? Let us stand together. Who is

My adversary? Let him come near Me. Surely the Lord God will help Me; Who is he who will condemn Me?" Here we find a complete declaration of the proper meaning of the term: to acquit and pronounce righteous upon trial. This meaning is also fully articulated in the preceding contrast.

In 1 Kings 8:31, 32 it states, "When anyone sins against his neighbor, and is forced to take an oath, and comes and takes an oath before Your altar in this temple, then hear in heaven, and act, and judge Your servants," where לְהַרְשִׁיעַ רָשָׁע means to condemn the wicked, charging his wickedness against him, while וּלְהַצְדִּיק צַדִּיק means to justify the righteous. These same words are repeated in 2 Chronicles 6:22, 23.

Psalm 82:3 says, "Do justice to the afflicted and needy," meaning to justify them in their cause against wrong and oppression. Exodus 23:7 declares, "For I will not justify the wicked," meaning to absolve, acquit, or pronounce him righteous. Job 27:5 reads, "Far be it from me That I should say you are right," meaning to pronounce judgment in your favor as if you were righteous. And Isaiah 53:11 states, "By His knowledge My righteous Servant shall justify many, For He shall bear their iniquities," the bearing of their iniquities being the basis for their absolution and justification.

The term is used once in the Hithpael form, indicating a reciprocal action, where a person justifies himself. In Genesis 44:16 Judah says, "What shall we say to my lord? What shall we speak?" and the phrase וּמַה־נִּצְטַדָּק means "and how shall we clear ourselves? God has found out the iniquity of your servants." They had no grounds to plead for their absolution from guilt.

The participle is used once to denote the outward instrumental cause of the justification of others, which is the only instance where there is any uncertainty about its meaning. In Daniel 12:3 it speaks of "those who turn many to righteousness," in the same sense that the preachers of the gospel are said to "save both yourself and those who hear you" (1 Timothy 4:16). In other words, individuals may be instrumental causes of the justification of others just as they are of their sanctification.

Therefore, although צָדַק in the Kal form signifies "to be just" and sometimes "to act justly," which may relate to inherent righteousness, when any action toward another is indicated this word signifies nothing but esteeming, declaring, pronouncing, and adjudging someone as absolved, acquitted, cleared, or justified. Thus there is no other kind of justification mentioned in the Old Testament.

Dikaioō is the word used for the same purpose in the New Testament, and it is the only term employed. This word is not used in any reputable author to signify making a person righteous through any means that produce internal righteousness in him. Rather, it means to absolve and acquit, to judge, esteem, and pronounce righteous, or conversely, to condemn. As Suidas states, "Dikaioun duo dēloi, to te kolazein, kai to dikaion nomizein;" — it has two significations: to punish, and to account righteous. He supports this interpretation with examples from Herodotus, Appianus, and Josephus. Again, he states, "Dikaiōsai aitiatikē, katadikasai, kolasai, dikaion nomisai" with an accusative case; that is, when it affects a subject, it is either to condemn and punish or to esteem and declare righteous. Hesychius mentions only the first meaning: dikaioumenon, kolazomenon, dikaiōsai, kolasai. They never considered any meaning of this word other than forensic.

In our language, to be justified was commonly used in the past to mean to be judged and sentenced, as it still is among the Scots. One of the articles of peace between the two nations at the surrender of Leith, during the reign of Edward VI, stated, "That if anyone committed a crime, he should be justified by the law upon his trial." In general, "dikaousthai" means "to take away justice in judgment," and "dikaiōsai" means "to consider, declare, pronounce just;" and how in Scripture it is constantly opposed to "condemnare," we shall see shortly.

However, we may consider the use of this word in the New Testament more distinctly, just as we have examined הַצַּדִּיק in the Old Testament. What we inquire about is whether this word is used in the New Testament in a forensic sense—denoting an act of jurisdiction—or in a physical sense, to express an internal change or mutation, such as the infusion of a habit of righteousness, or whether it signifies something other than the pardon of sin.

We can set this aside: surely no one has ever been so foolish as to claim that dikaioō signifies the pardon of sin, yet it is the only word used to express our justification in the New Testament. If it is taken only in the former sense, then what is argued by those of the Roman church under the name of justification, however good, useful, and necessary it may be, cannot properly be called justification, since it is entirely different from what the word signifies.

In Matthew 11:19 the Lord says, "But wisdom is justified by her children;" and there it does not mean made just, but approved and declared. In Matthew 12:37 He warns, "For by your words you will be justified, and by your words you will be condemned." That does not mean made just by them, but judged according to them, as is evident in the antithesis. In Luke 7:29 we read, "And when all the people heard Him, even the tax collectors justified God," not by making Him righteous in Himself, but by acknowledging and declaring His righteousness. In Luke 10:29 it is written, "But he, wanting to justify himself,"—to declare and maintain his own righteousness. Similarly, in Luke 16:15 Christ said, "You are those who justify yourselves before men; but God knows your hearts." They did not make themselves internally righteous, but approved of their own condition.

The Biblical Meaning of Justify

Our Savior makes this clear in Luke 18:14: "I tell you, this man went down to his house justified rather than the other;" that is, acquitted, absolved, pardoned, upon the confession of his sin and supplication for remission. In Acts 13:38-39 Paul proclaims the forgiveness of sins and justification by faith; and Romans 2:13 affirms that "but the doers of the law will be justified." These passages show the nature of our justification before God and clarify the meaning of the word: justification is not the making of us righteous by infusion.

Thus the word is used in Romans 3:4 where it reads, "That You may be justified in Your words," and in many other places — 1 Corinthians 4:4; 1 Timothy 3:16; Romans 3:20, 26, 28, 30; 4:2, 5; 5:1, 9; 6:7; 8:30; Galatians 2:16, 17; 3:11, 24; 5:4; Titus 3:7; James 2:21, 24, 25 — and in none of these instances can it bear any other meaning or denote the making of any man righteous by the infusion of a habit or principle of righteousness, or any internal change whatsoever.

It is not the case, therefore, in many places of Scripture, as Bellarmine admits, that the words we have discussed signify anything other than the declaration or judicial pronouncement of anyone as righteous. In all instances where they are used, they can only be understood in a forensic sense. This is especially evident when justification before God is mentioned.

Because this single consideration, in my opinion, sufficiently refutes all the claims of those in the Roman church regarding the nature of justification, I will address the objections raised against this observation and remove them from our discussion.

Lud. de Blanc, in his reconciliatory efforts on this article of justification ("Thes. de Usu et Acceptatione Vocis, Justificandi"), concedes to the Papists that the word dikaioō does, in several places of the New Testament, signify to renew, to sanctify, to infuse a habit of holiness or righteousness, as they argue. There is no reason to believe that he has based that concession on instances most relevant to that purpose; nor can we expect that anyone will provide a better justification for this concession than he has. Therefore, I will examine all the instances he cites for this purpose and leave the determination of the difference to the judgment of the reader.

I will only preface this with what I consider a reasonable request: if the meaning of the word in any or all the places he mentions seems doubtful to anyone (as it does not to me), the uncertainty of a very few instances should not lead us to question the proper meaning of a word whose sense is established in so many places where it is clear and unquestionable. The first instance he mentions is from the apostle Paul himself, Romans 8:30: "Moreover whom He predestined, these He also called; whom He called, these He also justified; and whom He justified, these He also glorified." He argues that "justified" in this passage refers to an internal work of inherent holiness in those who are predestined because, he says, it seems unlikely that the holy apostle, in this enumeration of gracious privileges, would omit the mention of our sanctification, by which we are freed from the service of sin and adorned with true internal holiness and righteousness. He claims sanctification must be included under the name and title of being justified; otherwise it is absurd to refer it to the head of glorification.

The grace of sanctification, by which our natures are spiritually washed, purified, and endowed with a principle of life, holiness, and obedience to God, is undoubtedly a great and excellent privilege, without which none can be saved. The same can be said for our redemption by the blood of Christ; the apostle declares, commends, and emphasizes both these truths in numerous other places. Whether he ought to have introduced the mention of them or either of them in this particular context, since he has not done so, I cannot judge.

If our sanctification is included or intended in any of the privileges expressed here, there is none of them, except predestination, that is more likely to be associated with justification than the others. Indeed, it seems to be expressly included in vocation. For since it is effectual vocation that is intended—wherein a holy principle of spiritual life or faith itself is communicated to us—our sanctification is fundamentally contained in it as the effect and adequate immediate cause.

Hence, we are said to be "called to be saints" (Romans 1:7), which is the same as being "sanctified in Christ Jesus" (1 Corinthians 1:2). In many other places, sanctification is included in vocation.

Whereas our sanctification, in the infusion of a principle of spiritual life and the exercise of it toward an increase in duties of holiness, righteousness, and obedience, is that by which we are made fit for glory. It is essentially of the same nature as glory itself, from "from glory to glory" (2 Corinthians 3:18), and glory itself is called "the grace of life" (1 Peter 3:7). For these reasons, sanctification is far more appropriately expressed by our being glorified than by being justified, which is a privilege of an entirely different nature. Nevertheless, there is no reason to depart from the general use and meaning of the word, nor does the text compel us to do so.

The next instance he concedes to this meaning is 1 Corinthians 6:11, "And such were some of you. But you were washed, but you were sanctified, but you were justified in the name of the Lord Jesus and by the Spirit of our God." He attempts to prove that justification here signifies the infusion of an inherent principle of grace, making us inherently righteous, by three reasons.

1. "Because justification is here ascribed to the Holy Spirit: 'But you were justified in the name of the Lord Jesus and by the Spirit of our God.'" He argues that renewing us is the proper work of the Holy Spirit.

2. "It is evident," he says, "that by justification the apostle signifies some change in the Corinthians, whereby they ceased to be what they were

before. For they were fornicators and drunkards, such as could not inherit the kingdom of God; but now they were changed: which proves a real inherent work of grace to be intended."

3. "If justification here signifies nothing but to be absolved from the punishment of sin, then the apostle's reasoning will be weak and unconvincing; for after he has stated what is greater, as a heightening of it, he adds the lesser; for it is more to be washed than merely to be freed from the punishment of sin."

All these reasons do not prove that it is the same to be sanctified and to be justified, which would have to be the case if the latter sense were correct. The apostle expressly distinguishes them and proceeds from one to another, ascending from the lesser to the greater.

The infusion of a habit or principle of grace, or evangelical righteousness, by which we are inherently righteous, is what he must show to make justification mean that here. But sanctification is distinguished here from washing: "But you were washed, but you were sanctified," so the apostle is speaking of positive habits of grace and holiness in that clause. Therefore, he cannot mean by being justified anything different from what he would have said by plain words to that effect.

Justification is attributed to the Spirit of God, who is the primary efficient cause in applying God's grace and the blood of Christ. He applies these to our souls and consciences, and He also works faith by which we are justified. Therefore, although we are said to be justified by Him, it does not follow that our justification consists in the renewal of our natures.

The change that occurred in the Corinthians, insofar as it was physical and involved inherent effects, the apostle explicitly attributes to their washing and sanctification. Thus, there is no need to suppose that this change is what the apostle denotes by their being justified.

The real change asserted — the renewal of their natures — constitutes the true and complete work of sanctification. Because of the sinful habits and practices mentioned, they were in a state of condemnation and had no right to the kingdom of heaven. Through their justification they were transferred from that state into another, where they had peace with God and the right to eternal life.

The third reason is based on a misunderstanding — that to be justified is merely to be "freed from the punishment due to sin." Justification includes both the non-imputation of sin and the imputation of righteousness, along with the privilege of adoption and the right to the heavenly inheritance, which are inseparable from it.

Although it does not appear that the apostle intended to present these privileges in a strict progression from lesser to greater, we can assert that in this life we cannot partake of a greater mercy or privilege than what is found in our justification. The reader can see how impossible it is to find any instance where the terms "justification" and "to justify" signify a real internal work and physical operation.

This learned man, who has much clarity and candor, attempted to prove his case by examples that give little support. He cites Titus 3:5-7: "not by works of righteousness which we have done, but according to His mercy He saved us, through the washing of regeneration and renewing of the Holy Spirit, whom He poured out on us abundantly through Jesus Christ our Savior, that having been justified by His grace we should become heirs according to the hope of eternal life." His argument is that because the apostle first states that "God saved us according to His mercy, through the washing of regeneration and renewing of the Holy Spirit," and then affirms that we are "justified by

His grace," regeneration and renewal must precede and be included in justification; therefore, justification must imply sanctification.

In response, the plain truth is that the apostle does not assert the necessity of our sanctification, regeneration, or renewal by the Holy Spirit prior to our justification, which is the foundation of this argument. He attributes our regeneration, renewal, and justification all alike to grace and mercy, in contrast to any works of our own, and does not lay down an order of precedence among them, except that justification precedes adoption in the order of nature: "that, having been justified by His grace, we should become heirs according to the hope of eternal life." All the things he mentions are inseparable. No one is regenerated or renewed by the Holy Spirit without also being justified; nor is anyone justified without being renewed by the Holy Spirit. All are equally acts of sovereign grace, opposed to any works of righteousness we have done.

We advocate the freedom of God's grace in sanctification just as much as in justification. Still, the apostle does not state in this passage that sanctification is necessary in order to be justified before God, who justifies the ungodly. Even if he had, that would not prove that the meaning of "to be justified" is "to be sanctified" or to have inherent holiness worked within us. The testimonies cited do not establish that point; these concepts are clearly distinguished, and no clearer examples can be found.

The last instance where he concedes this meaning of the word dikaioō is Revelation 22:11: "he who is righteous, let him be righteous still." This passage is often cited by Roman Catholics. Our author claims that few Protestants deny the word cannot be used in a forensic sense here, but rather that to be justified means to continue and grow in piety and righteousness.

In response, there is a significant objection to any argument based on these words, arising from the various readings of the passage. Many ancient copies read not "He who is righteous, let him be righteous still," as the Vulgate renders Justificetur adhuc, but rather "Let him who is righteous do still more righteousness," as the printed copy currently before me reads. This reading appears in the Complutensian edition, which Stephens praises, and in another ancient copy he used. It is also found in the Syriac and Arabic versions published by Hutterus, and in our own Polyglot.

Cyprian reads the words, "De bono patientiae; justus autem adhuc justiora faciat, similiter et qui sanctus sanctiora." I have little doubt this is the true reading, and that dikaioō has been supplied by some to agree with the hagiastheto that follows. The phrase used by John, "He who practices righteousness is righteous," appears in 1 John 2:29 and 1 John 3:7, and it clearly conveys what is expressed here. To understand the passage as the Vulgate does — "Let him be justified more" (if dikaiōthētō is retained) — would make it refer to an act of God that is neither prescribed as a duty nor capable of increase in degrees. Moreover, people are usually called dikaioi on account of inherent righteousness; if the apostle had meant justification here he would have written ho dikaiōtheis. All these considerations favor the Complutensian, Syriac, and Arabic readings over the Vulgate rendering. If the Vulgate reading is kept, it can only mean that the righteous should continue to do righteousness to secure and demonstrate their justified state before God and the world.

Now, while the words "dikaioō" and "dikaioumai" occur thirty-six times in the New Testament, objections have been raised only in these instances against their forensic meaning. Any impartial observer will see the ineffectiveness of those objections.

Other considerations also support this argument, such as the contrast between justification and condemnation. This contrast is evident in

Isaiah 50:8-9; Proverbs 17:15; Romans 5:16, 18; 8:33-34; and in several other passages noted earlier. Just as condemnation does not mean infusing a habit of wickedness into the condemned person, so justification does not mean changing someone from inherent unrighteousness to inherent righteousness by infusing a principle of grace. Rather, justification is a declarative sentence concerning his status before God.

Moreover, Scripture often expresses the intended meaning with equivalent terms that exclude any notion of infusing a habit of righteousness. The apostle speaks of the imputation of righteousness apart from works in Romans 4:6 and 4:11, and he refers to the blessedness we receive through pardon and the covering of iniquity in the same argument. He also calls it reconciliation with God in Romans 5:9-10. Being justified by the blood of Christ is spoken of as being reconciled by His death: "Much more then, having now been justified by His blood, we shall be saved from wrath through Him. For if when we were enemies we were reconciled to God through the death of His Son, much more, having been reconciled, we shall be saved by His life." (See also 2 Corinthians 5:20-21.) Reconciliation does not imply the infusion of a habit of grace, but the removal of enmity and causes of offense so that peace and love are established. The terms "to save" and "salvation" are used in the same connection: "He will save His people from their sins." (Matthew 1:21)

Acts 13:39 states, "and by Him everyone who believes is justified from all things from which you could not be justified by the law of Moses." This agrees with Galatians 2:16, where it says, "we have believed in Christ Jesus, that we might be justified by faith in Christ and not by the works of the law." It also accords with Acts 15:11: "but we believe that through the grace of the Lord Jesus Christ we shall be saved in the same manner as they."

Ephesians 2:8-9 affirms, "By grace you have been saved through faith, and that not of yourselves; it is the gift of God, not of works." Justification is also expressed by terms such as pardon or the remission of sins, as in Romans 4:5-6, and by receiving atonement, as in Romans 5:11. It is not about coming into judgment, as John 5:24 indicates, nor is it merely about blotting out sins and iniquities, as Isaiah 43:25 and related passages describe. Scripture also speaks of casting sins into the depths of the sea (Micah 7:19) and uses various other graphic expressions to illustrate the removal of sin.

The apostle likewise declares the effect of justification: "many will be made righteous" (Romans 5:19).

One may observe that all matters concerning justification in Scripture are presented within a judicial or forensic framework — as a trial, verdict, and sentence.

1. A judgment is presumed, concerning which the psalmist prays that God not enter into judgment with His servant (Psalm 143:2).

2. The judge is God Himself (Isaiah 50:7-8; Romans 8:33).

3. The tribunal where God sits in judgment is the "throne of grace" (Hebrews 4:16). "Therefore the Lord will wait, that He may be gracious to you; And therefore He will be exalted, that He may have mercy on you. For the Lord is a God of justice; Blessed are all those who wait for Him." (Isaiah 30:18)

4. The guilty party is the sinner, who is "guilty before God" (Romans 3:19) and whose mouth is stopped (Romans 1:32).

5. Accusers are present to bring charges against the guilty party: the law (John 5:45), conscience (Romans 2:15), and Satan (Zechariah 3:1; Revelation 12:10).

6. The charges are formally presented in a written record before the judge, serving as a barrier to the offender's deliverance (Colossians 2:14).

7. A plea is prepared in the gospel for the guilty party, which is grace through the blood of Christ, the ransom paid, the atonement made, and the everlasting righteousness brought in by the surety of the covenant (Romans 3:23-25; Daniel 9:24; Ephesians 1:7).

8. The sinner must rely solely on this plea, renouncing all other defenses (Psalm 130:2; 143:2; Job 9:2-3; 42:5-7; Luke 18:13; Romans 3:24-25; 5:11; 16-19; 8:1-3, 32-33; Isaiah 53:5-6; Hebrews 9:13-15; 10:1-13; 1 Peter 2:24; 1 John 1:7). There is no other plea for a sinner before God. Those who know God and themselves will not seek any other defense, nor will they trust in any other, even if they had the assurance of all the angels in heaven to plead for them.

9. To make this plea effective, we have an Advocate with the Father, who pleads His own propitiation for us (1 John 2:1-2).

10. The resulting sentence is absolution based on the ransom, blood, or sacrifice and righteousness of Christ, along with acceptance into favor as persons approved by God (Job 33:24; Psalm 32:1-2; Romans 3:23-25; 8:1, 33-34; 2 Corinthians 5:21; Galatians 3:13-14).

The significance of this process in the justification of a sinner has been partially addressed. If many were to seriously consider that all these elements are necessary for the justification of everyone who will be saved, they might not take such a light view of sin and the means of deliverance from its guilt. This understanding led the apostle to recognize the "terror of the Lord," which made him earnest in urging others to seek reconciliation (2 Corinthians 5:10-11).

I would not have elaborated on the meaning of these terms in Scripture, except that a correct understanding excludes the claims of Romanists regarding the infusion of a habit of charity as the formal cause of our justification before God. It may also prompt some to consider where they can place their own personal, inherent righteousness in relation to their justification before Him.

6. Justification as One Complete Act

Before we consider the nature and causes of justification, a few preliminary matters must be settled to avoid ambiguity or misunderstanding. I therefore affirm that the evangelical justification under discussion is singular and completed at once. We will not engage with any other form of justification before God. Those who would identify another may call it what they please or attribute whatever qualities they like to it. Let us, then, examine what is presented on this point.

The Roman Church grounds its entire doctrine of justification on a distinction between two justifications, which it calls the first and the second. They assert that the first justification involves the infusion or communication of an inherent principle or habit of grace or charity. By this, they say, original sin is extinguished and all habits of sin are expelled. They maintain that this justification is by faith, with the obedience and satisfaction of Christ as the only meritorious cause. Yet they occupy themselves with numerous questions about preparations for it and dispositions toward it.

Under these terms, the Council of Trent embraced the schoolmen's doctrine concerning the "meritum de congruo," as Hosius and Andradius acknowledge in defending the council. Though similar explanations are offered, the council cautiously avoided calling this first justification a true merit. In their view, faith here is merely a general assent to divine revelation that prepares the mind to receive "gratiam gratum facientem," a habit of grace that expels sin and renders us acceptable to God.

For them, to be "justified by faith" means that the mind is prepared by this sort of belief to receive that grace which justifies us. They argue Paul is speaking of this justification in his epistles when he excludes all works of the law. The second justification, in their scheme, follows as an effect or consequence of the first. Good works are the proper formal cause of this second justification, arising from the implanted principle of grace and love. Thus these works are reckoned the righteousness by which believers are considered righteous before God, and so are said to merit eternal life. They call this the righteousness of works and attribute it to the teaching of the apostle James.

They repeatedly contend that this results in being "justos ex injustis," a position shared by others. This is the usual way to reconcile the apparent contradiction between Paul and James. They say Paul treats only the first justification, excluding all works, while James addresses the second justification, achieved by good works. Bellarmine affirms this, and the decisions of the Council of Trent state it explicitly.

This distinction was devised solely to introduce confusion into the gospel. It undermines justification by the free grace of God, through faith in the blood of Christ. Sanctification is confused with justification and corrupted by making its fruits meritorious. The evangelical doctrine of justification — the gratuitous pardon of sin, the imputation of Christ's righteousness, and the declaration of a believing sinner as righteous, as the term itself implies — is wholly subverted by this distinction.

Others have also accepted this distinction, though not so absolutely. The Socinians, for example, must concede it in some form, as do all who believe our inherent righteousness causes or influences our justification before God. They admit a justification that, in order of nature, precedes genuinely gracious and evangelical works; yet they also posit a justification that follows such works. That later justification differs at least in degree, if not in kind, because its formal cause is our new obedience rather than the former principle.

They mostly insist, however, that what they mean is merely the continuation of our justification and an increase of it in degrees. If they are allowed to equate sanctification with justification and to treat growth or increase in either root or fruit as a new justification, they could just as well invent twenty justifications as two. Yet "the inward man is being renewed day by day" (2 Corinthians 4:16). Believers also "go from strength to strength," are "are being transformed into the same image from glory to glory" (2 Corinthians 3:18), and add one grace to another in their practice (2 Peter 1:5-8). The body of Christ "grows with the increase that is from God" (Colossians 2:19), and believers may "grow up in all things into Him who is the head—Christ—" (Ephesians 4:15). If their justification consists in these things, then, by their logic, believers would be justified anew every day.

Therefore, I will undertake two tasks:

1. Demonstrate that this distinction is both unscriptural and irrational.

2. Clarify what the continuation of our justification is and what it depends upon.

1. Justification by faith in the blood of Christ can be viewed in two ways: as to its nature and essence, or as to its manifestation and declaration. Its manifestation is twofold:

- First, initial, in this life.

- Second, solemn and complete, on the day of judgment, which we will discuss later.

The manifestation in this life relates either to the souls and consciences of those who are justified or to others, such as the church or the world. Each of these manifestations is called justification, although our actual justification before God remains one and the same.

A person may be truly justified before God yet lack the evidence or assurance of it in their own mind. That evidence or assurance is not part of the nature or essence of the faith by which we are justified, nor does it necessarily accompany our justification. When assurance is later attained, it is not a second justification. It is only the former justification applied to the conscience by the Holy Spirit, and it depends on various causes that are not essential to justification itself.

There is also a manifestation with respect to others, which likewise depends on causes different from those that determine our justification before God. Yet this is not a second justification either; it rests entirely on the visible effects of the faith by which we are justified, as the apostle James instructs. Still, it remains a single justification before God, evidenced and declared for His glory, for the benefit of others, and for the increase of our own reward.

There is also a twofold justification before God mentioned in Scripture. First, "by the works of the law" (Romans 2:13; 10:5; Matthew 19:16–19). This requires absolute conformity to the whole law of God — embracing our natures, all the faculties of our souls, and all the principles of our moral actions — with perfect actual obedience to every command in every instance of duty, both in substance and manner. For, "Cursed is everyone who does not continue in all things which are written in the book of the law, to do them" (Galatians 3:10), and "For whoever shall keep the whole law, and yet stumble in one point, he is guilty of all" (James 2:10). Hence the apostle concludes that no one can be justified by the law, because all have sinned.

Second, there is a justification by grace, through faith in the blood of Christ, which we will discuss. These two ways of justification are opposed to each other; they proceed on directly contradictory terms and cannot be made consistent or subservient to one another. As we will show later, the confusion that arises from mixing them is the very purpose of inventing a first and second justification. Nevertheless, the justification we have before God, in His sight and through Jesus Christ, is singular, full, and complete; this distinction is a vain and fanciful invention.

As explained by the Papists, this distinction greatly undermines the merit of Christ. It renders His work ineffective for us by reducing it to the mere infusion of a habit of charity. Once that habit is given, all that remains of our salvation is to be achieved by our own efforts. Christ, in this scheme, has only merited the first grace for us so that, through our subsequent merits, we may attain eternal life. The merit of Christ is thus confined in its effect to the first justification and has no immediate influence on any grace, privilege, mercy, or glory that follows; those things are all ascribed to the second justification, which is purely by works. This is plainly contrary to the tenor of Scripture; for although God has ordered our evangelical privileges so that we partake of them in sequence, one before another, they are all immediate effects of the death and obedience of Christ, who has "having obtained eternal redemption" (Hebrews 9:12) and is "the author of eternal salvation to all who obey Him" (Hebrews 5:9), "For by one offering He has perfected forever those who are being sanctified" (Hebrews 10:14).

Those who accept a secondary, if not a second, justification based on our own inherent personal righteousness are guilty of an error, though not to the same degree as others. They attribute to this supposed justification our acquittal from all charges of sin after the first justification, and they treat it as a righteousness accepted in judgment—complete and perfect, upon which our final absolution and reward depend. It is clear, however, that the immediate efficacy of Christ's satisfaction and merit is confined to the first justification. We will examine whether Scripture teaches any further effect to it.

Moreover, this distinction attributes more to our own workings—by virtue of inherent grace—regarding the merit and procurement of spiritual and eternal good than it does to the blood of Christ. According to this view, Christ's blood only procures the first grace and justification for us. Then, by means of that infused grace, we supposedly obtain, procure, or merit a second, complete justification: the continuation of God's favor, all its fruits, and ultimately eternal life and glory. Thus our works are said to perfect and complete Christ's merit, without which His merit would be imperfect.

Those who place the continuation of our justification—the effects of divine favor and grace—and our final justification before God on the basis of our own personal righteousness follow this reasoning, so far as I can discern. Such matters are open to debate; and in these discussions tradition, prejudice, and subtle reasoning often exert an incredible influence. They distract people from honestly considering their true condition before God. If such persons were made to reflect on how they will appear before the Most High—freed from the sentence of the law and the curse due to sin, and seeking a plea-worthy righteousness at God's judgment seat—their subtle arguments for the efficacy of their own righteousness would vanish like water at high tide, leaving nothing but mud and filth.

This doctrine of two justifications, as taught and advanced by the Roman Church, ultimately leaves us with no genuine justification at all. Some parts of what they call the first justification relate to sanctification, but nothing in that branch actually constitutes justification. Their "first justification," which they describe as the infusion of a habit or principle of grace to expel habits of sin, is sanctification and nothing more. We never maintained that our justification, in that sense, consists in the imputation of Christ's righteousness. If anyone insists on calling that sanctification a justification, then that so-called justification is capable of degrees—both in itself and in its fruits—as was already noted.

To call this infusion our justification, and to assert that it makes us personally and inherently righteous, while also claiming that it is the justification "by faith in the blood of Christ" declared in Scripture, is to exclude the true evangelical justification from religion altogether. This second branch resembles justification by the law but lacks the essence of what the gospel declares. Instead of providing us two gospel justifications, this distinction leaves us with none.

There is no warrant for this distinction in Scripture. Scripture does speak of a twofold justification—one by the law and one according to the gospel—but it gives no hint that either of these should be further divided into a first and second of the same kind, whether under the law or under the gospel. The second justification supposed by some does not correspond to what the apostle James discusses. James speaks of justification but mentions no addition or increase to it, and he does not delineate a first and second justification. He addresses those who boast of faith without works and calls that faith dead. Yet, by the admission of our adversaries, those who have the first justification possess a true, living faith, enlivened by charity. When James appeals to Abraham's justification—the same event Paul cites—he intends the same justification seen from a different perspective, not a different, second justification.

No believer learns anything of this supposed distinction from personal experience, nor would sober readers find it in Scripture unless they had some ulterior purpose. It is harmful to spiritual truth when people invent arbitrary distinctions without scriptural warrant and present them as doctrine. Such devices only distract attention from what truly matters and provoke endless disputes. If the authors of this distinction were to examine the scriptural passages that speak of our justification before God and try to sort them according to their scheme, they would quickly find themselves at a great loss.

Scripture ascribes much to what some call our first justification — if they insist on that label — leaving little or nothing for the fabricated second justification. The whole foundation of this distinction is a denial of those things that Scripture assigns to our justification by the blood of Christ. Consider some of the benefits Scripture attributes to that justification; you will then see how little remains for the pretended second justification.

1. In it, we receive the complete "the forgiveness of sins" (Romans 4:6-7; Ephesians 1:7; 4:32; Acts 26:18).

2. Through it, we are "made righteous" (Romans 5:19; 10:4).

3. We are freed from condemnation, judgment, and death (John 3:16, 19; 5:25; Romans 8:1).

4. We are reconciled to God (Romans 5:9-10; 2 Corinthians 5:21).

5. We have peace with Him, and by faith we have access into the grace in which we stand. We also enjoy the benefits and consolations that flow from a sense of His love (Romans 5:1-5).

6. We receive adoption and all its privileges (John 1:12).

7. We gain a right and title to the full inheritance of glory (Acts 26:18; Romans 8:17).

8. Eternal life follows from this (Romans 8:30; Romans 6:23).

These matters will be addressed again on another occasion. If anything remains for their so-called second justification to accomplish, let them claim it; yet all these things belong to the one justification we affirm. Therefore either the first justification negates the second, making it unnecessary, or the second robs the first by taking away what properly belongs to it. They cannot consistently coexist, so we must reject one or the other. The real motive behind inventing such distinctions, and many others, is a dislike of the doctrine of God's grace and of justification by faith in the blood of Christ. Some attempt to dismiss that doctrine as a futile endeavor so they may exalt their own righteousness to take its place and dignity.

There is greater substance and complexity in the arguments about the continuation of our justification. Those who are freely justified remain in that state until they are glorified. Justification truly changes their standing and condition; it establishes a new relationship with God and with Christ, and it alters their relation to the law and to the gospel. The question is on what their continuance in this state depends — what is required for them to remain justified until the end.

Some maintain that not faith alone but also the works of sincere obedience are required of all who are justified as they continue in that state before the coming glory. We must therefore examine whether faith is immediately set aside after our initial justification — its role and function transferred to works — so that the continuation of justification depends on our personal obedience rather than on the renewed application of faith to Christ and His righteousness.

Note that while all acknowledge the necessity of personal obedience in those who are justified, the apparent difference here is not about the substance of the doctrine of justification. It concerns the manner of expressing the order of God's grace and our duty toward edification. I will offer my thoughts on this matter in the following observations:

Justification is a work completed at once in all its causes and effects, though not yet in the full possession of all the rights and titles it confers.

1. All our sins—past, present, and future—were imputed to and laid upon Jesus Christ at once; we will inquire further into the sense of this later. "But He was wounded for our transgressions, He was bruised for our iniquities; The chastisement for our peace was upon Him, And by His stripes we are healed. All we like sheep have gone astray; We have turned, every one, to his own way; And the Lord has laid on Him the iniquity of us all" (Isaiah 53:5-6). "who Himself bore our sins in His own body on the tree" (1 Peter 2:24). The assertions being indefinite, without exception or limitation, are equivalent to universals. All our sins were on Him; He bore them all at once; and therefore, He died once for all.

2. He therefore "To finish the transgression, To make an end of sins, To make reconciliation for iniquity, To bring in everlasting righteousness" (Daniel 9:24). He expiated all our sins at once; for "by Himself purged our sins" and "sat down at the right hand of the Majesty on high" (Hebrews 1:3). "For by one offering He has perfected forever those who are being sanctified" (Hebrews 10:14). He will never do more than He has already accomplished regarding the expiation of all our sins from beginning to end; "there no longer remains a sacrifice for sins" (Hebrews 10:26).

I do not mean that our justification is already carried to its final consummation; rather, I mean that the meritorious, procuring cause of it was accomplished once for all and will never be repeated. The present question is how that benefit is renewedly applied to our souls and consciences—whether by faith alone or by the righteous works we perform.

3. By our actual believing with justifying faith, believing in Christ or His name, we receive Him; and thereby, upon our first justification, we become "children of God" (John 1:12); that is, "heirs of God and joint heirs with Christ" (Romans 8:17). Through this we gain a right and interest in all the benefits of His mediation, which constitutes complete justification. "and you are complete in Him" (Colossians 2:10). Through the faith that is in Him, we "receive forgiveness of sins and an inheritance among those who are sanctified" (Acts 26:18), being immediately "justified from all things from which you could not be justified by the law of Moses" (Acts 13:39). God, therefore, "has blessed us with every spiritual blessing in the heavenly places in Christ" (Ephesians 1:3). All these things are inseparable from our initial belief in Him; thus, our justification is complete at once.

In particular:

4. Upon our believing, all our sins are forgiven. "He has made alive together with Him, having forgiven you all trespasses" (Colossians 2:13-15). "In Him we have redemption through His blood, the forgiveness of sins, according to the riches of His grace" (Ephesians 1:7); this one verse addresses all the objections some raise against the consistency of God's free grace in the pardon of sins and the satisfaction of Christ in procuring it.

5. There is nothing that can be charged against those who are justified. "Most assuredly, I say to you, he who hears My word and believes in Him who sent Me has everlasting life, and shall not come into judgment, but has passed from death into life" (John 5:24). "Who shall bring a charge against God's elect? It is God who justifies. Who is he who condemns? It is Christ who died" (Romans 8:33-34). "There is therefore now no condemnation to those who are in Christ Jesus" (Romans 8:1); for "Therefore, having been justified by faith, we have peace with God through our Lord Jesus Christ" (Romans 5:1).

6. We have the blessedness of which we are capable in this life (Romans 4:5-6). From all this it is clear that our justification is complete at once.

7. It must be so, or no person can be justified in this world. No time can be assigned, nor any measure of obedience fixed, upon which it may be supposed that anyone becomes justified before God if they are not justified upon their first belief; Scripture gives no such time or measure.

To assert that no one is completely justified in the sight of God in this life is to undermine all Scripture teaches concerning justification, and consequently to destroy all peace with God and comfort for believers. A person acquitted in a legal trial is immediately discharged from all that the law has against them.

Upon this complete justification, believers are obligated to universal obedience to God. The law is not abolished but established by faith. It is neither annulled nor dispensed with so as to remove its obligation regarding anything it requires, nor in the degree and manner in which it requires it. This is impossible, for the law is the rule of obedience that the nature of God and of man makes necessary between One and the other.

Antinomianism of the worst sort, most derogatory to the law of God, asserts that the law is divested of its power to obligate perfect obedience so that anything less than that will be accepted as if it were perfect and thus would fulfill the law's requirements. There is no middle ground. Either the law is entirely abolished, in which case there is no sin (for where there is no law there is no transgression), or it must be acknowledged that it requires the same obedience it did at its institution, and to the same degree.

It is beyond the power of any living person to keep their conscience from judging and condemning them for any failure to meet the law's perfection. Therefore the commanding power of the law in its positive precepts and prohibitions, to which justified persons remain subject, makes all their failures to conform to it truly and properly sins in their nature, just as they would be if their persons were subject to the curse of it. They are not, nor can they be, for to be subject to the curse of the law and to be justified are contradictory. But to be subject to the law's commands and to be justified are not contradictory.

It is subjection to the commanding power of the law, and not obligation to the curse of the law, that constitutes the nature of sin in its transgression. Therefore that complete justification which is present at once, while it dissolves the sinner's obligation to punishment by the curse of the law, does not annihilate the commanding authority of the law over those who are justified, so that what is sin for others should not be sin for them. See Romans 8:1, 33, 34.

Thus, in the first justification of believing sinners, all future sins are remitted as far as any actual obligation to the curse of the law is concerned, unless they commit sins that, by their very nature, would forfeit their justified status and transfer them from the covenant of grace to the covenant of works—something we trust God, in His faithfulness, will preserve them from. Although sin cannot be actually pardoned before it is committed, the obligation to the curse of the law may be virtually removed from such sins in justified persons if those sins are consistent with a justified state or with the terms of the covenant of grace, even before they are actually committed.

God, in this sense, "Who forgives all your iniquities, Who heals all your diseases; Who redeems your life from destruction, Who crowns you with lovingkindness and tender mercies" (Psalm 103:3–4). Future sins are not pardoned in such a way that, when committed, they are no longer sins; that cannot be the case unless the commanding power of the law is abrogated. Their relation to the curse of the law, however, or the power of the law to obligate the justified person, is taken away.

Nevertheless, the true nature of sin remains in every failure to conform to, or transgression of, the law by justified persons, and this requires daily actual pardon. For "for there is no one who does not sin" (1 Kings 8:46), and "If we say that we have no sin, we deceive ourselves" (1 John 1:8). No one is more conscious of the guilt of sin, more troubled by it, or more earnest in seeking pardon for it than justified persons. This is the effect of Christ's sacrifice applied to believers' souls, as the apostle declares in Hebrews 10:1-4, 10, 14. It removes the sinner's condemnation so far as the curse of the law is concerned, but it does not remove the conscience's sense of condemnation for sin, which, before God, themselves, the law, and the gospel, requires repentance from the sinner and actual pardon from God.

Since one essential part of justification consists in the pardon of our sins, and sins cannot be actually pardoned before they are committed, our present inquiry concerns the basis on which the continuation of our justification depends despite sin occurring after we are justified. We ask how such sins are actually pardoned and how our persons remain in acceptance with God, maintaining their right to life and glory without interruption. Justification is complete at once in the imputation of perfect righteousness, the grant of a right and title to the heavenly inheritance, the actual pardon of all past sins, and the virtual pardon of future sins. We must now explore by what means, on what terms and conditions, this state is continued for those once justified, ensuring their righteousness is everlasting, their title to life and glory indefeasible, and all their sins are actually pardoned.

To answer this inquiry, I say:

1. "It is God who justifies"; therefore the continuation of our justification is also His act. This depends on the immutability of His counsel, the unchangeableness of the everlasting covenant, which is ordered in all things and sure, the faithfulness of His promises, the efficacy of His

grace, His pleasure in the propitiation of Christ, the power of His intercession, and the irrevocable grant of the Holy Spirit to those who believe. These matters, however, are not the focus of our present inquiry.

2. Some argue that the continuation of our justification depends on the condition of good works, suggesting that they hold the same significance and purpose as faith itself in this matter. While they may concede that faith has a unique role in our justification, they assert that both faith and works equally influence its continuation. Some even attribute this continuation specifically to works, provided they are performed in faith. I cannot comprehend how the continuation of our justification could depend on anything other than the same factors that justified us in the first place. Just as faith alone is necessary for our initial justification, so faith alone is required for its continuation, even though the expressions and outcomes of faith in justification and in its continuation may differ.

To clarify this assertion, two points should be noted:

1. The continuation of our justification is the ongoing imputation of righteousness and the pardon of sins. I maintain that the imputation of righteousness is essential to our justification, although we have yet to examine precisely what righteousness is being imputed. The apostle explicitly affirms that God imputes righteousness to us in our justification, and this cannot be disputed. The initial act of God in imputing righteousness cannot be repeated, and the actual pardon of sin following justification is a result of that imputation. If anyone sins, there is a propitiation: "Then He is gracious to him, and says, 'Deliver him from going down to the Pit; I have found a ransom.'" Therefore, for this actual pardon, nothing is required except the application of that righteousness which effects it, and this application is accomplished solely through faith.

2. The continuation of our justification before God, or in His sight, is as significant as our absolute justification. We are not discussing how it appears to our own souls for peace with God, nor how it is demonstrated to others by its effects. Rather, we mean its persistence in the sight of God. Thus, whatever means, conditions, or causes are involved must be presented before God and argued accordingly.

The question then is: When a justified person, who is in some measure guilty of sin daily, is burdened by conscience and fears that this guilt threatens his justified state, favor with God, and claim to glory, what does he turn to? What does he plead for the continuation of his state and for the pardon of his sins? What is effective in this regard? It is evident that this does not involve his own obedience, personal righteousness, or the fulfilling of the conditions of the new covenant.

First, consider the experience of believers themselves, whose consciences are continually engaged with this matter. What do they rely on, and what do they plead with God for the continuation of the pardon of their sins and for the acceptance of their persons before Him? Is it anything other than sovereign grace and mercy through the blood of Christ? Are not all the arguments they present drawn from the attributes of God—His mercy, grace, faithfulness, tender compassion, covenant, and promises—all manifested and exercised through the Lord Christ and His mediation alone? Do they not place their sole trust and confidence in this, that their sins may be pardoned and their persons, though unworthy in themselves, accepted by God? Do any other thoughts enter their minds? Do they plead their own righteousness, obedience, and duties for this purpose? Do they abandon the prayer of the publican and adopt that of the Pharisee? Is it not by faith alone that they approach the mercy of God through the mediation of Christ?

It is true that faith expresses itself through godly sorrow, repentance, humiliation, self-examination, fervent prayer, and a humble expectation of peace from God, along with commitments to renewed obedience. Nevertheless, it is faith alone that seeks grace in the blood of Christ for the continuation of our justified state. These other actions and effects manifest faith, but a believing soul does not expect the mercy sought from them.

The Scripture explicitly declares this to be the only means for the continuation of our justification. "My little children, these things I write to you, that you may not sin. And if anyone sins, we have an Advocate with the Father, Jesus Christ the Righteous. And He Himself is the propitiation for our sins." It is required of those who are justified that they do not sin; it is their duty not to sin. Yet this is not required in such a way that if they fail in any aspect of their duty, they immediately lose the privilege of their justification. Therefore, given the possibility of sin, if anyone sins (for there is no man who lives and does not sin), what course is prescribed? What should they apply themselves to so that their sins may be pardoned and their acceptance with God maintained, which is essential for the continuation of their justification?

The course directed by the apostle is nothing other than the application of our souls by faith to the Lord Christ, our Advocate with the Father, based on the propitiation He has made for our sins. Considering His dual role in His priestly office — His sacrifice and His intercession — He is the object of our faith in both our absolute justification and the continuation of it. Thus, our whole progression in our justified state, in all its stages, is attributed solely to faith.

It is not part of our inquiry what God requires of those who are justified. There is no grace or duty, in substance or manner of performance, that is not required by either the law or the gospel. When these duties are neglected, the guilt of sin is incurred, often accompanied by aggravations that some may refuse to acknowledge or confess to God. Believers are particularly and continually engaged in godly sorrow, repentance, humiliation for sin, and confession before God, because of their awareness of its guilt.

These duties are necessary for the continuation of our justification, because a justified state cannot coexist with sins and vices that oppose it. The apostle affirms, "For if you live according to the flesh you will die;" (Romans 8:13). Just as one cannot carelessly fall into fire, water, or other things that would destroy natural life, one cannot maintain spiritual life while neglecting these duties. However, these duties do not constitute the foundation of our life.

The question here is not which duties obedience requires of us, but what the continuation of our justification depends on. If one claims that the continuation of justification relies on our own obedience and good works—that God requires good works and obedience from all who are justified, so that a justified state is incompatible with neglecting them—then I readily grant that point and will not dispute how some choose to express it.

But if the inquiry is how we actively participate in the continuation of our justified state—specifically, in the pardon of our sins and our acceptance with God—we assert that it is faith alone. "The just shall live by faith." (Romans 1:17). The apostle uses this divine testimony to affirm that our initial justification is by faith alone, and he applies it likewise to the continuation of our justification, as the same means. He makes this clear in Hebrews 10:38-39: "Now the just shall live by faith; But if anyone draws back, My soul has no pleasure in him. But we are not of those who draw back to perdition, but of those who believe to the saving of the soul." (Hebrews 10:38-39).

Drawing back to perdition includes the loss of a justified state, whether truly or only in profession. In contrast, the apostle emphasizes "believing to the saving of the soul," which pertains to the continuation of justification until the end. The life "which I now live in the flesh I live by faith in the Son of God, who loved me and gave Himself for me." (Galatians 2:20). This life, characterized by righteousness and acceptance with God, stands opposed to a life of legal works. As the next verse declares, "I do not set aside the grace of God; for if righteousness comes through the law, then Christ died in vain." (Galatians 2:21).

Thus, this life is sustained by faith in Christ — the same faith that trusts He loved us and gave Himself for us as a propitiation for our sins. Therefore this is the only means, on our part, for preserving that life and for the continuation of our justification. And we are "kept by the power of God through faith for salvation."

If the continuation of our justification depended on our own works of obedience, then the righteousness of Christ would be imputed to us only for our initial justification. This is, in fact, the doctrine of the Roman school. They teach that Christ's righteousness is imputed to us so that, on that basis, God grants us justifying grace and the remission of sins as they understand it. They then assert that, after receiving that grace, we remain justified before God by the works we perform through the grace received.

Some maintain that this grace and the works arising from it require no further reference to Christ's righteousness to merit our second justification and eternal life. As Vasquez explicitly states (1, 2, q. 114, disp. 222, cap. 3), many nonetheless affirm that it is still on the merit of Christ that our works are regarded as meritorious. Their position is that our own works, though imperfect, are accepted by God because of Christ's righteousness, and so the continuation of our justification depends on them. The apostle, however, explains the matter differently in Romans 5:1-3, distinguishing three aspects:

1. Our access into the grace of God.

2. Our standing in that grace.

3. Our rejoicing in that state against all opposition.

The first expresses our absolute justification, the second our continuation in the state into which we are admitted, and the third the assurance of that continuation despite all opposition. The apostle attributes all three equally to faith, without mixing in any other cause or condition. Other passages could be cited to support this same point.

3. The examples of those who believed and were justified, as recorded in Scripture, all testify to the same truth. The continuation of Abraham's justification before God is shown to have been by faith alone, as indicated in Romans 4:3. The instance of his justification, which the apostle cites from Genesis 15:6, occurred long after he was initially justified. If our first justification and its continuation did not depend on the same cause, the example of one could not be used to prove the means of the other.

Moreover, David, as a justified believer, locates the blessedness of a man in the free remission of sins, contrasting this with dependence on works in general (Romans 4:6-7). He also attributes the continuation of his justification and his acceptance before God to grace, mercy, and forgiveness alone — gifts received by faith (Psalm 130:3-5; Psalm 143:2). All other works and duties of obedience accompany faith as necessary fruits and effects of continuing in a justified state, but they are not causes, means, or conditions on which that state depends. It is patient waiting by faith that brings about the full realization of the promises (Hebrews 6:12, 15).

Therefore, there is only one kind of justification at issue here — the justification of an ungodly person by faith. Scripture mentions no other kind. If there were a second justification, it must either be the same kind as the first or a different kind. If it were the same kind, the same person would be justified repeatedly by the same justification; by that logic, one might argue for repeated baptism. If it were a different kind, then a person would be justified before God by two distinct types of justification—something for which Scripture gives no ground. Thus, the continuation of our justification depends on the same causes as our initial justification.

7. Personal Righteousness and the Final Judgment

The points we have discussed about a first and second justification, and about the continuation of justification, are intended solely to remove matters that do not properly belong to the main question. Until we separate what is truly heterogeneous or superfluous, we cannot rightly understand the nature and causes of our justification before God. We intend to focus on one justification only—namely, that by which God freely justifies a convinced sinner through faith in the blood of Christ. Whatever else people may call "justification" is not the concern of this discussion, nor does it trouble the consciences of believers. I will briefly consider the usual debates about personal righteousness and any justification said to rest on it, as well as the so-called sentential justification at the day of judgment, only so far as necessary to keep the principal subject distinct from them. Differences in expression about spiritual matters arise from the partialness of our knowledge; they affect more how we speak than the substance of the doctrine. Such differences should not break charity, provided mutual liberty of thought is respected.

Some hold that there is an evangelical justification based on our own personal, evangelical righteousness. They distinguish this from the justification by faith through the imputation of Christ's righteousness, which they also acknowledge. They admit that Christ's righteousness is our legal righteousness, by which we receive pardon and acquittal through His satisfaction and merit. Yet they argue that, because a personal, inherent righteousness is required of us, there is also a gospel justification based on that righteousness. Thus, by our faith and its plea we are justified against the charge of unbelief; by our sincerity and its plea we are justified against the charge of hypocrisy; and similarly, by other graces and duties we are justified against charges of contrary sins in commission or omission, insofar as those sins conflict with the covenant of grace.

Those who explain the distinction say that this differs from a second justification before God, which some claim is achieved by works after the pardon of sin, combined with the infusion of a habit of grace that enables those works. They describe how, on that view, pardon and infused grace prepare the way for works that then secure a further justification.

Some add that this inherent, personal evangelical righteousness is the condition on our part for our legal righteousness, or for the imputation of Christ's righteousness to our justification, or for the pardon of sin. Those who deny Christ's satisfaction and merit make it the sole condition of absolute justification before God. This is the constant position of the Socinians, who deny that Christ's obedience is either the meritorious or efficient cause of our justification; instead, they call it merely a condition without which God has decreed we shall not partake of the benefits. Socinus himself writes: "Our works, that is, our obedience to Christ, though neither efficient nor meritorious, is a cause (as they say) without which justification before God and our eternal life cannot occur." Again he warns, "We must be careful not to believe that the holiness and innocence of life are the effects of our justification before God, nor should we affirm that they are the efficient or impulsive cause of our justification; but only a cause without which God has decreed that we cannot attain justification." Throughout their writings they maintain that personal righteousness and holiness, or obedience to Christ's commands — what they regard as the essence of faith — is the condition upon which we obtain justification or the remission of sins.

Given their views of Christ's person and their denial of His satisfaction and merit, they cannot conceive of any other idea of justification. I am unsure why some among us would align with them on this point, when they are not committed to the same prior conclusions about Christ's person and mediation.

For now, I will examine only that particular evangelical justification claimed to result from our own personal righteousness or to be granted on that basis. We should note that God requires sincere obedience from all who believe, performed in and through their own persons, though with grace supplied to them by Jesus Christ. He requires obedience, duties, and works of righteousness from everyone. But works done before believing are excluded from any causal role in our justification before God. Some may discuss such pre-conversion works as preparatory to believing (a point addressed earlier), yet none include them among evangelical works of faith, for to do so would be contradictory.

Nevertheless, all agree that such works are necessary for believers. We will inquire later into the reasons and ends for which they are required. These are declared in Ephesians 2:10.

It is also acknowledged that believers are called righteous in Scripture because of their obedience and works of righteousness, as seen in Luke 1:6 and John 3:7. However, this designation is not based on an inherent grace but on the effects of that grace as shown in their obedience. For example, Scripture says, "And they were both righteous before God, walking in all the commandments and ordinances of the Lord blameless" (Luke 1:6), the latter clause explaining the former. Likewise,

"He who practices righteousness is righteous," indicating that the title derives from action.

Bellarmine, trying to prove that habitual rather than actual righteousness is the formal cause of our justification before God, could not find a single Scripture where anyone is called righteous on the ground of habitual righteousness (De Justificat., lib. ii. cap. 15). He ends up with the strained argument that "we are justified by the sacraments, which do not produce actual but habitual righteousness." This exposes the weakness of any claim that our own righteousness, as so designated, bears on justification, since that designation does not concern the principal aspect of righteousness.

This inherent righteousness—understood as both habitual and actual—is essentially our sanctification; the terms name the same reality. Sanctification involves an inward renewal of our nature that issues in a new life of obedience to God through Christ and in works of righteousness.

Nevertheless, Scripture consistently distinguishes sanctification from justification, whatever causal relation one might assert between them. Those who confuse the two, as the Papists do, are not merely disputing the nature of justification; they deny its distinct existence. They argue that what should strengthen justification—the pardon of sin—is instead removed or extinguished by the infusion of inherent grace, which does not properly belong to justification.

Through this inherent, personal righteousness, believers may be said to be justified in several ways.

1. In our own consciences, for it serves as evidence that we partake of the grace of God in Christ Jesus and are accepted with Him, which greatly affects our peace. The apostle says, "For our rejoicing is this: the testimony of our conscience, that in simplicity and godly sincerity, not

with fleshly wisdom but by the grace of God, we have had our conduct in the world" (2 Corinthians 1:12). Yet he denies any confidence in this for his justification before God, saying, "I know nothing against myself, yet I am not justified by this" (1 Corinthians 4:4).

2. We may also be said to be justified before men — that is, acquitted of charges brought against us and acknowledged as righteous and blameless. The truth is that professors of the gospel have always been, and will continue to be, accused as evildoers. Their way of acquitting themselves so that, ultimately, those not entirely blinded by wickedness may justify them is to live in holiness and fruitfulness, abounding in good works (1 Peter 2:12; 3:16).

3. This righteousness can be pleaded for our justification against all accusations from Satan, the great accuser of the brethren. Whether he brings his charges privately into our consciences, as he did with Job, or urges them through his instruments in reproaches and slanders, this righteousness stands as a defense for our justification.

Taken in its proper context and use (which I will elaborate on later), personal righteousness does not constitute an evangelical justification by which believers are justified in God's sight on the basis of their own inherent righteousness. The imputation of Christ's righteousness for our absolute justification before God does not depend on it.

No one possesses this personal righteousness unless already justified in God's sight. It is the obedience of faith that springs from true and saving faith in God through Jesus Christ. As already noted, works done prior to faith are universally excluded from any role in our justification. We have shown they are neither conditions, dispositions, nor preparations for justification in the proper sense.

Every true believer is justified immediately upon believing. There is no time when a person is a true believer, as required by the gospel, and yet not justified. Because believers are united to Christ—the ground of our justification—the whole Scripture testifies that he who believes is justified. This shows an infallible connection, ordained by God, between true faith and justification. Therefore personal righteousness cannot be a condition for justification before God; it is a consequence of it. Any attempts to posit a second justification or different causal principles for the beginning and continuance of justification have already been refuted.

Justification before God is a release and absolution from charges against us—at least that element is included. Such charges must come either from the law or from the gospel. But neither the law nor the gospel indicts true believers for unbelief, hypocrisy, or similar faults; "Who shall bring a charge against God's elect? It is God who justifies" (Romans 8:33). Accusations may come from Satan, sometimes from the church through misunderstanding, or from the world, as in Job's case. Against these, our righteousness may be pleaded.

What is charged directly before God, however, is charged by God Himself—either under the law or under the gospel—and God's judgment corresponds with truth. If the charge comes from the law, then justification must be by the law. But sincere obedience cannot justify us under the law, which demands full and perfect satisfaction. If the gospel itself lays any charge against persons before God, then justification cannot occur unless we suppose the gospel is making a false charge; how can one be justified whom the gospel condemns? If justification by the gospel removes the charge of the law, then Christ's death is rendered ineffective; a justification without a charge is inconceivable.

This supposed justification is entirely unnecessary and serves no purpose. Scripture's teaching about our justification before God through faith in the blood of Christ—already discussed—makes this plain. There is no need or role for a new justification based on our personal righteousness, whether it is supposed to be prior to and supportive of justification, or subsequent and intended to perfect it.

This claimed evangelical justification does not resemble any justification taught in Scripture—neither that of the law nor that of the gospel. Justification by the law states, "The man who does those things shall live by them." That does not apply here.

Nor does this idea fit with evangelical justification. In the gospel the charge against the person who is justified is true: he has sinned and fallen short of the glory of God. But in the present scheme the charge is false: a believer is not an unbeliever, a sincere person is not a hypocrite, one who bears fruit is not altogether barren. That false charge is presumed to be brought in God's name and before Him.

In true evangelical justification our acquittal rests on the pardon of sin; in this scheme it rests on a vindication of our own righteousness. In the gospel the plea of the person being justified is, "Guilty"—all the world is guilty before God. Here the plea is, "Not guilty," followed by proofs and evidence of innocence and righteousness. But that plea the law will not accept, and the gospel disavows.

If we are to be declared righteous before God on the basis of our own personal righteousness, then God is judging us by something within ourselves and acquitting us accordingly. Justification is a judicial act, part of God's judgment, which must be according to truth.

The psalmist did not suppose God would enter into judgment with His servant on the basis of personal righteousness (see Psalm 130:2-3; 143:2), and neither did the publican in Luke 18.

This personal righteousness cannot be regarded as a subordinate righteousness that supports our justification by faith in the blood of Christ. In the gospel God justifies the ungodly and excludes reliance on works; personal righteousness is explicitly set aside from any role in our justification (see Ephesians 2:7-8).

This personal, inherent righteousness that is said to justify us in this evangelical scheme is our own righteousness. The terms "personal righteousness" and "our own righteousness" mean the same thing here. But our own righteousness is not the material cause of any justification before God.

1. It is unfit for such a purpose (Isaiah 64:6).

2. It directly opposes the righteousness by which we are justified, as it is inconsistent with it for that end (Philippians 3:9; Romans 10:3-4).

It may be argued that our own righteousness is the righteousness of the law, while this personal righteousness is evangelical. However, first, it is hard to show that this personal righteousness is anything other than our own righteousness, and those passages explicitly reject our own righteousness from any role in justification.

Second, the righteousness called "evangelical," considered as to its efficient cause, motives, and particular ends, is legal in its formal reason and in our obligation to it. There is no separate duty attached to it; rather, we are generally obliged to perform it by virtue of the first commandment, which calls us to take the Lord as our God. By acknowledging His essential truth and sovereign authority, we are bound to believe all He reveals and to obey all He commands.

3. The good works excluded from any role in our justification are those for which we are "created in Christ Jesus" (Ephesians 2:8-10); they are the "works of righteousness which we have done" (Titus 3:5), and they include the case of the Gentiles, who did not seek righteousness by the works of the law (Romans 9:30).

Yet, one might still insist these points are self-evident. God requires an evangelical righteousness from all who believe; but this is not Christ's righteousness, nor is it the righteousness of Christ. He may be regarded as our legal righteousness, yet He is not our evangelical righteousness. If we possess any righteousness at all, we are justified by it. By this evangelical righteousness we must be judged: if we have it we will be acquitted, and if we lack it we will be condemned. Therefore, there is a justification according to it.

In reply, some proponents of this view see no reason why the Lord Christ cannot be reckoned our evangelical righteousness as well as our legal righteousness. They deny that our legal righteousness is founded on a proper imputation of His righteousness to us, and instead explain it by the communication of the fruits of what He did and suffered for us. Thus, in their view, He is also our evangelical righteousness, since our sanctification is a fruit of what He accomplished for us (Ephesians 5:26–27; Titus 2:14).

Only those who are, at least in the order of nature, justified before they actually possess this evangelical righteousness can truly have it. This righteousness is required of all who believe and are justified on that basis. There is no need to ask how a person is justified after they have already been justified.

God has not appointed this personal righteousness as the ground of our justification before Him in this life, although He has appointed it to manifest our justification before others and even before Himself, as will be shown. He accepts and approves it on the footing of the person's free justification, through whom it is performed, just as He had "And the Lord respected Abel and his offering." However, it does not acquit us from any real charge in God's sight, nor does it procure the remission of sins on its own account. Those who make remission of sins the whole of justification, and place this personal righteousness as its condition, as the Socinians do, leave no room for the righteousness of Christ in our justification.

If, in any sense, we were justified before God by this personal righteousness, we would have grounds for boasting before Him. We might not boast absolutely or claim merit, but we could boast comparatively—over others who cannot claim the same. Yet all boasting is excluded; it avails nothing to say that this personal righteousness is a free gift of God to some and not to others, for it must be presented as a duty, not as God's free grace.

Suppose a person is freely justified by the grace of God through faith in the blood of Christ, apart from any works, obedience, or righteousness of their own. We freely acknowledge that:

1. God does require personal obedience from them, which may be called their evangelical righteousness.

2. God does approve and accept this righteousness, as performed in Christ.

3. This righteousness serves to evidence, prove, and manifest the faith by which we are justified, both before God and before men.

4. This righteousness can be pleaded for acquittal against any charge from Satan, the world, or our own consciences.

5. Based on it, we shall be declared righteous on the last day, and without it none shall be.

If anyone wishes to conclude from this that there is an evangelical justification, or to call God's acceptance of our righteousness by that name, I will not contend with them. Whenever this question arises— not about how a sinner, guilty of death and under the curse, is pardoned, acquitted, and justified by the righteousness of Christ alone imputed to him—but about how a person who professes evangelical faith, or faith in Christ, is to be tried and judged, and on what grounds they shall be declared righteous, we agree it must be based on their own personal, sincere obedience.

These remarks are not made to contend with anyone or oppose anyone's opinions. They are offered solely to clarify the main question by removing elements that do not pertain to it.

A few words will also clarify our inquiry regarding what is called sentential justification on the day of judgment. Whatever its nature, the person concerning whom that sentence is pronounced was:

1. Actually and completely justified before God in this world;

2. Made a partaker of all the benefits of that justification, even unto a blessed resurrection in glory: "It is raised in glory" (1 Corinthians 15:43).

3. Most souls will long before have enjoyed a blessed rest with God, fully discharged and acquitted from all their labors and sins; only the actual admission of the whole person into eternal glory remains.

Thus this judgment can only be declaratory. It serves to glorify God and to give everlasting refreshment to those who have believed. This does not make it a new justification, nor is it called such in Scripture. Its purposes are plain: to manifest the wisdom and righteousness of God in appointing the way of salvation through Christ and in giving the law; to publicly convict those who transgressed the law and despised the gospel; to vindicate the righteousness, power, and wisdom of God in governing the world by His providence, where His paths are often deep and His footsteps unknown; to glorify Jesus Christ, who triumphs over all His enemies and makes them His footstool; and to exalt grace in all who believe.

Thus it becomes clear how weak is the argument that some urge as decisive here. They say, "As everyone shall be judged by God on the last day in the same way and on the same grounds as they are justified before God in this life; but everyone shall be judged at the last day by works, and not by faith alone; therefore, everyone is justified before God in this life by works, and not by faith alone."

However, it is nowhere said that we shall be judged at the last day "according to works"; rather, Scripture says God will render to men "according to their works." Yet God does not justify anyone in this life "according to works." We are justified freely by His grace, not according to the works of righteousness we have done. Scripture consistently says we are justified in this life "by faith," but never "for faith"; it speaks of being justified "according to faith," that is, by faith, but not for our faith, nor according to our faith. We must adhere to Scripture's expressions, where this distinction is consistently observed.

It is somewhat strange to say a person will be judged on the last day and justified in this life in the same way — specifically regarding faith and works — when Scripture attributes our justification before God to faith alone, without works. Moreover, the judgment on the last day is described as being based on works, with no mention of faith.

If justification and the final judgment were to rest entirely on the same grounds, reasons, and causes, then those who had not committed the sins for which they will be condemned on the last day would already have been justified in this life. However, many will be condemned solely for sins committed without the law, as stated in Romans 2:12 — that is, having never had the written law or the gospel revealed to them. Therefore, for such persons, refraining from sins committed without the law would suffice for their justification, even without any knowledge of Christ or the gospel.

The proposition that God pardons men their sins and grants them adoption as children, with a right to the heavenly inheritance, on the basis of their works is not only foreign to the gospel but contradicts and destroys it. This runs counter to every explicit testimony of Scripture in both the Old and New Testaments. Yet it is true, as Scripture affirms, that God will judge all men and render to each according to his works at the last judgment.

In our justification in this life by faith, Christ is presented as our propitiation and advocate—the One who has atoned for sin and brought in everlasting righteousness. But on the last day, at the final judgment, He is regarded as Judge.

The purpose of God in our justification is the praise of the glory of His grace, as stated in Ephesians 1:6. By contrast, the purpose of God in the last judgment is the praise of His remunerative righteousness, as noted in 2 Timothy 4:8.

The representations of the final judgment in Matthew 7 and 25 pertain only to the visible church. There the profession of faith is common to all—the same outward plea is made by everyone. On that common plea it is tested whether the faith is sincere and living or merely dead and barren. That trial is carried out solely by the fruits and effects of that faith; in a public declaration addressed to all, it cannot be otherwise determined. Thus the faith by which we are justified does not itself come into judgment on the last day (see John 5:24; Mark 16:16).

8. Imputation of Christ's Righteousness

The first clear statement about justification in Scripture shows that it is by imputation, as in Genesis 15:6. This chapter will explain why the doctrine matters, define what imputation means as Paul uses the term, and answer the objections leveled against it. The importance of the doctrine of imputed righteousness is widely recognized, including by the Reformed churches and especially by the Church of England.

We will examine who opposes this doctrine and on what grounds, what the word imputation signifies, and how it differs from the term reckoning. There are two kinds of imputation:

Imputation of something that already belongs to the person, whether good or bad. Examples of both types exist. In this case, what is imputed is credited to the person just as it is.

Imputation of something that did not belong to the person beforehand but becomes theirs by imputation. This will be discussed more fully, showing that this kind of imputation does not mean blaming someone for something they did not do.

Several distinct grounds for this kind of imputation will be discussed:

By justice

Because of a covenant relationship

Because of a natural relationship

By voluntary commitment.

For example, in Philemon 18, where Paul tells Philemon to charge any debts to him, and in Genesis 43:9, where Judah offers himself as surety for Benjamin. These are examples of taking responsibility for another's actions by choice.

By wrongdoing or harm, as in 1 Kings 1:21, where blame or consequence falls on someone because of injury or injustice done.

By pure grace, as explained in Romans 4, where imputation happens not because it is owed, but as a gift of grace.

The chapter will also explore the difference between imputing our own works versus imputing the righteousness of God. If someone's own righteousness is imputed on the basis of justice, it cannot at the same time be by grace. As Romans 11:6 says, "And if by grace, then it is no longer of works; otherwise grace is no longer grace."

Both types of imputation (our works and Christ's righteousness) will be compared, and the real meaning of justification by the imputation of righteousness will be clarified. The righteousness of Christ is what is imputed, not just its effects. This stands in opposition to what groups like the Socinians teach.

The first person whose justification is explicitly recorded in Scripture is Abraham. Although others were justified before him (and Scripture gives enough proof of that), Abraham's justification is the first recorded in detail and serves as the example for all believers. Genesis 15:6 says, "And he believed in the Lord, and He accounted it to him for righteousness." The original Hebrew word means "it was credited" or "imputed." The Greek translation says it was "counted" or "reckoned." Paul adds in Romans 4:23-24 that this was not written for Abraham alone but for us too—to whom righteousness will also be imputed if we believe.

Therefore, the first clear teaching about justification in the Bible shows that it happens through imputation—specifically, the imputation of something that results in righteousness. This was recorded as the pattern and example for everyone who will be justified. The way Abraham was justified is the way we are justified. There is no other.

Under the New Testament, there was a necessity for a more complete and clear declaration of the doctrine of justification, as it is one of the first and most essential parts of the heavenly mystery of truth that was to be revealed by the gospel. Additionally, from the beginning, there was strong and dangerous opposition to this doctrine. The matter of justification, the doctrine itself, and its necessary components were the reasons why the Jewish church broke away from God, rejected Christ and the gospel, and perished in their sins, as explicitly stated in Romans 9:31 and 10:3-4.

Similarly, a dislike of this doctrine and opposition to it has always been, and will continue to be, a principle and cause of the apostasy of any professing church from Christ and the gospel, as was the case later in the churches of the Galatians. In this context, the doctrine of justification was fully declared, established, and defended by the Apostle Paul in a unique manner. He does this particularly by affirming and proving that the righteousness by which and with which we are justified is through imputation; that our justification consists in the non-imputation of sin and the imputation of righteousness.

Despite the fact that the first recorded instance of justification — which was documented to serve as an example and represent the justification of all who would be justified until the end of the world — is expressed through imputation and righteousness imputed, and that the doctrine of it is articulated in the significant case concerning the eternal welfare or ruin of the Jewish church, it has unfortunately become the case in our days that nothing in religion is more maligned, reproached, or despised than the concept of imputed righteousness.

Some among us refer to it as "a putative righteousness, the shadow of a dream, a fancy, a mummery, an imagination." Socinus describes it as "fœda, execranda, pernitiosa, detestanda." Opposition to this doctrine arises daily from a wide variety of principles. Those who oppose and reject it can hardly agree on what to propose as a substitute.

However, the weight and importance of this doctrine are acknowledged by all, whether it is true or false. This is not a dispute about mere notions, terms, or idle speculations — those small controversies that have little bearing on Christian practice. Rather, it has an immediate influence on our present duties and on our eternal welfare or ruin.

Those who reject the imputation of righteousness assert that the faith and doctrine surrounding it undermine the necessity of gospel obedience, personal righteousness, and good works. They say this leads to antinomianism and libertinism in life. Consequently, they treat the doctrine as destructive of salvation and shape their practices around that belief.

On the other hand, those who accept this doctrine insist that it is impossible for anyone to be justified before God in any other way than through the imputation of Christ's righteousness. They therefore conclude that, without it, no one can be saved.

A learned man recently stated, "Thus far of the imputation of the righteousness of Christ; without which no man was ever saved, nor can any so be." They do not mean that every person who cannot grasp or who denies the doctrine is therefore excluded from salvation. Rather, they mean that those to whom that righteousness is not truly imputed are excluded. They regard imputation as the foundation of acceptance with God and eternal salvation.

These positions are significantly different. To believe the doctrine of imputation, or to deny it as explained, is one thing; to possess its reality, or not to possess it, is another.

I have no doubt that many receive more grace from God than they understand or acknowledge. The efficacy of that grace may operate in them more than they suppose. People may be genuinely saved by grace they doctrinally deny, and they may be justified by the imputation of righteousness even though, in opinion, they deny that it is imputed. Their faith in it may be included in the general assent they give to the truth of the gospel, and such adherence to Christ may secure them a real interest in salvation despite their misunderstandings about how they are saved.

For my part, I must say that despite all the disputes I see and read about justification—many full of offence and scandal—I do not think the authors of these disputes (unless they are avowed Socinians, denying the merit and satisfaction of Christ) distrust Christ's mediation for the pardon of their sins and their acceptance with God in favour of trusting their own works or obedience. I will not believe otherwise until they expressly declare it.

We will address the objection about the danger of the doctrine of imputation in relation to the necessity of holiness and good works later.

The judgment of the Reformed churches on this matter is well known and must be acknowledged, unless we intend to increase and perpetuate contentions by vain arguments. The Church of England, in particular, is explicit in her doctrine regarding the imputation of Christ's righteousness—both active and passive, as commonly distinguished.

This has been thoroughly demonstrated from her authentic writings: the Articles of Religion, the Books of Homilies, and other publicly authorized documents. That demonstration makes further proof unnecessary. Those who claim to hold a different view are not worth contending with; what purpose is there in disputing with those who would deny the sun shines when they cannot bear the heat of its rays? In what follows I shall not deviate from the ancient doctrine of the Church of England. My aim is only to declare and vindicate it, as God enables me.

There are indeed differences among learned, sober, and orthodox men—if that phrase offends, I mean only those who hold to the faith—about how best to explain justification by the imputation of Christ's righteousness. Yet they all agree on the substance of it, especially as to the grace of God, the honour of Christ, and the peace of the soul.

As far as possible, I shall refrain from engaging those differences for mere contention. What purpose is there in arguing over arrangement and ornament while the substance of the doctrine itself is openly opposed and rejected? Why debate the best arrangement of rooms in a house when the whole structure is on fire? Once that fire is put out, we may consider how to best order and adorn the various parts.

Two major parties oppose justification by the imputation of Christ's righteousness: the Papists and the Socinians. They operate on different principles and to different ends. The former aim to exalt their own merits; the latter seek to undermine the merit of Christ.

Besides these, there are many interlopers who, riding on their coattails, borrow from both as they please. We will address all of them in our discussion—not the individuals themselves, nor the particular manner in which they express their views, but their opinions insofar as they oppose the truth. It is lamentable to see professed religious people quarrelling over expressions, contending about words, and trying to force opinions on others they do not hold, all while mutually reviling one another and publishing their disputes as great achievements. That is no way to teach the gospel or promote the edification of the church.

Yet the importance of this cause, the magnitude of the opposition, and the high stakes for souls require a renewed declaration and vindication of the doctrine. I undertake this task convinced that the life and continuity of any church—or, on the other hand, its apostasy and ruin—depend greatly on whether this article of religion is preserved or rejected, as it has been professed and believed in the Church of England in former days.

The first thing to consider is the meaning of the words "to impute" and "imputation." A clear definition of these terms will show that many charges made against the doctrine we defend are unfounded or arise from misunderstanding.

חָשַׁב, the Hebrew word first used for this purpose, signifies to think, to esteem, to judge, or to attribute a matter to someone; to impute, or to be imputed, for good or evil. See Leviticus 7:18; 17:4; and Psalm 106:31. וַתֵּחָשֶׁב לוֹ לִצְדָקָה, — "and He accounted it to him for righteousness." This denotes to judge or esteem something as good or evil belonging to a person.

The Septuagint renders it with logizō and logizomai, as do the writers of the New Testament. These are variously translated reputare, imputare, acceptum ferre, tribuere, assignare, ascribere. Yet there is a distinction among these terms. To be reputed righteous and to have righteousness imputed are cause and effect, not identical things.

For a person to be reputed righteous—i.e., to be judged or esteemed as righteous—there must be a real basis for that reputation; otherwise the judgment is mistaken. A man may be reputed wise though he is a fool, or reputed rich though he is a beggar. Therefore, one who is reputed righteous must either possess a righteousness of his own or have another righteousness imputed to him as the foundation of that reputation.

Thus, to impute righteousness to someone who has none of his own does not mean merely to call a truly unrighteous person righteous. It means to communicate a righteousness to him so that he may justly and rightly be esteemed, judged, or reputed as righteous.

"Imputare" is a term recognized in the Latin language in the sense used by theologians. Seneca states, "You have deserved well of the worst, to whom the uncorrupted faith of things has been attributed," and Pliny, in his apology for the earth, our common parent, writes, "We burden it with our faults and charge our guilt upon it."

In this context, to impute something to another means, if it is evil, to charge it to him, to burden him with it. Pliny states, "We impute our own faults to the earth, or charge them upon it." If it is good, it means to ascribe it to him as his own, whether it originally belonged to him or not: "Attributed to the great author." Vasquez, in Thom. 22, vol. ii, disp. 132, attempts to explain the term but confuses it with "reputare": "To impute or to reputare something to someone is the same as to enumerate and count it among those things that belong to him." This is proper to "reputare"; "imputare" includes an act that precedes this accounting or estimation of a thing as belonging to any person.

However, since that which may be imputed to us must be truly our own prior to that imputation, the term must have a dual meaning, as seen in the examples from Latin authors mentioned earlier. To impute to us that which was genuinely ours before that imputation involves two aspects: (1) An acknowledgment or judgment that the thing imputed is genuinely and truly ours or in us. When someone imputes wisdom or learning to a person, they first acknowledge that the person is wise or learned. (2) A response to them based on this acknowledgment, whether it be good or evil. For instance, when a person is acquitted after being found righteous, they are first judged and esteemed as righteous, and then treated as a righteous person — his righteousness is imputed to him. This is exemplified in Genesis 30:33.

To impute to us that which is not our own prior to that imputation also involves two aspects: (1) A grant or donation of the thing itself to us, making it ours based on some just ground or foundation; for a thing must be made ours before we can justly be dealt with according to what is required of it. (2) A willingness to deal with us, or an actual dealing with us, according to that which has been made ours. In this matter we discuss, the most holy and righteous God does not justify anyone — meaning He does not absolve them from sin, pronounce them righteous, and grant them the right and title to eternal life — except upon the basis of a true and complete righteousness, which is truly and completely made the righteousness of those who are to be justified in the order of nature prior to their justification. These matters will be made clearer through examples, and it is necessary that they should be so.

There is an imputation to us of that which is truly our own, inherent in us, and performed by us prior to that imputation, whether it be evil or good. The rule and nature of this is expressed in Ezekiel 18:20: "The righteousness of the righteous shall be upon himself, and the wickedness of the wicked shall be upon himself." We have examples of both types of imputation.

First, consider the imputation of sin, where a person guilty of it is judged and recognized as a sinner and dealt with accordingly. Shimei expressed this when he said to the king in 2 Samuel 19:19, "Do not let my lord impute iniquity to me," — אַל־יַחֲשָׁב־לִי אֲדֹנִי עָוֺן, the same term used for the imputation of righteousness in Genesis 15:6. He acknowledged his guilt but asked that it not be imputed to him in a way that reflected the full weight of his sin. Similarly, Stephen asked for the sin of those who stoned him to not be imputed to them, as noted in Acts 7:60: "Lord, do not charge them with this sin." On the other hand, Zechariah, son of Jehoiada, who died in a similar manner to Stephen, prayed that the sin of those who killed him might be charged against them, as recorded in 2 Chronicles 24:22. Therefore, to impute sin is to lay it to the charge of someone and to deal with them according to its consequences.

To impute something good to someone is to judge and acknowledge it as belonging to them and to deal with them accordingly, in relation to the law of God. As stated, "The righteousness of the righteous shall be upon himself." Jacob, for instance, ensured that his "So my righteousness will answer for me in time to come" (Genesis 30:33). We see this in God's dealings with people, as in Psalm 106:30-31: "Then Phinehas stood and executed judgment, and so the plague was stopped. And it was counted to him for righteousness." Although it seemed he lacked sufficient justification for his actions, God, who knew his heart and the guidance of His Spirit, approved his act as righteous and rewarded him as a sign of that approval.

It must be noted regarding this imputation that whatever is truly our own before it, which is an act of God, can never be imputed to us for anything more or less than what it actually is. This imputation consists of two parts:

1. A judgment that the thing is ours, that it is in us, or that it belongs to us.

2. A will to deal with us, or an actual dealing with us, according to it.

Thus, in the imputation of anything to us that is genuinely ours, God does not regard it as anything other than what it is. He does not consider an imperfect righteousness to be perfect; to do so would imply either a misunderstanding of the thing being judged or a flaw in the judgment itself. Therefore, if, as some claim, our faith and obedience are imputed to us for righteousness, since they are imperfect, they must be imputed to us as an imperfect righteousness, not as a perfect one. The judgment of God, which is based on truth, is involved in this imputation. An imputation of imperfect righteousness, regarded only as such, will not benefit us in this matter. Furthermore, the idea of acceptilation, which some propose by misapplying a legal fiction to interpret the mystery of the gospel, undermines all imputation, as well as the satisfaction and merit of Christ. It is important to note that this imputation is a purely just act, without any mixture of grace, as the apostle states in Romans 11:6. It consists of two parts:

1. An acknowledgment and judgment that something is truly in us.

2. A will to deal with us according to that acknowledgment. Both of these are acts of justice.

The imputation to us of that which is not our own prior to that imputation — at least not in the same manner as it becomes afterwards — depends on the grounds and causes on which it is based. It must be emphasized that no imputation of this kind implies that those to whom something is imputed have actually done the things themselves. That would be a misjudgment and would completely undermine the nature of gracious imputation. Rather, it means that something is made ours by imputation which was not ours before, so that for all practical purposes it serves as if it had been truly our own even without any prior possession.

It is a clear misunderstanding that some use to criticize the doctrine of imputation. They argue, "If our sins were imputed to Christ, then He must be considered to have done what we have done wrong and thus be the greatest sinner that ever was." Conversely, they say, "If His righteousness is imputed to us, then we are viewed as having done what He did, and therefore stand in no need of forgiveness for sin." But this contradicts the nature of imputation. Imputation does not mean that Christ actually committed our sins, nor that we actually performed His obedience. On the contrary, it recognizes that we have not done what is imputed to us, and that Christ has not done what was imputed to Him.

To clarify this imputation more distinctly, I will consider its various kinds, or rather the different grounds from which it arises. The imputation to us of what is not our own prior to that imputation may be classified as follows:

1. "Ex justitia" (from justice)

2. "Ex voluntaria sponsione" (from voluntary sponsorship)

3. "Ex injuria" (from injury)

4. "Ex gratia" (from grace)

All of these will be exemplified. I do not present them as if they could not overlap in the same imputation — they can and sometimes do. I will refer each kind of imputation to its primary cause.

1. Things that are not originally, personally, or inherently ours may still be imputed to us "ex justitia" (from justice), according to the rule of

righteousness. This can occur in relation to those to whom they belong in two ways:

1. Federal

2. Natural

Actions performed by one person may be imputed to others "propter relationem fœderalem" (because of a covenant relationship between them). For example, the sin of Adam was and is imputed to all his descendants; I will explain this more fully later. The basis is that we all stood in the same covenant with him as our head and representative. The corruption and depravity of nature that we inherit from Adam is imputed to us under the first type of imputation — that of what is ours prior to imputation. However, his actual sin is imputed to us as something that becomes ours through that imputation, which it was not before. Bellarmine himself states, "Peccatum Adami ita posteris omnibus imputatur, ac si omnes idem peccatum patravissent" (The sin of Adam is so imputed to all his posterity, as if they had all committed the same sin) in De Amiss. Grat., Book IV, Chapter 10. He thus acknowledges an imputation that transfers the sin to us and a dealing with us as if we had committed it; this accords with the apostle's doctrine in Romans 5.

There is an imputation of sin to others "ex justitia propter relationem naturalem" (from justice on account of a natural relation) — based on a natural relationship between them and those who have actually incurred the guilt.

However, this applies only to some outward, temporary effects of it. For instance, God speaks of the children of the rebellious Israelites in the wilderness, saying, "And your sons shall be shepherds in the wilderness forty years, and bear the brunt of your infidelity" (Numbers 14:33). Their sin shall be imputed to their children insofar as the children will suffer for it — being afflicted in the wilderness — because of their relationship with them. This is just because of the connection between them, as similar actions of divine justice are frequently noted elsewhere in Scripture. Thus, where there is a proper foundation for it, imputation is an act of justice.

Imputation may justly occur "ex voluntaria sponsione" (from voluntary undertaking) when one person freely and willingly agrees to take responsibility for another. A notable example of this is found in the apostle's letter to Philemon regarding Onesimus, specifically in verse 18: "If he has wronged you or owes you anything, charge that to my account." (touto emoi ellogei). The apostle suggests that Philemon might have two claims against Onesimus:

1. "Injuriarum" (of wrongs): "If he has wronged you" (Ei de ti ēdikēse se), meaning that if he has wronged you in such a way that he deserves punishment.

2. "Damni" (of loss): "If he owes you anything" (Ē opheilei), indicating that he is in debt to you and thus liable for payment or restitution.

In this situation, the apostle intercedes by a voluntary sponsorship, stating, "I, Paul, write this with my own hand:" (Egō apotisō). He effectively takes on Onesimus's liabilities. He offers to answer for the whole, taking on both debts himself, since the nature of the offense allows such a defense (it is not capital). The imputation of these debts to him is justified by his voluntary undertaking. "Consider me," he says, "the one who has committed these acts, and I will make restitution, so that nothing is charged to Onesimus."

Similarly, Judah voluntarily pledged to Jacob for Benjamin's safety, binding himself to perpetual guilt should he fail, as seen in Genesis 43:9: "I myself will be surety for him; from my hand you shall require him. If I do not bring him back to you and set him before you, then let me bear the blame forever." (וְחָטָאתִי לְךָ כָּל־הַיָּמִים). This illustrates the nature and role of a surety; what he undertakes is justly required of him, as if he were originally and personally involved. This voluntary sponsorship is one basis for the imputation of our sins to Christ. He assumed the identity of the entire church that had sinned to answer for what they had done against God and the law. Thus, this imputation is "fundamentaliter ex compacto, ex voluntaria sponsione" (fundamentally based on agreement and voluntary undertaking); it is rooted in his voluntary commitment. However, on this basis, it is also "ex justitia" (from justice), as it is right for him to answer for it and fulfill what he has undertaken, given the glory of God's righteousness and holiness is significantly at stake.

There is an imputation "ex injuria" (from injury) when something is charged to someone who is not guilty of it. For instance, Bathsheba says to David, "It shall come to pass, when my lord the king rests with his fathers, that I and my son Solomon will be counted offenders." (חַטָּאִים) (1 Kings 1:21); meaning, we shall be treated as offenders, as guilty persons, having sin imputed to us for one reason or another, leading to our destruction. We shall be regarded as sinners and treated accordingly.

In Scripture, the designation of sinners follows the imputation as well as the presence of sin, which sheds light on the apostle's statement, "For He made Him who knew no sin to be sin for us" (2 Corinthians 5:21). This type of imputation has no place in God's judgment. It is inconceivable that the righteous should be treated as the wicked.

There is an imputation "ex mera gratia" (from mere grace and favor). This occurs when something that was not ours, not inherent in us, and not performed by us—something we had no right or claim to—is granted to us and considered ours, so that we are judged and treated according to it. This imputation, in both its aspects—negative in the non-imputation of sin and positive in the imputation of righteousness—is what the apostle passionately argues for and frequently asserts in Romans 4. He affirms the reality of this imputation and declares that it is purely by grace, without any regard to anything within ourselves.

If this type of imputation cannot be fully exemplified in any other instance but the one we are discussing, it is because its foundation, in the mediation of Christ, is unique and has no parallel in any other case among men.

From the discussion regarding the nature and grounds of imputation, several points become clear that greatly illuminate the truth we advocate for, at least in terms of understanding and articulating the matter under debate.

The distinction is clear between the imputation of our own works and the imputation of the righteousness of faith apart from works. The imputation of works—whatever their nature, even faith itself when regarded as a work of obedience—is the imputation of what was already ours prior to that imputation. By contrast, the imputation of the righteousness of faith, or the righteousness of God that comes by faith, is the imputation of what is made ours by virtue of that imputation.

These two kinds of imputation differ fundamentally. The first consists in judging that something is in us which already is so. The second consists in communicating to us something that was not ours before. No one can comprehend the apostle's argument—indeed, cannot understand any part of it—unless they acknowledge that the righteousness he speaks of is made ours by imputation and was not ours beforehand.

The imputation of works, whatever they may be, including faith itself taken as a work and all acts of obedience, is "ex justitia" (from justice), not "ex gratia" (from grace). Though the bestowal of faith upon us and the producing of obedience within us may be acts of grace, to impute these to us as if they were ours is an act of justice. Such imputation, as shown above, is simply a judgment that certain things are in us or are ours—which indeed they are—and we are treated accordingly. This is an act of justice, as its description indicates.

In contrast, the imputation of righteousness that the apostle speaks of is "ex mera gratia" (from mere grace), as he explicitly affirms—dōrean tē chariti autou. Moreover, he teaches that these two kinds of imputation are incompatible and cannot be mixed, so that anything could be partly one and partly the other. As he puts it in Romans 11:6, "And if by grace, then it is no longer of works; otherwise grace is no longer grace. But if it is of works, it is no longer grace; otherwise work is no longer work."

For example, if faith itself, viewed as a work of ours, is imputed to us, then since it existed in us before that imputation, the imputation is merely an acknowledgment that it is in us and ours—an attribution of it for what it is. To ascribe to us anything for what it is not is not true imputation but an error. Therefore this is an imputation "ex justitia" of works; and consequently what is of mere grace, in the apostle's sense, cannot apply. If what is imputed is what is within ourselves, grace in that sense is excluded. Conversely, if the righteousness of Christ is imputed to us, it must be "ex mera gratia" (from mere grace), because what is imputed was not ours before and is thereby communicated to us. In that case there is no place for works or any pretense of them. In one instance the basis lies within ourselves; in the other it lies in another—two irreconcilable grounds.

Both types of imputation agree in this: whatever is imputed to us is imputed for what it is, not for what it is not. If a perfect righteousness is imputed to us, it is regarded and judged as such, and we are treated as those who possess perfect righteousness. If what is imputed as righteousness is imperfect, it must be judged as imperfect, and we are treated as those who possess imperfect righteousness — nothing more.

Therefore, since our inherent righteousness is imperfect (those who think otherwise should be pitied or dismissed), if that is what is imputed to us, we cannot be accepted as perfectly righteous without a judicial error.

Thus the true nature of the imputation we maintain (which many cannot or will not understand) is plain, both negatively and positively.

Negatively: First, it is not a judgment or estimation of persons as righteous when they are not so. Such a judgment cannot be grounded in any of the foregoing kinds of imputation. It would resemble "ex injuria" (from injury), a false charge, though the comparison is not exact: the one involves evil, the other involves a false ascription of good. Accordingly, the accusations of Papists and others — that we assert God regards the wicked as righteous — are simply expressions of ignorance or malice. Those charges fall most heavily on those who insist that we are justified before God by our own inherent righteousness; for on that view a man would be held righteous who is not truly so, and no one who is not perfectly righteous can be justified in God's sight.

Secondly, it is not a bare declaration that someone is righteous without a just and sufficient basis for God's judgment. God does not pronounce anyone righteous except those who are so; the whole question concerns how one becomes so.

Thirdly, it is not the transmission or transfusion of another's righteousness into those being justified so that they thereby become subjectively and inherently and perfectly righteous. One person's righteousness cannot literally be transferred into another to become inherently theirs. Yet it is a serious mistake to infer from that impossibility that one person's righteousness therefore cannot be made the righteousness of another; to deny that would deny all imputation.

Positively, this imputation is an act of God "ex mera gratia" (from mere grace). Considering Christ's mediation, God makes an effective grant and donation of true, real, perfect righteousness—specifically, the righteousness of Christ Himself—to all who believe. By this gracious act He accounts it as theirs, absolves them from sin, and gives them the right and title to eternal life.

In this imputation, the thing itself is first imputed to us, not merely its effects. Those effects become ours by virtue of that imputation. To say that the righteousness of Christ—His obedience and sufferings—is imputed to us only as to their effects is to deny the reality of imputation itself. This is the Socinian position; they thus undermine all true, real imputation.

"For it is not necessary that we should be justified through Christ's righteousness for it to become our righteousness; it suffices that Christ's righteousness is the cause of our justification; and to this extent, we can concede that Christ's righteousness is our righteousness, inasmuch as it redounds to our benefit," says Schlichtingius in his work against Meisner. It is discouraging to see some among ourselves adopt these sentiments and words in arguing against the Protestant doctrine on this point, especially the doctrine of the Church of England.

The view that Christ's righteousness is imputed to us only in terms of its effects carries this implication: those effects are made ours because of that imputation. It implies that God truly communicates all the effects of Christ's righteousness to us.

But to claim that Christ's righteousness itself is not imputed, only its effects, undermines the very notion of imputation. If His righteousness itself is not imputed, then the idea of imputation becomes irrelevant. It also fails to explain why the apostle emphasizes imputation so frequently, as in Romans 4.

The Socinians, who explicitly reject the imputation of Christ's righteousness and insist we merely participate in its effects, wisely deny any notion that Christ's righteousness is satisfactory or meritorious in a way that could be imputed to us. They accept that what they allow Christ's righteousness to consist of cannot be imputed to us, however many benefits we may derive from it.

I cannot see how those who hold that Christ's righteousness consists primarily in His satisfaction for us, in our stead, can conceive of imputation of its effects without also imputing the righteousness itself. We partake of the benefits because that righteousness is made ours.

The definition and examples of imputation show there can be no imputation of anything unless the thing itself is imputed. Nor can we participate in the effects of anything without the foundation of the imputation of the thing itself. Therefore, in our case, no imputation of Christ's righteousness is coherent unless we acknowledge that the righteousness itself is imputed. And we cannot partake of its effects apart from that presupposition and foundation.

The irrelevant objections some have recently raised—echoing Papists and Socinians—claiming that if this is true we are as righteous as Christ, that we have redeemed the world or satisfied for others' sins, that the pardon of sin is impossible, or that personal righteousness is unnecessary, will be answered later, since they require separate discussion.

All we aim to demonstrate is one of two things: either the righteousness of Christ itself is imputed to us, or there is no imputation in our justification. Whether that is true will be considered later.

As already stated, the effects of Christ's righteousness cannot properly be said to be imputed to us apart from the imputation of the righteousness itself. Take the pardon of sin: it is a chief effect of Christ's righteousness. Our sins are forgiven on account of it; God forgives us all our sins for Christ's sake. Yet the pardon itself is not what is imputed to us. Likewise, adoption, justification, peace with God, and all grace and glory are effects of Christ's righteousness; by their nature these things are not imputed to us, nor can they be. We receive them only on the basis of the imputation of Christ's righteousness to us.

This is enough for now about the nature of the imputation of Christ's righteousness. Next, we shall examine the grounds, reasons, and causes of it. I have no doubt that our inquiry will show this is not some wild invention of the ignorant. Rather, it is a solemn truth woven into the deepest mysteries of the gospel and inseparable from the grace of God in Christ Jesus.

9. Our Sins Imputed to Christ, Our Surety

Those who affirm that Christ's righteousness is imputed to believers for the justification of life also unanimously maintain that the sins of all believers were imputed to Christ. They base this on many testimonies of Scripture that directly attest the fact; some of those texts will be produced and vindicated later. For the present, we will focus on the general notion and state the nature of what will be proved in due course.

First, we will inquire into the foundation and equity of this divine arrangement—that is, the grounds on which it was resolved. Without understanding that foundation, the whole matter cannot be well comprehended.

The principal foundation for this is that Christ and the church, in this design, are one mystical person. They actually coalesce into this state through the uniting efficacy of the Holy Spirit. He is the head, and believers are the members of that one person, as the apostle declares in 1 Corinthians 12:12-13.

Thus, as what He did is imputed to them as if done by them, so what they deserved on account of sin was charged upon Him. A learned prelate expressed it this way: "He sustained our cause, who united our flesh to Himself, and thus, being closely joined to us, made what was ours His own." Furthermore, he stated, "Is it any wonder that, being constituted in our person and clothed with our flesh..."

The ancients spoke similarly. Leo, in Sermon 17, said, "Therefore, the divine power preserved human infirmity, so that while God makes what is ours to be His, He makes what is His to be ours." In Sermon 16, he added, "Our head, the Lord Jesus Christ, transforms all the members of His body into Himself, as He cried out on the cross in the voice of His redeemed." Augustine also spoke to this in Epistle 120 to Honoratus, saying, "We hear the voice of the body from the mouth of the head. The church suffered in Him when He suffered for the church; as He suffers in the church when the church suffers for Him."

We may also look back further into the understanding of the ancient church on this matter. Irenaeus stated, "Christ recapitulated all nations scattered from Adam and the generation of mankind in Himself; hence, Paul called Him the type of the future Adam" (Book III, Chapter 33). He further explained, "Recapitulating the entire human race in Himself from beginning to end, He also recapitulated His death."

In this recapitulation, there is no doubt that he referred to the anakephalaiōsis mentioned in Ephesians 1:10. It may be that this was what Origen intended enigmatically when he said, "The soul of the first Adam was the soul of Christ, as it is charged on Him." Cyprian, in Epistle 62, spoke of bearing the administration of the sacrament of the Eucharist, saying, "Christ bore us all; He who also bears our sins."

Athanasius affirmed the voice He used on the cross, saying, "It was not the Lord alone who suffered; rather, we suffered in Him." Eusebius also spoke extensively on this subject in Demonstratio Evangelica, Book X, Chapter 1, explaining the psalmist's words, "Heal my soul, for I have sinned against You," and applying them to our Savior in His sufferings. He stated, "Because He took our sins to Himself;" communicating our sins to Himself, making them His own.

He further elaborated, "How does He make our sins His own? And how does He bear our iniquities? Is it not because we are said to be His body? As the apostle says, 'Now you are the body of Christ, and members individually.' And just as when one member suffers, all the members suffer, so the many members sinning and suffering, He, according to the laws of sympathy in the same body (seeing that, being the Word of God, He made Himself of no reputation, taking the form of a bondservant, and was joined to our common nature), took the sorrows or labors of the suffering members upon Himself, making all their infirmities His own.

According to the laws of humanity, He bore our sorrow and labor for us. The Lamb of God did not only these things for us but also underwent torments and was punished for us; that which He was not exposed to for Himself, but we were so by the multitude of our sins. Thus, He became the cause of the pardon of our sins — namely, because He underwent death, stripes, and reproaches, transferring what we deserved unto Himself, and was made a curse for us, taking upon Himself the curse that was due to us; for what was He but a substitute for us, a price of redemption for our souls?

In our person, therefore, the oracle speaks, whilst freely uniting Himself to us and us to Himself, making our sins or passions His own, "I said, 'Lord, be merciful to me; Heal my soul, for I have sinned against You.'" I have transcribed this passage at length because, as I mentioned, what I intend to prove in this discourse is fully declared therein. Thus, he speaks: "How, then, did He make our sins His own, and how did He bear our iniquities? Is it not because we are said to be His body? As the apostle speaks, 'Now you are the body of Christ, and members individually.' And just as when one member suffers, all the members suffer, so the many members sinning and suffering, He, according to the laws of sympathy in the same body (seeing that, being the Word of God, He made Himself of no reputation, taking the form of a bondservant and was joined to our common nature), took the sorrows or labors of the suffering members upon Himself, making all their infirmities His own.

According to the laws of humanity, He bore our sorrow and labor for us. The Lamb of God did not only these things for us but also underwent torments and was punished for us; that which He was not exposed to for Himself, but we were so by the multitude of our sins. Thus, He became the cause of the pardon of our sins — namely, because He underwent death, stripes, and reproaches, transferring what we deserved unto Himself, and was made a curse for us, taking upon Himself the curse that was due to us; for what was He but a substitute for us, a price of redemption for our souls?

In our person, therefore, the oracle speaks, freely uniting Himself to us and us to Himself, and making our sins or passions His own: "I said, 'LORD, be merciful to me; heal my soul, for I have sinned against You.'" That our sins were transferred to Christ and made His, that He underwent the punishment due to us for them, and that the ground of this — where its equity is resolved — is the union between Him and us, is fully declared in this discourse.

The learned and passionate author of the Homilies on Matthew (Chrysostom), Homily 54, the last of them, stated, "In His flesh, He received all flesh; crucified, He crucified all flesh in Himself." He speaks of the church. Others often say that "He bore us," that "He took us with Him on the cross," that "we were all crucified in Him." As Prosper stated, "He is not saved by the cross of Christ who is not crucified in Christ."

This, then, is the foundation of the imputation of the sins of the church to Christ—namely, that He and the church are one person. We must inquire into the grounds of this.

However, various discussions and inquiries arise about what a person is: in what sense the word may be used, how many senses it has, what the true notion of it is, what a natural person is, and what a legal, civil, or political person is. In explaining these, some have fallen into mistakes. Were we to enter this field, we would find ample material for debate and contention.

I must say that these matters do not pertain to our present occasion; they do not clarify the union of Christ and the church but rather obscure it. Christ and believers are neither one natural person, nor a legal or political person, nor any such person as the laws, customs, or usages of men recognize. They are one mystical person. Although there may be some imperfect resemblances found in natural or political unions, the union between Him and us is of such a nature and arises from such reasons and causes that no personal union among men (or the union of many persons) has any real relevance to it.

To represent it to our weak understandings, which cannot comprehend the depths of heavenly mysteries, it is compared to unions of various kinds and natures. It is represented by the union of man and wife—not in terms of mere mutual affections that give only a moral union, but from the extraction of the first woman from the flesh and bone of the first man and the institution of God for the individual society of life based on that.

The apostle elaborates on this in Ephesians 5:25-32, and concludes that from the union thus represented, "We are members of His body, of His flesh and of His bones" (verse 30); or that we have such a relation to Him as Eve had to Adam when she was made from his flesh and bone, thus becoming one flesh with him.

It is also compared to the union of the head and members of the same natural body (1 Corinthians 12:12) and to a political union between a ruling or political head and its political members; but never exclusively to the union of a natural head and its members as described in the same expression (Ephesians 4:15; Colossians 2:19). It is also compared to various things in nature, such as a vine and its branches (John 15:1-2).

The relationship between Adam and his posterity, established by God's institution and the law of creation, is also declared in Romans 5:12, etc. The Holy Spirit, by representing the union between Christ and believers through such a variety of resemblances—things that agree only in the common or general notion of union—on various grounds sufficiently demonstrates that it is not of, nor can be reduced to, any one kind of them.

This will become even more evident when we consider the causes of it and the grounds upon which it is resolved. Since treating them in full would require much time and diligence, which the present mention does not allow, I will briefly refer to the main points. The first cause of this union, and of all the other causes, lies in that eternal compact between the Father and the Son concerning the recovery and salvation of fallen mankind. Among other effects of that compact, the assumption of our nature—the foundation of this union—was designed. I have previously declared the nature and terms of this compact, counsel, and agreement; therefore I will not dwell on it here. The relation between Christ and the church, resulting from this and being an effect of infinite wisdom in the counsel of the Father and Son, made effective by the Holy Spirit, must be distinguished from all other unions or relations.

The Lord Christ, regarding the nature He was to assume, was predestined unto grace and glory. He was foreordained before the foundation of the world (1 Peter 1:20); that is, He was predestined not only in terms of His office but also for all the grace and glory required and consequent to it. All the grace and glory of the human nature of Christ was an effect of free divine preordination. God chose it from all eternity for participation in all that it received in time. No other cause for the glorious exaltation of that portion of our nature can be assigned.

This grace and glory to which He was predestined were twofold: (1) that which was unique to Himself; and (2) that which was to be communicated through Him to the church.

The first type was the grace of personal union—the unique effect of divine wisdom, with no shadow or resemblance in any other works of God, whether in creation, providence, or grace. His nature was filled with this grace: "full of grace and truth." All His personal glory, power, authority, and majesty as mediator, demonstrated in His exaltation at the right hand of God, belong to this category. These aspects were unique to Him and are all effects of His eternal predestination.

However, He was not predestined absolutely. He was also predestined with respect to the grace and glory that were to be communicated through Him to the church. He was so as the pattern and exemplary cause of our predestination, for we are "predestined to be conformed to the image of His Son, that He might be the firstborn among many brethren." (Romans 8:29) Hence, He will "transform our lowly body that it may be conformed to His glorious body" (Philippians 3:21). Thus, when He is revealed, we shall be like Him (1 John 3:2).

He is also the means and cause of communicating all grace and glory to us, for, as Scripture puts it, "just as He chose us in Him before the foundation of the world, that we should be holy and without blame before Him in love, having predestined us to adoption as sons by Jesus Christ to Himself" (Ephesians 1:3-5). He was designated as the only procuring cause of all spiritual blessings in the heavenly places for those who are chosen in Him.

Furthermore, He was foreordained as the head of the church, for it was God's design to gather all things into a head in Him (Ephesians 1:10).

All the elect of God were, in His eternal purpose and design and in the everlasting covenant between the Father and the Son, committed to Him to be delivered from sin, the law, and death, and to be brought into the enjoyment of God: "They were Yours, You gave them to Me" (John 17:6). This is the source of His love for them, with which He loved them and gave Himself for them, before there was any goodness or love in them (Ephesians 5:25-26; Galatians 2:20; Revelation 1:5-6).

In fulfilling this divine design and the everlasting covenant, in the fullness of time He took upon Himself our nature, uniting it personally to Himself. The special relationship that followed between Him and the elect children is elaborated by the apostle in Hebrews 2:10-17; I refer the reader to our exposition of that passage.

On these foundations, He undertook to be the surety of the new covenant (Hebrews 7:22), "by so much Jesus has become a surety of a better covenant." This aspect of the imputation of our sins to Christ is what I will focus on, aiming to clarify some misconceptions about the nature of His suretyship and its relation to the covenant for which He was the surety. I will draw from our exposition of this passage in the seventh chapter of this epistle, which has not yet been published, with minimal variation from what I have previously discussed on that occasion, without any regard to our current subject.

The word "enguos" is found in Scripture only in this context. However, the argument some make from this — that since it appears only once, it is not significant or worthy of emphasis — is both unreasonable and absurd.

1. This single instance is of divine revelation and thus holds the same authority as twenty testimonies to the same effect. One divine testimony makes our faith no less necessary, nor does it make it any less secure from deception than a hundred.

The meaning of the word is clear from its usage and from what it signifies among people; therefore there can be no doubt about its sense and importance, even if it occurs only once. This answers the difficulty and danger commonly urged about "hapax legomena."

The concept is so fully explained by the apostle in this passage and is taught elsewhere throughout Scripture that the word's singular occurrence may add nuance but does nothing to lessen its significance.

Something may be said about the meaning of the word "enguos" that will clarify the author's intent. "Gualon" denotes the palm of the hand; accordingly "enguos" or "eis to gualon" means to deliver into the hand. "Enguētēs" bears the same sense. Thus being a surety is represented as striking the hand. Proverbs 6:1 states, "My son, if you become surety for your friend, If you have shaken hands in pledge for a stranger." This illustrates the gesture and idea behind the term.

This corresponds to the Hebrew עָרַב, which the LXX renders with forms of enguaō (see Proverbs 6:1; 17:18; 20:16) and by dienguaō in Nehemiah 5:3. The root עָרַב originally signifies to mix or mingle; from this conjunction and union between a surety and the person for whom he stands, they are, for the purpose of that suretyship, treated as one.

A surety answers for another whatever befalls that person. Genesis 43:9 captures this: "I will be surety for him; from my hand you shall require him." In taking on Judah's suretyship for Benjamin, he undertook to answer for his safety and preservation. He adds, "If I do not bring him back to you and set him before you, then let me bear the blame forever."

This obligation extends to everything for which the person bound by the surety is liable, whether in criminal or civil matters, so far as the suretyship reaches. A surety is an undertaker for another or others, and is justly and legally accountable for what is owing to or from them; the term is not used otherwise. See Job 17:3; Proverbs 6:1; 11:15; 17:18; 20:16; 27:13. Thus Paul acted as a surety to Philemon for Onesimus (Philemon 18).

"Enguē" denotes sponsio, expromissio, fidejussio — an undertaking or providing security for someone or something to another, producing an agreement. Sometimes this was effected by a pledge or earnest, as in Isaiah 36:8: "Now therefore, I urge you, give a pledge to my master the king of Assyria, and I will give you two thousand horses — if you are able on your part to put riders on them!" Hence the Hebrew עֵרָבוֹן, arrhabōn, means a pledge or earnest (see Ephesians 1:14). Therefore "enguos" signifies a sponsor or fidejussor — one who voluntarily takes on another's cause or condition, to answer, undergo, or pay what is due, and so becomes justly and legally bound to perform. This is the sense in which the apostle uses the word here.

In our inquiry about the nature of Christ's suretyship, everything reduces to one question: Was the Lord Christ made surety only on God's part, to assure us that the covenant promise would be fulfilled? Or was He also, and primarily, an undertaker on our part — performing what was required, or acting with respect to us so that the promise might be accomplished?

The first view is strongly pressed by the Socinians and is followed in this passage by Grotius and by Hammond in his annotations.

Schlichtingius argues: Jesus is called the surety of the covenant because, in God's name, He promised us that God would fulfill the covenant's promises. But, he insists, Christ did not promise God on our behalf, nor did He take upon Himself the payment of our debts. We did not send

Christ; God sent Him, and God—whose name Christ bore to us—established and pledged the covenant's truth. Thus, Schlichtingius concludes, Christ is the surety of the covenant. He confirmed the covenant's truth not only by word but by a life of perfect innocence and holiness, by the divine works He performed, and by the violent death He suffered in vindication of His doctrine.

Following this, he offers a lengthy discourse on the evidences we have of Christ's veracity. He gives a brief account of their entire opinion regarding Christ's mediation. Grotius likewise observes, "Christ promised; that is, He made us certain of the promise, not only with words but through His continual sanctity of life, the death He endured for this reason, and through many miracles." This summarizes Schlichtingius's position. Dr. Hammond agrees in the same vein, interpreting that Christ was a surety for God in confirming the promises of the covenant.

On the other hand, the majority of interpreters—both ancient and modern, from the Roman and Protestant churches—affirm that the Lord Christ, as surety of the covenant, was properly a surety or undertaker to God for us. He was not a surety and undertaker to us for God. Because this is a matter of great importance, and because the faith and consolation of the church depend on it, I will elaborate a little further.

First, consider the argument offered to prove that Christ was only a surety for God on our behalf. This argument does not come from the name or the nature of the office or work of a surety, nor from the nature of the covenant he guaranteed, nor from the office in which he served. The sole argument insisted upon is this: we did not give Christ as a surety of the covenant to God; He gave Him to us. Therefore, it is said, He is a surety for God and for the fulfillment of His promises, not for us to pay our debts or to answer for what is required of us.

This argument is weak, for it does not touch the nature of a surety or what makes someone such. What is required is the voluntary assumption of the office and its work, regardless of how the person was designated or induced to undertake it. Whoever voluntarily undertakes for another is that person's surety, whatever the grounds or considerations that moved him.

The Lord Christ did precisely that on behalf of the church. When it was said, "Sacrifice and offering You did not desire," or when sacrificial rites were declared insufficient to make the atonement required for the covenant to be established for us, He said, "To do Your will, O God" (Hebrews 10:5, 7). He willingly and voluntarily, out of His abundant goodness and love, took upon Himself the task of making atonement for us. In this, He was our surety.

Accordingly, this undertaking is attributed to the love He exercised therein (Galatians 2:20; 1 John 3:16; Revelation 1:5). He also took upon Himself our nature—the seed of Abraham—and in that act He became our surety. Though we neither appointed nor could appoint Him, He assumed that which constituted His suretyship. That voluntary engagement and His taking our nature for that purpose constitute the formal reason He was instated in that office, despite prior transactions between the Father and Him in the matter.

It is unreasonable and contrary to common experience to assert that no one can be a surety for others unless those others appoint him. The principal instances of suretyship have involved voluntary undertakings by those not compelled by those for whom they undertook. In such cases, the one who becomes surety is no less concerned for the creditor's satisfaction than for the debtor's safety. For example, when Judah on his own accord became a surety for Benjamin, he cared as much for his father's satisfaction as for his brother's safety. Likewise, in undertaking to be our surety, the Lord Christ considered the glory of God as well as our safety.

Secondly, consider the arguments showing that He neither was nor could be a surety to us for God, but was a surety for us to God. The Greek term enguos (or enguētēs), meaning "a surety," denotes one who undertakes for another where that person is deficient—either in fact or in reputation. The undertaking may be a promise in words, the deposit of real security with an arbitrator, or any personal engagement of life and body. In every case the surety addresses the deficiency of the person for whom he becomes surety.

Such a person is a sponsor or fidejussor, in common usage. If someone has absolute credit and unquestionable reputation, a surety is unnecessary, except perhaps because of mortality. The words a surety uses on behalf of another whose ability or reputation is doubtful are: "I accept responsibility; he will do it, or I will do it." When enguos is taken adjectively, it sometimes signifies being liable to payments for others who are unable to pay.

God, therefore, cannot have a surety in the proper sense, because there can be no notion of defect in Him. There might be a question whether a word or promise is indeed God's; to assure us of that is the work of a witness or other means that provide evidence. But if it truly is His word or promise, there can be no fear of defect on His part, and so no need for a surety for its performance. He uses witnesses to confirm His word—testifying that He has made such promises and will fulfill them.

The Lord Christ served as such a witness. As Scripture says, "You are My witnesses," says the Lord, "And My servant whom I have chosen" (Isaiah 43:10). He also declared that He came into the world "that I should bear witness to the truth" (John 18:37). He was the minister of the circumcision for the truth of God's promises to the fathers (Romans 15:8). But a surety for God, properly so called, He was not, nor could He be.

The distinction between a witness and a surety matters. A surety must enhance the debtor's credit or reputation; otherwise his suretyship is pointless. No one can fulfill that role for God, not even the Lord Christ, who in His entire work was the Father's servant. The apostle does not use enguos in a loose sense meaning any form of assurance; if he did, he would attribute nothing unique to Christ. All the prophets and apostles, in some sense, confirmed God's word with their lives. But the surety the apostle names is one who undertakes to do for others what they cannot do for themselves, or at least are not regarded as able to do.

The apostle has already declared at length who and what God's surety is in the matter of the covenant, and how impossible it is for there to be any other. That surety is God Himself, interposing by His oath. "For when God made a promise to Abraham, because He could swear by no one greater, He swore by Himself" (Hebrews 6:13). Therefore, if God were to provide any other surety besides Himself, it would have to be one greater than He. That is impossible; thus He swears only by Himself.

God may and does use many means to declare and testify His truth to us, so that we may know and believe it is His word. In this, the Lord Christ in His ministry was the principal witness of God's truth. But God can have no surety other than Himself.

When God intends that we come to a full assurance of faith in His promises and find strong consolation in them, He rests that assurance on the immutability of His counsel—declared by His promise and His oath (Hebrews 6:18-19). Thus, neither is God capable of having a proper surety, nor do we need one from His side to secure our highest consolation.

In every respect we need a surety to act on our behalf. Without such a surety, no covenant between God and us could be firm or stable. It could not be an everlasting covenant, ordered in all things and secure.

In the first covenant made with Adam there was no surety; God and man were the immediate covenanters. Although humanity then was in a condition to fulfill the covenant's terms, it was nevertheless broken and annulled. If that failure had been God's rather than ours, a surety for God would have been necessary when making a new covenant so that it might be stable and everlasting. But that idea is false and blasphemous to imagine. It was man alone who failed and broke that covenant.

Therefore, when the new covenant was made with the intention that it should not be annulled like the former, we needed a surety to undertake for us. If the first covenant proved unstable despite our original ability to meet its terms because there was no surety for us, how much less could any covenant be stable now that our natures are depraved and sinful! Thus only we could have a proper surety; only we stood in need of one. Without such a surety, the covenant could not be firm and inviolable on our part. Therefore, the surety of this covenant is with God for us.

The apostle is addressing Christ's priesthood in this passage and nothing else. He is a surety by virtue of being a priest and in the discharge of that office; therefore, he is a surety with God on our behalf. Schlichtingius notices this and anticipates the objections that may be raised, which he tries to answer.

"It may seem strange," he says, "to some why the divine author, discussing the priesthood of Christ in the preceding and following passages, suddenly calls Him the surety of the covenant and not simply a priest. Why does he not say, 'Jesus has become a priest of a much greater covenant?' This seems to be required by the entire context of the discourse. It is credible that in the term 'surety,' the priesthood of Christ is also understood. For it is not the role of a surety to promise anything in another's name, and to interpose his faith for another; but also, if the situation demands it, to fulfill what he has promised in the name of another. In human affairs, if the one for whom the surety has pledged does not fulfill his obligation, the surety is held accountable; but here, due to the contrary cause (for the former cannot apply), namely, inasmuch as the one for whom Christ pledged presents His promises to us through Christ Himself; this is where the essence of Christ's priesthood is contained."

It may indeed appear odd to anyone who thinks of Christ's suretyship in a narrow, particular sense that the apostle would name Him a surety when describing His priestly office. But if we grasp what a surety properly does, and for whom the Lord Jesus acts as surety, it becomes clear that the term is both appropriate and highly relevant in that context.

He admits that his reading — that Christ is a surety for God — seems to conflict with the human notion of a surety. By common understanding, a surety steps in only when the one for whom he vouches is absent or unable. The surety pays what the other owes and does what the other cannot do. If that is not the sense here, then the apostle would be using a term in a way it is never used elsewhere in Scripture, which would be unlikely and absurd.

Therefore, the apostle's purpose in choosing the word is to let us understand its meaning by reference to its ordinary use, and then to apply that meaning to what he attributes to the Lord Jesus under that title.

The only way some can reconcile the apostle's calling of Christ a surety in the description of His priesthood is by weakening the nature of that priesthood. To make it appear that Christ, as priest, was a surety for

God, they suggest the priesthood consists in making God's promises effective for us or in actually communicating the promised blessings.

I have already refuted that mistaken view. Since the Lord Christ is a surety of the covenant as priest, and all His priestly acts have God as their immediate object and are performed on our behalf, He is therefore a surety for us.

The Lord Christ became our surety by a voluntary undertaking, out of abundant grace and love, to fulfill everything required on our part so that we might enjoy the covenant's benefits—the grace and glory prepared, proposed, and promised in it, according to divine wisdom. This can be summarized in two main points. First, His atonement for our transgressions against the first covenant. Second, His securing of the grace of the new covenant.

He himself declared the substitutionary aspect of his work: "having become a curse for us (for it is written, 'Cursed is everyone who hangs on a tree'), that the blessing of Abraham might come upon the Gentiles in Christ Jesus," (Galatians 3:13-14).

As the covenant's surety, He undertook to answer for all the sins of those who would partake of its benefits. He bore the punishment due for their sins and made atonement by offering Himself as a propitiatory sacrifice. He redeemed them with the price of His blood from their misery and bondage under the law and its curse. (See Isaiah 53:4-6, 10; Matthew 20:28; 1 Timothy 2:6; 1 Corinthians 6:20; Romans 3:25-26; Hebrews 10:5-8; Romans 8:2-3; 2 Corinthians 5:19-21; Galatians 3:13.)

This undertaking was absolutely necessary for the covenant's grace and glory to be communicated to us. Without it, the righteousness and faithfulness of God would not permit sinners—those who turned from Him, despised His authority, and rebelled against Him, thereby falling under the law's sentence and curse—to be received back into His favor and made partakers of grace and glory. The Lord Christ therefore took this upon Himself as the covenant's surety.

Those included in the covenant were to receive grace enabling them to meet its terms, fulfill its conditions, and produce the obedience God requires. By God's appointment, Christ procured and merited the Holy Spirit and all necessary supplies of grace for them. He secured their being made new creations and enabled them to obey God from a new principle of spiritual life, persevering faithfully to the end.

Thus He is the surety of this better testament. The detailed treatment of these points will follow in the section from which these observations are drawn, since they belong to that larger argument.

However, some hold a different view. They claim that "Christ, by His death and His obedience therein, whereby He offered Himself as a sweet-smelling sacrifice to God, procured for us the new covenant."

They argue that everything we receive through Christ's death is simply what we owed under the covenant of grace. In this view, He did and suffered what God required and freely appointed Him to do and suffer. This is not said to be because God's justice required anything of Him regarding the sins of those for whom He died, nor because the law demanded a substitute. Rather, it was what the divine wisdom and sovereignty freely ordained.

Accordingly, they maintain, God was pleased to relax the terms of the old covenant and to establish a new covenant with humanity on terms more suitable to our reason and abilities. These new terms, they say, are faith and sincere obedience — an assent to the truth of divine revelation that leads to obedience to God's will, encouraged by the promises of eternal life or future rewards contained in that revelation.

They conclude that our justification, adoption, and future glory depend on fulfilling these conditions, because these conditions constitute the righteousness before God by which He pardons our sins and accepts us "as if we were perfectly righteous." Thus, by attributing the procuring of the new covenant to Christ's death, they imply either the abrogation of the old covenant or at least a modification of it. Under their view, the old covenant would no longer demand sinless obedience or threaten punishment for failure, nor require perfect righteousness for justification. Instead, a new law of obedience, suited to our present state, would be established, and observance of that law alone would secure all the promises of the gospel.

Others assert that, in the death of Christ, a real satisfaction was made to God—not to the law, nor to God according to what the law required, but to God absolutely. They mean that He did what pleased God without regard to God's justice or the curse of the law.

They further maintain that, as a result, the whole righteousness of Christ is imputed to us so that we become partakers of its benefits. They add that the means by which these benefits are conveyed is the new covenant, which the Lord Christ procured by His death.

According to them, the conditions of that covenant are set within the covenant itself; upon those conditions God will bestow all its benefits and effects, among which are faith and obedience. Thus what the Lord Christ has done for us is accepted as our legal righteousness to the degree that God, on the basis of our faith and obedience toward it, releases and pardons all our sins of omission and commission.

On this view there is no need for any positive, perfect righteousness for our justification or salvation. Instead, our own personal righteousness is accepted by God in its place, by virtue of the new covenant which Christ procured. This is the way Curcellæus and his followers have stated the doctrine.

There are several aspects of these opinions that deserve examination, and most of them will arise as we proceed. Our primary question concerns the Lord Christ as the surety of the covenant — the foundation of the views under review — and specifically whether Christ, by His death, procured the new covenant for us.

Some insist that everything we receive comes through that procuring; if that claim fails, they say, we owe nothing to it. But these matters require careful scrutiny. The phrase "procured the new covenant" is ambiguous. It has not been made clear how the Lord Christ procured it — whether by His satisfaction and obedience as the meritorious cause, or by some other means. Until this is settled, the relation of the new covenant to Christ's death remains uncertain.

To assert simply that we owe the new covenant to Him does not clarify matters; it only makes the terms more obscure. It is also unclear whether the claim concerns the constitution of the covenant itself or only the communication of its benefits. In general, people mean that God was so pleased with what Christ did that He made and entered into a new covenant with mankind.

Those who deny any true satisfaction and merit in Christ may accept this vague notion. If by it they mean that the Lord Christ, through His obedience and sufferings, meritoriously procured the making and establishment of the new covenant — and that this is all He procured and the full effect of His death — then their statement can be understood. Yet taken that way it undermines the whole nature of Christ's mediation.

This opinion earns strong criticism because it concerns a fundamental article of our faith — one closely tied to the church's eternal welfare — yet it is not mentioned in Scripture. It seems strange that, if this were truly the sole effect of Christ's death as some claim, Scripture attributes many other effects and fruits to His death but nowhere states—or reasonably implies—this particular point.

Redemption, the pardon of sins, the renewal of our natures, our sanctification, justification, peace with God, and eternal life are repeatedly ascribed to Christ's death in many passages. But Scripture never says that Christ, by His death, merited, procured, or obtained the new covenant, nor that God should enter into a new covenant with mankind. In fact, as we shall see, Scripture frequently asserts the contrary.

To clarify the truth, we must examine the various notions and causes of the new covenant and the true relation of Christ's death to it. That relation is presented to us in several distinct ways:

1. In the designation and preparation of its terms and benefits in the counsel of God. Though this takes the form of an eternal decree, it is not identical with the decree of election, as some suppose. The decree of election concerns the persons for whom grace and glory are prepared; this counsel concerns how that grace and glory are prepared to be communicated.

Some learned writers hold that this counsel and purpose of God's will—to grant grace and glory through Jesus Christ to the elect, in the manner He ordained—is formally the covenant of grace or at least contains its essence. But it is clear that more is needed to constitute a covenant fully. Moreover, this counsel or purpose is not called "the covenant" in Scripture; it is presented as the source and foundation of the covenant, as seen in Ephesians 1:3–12.

To exemplify the covenant of grace fully, there must be a declaration of this counsel of God's will, the means and powers necessary for its fulfillment, and a prescription of the way we are to be involved and partake of its benefits. In asking what procured the new covenant, this aspect must come first. Nothing can be the procuring cause of the covenant that is not also the cause of this source and foundation of it — of the idea in God's mind and of the preparation of its terms and benefits.

Yet Scripture nowhere affirms that this is the effect of Christ's death or mediation. To attribute it to Him would undermine the entire freedom of eternal grace and love. And nothing that is absolutely eternal — such as this decree and counsel — can reasonably be said to be produced or procured by anything external and temporal.

2. It may also be considered with respect to the federal transactions between the Father and the Son that relate to the fulfillment of this counsel of His will. I have treated these transactions in detail in my earlier work, Exercitat., vol. ii. I do not call this, in an absolute sense, the covenant of grace, nor is it so called in Scripture.

Still, some do not distinguish between the covenant of the mediator and the covenant of grace, since the promises of the covenant are spoken of as made to Christ, as noted in Galatians 3:16, and He is the first recipient of all its grace. In the covenant of the mediator, Christ stands for Himself and undertakes obligations for Himself alone; in the covenant of grace, He represents the church.

This is the place where the covenant was settled so that every way, means, and end of its fulfillment were arranged to secure its effect for the eternal display of God's wisdom, grace, righteousness, and power. Therefore the covenant of grace could not be procured by any cause other than that which procured the covenant between the Father and the Son — the engagements made as the Son undertook the work of mediation.

Since Scripture does not ascribe this to Christ's death, to assert it contradicts sound spiritual reason. Who can conceive that Christ, by

His death, procured the agreement between God and Himself that He should die?

3. With respect to its declaration by special revelation, we may speak of God's making or establishing the covenant—though Scripture primarily, if not exclusively, applies the term "making" the covenant to its execution or its actual application to individuals, as seen in 2 Samuel 23:5 and Jeremiah 32:40. This public declaration of God's grace, together with the provisions in the mediator's covenant for making it effective to His glory, is most commonly called the covenant of grace.

This may be regarded as a single, absolute promise. It was first declared and established with Adam and later reiterated with Abraham. The promise declares God's previously determined purpose or the free determination of His will concerning His dealings with sinners, assuming the fall and the forfeiture of the original covenant condition. This promise flows solely from God's grace and will, as noted in Hebrews 8:8. Christ's death cannot be the means by which it was procured, for Christ Himself—and all that He was to do for us—forms the substance of that promise.

That promise, insofar as it declares God's purpose to communicate grace and glory to sinners by Christ's mediation according to the ways and terms prepared in His sovereign wisdom, is formally the new covenant. Yet something more must be added to complete its application to us.

The essence of that first promise—wherein the whole covenant of grace was virtually contained—directly addressed and expressed the giving of Christ for the recovery of mankind from sin and misery through His death, as indicated in Genesis 3:15. Therefore, if He and all the benefits of His mediation, including His death and its effects, are contained in the promise, then His death was not the procuring cause of the covenant, and we do not owe the covenant to Him.

4. Finally, consider the specification of the way and means by which God's will is that we enter into covenant fellowship with Him and share its benefits. This is virtually included in the absolute promise — every promise of God implicitly requires faith and obedience from us — and it is expressed elsewhere as the condition required of us.

This specification is not the covenant itself but the establishment of the terms on our part that enable us to partake of it. The establishment of these terms is not an effect of Christ's death, nor is it procured by it; it is solely the effect of God's sovereign grace and wisdom.

The things themselves, as they are given to us, communicated to us, and worked in us by grace, are all effects of Christ's death. However, establishing them as the terms and conditions of the covenant is an act of pure sovereign wisdom and grace. "For God so loved the world that He gave His only begotten Son," not so that faith and repentance might be the means of salvation, but so that all His elect might believe, and that all who believe "should not perish but have everlasting life." It is acknowledged that the establishment of these terms of the covenant does relate to the federal transaction between the Father and the Son, in which they were arranged to praise the glory of God's grace. Thus, although their establishment was not procured by His death, it would not have been conceived without reference to it. Therefore, the sole cause of God's making the new covenant was the same as that of giving Christ Himself to be our mediator — namely, the purpose, counsel, goodness, grace, and love of God, as expressed throughout Scripture.

5. The covenant can also be considered in terms of the actual application of its grace, benefits, and privileges to individuals — by which they become true participants in it or enter into covenant with God. This is what Scripture means when it speaks of God's making a covenant with someone. It is not a mere general declaration of the covenant's terms and nature (some call that a universal conditional

covenant, for reasons known only to them). Making a covenant in its proper sense includes the actual acceptance of it and participation in its benefits. Rather, Scripture speaks of God's making His covenant with a person when His grace is communicated to them, accompanied by a prescription of obedience. All biblical instances of God's "making" a covenant point to this actual communication and summons to obedience.

It may therefore be asked what connection the covenant of grace has to the death of Christ, or how His death influences it.

I answer, on the assumption already made about His being the surety of the covenant: the connection is threefold.

1. The covenant—its prepared grace and glory in God's counsel, its terms established in the mediator's covenant, and its declaration in the promise—was confirmed, ratified, and made irrevocable by His death. The apostle treats this in detail in Hebrews 9:15-20, comparing Christ's blood, in His death and sacrifice, to the sacrifices and their blood that confirmed the old covenant (see especially verses 18-19). Those sacrifices did not procure the covenant or move God to make it; they ratified and confirmed what was already ordained. In the new covenant the blood of Christ accomplishes this same confirmation.

2. By His death He endured and fulfilled all that righteousness and wisdom required of God, so that the effects, fruits, benefits, and grace intended and prepared in the new covenant might be accomplished and communicated to sinners. Therefore, although He did not procure the covenant's establishment by His death, He was, in His person, mediation, life, and death, the only cause and means by which the covenant's full saving effect is made effective for us.

3. All the benefits of the covenant were procured by Him. In other words, all the grace, mercy, privileges, and glory that God prepared in

the counsel of His will—those things fixed regarding the way of communicating them in the mediator's covenant and set forth in its promises—were purchased, merited, and procured by His death. These benefits are then effectively communicated or applied to the covenanters by virtue of His death and other mediatory acts. This is a far more significant procuring of the new covenant than the notion that His death merely procured its terms and conditions. If His mediation had procured only a rule, law, or promise that whoever believes would be saved, without also procuring the means whereby sinners are actually converted and saved, then, given our condition, no one could be saved by that alone.

To summarize: we must ask which aspect of the new covenant is meant when it is said to have been procured by Christ's death. If the claim is that His death procured the actual communication of all the grace and glory prepared in the covenant and offered to us in its promises, that is true. All the grace and glory promised in the covenant were purchased for the church by Jesus Christ. In this sense, by His death He procured the new covenant. Scripture attests this from the first promise to the last. It is in Him alone that God "has blessed us with every spiritual blessing in the heavenly places in Christ." If we sum up all the good things mentioned or promised in the covenant, whether explicitly or by necessary consequence, it will not be hard to show that they were all procured for us by Christ's obedience and death.

However, many who hold the opposite opinion deny that the covenant's saving effects—conversion, remission of sins, sanctification, justification, adoption, and the like—are the effects or procurements of Christ's death. They claim instead that what was procured was God's making of the covenant itself, meaning the arrangement of its terms and conditions and their proposal to humanity for recovery. That position is fundamentally flawed. The Lord Christ Himself, and the whole work of His mediation as God's ordinance for the recovery and salvation of lost sinners, was the subject of the first promise and virtually contained the whole covenant. His incarnation and mediatorial work, and our deliverance through them, were the substance of that promise. He was also the means by which the promise was renewed to Abraham when solemnly confirmed by God's oath, as set forth in Galatians 3:16-17. Christ did not, by His death, procure the promise of His incarnation or His coming into the world to die.

Scripture consistently ascribes the making of this covenant — not to the death of Christ — but to the love, grace, and wisdom of God alone. Just as the sending of Christ to die is ascribed to God's love and wisdom, so the making of the covenant is attributed to them; never is it attributed to Christ's death. The actual communication of all grace and glory is ascribed solely to God. Consider every passage that speaks of the giving of the promise, the sending of Christ, or the making of the covenant: in none is this act assigned to any cause other than the grace, love, and wisdom of God alone, though all of these are made effective for us through Christ's mediation.

The assertion that the sole purpose of Christ's death was merely to procure the new covenant, as argued, undermines the efficacy of both Christ's death and the covenant itself.

First, the covenant they mean is simply the establishment and proposal of new terms and conditions for life and salvation to all people. Because acceptance and fulfillment of these conditions depend on individuals' wills — which, they hold, are not governed by effective grace — it could happen that, despite all Christ accomplished by His death, no sinner would be saved. That possibility would make the whole design and purpose of God in this matter futile.

Second, the real advantage claimed for these new terms is that God will now, for Christ's sake, accept an obedience short of what the law requires. In other words, the grace of Christ would not raise anything to conform to the holiness and will of God as declared in the law, but would rather accommodate everything to our present condition. Nothing could be more dishonoring to Christ and the gospel. It would make Christ a minister of sin by nullifying the law's holiness without providing anything worthy to replace it.

Moreover, it would be inconsistent with divine wisdom, goodness, and immutability to impose a law of obedience on humanity and attach the severest penalties for its breach when God could, justly and honorably, have given them a law that allowed for many failings. If He can do that now, He could have done it before. The implications for the glory of God's attributes are serious.

Additionally, this notion contradicts Scripture, which affirms that the Lord Christ did not come to destroy the Law or the Prophets but to fulfill them; that He is the end of the law for righteousness to everyone who believes; and that through faith the law is not annulled but established. Finally, the Lord Christ is declared to be Mediator and surety of the new covenant, by whom it was ratified, confirmed, and established. Therefore the constitution of the covenant was not procured by Him; all His acts belong to His office of mediation, and it is hard to see how any mediatorial act intended to establish the covenant and make it effective could be said to procure it.

To return from that digression: the essence of the union between Christ and believers—the bond that makes them one mystical person—lies in the communication of His Spirit, the same Spirit that dwells in Him, to them. This Spirit abides in, animates, and guides the whole mystical body and all its members. This subject has been treated at length elsewhere, so I will only note it briefly here.

Consider what has been shown: by these considerations the Lord Christ became one mystical person with the church, bearing the person of the church in all that He did as mediator. By the holy and wise arrangement of God—the Author of the law and the supreme Governor of all mankind in their temporal and eternal concerns — and by His own consent, the sins of all the elect were imputed to Him. This has been the faith and language of the church through the ages, grounded on explicit testimonies of Scripture and on all the promises and declarations concerning His incarnation from the first. That position cannot now be reasonably denied.

Consequently, even the Socinians concede that our sins may be said to be imputed to Christ, and that He suffered for them to the extent that the evils and afflictions He endured in this life — including the death He suffered — were caused by our sins. Had we not sinned, His suffering would not have been necessary. Yet, despite this concession, they deny His satisfaction; they assert that He did not properly undergo the punishment due for our sins, and so deny any real imputation of those sins to Him. Others attempt a distinction, saying our sins were imputed to Him "quoad reatum pœnæ" (as to the obligation to punishment), but not "quoad reatum culpæ" (as to the guilt of fault). I confess that distinction seems to me inanem sine mente sonum — a sound without sense. Feuardentius stresses this distinction heavily (Dialog v. p. 467), and others follow him.

His aim is to prove that the Lord Christ did not present Himself before the throne of God laden with our sins as if to answer for them before God's justice. Hence "reatus" or "guilt" may mean either "dignitatem pœnæ" (the dignity of punishment) or "obligationem ad pœnam" (the obligation to punishment), as Bellarmine distinguishes (De Amiss. Grat., lib. vii. cap. 7). In relation to Christ, only the latter should be accepted. Their chief argument runs: if our sins are imputed to Christ as the guilt of fault, then He must be stained by them and therefore a sinner in every respect. That would follow if our sins could be transferred to Christ by transfusion, making them inherently and subjectively His. But imputation does not require that. There is a notion of legal uncleanness without inherent defilement — for example, the priest who offered the red heifer and the one who burned her were said to be unclean (Numbers 19:7-8).

In reply, they insist that Christ died and suffered by special command of God, not because His death and suffering were due to our sins or required by justice; and this view fundamentally undermines the doctrine of Christ's satisfaction.

Therefore, the aim of this distinction is to deny that the guilt of our sins was imputed to Christ. I cannot see in what acceptable sense they could be said to be imputed to Him. We are not bound by arbitrary niceties or by the private meanings anyone chooses to impose on these terms.

Accordingly, I will first examine what is meant by the words "guilt" and "guilty," so that we may understand more clearly what is intended by this distinction.

The Hebrews have no other word to signify "guilt" or "guilty" but אָשָׁם (asham). This term is used for sin, the guilt of sin, the punishment due for it, and even a sacrifice for it. When speaking of the guilt of blood they do not use any special word for guilt but simply say דָּם לוֹ (dam lo) — literally "it is blood to him." Thus, David prays מִדָּמִים (mi-damim), "Deliver me" — which we render as "from blood," or more fully "blood-guiltiness" (Psalm 51:14).

By God's constitution, anyone guilty of blood was to die by the hand of the magistrate or by God Himself. The word אָשָׁם (asham) is never used merely for guilt in the abstract; it indicates the relation of the sin in question to punishment. No other senses for it are to be sought in the Old Testament.

In the New Testament, a person who is guilty is referred to as hupodikos (Romans 3:19), meaning one who is liable to judgment or vengeance for sin — someone whom "yet justice does not allow to live"

(Acts 28:4) — and by enochos (1 Corinthians 11:27), a word of similar meaning. It is also expressed by opheilō (Matthew 23:18), meaning to owe or to be indebted to justice. To be liable to justice, vengeance, or punishment for sin is to be guilty.

"Reus," meaning "guilty" in Latin, has a wide application. One who is "crimini obnoxious" (exposed to crime), "pœnæ propter crimen" (liable to punishment for a crime), "voti debitor" (debtor of a vow), "promissi" (debtor of a promise), or "officii ex sponsione" (bound to an office by sponsorship) is called "reus." In particular, every sponsor or surety is legally considered "reus."

Thus, when a servant has agreed to pay for his freedom and has given a surety, even if the servant is later freed by another, the surety remains bound. A person who undertakes another's obligation is "reus" — a usage consistent in the best Latin authors.

Livy illustrates this usage. He says that every commander should tend his assigned station so that, if anything goes wrong, the fault may be imputed to him ("Opportuna loca dividenda præfectis esse ac suæ quique partis tutandæ reus sit," De Bello Punico, v.30). Again, he asks whether anyone, by proximity or kinship, should suffer death for another's fault ("An, quicunque aut propinquitate, aut affinitate, regiam aut aliquibus ministeriis contigissent, alienæ culpæ rei trucidarentur," iv.22).

Thus, in Latin a "reus" is one who is liable to punishment or payment for himself or for another.

"Reatus" is a term recently introduced into Latin, derived from "reus." Quintilian notes this in his discussion of obsolete and new words (book viii, ch. 3): "Quæ vetera nunc sunt, fuerunt olim nova, et quædam in usu perquam recentia" (What are now old were once new, and some that are in use are quite recent). He cites "reatum," first used by Messala, and says Augustus first used "munerarium."

At its inception, however, "reatus" did not have the sense it bears today. I mention this to show we are not bound by arbitrary definitions that men impose. Some lawyers at first used it "pro crimine" (for a crime), meaning a fault that exposes one to punishment.

But the earlier, established meaning — confirmed by long usage — was different. It signified the outward state and condition of one who was "reus" after being publicly accused in a criminal case, yet before acquittal or condemnation. Romans thus accused would put on a poor, squalid appearance. They wore sorrowful expressions and let their hair and beards grow unkempt, hoping to move those who judged them to compassion. Milo aggravated the disgrace of his banishment by refusing to adopt this custom, which made him seem cowardly and base. That state of sorrow and distress was called "reatus"—and nothing else.

Over time the word came to denote the condition of those held in custody awaiting trial, when the government became unpopular; in that context the custom served a purpose. If the term bears on our present argument, it properly denotes the state of an individual after conviction of sin and before justification. That is their "reatus"—a condition in which even the proud show inner sorrow and anxiety by outward signs. Beyond this historical usage, we are not bound; we must focus on the real matter we intend to express.

According to Scripture, guilt denotes the relation of sin to the law's sanction, which renders the sinner liable to punishment. To be guilty is to be hupodikos tō Theō — liable to punishment from God, the supreme Lawgiver and Judge. Thus, "reatus" is aptly defined as "obligatio ad pœnam, propter culpam, aut admissam in se, aut imputatum, justè aut injustè"—the obligation to punishment on account of guilt, whether inherent or imputed, justly or unjustly.

For example, Bathsheba tells David that she and her son Solomon should be חַטָּאִים (chattā'īm)—sinners; that is, they should be regarded as guilty or liable to punishment for some evil laid against them (1 Kings 1:21). The distinction between "dignitas pœnæ" (the dignity of punishment) and "obligatio ad pœnam" (the obligation to punishment) is simply another way of expressing sin's relation to the law's sanction. Even if that distinction seems different in words, in practice they are inseparable: there can be no "obligatio ad pœnam" without some "dignitas pœnæ."

There is little real difference between "reatus culpæ" (the guilt of sin) and "reatus pœnæ" (the guilt as to punishment), for "reatus culpæ" is simply "dignitas pœnæ propter culpam"—the dignity of punishment due to sin. Sin has other aspects, such as its formal character as a transgression and the moral stain it leaves on the soul. But the guilt of sin fundamentally concerns its relation to punishment as the law defines it. Thus "reatus culpæ" and "reatus pœnæ" amount to the same thing: sin's deserving of punishment.

Where there is no "reatus culpæ," there can be no true "pœnæ"; for "pœnæ" is "vindicta noxæ"—the vengeance due to sin. Therefore punishment and "reatus pœnæ" cannot exist without "reatus culpæ," which regards sin together with its guilt. The notion of a "reatus pœnæ" imagined apart from the guilt of sin is merely the acknowledgment of possible suffering on account of sin—a position the Socinians accept regarding Christ's sufferings, while they reject the idea that those sufferings constituted a proper satisfaction.

If this distinction is to be understood in terms of "reatus," with respect to sin and punishment, both parts must bear the same meaning; otherwise the subject equivocates. "Reatus pœnæ" denotes a liability or exposure to punishment under the law, making a sinner hupodikos tō Theō—liable to God. Consequently, "reatus culpæ" would have to imply a liability to sin, which is an unusual notion.

Thus, there can be no imputation of sin where there is no imputation of its guilt. A guilt of punishment that is disconnected from the desert of sin is a mere fiction—there is no such thing in rerum natura. Guilt exists only in relation to punishment.

What we affirm is that our sins were so transferred to Christ that he became אָשָׁם (asham), hupodikos tō Theō (responsible to God), and liable to punishment in God's justice for them. He was alienæ culpæ reus—perfectly innocent in himself—yet he took upon himself our guilt, our liability to punishment for sin.

In this sense, he may be called the greatest debtor in the world, though he never owed anything on his own account, if he becomes surety for the greatest debts of others. This is analogous to Paul becoming a debtor to Philemon by undertaking for Onesimus, who owed him nothing.

Two elements contributed to the imputation of sin to Christ:

1. The act of God imputing it.

2. The voluntary act of Christ himself in undertaking it or accepting the charge.

The act of God in imputing the guilt of our sins to Christ is expressed in Scripture as "And the Lord has laid on Him the iniquity of us all," and "For He made Him who knew no sin to be sin for us," as the supreme governor, lawgiver, and judge, it was his responsibility to ensure that his holy law was observed or that offenders were punished.

Upon the transgression of the law, he accepted the suretyship of Christ to answer for the sins of humanity (Hebrews 9:5–7).

To accomplish this, God placed Christ under the law, so the law had authority over him to demand and inflict the penalty due for the sins of those for whom he undertook (Galatians 3:13; 4:4, 5). In declaring his righteousness by presenting Christ as a propitiation and by bearing our iniquities, God transferred the guilt of our sins to him as part of his righteous judgment, treating him as the guilty party—much as public sureties are treated in many cases.

The Lord Christ's voluntary acceptance of the role of surety, or undertaker for the church, was essential for appearing before the throne of God's justice on their behalf and answering for whatever charges were laid against them. He did this willingly. His own will was engaged in all those divine acts that constituted him and the church as one mystical person. Out of his love and grace, he stood in our place before God when he made atonement for sin, taking upon himself the punishment it deserved. Therefore, it was just and right that he should suffer, "For Christ also suffered once for sins, the just for the unjust, that He might bring us to God,".

If this is not the case, I would like to know what has become of the guilt of believers' sins. If it was not transferred to Christ, it either remains upon them or it is nonexistent. Some may argue that guilt is removed through a free pardon of sin. But if that were true, there would be no need for punishment at all—the very conclusion the Socinians draw, though others reject it. For if punishment is not for guilt, then it is not punishment.

However, it is strongly objected against our assertion that if the guilt of our sins was imputed to Christ, then he would be considered a sinner, since it is the guilt of sin that defines someone as a true sinner. Bellarmine advances this argument in his work, "De Justificat," not to uphold it for its own sake, but to refute the imputation of Christ's righteousness to us. He goes on: "If we are made righteous and children of God through the imputation of Christ's righteousness, then he was made a sinner, and what horrifies the mind to consider, a son of the devil, by the imputation of our sins or unrighteousness to him." Others repeat this objection and offer further consequences, which I wish had been avoided for many reasons.

In response, I assert:

1. Nothing is more absolutely true, nothing more sacredly or assuredly believed by us, than that nothing Christ did or suffered, nothing he undertook or endured, could or did make him subjectively, inherently, or personally a sinner, or guilty of any sin of his own. To bear the guilt or blame of others' faults — to be "alienæ culpæ reus" — does not make one a sinner unless one undertakes it unwisely or irregularly. For Christ to admit any aspect of sin into himself would not only contradict the hypostatic union but would also render him unfit for every other duty of his office (Hebrews 7:25, 26).

I find it scandalous that Socinus, Crellius, and Grotius assert that, in some sense, Christ suffered for his own sins, and seek to prove this from a passage that explicitly denies it (Hebrews 7:27). This denial must be firmly established, and no word or thought should entertain the possibility of the contrary under any circumstances.

2. No one has ever suggested a transfusion or propagation of sin from us to Christ, such as occurred from Adam to us. Adam was a common representative for us; we are not such for Christ — rather, he is our representative. The imputation of our sins to him is a special act of divine dispensation, and no harmful consequences follow from it.

To imagine that our sins are imputed to Christ in such a way that they cease to be our sins and become his entirely contradicts what has been affirmed. If that were so, Christ could not suffer for our sins, because they would no longer be ours before his suffering. Yet the guilt of our sins was transferred to him so that, by his suffering for that guilt, it might be pardoned for us.

Having established these points, I will say the following:

1. Sin involves a transgression of the law's preceptive part, and that transgression brings punishment by the law's sanction. This transgression gives sin its formal nature; where it is absent, no one can be formally considered a sinner. A person may be called a sinner for a particular purpose, but without such a transgression they cannot be formally reckoned a sinner, no matter what is imputed to them. Conversely, where the transgression exists, merely not imputing the sin with respect to punishment does not prevent a person from being formally a sinner.

For example, when Bathsheba said to David that she and her son Solomon would be חַטָּאִים (sinners) because crimes were attributed to them, or when Judah told Jacob that he would be a sinner before him for any calamity that befell Benjamin, neither of them became a formal sinner by those declarations alone. Likewise, when Shimei asked David not to impute sin to him to avoid punishment, that non-imputation did not free him from being a sinner in the formal sense.

Thus, sin, as a transgression of the law, cannot be transferred from one person to another except where a corrupt principle or habit is propagated. Even then, one person's inherent sin cannot become another's personal sin. Adam's personal sin communicated a corrupt nature to all his descendants, and the guilt of his actual sin is imputed to them as if they had committed it themselves. Still, his specific personal sin could never become any descendant's personal sin except through the imputation of its guilt. Therefore, our sins cannot be imputed to Christ in such a way that they become his in a subjective sense, since they are transgressions of the law. A physical transfer or transfusion of sin is both naturally and spiritually impossible; the horrendous consequences some imagine rest solely on this false assumption.

The guilt of sin is an external aspect that concerns only the law's sanction. This can be separated from sin itself; if it could not be, no sinner could ever be pardoned or saved. Thus, guilt may be attributed to another by imputation without making that person formally a sinner. This is what was imputed to Christ, rendering Him subject to the curse of the law, for the law cannot declare anyone accursed except the guilty, as stated in Deuteronomy 27:26.

There is a significant difference between the imputation of Christ's righteousness to us and the imputation of our sins to Christ. He is not made a sinner in the same way that we are made righteous. Our sins were imputed to Christ only in his role as our surety and for a time, with the purpose of taking them away, destroying them, and abolishing them. They were never imputed to him in a way that fundamentally altered his personal state or condition.

In contrast, his righteousness is imputed to us to remain with us, to be ours forever, and to effect a complete change in our standing with God. Our sins were imputed to him temporarily, not absolutely, while he served as surety with the specific aim of destroying sin. That was conditional upon his righteousness being made ours eternally. The imputation of his righteousness to us, however, is absolute and permanent; it remains with us forever, changes our state before God, and is an expression of superabounding grace.

It may be argued that if the guilt of our sins were imputed to Christ, then God must hate Christ, since God hates the guilty. I am not sure why I raise these points, for they are the sort of objections some may make against any of the gospel's mysterious truths. Nevertheless, since the objection has been brought up, I will address it.

First, Christ's acceptance of the guilt of our sins was a profound act of obedience to God, as noted in Hebrews 10:5-6, and it is for this obedience that the Father loved Him (John 10:17-18). Therefore, there is no reason to suppose God would hate Christ for taking on our debt and paying it in supreme obedience to the Father's will.

Second, here God is presented as ruler and judge. A strict judge need not hate the guilty person, even when guilt exists by imputation rather than by inherent sin. The judge's duty is to acknowledge guilt and pronounce the sentence.

Third, consider a person who, out of heroic generosity, takes on another's punishment, as Judah did for Benjamin to secure his freedom. Would the most cruel tyrant, who then takes that person's life, really hate them in such a case? Would he not rather admire their worth and virtue? Christ suffered in this manner and in no other.

Fourth, this objection depends on ambiguity in the term "hate." It can mean either a moral aversion or a desire to punish, the latter often attributed to God. In the first sense, there is no reason for God to hate Christ because Christ became "non propriæ sed alienæ culpæ reus" — guilty not of his own but of another's fault. Inherent sin pollutes the soul and makes it the object of divine aversion; but for one who is perfectly innocent, holy, harmless, and undefiled to take upon himself the guilt of others' sins to fulfill God's design — to display his glory, wisdom, grace, goodness, mercy, and righteousness in the expiation and destruction of sin — nothing could make him more glorious and lovely before God and man. Yet, regarding God's desire to punish where sin is imputed, that point cannot be denied without rejecting the satisfaction of Christ.

To conclude, unless the guilt of sin was imputed to Christ, then sin was not imputed to him in any sense, for the punishment of sin is not sin itself. Those who object cannot clearly define what aspect of sin is imputed. Scripture is clear that "And the Lord has laid on Him the iniquity of us all" and "made Him to be sin for us," which could only occur through imputation.

There can be no punishment without reference to the guilt of sin, whether personally contracted or imputed. Only guilt gives what is materially evil and afflictive its formal nature as punishment; nothing else does. Therefore those who value conceptual consistency and will speak plainly say that if one of these notions is denied, the other must also be denied; and if one is accepted, both must be accepted.

If guilt was not imputed to Christ, then, they argue, he could not undergo the punishment of sin. He might endure sufferings related to sin, but he could not bear the punishment due for sin. Conversely, if the guilt of sin was imputed to him, they cannot deny that he underwent the punishment for it; and if he did suffer that punishment, they cannot deny that the guilt was imputed to him, since these ideas are inseparably linked.

Christ has redeemed us from the curse of the law, having become a curse for us (Galatians 3:13–14). The curse of the law pertains only to the guilt of sin. Where there is no guilt, the curse cannot apply in any sense; where guilt exists, the curse follows, as indicated in Deuteronomy 27:26.

The clear testimonies of Scripture on this matter cannot be evaded without distorting their words and meanings. God is said, in Isaiah 53:6, "And the Lord has laid on Him the iniquity of us all," and he bore them as his burden; the word signifies this burden. In verse 11 it says, "For He shall bear their iniquities."

This is the intent of עָוֹן (when paired with any word denoting sin), as seen in passages such as Psalm 32:5, "And You forgave the iniquity of my sin"—meaning the guilt of it, which is the aspect removed by pardon. Likewise the texts speak of "When You make His soul an offering for sin," of Him being "to be sin for us," and that "He condemned sin in the flesh," etc.

This was symbolically represented in all the sacrifices of old, especially the great annual sacrifice on the Day of Atonement and the ordinance of the scapegoat, as explained above.

Without this assumption, it is impossible to understand how Christ should be our Antipsuchos, or suffer anti hēmōn, in our stead. The only alternative would be to accept the interpretation of Mr. Ho, a recent writer, who, while listing the things Christ did on our behalf, adds merely that it is to benefit us. If he can conceive of anything more foolish and nonsensical, he possesses a singular talent for such endeavours.

10. The Righteousness by Which We Are Justified

The principal differences regarding the doctrine of justification can be categorized into three main areas:

The nature of justification: whether it consists in an internal change in the justified person through the imputation of inherent grace or righteousness, or whether it is a forensic act—judging, declaring, and pronouncing a person righteous, thereby absolving them from all sins and granting them the right to eternal life.

In this discussion we will focus only on the Roman Catholic perspective, since all others, including Protestants and Socinians, agree on the forensic meaning of the term and the nature of what it signifies. I have already addressed this sufficiently for our present purpose, and I shall now present evidence of truth that cannot be easily set aside.

We ought not suppose we have lingered too long on this subject, as if it were an antiquated opinion long refuted. I think otherwise. Those who avoid engaging Romanists on these controversies may appear fearful rather than contemptuous. In the end, if the doctrine of free justification through the blood of Christ and the imputation of His righteousness cannot hold its place in people's minds, the Roman doctrine of justification will inevitably resurface, together with all its consequences.

So long as there is any knowledge of the law or the gospel among us, consciences will, at some point—whether in life or in death—be truly affected by a sense of sin, guilt, and danger. This conscience-driven unrest will press people, however unwilling, to seek relief and satisfaction.

What will people not attempt when faced with the condition described in Micah 6:6-7? If the true and only relief for the distressed consciences of sinners—those burdened and weary—is hidden from their eyes, if they lack understanding or trust in what alone can stand between them and the sentence of the law and provide shelter from the storms of divine wrath that await unbelievers, they will turn to anything that confidently promises immediate ease and relief.

Consequently, many individuals, throughout their lives, remain ignorant of God's righteousness. Often, on their sickbeds or in their dying moments, they are attracted to the false assurances of rest and peace that Romanists propose. They wait for such advantageous moments to bolster their own reputation for zeal, a practice that ultimately brings scandal to the Christian faith.

When they meet people whose consciences are troubled and who are unaware of—or disbelieve—the heavenly relief offered in the gospel, they are quick to offer remedies. They claim these remedies have the endorsement of countless devout souls through many ages. This is their doctrine of justification, supplemented by confession, absolution, penances, and intercessions from saints and angels, particularly the blessed Virgin. All these means are warmed by the fires of purgatory and confidently administered to those suffering from ignorance, darkness, and sin.

Let no one take comfort in dismissing these matters. If the truth regarding evangelical justification is once disbelieved among us or erased from men's minds by any means, people will inevitably turn to these alternatives. The new schemes and proposals for justification that some now offer are ill-suited and incapable of providing relief or satisfaction to a conscience genuinely troubled by sin and earnestly seeking peace with God.

Therefore, I boldly assert — regardless of who may be offended — that if we abandon the ancient doctrine of justification through faith in the blood of Christ and the imputation of His righteousness to us, public profession of religion will swiftly lead to either Roman Catholicism or atheism, or, at the very least, to something closely resembling them.

The second principal controversy concerns the formal cause of justification, as expressed and defined by those of the Roman Church. Some Protestant theologians have agreed to debate this matter. I will not engage in a dispute over terminology that the Romanists might apply to our inquiry.

Some of our theologians assert that the imputed righteousness of Christ is the formal cause of our justification, while others claim that the imputation of Christ's righteousness serves as the formal cause. Still others argue that there is no formal cause of justification; rather, the righteousness of Christ performs the role of a formal cause. I will not concern myself with these distinctions, although I believe the latter perspective is the most appropriate and meaningful.

The essence of our inquiry is this: What is the righteousness by which and with which a believing sinner is justified before God? This is the righteousness that enables a person to be accepted by God, have their sins pardoned, be received into grace and favor, and be granted a title to the heavenly inheritance. I present this question because it encapsulates what convicted sinners seek in and through the gospel.

It is agreed by all, except the Socinians, that the procuring cause of the pardon of our sins and our acceptance with God is the satisfaction and merit of Christ. Yet it cannot be denied that some, while retaining the terminology, seem to renounce or disbelieve the underlying concepts. We need not address them further until they more frankly express their views.

Concerning the righteousness in question, there is disagreement among those who all deny it to be the righteousness of Christ imputed to us. The Roman Church asserts that upon the infusion of a habit of grace—expelling sin and renewing our natures, what they call the first justification—we are actually justified before God by our own works of righteousness. They then debate the merit and sufficiency of those works, including whether they are worthy of the reward of eternal life.

Others, like the Socinians, openly deny any merit in our works. Some, perhaps out of respect for the antiquity of the term and the vagueness of its meaning, have tried—though weakly—to accommodate it. In effect, however, they all agree that what the Papists call "justitia operum" (the righteousness of works) is a personal, inherent, evangelical righteousness. We have discussed that notion earlier.

The Papists nevertheless maintain that this righteousness of works is not absolutely perfect and cannot of itself justify us before God; it receives its worth from the merit of Christ. They further claim that this evangelical righteousness is the condition on which we receive the benefits of Christ's righteousness—namely, the pardon of sins and acceptance with God. For those who acknowledge no other righteousness by which we are justified, the meaning remains the same: whether we say that, on the basis of this righteousness, we partake of Christ's benefits, or that it is Christ's righteousness that makes our righteousness acceptable to God. These questions will require further examination.

The third question in dispute asks what is required on our part for justification, assuming we must be made participants in the righteousness of Christ. Some insist that faith alone suffices. Others contend that both faith and works are required in the same way.

Our present focus is the second point proposed. This is the heart of the entire controversy over our justification before God. How this is resolved will determine the outcome of the other related questions.

Therefore I affirm: The righteousness of Christ — rendered complete by His obedience and His suffering for us — and imputed to believers as they are united to Him by His Spirit, is the righteousness by which they are justified before God. On this ground their sins are pardoned, and they acquire a right to the heavenly inheritance.

This statement sums up the doctrine we defend in this crucial article of evangelical truth. I express it in this form because it reflects the thesis defended by the learned Davenant and endorsed by the common doctrine of the Reformed churches. It is the shield of truth in the whole debate over justification. So long as it is preserved, the disputes among scholars over finer points need not disturb the conscience. It remains the only refuge for distressed consciences, where they may find rest and peace.

To confirm this assertion, I will undertake three tasks:

1. Reflect on what is necessary to explain it.

2. Address the chief general objections raised against it.

3. Demonstrate its truth by arguments and testimony drawn from Holy Scripture.

As for the first point—what is necessary to explain this assertion—we treated it at length earlier. I will only summarize the key matters briefly now.

The foundation of the imputation we assert is union. Many grounds and causes for this have been explained previously. My immediate focus here is the union by which the Lord Christ and believers are joined into one mystical person. This union is effected by the Holy Spirit, who dwells in Christ as the head of the church in all fullness and dwells in believers according to their measure, thereby making them members of His mystical body.

The existence of such a union between Christ and believers is the faith of the universal church and has been held in every age. Those who now appear to deny or question it either do not understand what they say or are influenced by those who deny the divine persons of the Son and of the Spirit. Given this union, reason will concede that the imputation we advocate is reasonable; at the very least, it supplies a singular basis that cannot be paralleled in any natural or political relation among men.

The nature of imputation has been fully discussed elsewhere; I refer the reader to those sections for a clearer understanding of the term.

What is imputed is the righteousness of Christ. In short, this comprises His whole obedience to God in all that He did and suffered for the church. That righteousness is imputed to believers and is their only righteousness before God for the justification of life.

If other expressions have been used in explaining this truth, and those expressions have given rise to disputes, I will not concern myself with them—even if they are true and defensible. I am defending the essence of the truth as I have stated it. Where that is accepted, I will not argue about methods of expression or the particular terms others have employed.

For example, some have said that "what Christ did and suffered is so imputed to us that we are judged and esteemed in the sight of God to have done or suffered it ourselves in Him." I will not enter into that controversy. Though it may admit of a sound interpretation and was used by some of the ancients, it has caused offence. The essence of the truth we advocate is better expressed otherwise. We do not assert that God judges or esteems that we ourselves did and suffered in our persons what Christ did and suffered; rather, we maintain that He did and suffered it in our stead, and on that ground He grants and bestows it to believers upon their faith for their justification before Him. The same may be said of many similar phrases.

With these points established, I will now consider the general objections raised against the imputation we advocate. I shall handle only the principal objections, for most others can be resolved by these. It would be endless to take up every possible objection that might be imagined.

We must keep some general considerations in view. The doctrine of justification is a part — indeed a significant part — of the mystery of the gospel. Therefore it is not surprising that common reason cannot easily comprehend it. True spiritual apprehension of such mysteries requires more. Unless we mean to renounce the gospel, we must admit that corrupted reason — and the carnal mind, apart from divine revelation — will oppose these truths and rise in enmity against them. Scripture affirms this (Romans 8:7; 1 Corinthians 2:14).

Consequently, the minds and inventions of men are remarkably fertile in framing objections to evangelical truths. They rarely lack an endless array of sophistical difficulties which they imagine to be unanswerable. If carnal reason is permitted to act freely and boldly against spiritual mysteries under the pretence of truth, it becomes subtle in its arguments and prolific in its inventions.

For instance, consider the endless sophisms of the Socinians against the doctrine of the Trinity. They take pride in these objections as if they were unanswerable. Under the cover of such objections they dismiss the force of the plainest testimonies of Scripture, testimonies that are multiplied on every occasion.

In like manner they treat the doctrine of Christ's satisfaction much as the Pelagians of old treated the doctrine of His grace. Therefore anyone who is easily disturbed by subtle or plausible objections to gospel mysteries — mysteries that are plainly revealed and sufficiently attested in Scripture — is unlikely to find much stability in his profession of faith.

Most objections raised against the truth we assert arise from a failure to understand properly the order of God's grace and our duty in complying with it, as noted above. These objections often set out opposing elements that, while apparently inconsistent, are in fact consistent and mutually supportive when seen in their proper context.

This becomes evident in the experience of true believers. Examples have already been given, and more will soon be presented. Considering these cases helps us see the origin and real weight of the objections.

All the objections against the truth we defend rest on supposed consequences that would follow from accepting it. This is the usual method for perpetuating controversies and making them endless.

In my observation, I have yet to meet anyone who, to make the alleged absurdity of those consequences seem stronger, has not framed the suppositions or the state of the question in a way that unfairly disadvantages those he opposes. I wonder why good men are not weary or ashamed of this tactic.

It is objected that "the imputation of the righteousness of Christ undermines all remission of sins on God's part." Socinus advances this argument in De Servatore, book 4, chapters 2-4, and others have used it as well.

This charge seems confident to those who think that without such imputation there could be no remission of sin. They insist that "he who has a righteousness imputed to him that is absolutely perfect, so as to be made his own, needs no pardon, has no sin that should be forgiven, nor can he ever need forgiveness."

Since this objection will recur in defending a later point, I will address it briefly here. Grotius replies that when we say Christ has procured for us two things—freedom from punishment and a reward—the ancient church attributed one to His satisfaction and the other to His merit.

He explains: "Satisfaction consists in the translation of sins (from us to Him); merit consists in the imputation of His most perfect obedience, performed for us, to us." In his view, the remission of sins and the imputation of righteousness are as consistent as Christ's satisfaction and merit; indeed, they are consistent.

Had we not been sinners, we would have had no need for the imputation of Christ's righteousness to make us righteous before God. Because we are sinners, the primary purpose for which that righteousness is imputed is the pardon of sin. Without pardon, we could not be made righteous by the imputation of the most perfect righteousness.

Thus these concepts are compatible: Christ's satisfaction is imputed for the pardon of sin, and Christ's obedience is imputed to make us righteous before God. Not only are they consistent, but neither alone is sufficient for our justification.

The same author and others argue that "the imputation of the righteousness of Christ undermines the necessity of repentance for sin in order to receive remission or pardon; indeed, it renders repentance altogether unnecessary." They press the point this way: If, by imputation, a person is already regarded as completely just before God, what need is there for repentance? If Christ satisfied for all sins on behalf of the elect, paid all our debts as our surety, and his righteousness is made ours before we repent, then repentance seems needless.

These arguments are developed at length in the work already mentioned.

We must remember that evangelical faith is required, in the order of nature, prior to our justification by the imputation of Christ's righteousness; this faith is also necessary for its continuance. Therefore whatever is necessary for justification is likewise required for believing. Among these requirements are sorrow for sin and repentance from it.

Whoever is truly convinced of sin—seeing its evil and guilt both because it violates the preceptive part of the holy law and because of its inevitable consequences, including the wrath and curse of God—cannot help but be troubled in mind for having fallen into sin. That state is accompanied by shame, fear, sorrow, and other distressing emotions. From this arises a resolution to abstain from sin in the future, with sincere efforts toward that end, and, time permitting, a reformation of life.

True repentance includes a sense of sin, sorrow for it, fear about it, abstinence from it, and reformation of life. This repentance is often called legal because its motives primarily arise from the law, though it also requires the temporary gospel faith described earlier. Because it typically produces effects such as confession, humiliation, and a change of life (as in Ahab and the Ninevites), it commonly precedes true saving faith and the justification that follows.

Thus the doctrine of the imputation of Christ's righteousness neither diminishes the necessity of this repentance nor makes it irrelevant; rather, it strengthens and gives effect to it. Without repentance, in the order of the gospel, one cannot obtain an interest in that imputation. The Old Testament frequently presents this kind of repentance as the means and condition for averting the judgments threatened for sin; it is true and sincere in its kind.

The Socinians, by contrast, do not require evangelical repentance for justification. They deny true evangelical repentance in its specifics and require only that which may precede faith in the natural order. On that basis their objection is baseless and merely a pretense.

Justifying faith inherently includes the whole principle of evangelical repentance, so it is impossible for someone to be a true believer without being truly penitent at the same time. That is why Scripture often conjoins the two as one simultaneous duty. Indeed, the gospel call to repentance is a call to faith that expresses itself through repentance.

The reason the call to repentance is linked to the forgiveness of sins (Acts 2:38) is that the promise proposed becomes the object of faith (verse 39). The thoughts and feelings a person has about sin—sorrow for it and resolution to turn from it—when enlivened and made evangelical by the introduction of faith, become evangelical repentance. Thus faith cannot exist without repentance.

Although the first act of faith regarding justification focuses on God's grace in Christ and the way of salvation he proposes, this act does not, and cannot, precede the expressions of self-abhorrence, godly sorrow, and a universal turning from sin to God. Faith virtually and fundamentally contains all these elements. Yet evangelical repentance is not the condition for justification in the sense that it directly influences or merits it; we are not said to be justified by repentance, nor does repentance have the same proper object as justification, nor is it the immediate act of giving glory to God for his wisdom and grace in Christ Jesus. Still, repentance is essential for any true sense or comfort of forgiveness in the soul.

These truths appear clearly in the divine method of our justification, in the order of duty prescribed by the gospel, and in the experience of believers. Considering the necessity of legal repentance before believing, the sanctification of the affections exercised there by faith (which makes them evangelical), and the nature of faith as including a principle of universal conversion to God—especially repentance motivated primarily by love for God and for Jesus Christ, together with the grace communicated from that love—the necessity of true repentance is firmly established on its proper foundation.

On the objection about Christ's suffering on behalf of the elect, I do not know whether anyone has previously answered it, and I will not quarrel about the terms. He suffered in their stead, a point affirmed by many writers, ancient and modern. In his suffering he bore the person of the church.

As I have stated, Christ and believers constitute one mystical person—the one living body, head and members. To deny this is to undermine the church and its faith. Hence what he did and suffered is imputed to them. It is acknowledged that, as the covenant's surety, he paid our debts and answered for our faults, and that his righteousness is truly communicated to us.

"Why, then," some ask, "is there any need for repentance? Everything has already been accomplished for us." But why accept part of the gospel and reject another? Was it not God's freedom to appoint the method and order by which these blessings are communicated?

According to the design of his wisdom and grace, two things were necessary:

1. That the righteousness of Christ should be communicated to us and made ours so that he himself might be glorified in it—as he has arranged all things in this economy for "the praise of the glory of His grace" (Eph. 1:6). This was to be done through faith on our part. It could be no other way, for the faith by which we are justified is our acknowledgement of God's glory in his wisdom, grace, and love. Whatever does this is faith; nothing else can be.

2. Furthermore, since our nature was so corrupted and depraved that, if it remained in that state, it could not participate in the righteousness of Christ or benefit from it for God's glory and our good, it was also necessary that our nature be renewed and changed. Unless this renewal occurred, the purpose of God in the mediation of Christ—namely, our complete recovery to himself—could not be achieved.

Therefore, as faith in its formal consideration was necessary to the first purpose—namely, to give glory to God—it was also necessary that this faith be accompanied by, and contain within itself, the seeds of all the other graces that constitute the divine nature, of which we are to become partakers. Thus not only the act of communicating the righteousness of Christ to us, but also the way, manner, and means of it depend on God's sovereign order and arrangement.

Accordingly, although Christ made satisfaction to the justice of God for all the sins of the church, and did so as a common person (for no one in their right mind can deny that a mediator and surety is, in some sense, a common person), and although he paid all our debts, the particular interest of this or that individual in what he did and suffered depends on the way, means, and order that God has designed for that purpose. This, and this alone, establishes the true necessity of all the duties required of us, together with their order and ends.

It is objected that "the imputation of the righteousness of Christ, which we defend, undermines the necessity of faith itself." This is indeed a serious claim. "Aliquid adhærebit" is the aim of all these objections; yet those who make this claim have reason to defend themselves.

They argue: On this assumption, the righteousness of Christ is ours before we believe; for Christ satisfied for all our sins as if we had satisfied for them ourselves. Therefore, one who is considered to have satisfied for all his sins in his own person is acquitted from them all and deemed just, whether he believes or not; thus there is no reason for him to be required to believe.

If the righteousness of Christ is truly ours because, in God's judgment, we are considered to have accomplished it in him, then it is ours before we believe. If it is not, then it is clear that this righteousness can never be made ours through believing; only the fruits and effects of it may be contingent upon our believing, through which we may partake of them. Moreover, if Christ made any such satisfaction for us as is claimed, it is indeed ours without any further imputation; for, having been performed for us and in our stead, it would be the highest injustice not to have us regarded as pardoned and acquitted without any further imputation on God's part or faith on ours.

I have transcribed these points from Socinus, De Servatore, book 4, chapters 2–5; I would not have done so had I not found others who have previously addressed this issue, albeit for a different purpose. He concludes with a confidence that others seem to have learned from him, stating to his opponent, "Your view, and that of your followers, is so foul and abominable that I cannot believe a more pestilential error has arisen among mankind." He speaks of the satisfaction of Christ and its imputation to believers.

Indeed, his cunning wit was fertile in inventing objections against all the mysteries of the gospel. He was not bound by any of them, so as to contradict himself regarding any other of them; for, denying the deity of Christ, his satisfaction, sacrifice, merit, righteousness, and undermining the entire nature of his mediation, nothing stood in his way to oppose. However, I am somewhat surprised that others can utilize his inventions in this regard. If they considered their proper implications, they would find them utterly destructive of what they claim to support.

This is true in the present objection against the imputation of the righteousness of Christ. If it held any weight—which it does not—it would serve to prove that the satisfaction of Christ was impossible; and that was his intention. But this can be easily addressed.

I respond, first, in general, that the entire fallacy of this objection lies in opposing one part of the design and method of God's grace in this mystery of our justification to another; or in taking one part of it to represent the whole, which, in terms of efficacy and perfection, depends on something else. We warned the reader of this in our previous discussions.

The whole argument is based on the assumption that the satisfaction of Christ, if it exists, must have its full effect without our believing, which contradicts the entire declaration of God's will in the gospel. However, I will primarily address those who utilize this objection yet do not deny the satisfaction of Christ.

I assert that when the Lord Christ died for us and offered himself as a propitiatory sacrifice, "And the Lord has laid on Him the iniquity of us all" (Isa. 53:6); and he then "who Himself bore our sins in His own body on the tree" (1 Pet. 2:24). He suffered in our place and made full satisfaction for all our sins; for he "has appeared to put away sin by the sacrifice of Himself" (Heb. 9:26); and "For by one offering He has perfected forever those who are being sanctified" (Heb. 10:14).

He whose sins were not actually and absolutely satisfied for in that one offering of Christ shall never have them expiated for eternity; for "knowing that Christ, having been raised from the dead, dies no more" (Rom. 6:9), and "there is no longer an offering for sin" (Heb. 10:18). The repetition of a sacrifice for sin, which would require the crucifying of Christ afresh, undermines the foundation of the Christian faith.

Despite this full and complete satisfaction once made for the sins of the world that will be saved, all men continue to be born by nature as "children of wrath." While they do not believe, "the wrath of God abides on them" (John 3:36); that is, they are subject to and under the curse of the law.

Therefore, based solely on the making of that satisfaction, no one for whom it was made in the design of God can be said to have suffered in Christ, nor to have an interest in his satisfaction, nor can they in any way be made partakers of it prior to another act of God in its imputation to them. This satisfaction is only one part of God's purpose of grace regarding our justification by the blood of Christ—namely, that he should make satisfaction for our sins—and it must not be separated from what also pertains to it in the same purpose of God.

Therefore, from the acknowledgment of the satisfaction of Christ no argument can be drawn to negate the necessity of a consequential act of its imputation to us; nor, consequently, of our faith in believing and receiving it, which is no less an appointment of God than the requirement for Christ to make that satisfaction.

Thus, what the Lord Christ paid for us is as truly paid as if we had paid it ourselves. As stated in Psalm 69:5, "O God, You know my foolishness; And my sins are not hidden from You." He did not rob God of his glory;

rather, what was done in that regard by us, he returned to him. What he endured and suffered, he did so in our place.

However, the act of God in laying our sins on Christ did not convey any actual right or title to us regarding what he did and suffered. They are not immediately ours by that act; because God has appointed something else, not only prior to that act but also as the means of it, for his own glory. These matters, both in their existence and order, depend on the free ordination of God.

Still, it cannot be said that this satisfaction was made for us under a condition that would absolutely suspend the outcome and render it uncertain whether it would ever be for us or not. Such a condition may be justifiable in monetary transactions. A person may pay a large sum of money for another's discharge under a condition that may never be fulfilled; if the condition fails, his money may and should be returned to him, as he has suffered no injury or loss. However, in the case of penal suffering for crimes and sins, there can be no just constitution that would make the outcome and efficacy depend on a condition that is absolutely uncertain and may not come to pass or be fulfilled; for if the condition fails, no recompense can be made to the one who has suffered. Therefore, the means by which the satisfaction of Christ is applied to those for whom it was made is certain and steadfast in the purpose of God.

God has appointed that there shall be an immediate foundation for the imputation of the satisfaction and righteousness of Christ to us. This allows us to be said to have done and suffered in Him what He did and suffered in our place, through the grant, donation, and imputation of it to us. This is what we contend for: that we may have an interest in it, and that it may be made ours. This is our actual union into one mystical person with Him by faith. The necessity of faith originally depends on this.

If we also consider the necessity of faith in relation to the special glory of God that He intends to exalt in our justification by Christ, as well as to all the purposes of our obedience to God and the renewal of our natures into His image, its position is sufficiently secured against all objections. Our actual interest in the satisfaction of Christ depends on our actual incorporation into His mystical body by faith, according to God's appointment.

It is objected, "If the righteousness of Christ is made ours, we may be said to be saviors of the world, as He was, or to save others, as He did; for He was so and did so by His righteousness, and no otherwise." This objection is of the same nature as those previously mentioned — a mere sophistical argument.

The righteousness of Christ is not infused into us so as to become inherently and subjectively ours as it was in Him, which would be necessary for the effect of saving others. Whatever we may do, or be said to do, with respect to others by virtue of any power or quality inherent in ourselves, we cannot do anything for others based solely on what is imputed to us for our own benefit. For any righteousness of ours to benefit another, it is absolutely necessary that it be produced by ourselves.

Even if the righteousness of Christ could be infused into us and made inherently ours, we still could not be considered saviors of others. Our individual nature is not "subjectum capax," that is, capable of receiving and retaining a righteousness useful and effective for that purpose. That capacity was granted to human nature in Christ by the hypostatic union, and in no other way.

The righteousness of Christ, as performed in human nature, would not have sufficed for the justification and salvation of the church had it not been the righteousness of His person, who is both God and man; for "which He purchased with His own blood."

The imputation of Christ's righteousness to us is determined by the will of God and by His purpose in making that imputation. God's purpose is that this righteousness should be the righteousness of those to whom it is imputed, and nothing else.

We do not claim that the righteousness of Christ, provided for the whole church, is indiscriminately imputed to every believer apart from God's will. Rather, Christ's satisfaction for each believer is imputed to that person according to God's will — not merely with respect to broad or general purposes, but according to each individual's particular interest. Every believer receives his own portion of this bread of life, and all are justified by the same righteousness.

The apostle teaches, as we will show later, that just as Adam's actual sin is imputed to us for condemnation, so the obedience of Christ is imputed to us for justification and life. Yet Adam's sin is not imputed to anyone in such a way that Adam thereby becomes the direct cause of sin and condemnation in every other person. Rather, by his sin he rendered himself guilty before God, and that guilt is reckoned to his posterity.

The same principle holds in the opposite direction. Just as we are made guilty by Adam's actual sin — guilt that is not inherent in us but imputed to us — we are made righteous by the righteousness of Christ, which likewise is not inherent in us but is imputed to us. It is imputed to us because He was righteous in it, not for Himself, but for us.

It has been argued that if we insist on the personal imputation of what Christ did to every believer — if we say that any believer is personally righteous in the very individual acts of Christ's righteousness — many absurdities would follow. Yet when opponents try to discredit a view by pointing to supposed absurd consequences, they often misstate the view to make it seem absurd. Even the most candid and worthy disputants can fall into this in the heat of debate.

I fear that has happened here. When it comes to the phrase "personal imputation," I do not fully understand how the term is being used. All imputation is to a person and involves the person; yet I hesitate to call it a personal imputation in the sense that some suggest. If an imputation is proposed that does not properly pertain to persons — specifically, to all believers — its exact nature has not, as far as I can see, been clearly defined.

I know of no one who has explicitly said that "every believer should be personally righteous in the very individual acts of Christ's righteousness." I have neither read nor heard such a claim clearly made. Some may have insinuated it, but I will not defend that position; it effectively assumes that Christ performed every individual act required of us and that those acts are made inherently our own — both false and impossible.

What is truly meant by this imputation is that what the Lord Christ did and suffered as mediator and surety of the covenant — in response to the law, for them and in their stead — is imputed to each believer for the justification of life. That imputation suffices for justification without adopting those impossible assumptions.

1. From the dignity of the person who rendered this obedience, which made it both satisfactory and meritorious, and therefore imputable to many.

2. From the nature of the obedience itself: it was a perfect compliance with the law, fulfilling and satisfying all its demands. On the basis of God's sovereign act — by which a public representative of the whole church was appointed to answer the law — this obedience becomes the

foundation for His righteousness being counted to them and being wholly sufficient for their justification.

3. From God's constitution that what Christ did and suffered as our public person and surety should be reckoned to us as if we had done it ourselves. Just as Adam, as a public person representing his entire posterity, had his sin imputed to all his offspring, so Christ's obedience, as public person, is imputed to believers.

Bellarmine himself acknowledges this point: "We sinned in the first man when he sinned, and his transgression was also our transgression. For we would not truly be constituted sinners by Adam's disobedience unless his disobedience were also our disobedience," De Amiss. Grat. et Stat. Peccat., lib. v. cap. 18. He further says that Adam's actual sin is imputed to us as if we had all committed that sin—indeed, as if we had broken the whole law of God. The apostle uses this very illustration to explain the imputation of Christ's righteousness to believers, and it can be criticized for absurdity just as easily as other analogies.

We do not mean that God counts us to have done those very acts and endured those very penalties that the Lord Christ did and endured; to say that would undermine the idea of imputation. Rather, Christ's acts and sufferings are imputed to believers for the justification of life, as if they had been done by the believers themselves. His righteousness, as a public person, is made theirs by imputation—just as Adam's sin, in his public person, is reckoned to all his posterity by imputation.

None of the supposed absurdities follow from this. It does not mean that Christ, in His own person, performed every individual act we are required to perform in our circumstances. Nor was there any need for Him to do so. As I have shown, the imputation is founded on other grounds.

Moreover, it does not follow that every saved person's righteousness before God is numerically identical to Christ's in His public capacity as mediator. That objection contradicts itself by affirming that it was His righteousness—the righteousness of the God-man—and therefore has a special relation to His person. It is the same righteousness that Christ worked or achieved in His public capacity, but there is an important difference in how it is regarded: as His absolutely and as made ours.

It was formally inherent in Him; it is only materially imputed to us. It was actively His; it is passively ours. It was accomplished in the person of the God-man for the whole church; it is imputed to each individual believer for his own interest. Adam's sin, as imputed to us, is not merely the sin of a representative, though it proceeds from him; rather, it is treated as the particular sin of each one of us. I will address this objection further when it arises later.

It does not follow from this assumption that we must be considered to have done what was done long before we were capable of doing anything. What is done for us and in our stead, before we exist in any such capacity, may be imputed to us—just as Adam's sin is imputed. In a sense, therefore, men may be said to have done what was done for them and in their name before their actual existence. There is no absurdity in that.

As for the additional point that Christ did not do or suffer the exact "idem" that we were obliged to do: while He did what the law required and suffered what the law threatened the disobedient, which covers all that we are obliged to do, this will not be easily proven by opponents, nor will objections be quickly answered. Scripture plainly affirms that Christ sustained the role of a surety, and that He is the surety of the new covenant cannot be denied. I have already shown that sureties may exist in both criminal and civil cases.

What is said about the uniqueness of Christ's obedience as mediator only shows that His righteousness, as formally and inherently His, was peculiar to Himself. The attributes that arise from its relation to His person, insofar as it was inherent in Him, are not communicable to those to whom it is imputed.

Moreover, it is argued: "If we accept the supposed imputation of the righteousness of Christ, it will follow that every believer is justified by the works of the law; for the obedience of Christ was a legal righteousness, and if that is imputed to us, then we are justified by the law, which contradicts many clear testimonies of Scripture."

1. I find nothing more common in the writings of some learned men than the assertion that the righteousness of Christ is our legal righteousness. Still, I presume they can free themselves from this objection.

2. If this follows in the true sense of being justified by the law or its works, which is denied in Scripture, it is unfortunate for those who see no other means by which we can be freed from the obligation to be justified by the law than through this imputation of the righteousness of Christ.

3. Scripture states that "Therefore by the deeds of the law no flesh will be justified," and it likewise affirms, "Do we then make void the law through faith? Certainly not! On the contrary, we establish the law." It also says "that the righteous requirement of the law might be fulfilled in us who do not walk according to the flesh but according to the Spirit." Christ declared, "Do not think that I came to destroy the Law or the Prophets. I did not come to destroy but to fulfill." And Scripture teaches, "For Christ is the end of the law for righteousness to everyone who believes." We will prove later that the law must be fulfilled; otherwise we cannot be justified.

4. We are not justified by the law or its works in the only sense of that proposition in Scripture; it is not safe to create new meanings or interpretations of it. The meaning in Scripture is that only "but the doers of the law will be justified" (Romans 2:13); and that "The man who does those things shall live by them" (Romans 10:5) — namely, in his own person, through personal duty, which is all the law requires. However, if we, who have not fulfilled the law through inherent personal obedience, are justified by the imputation of the righteousness of Christ to us, then we are justified by Christ, and not by the law.

However, it is argued that this perspective does not provide relief. If Christ's obedience is imputed to us in such a way that God considers us to have done what Christ did, then we are justified by the law as if we had personally performed an unsinning obedience to it. I confess I cannot comprehend this reasoning. The nature of this imputation is presented here, as it has been previously, in a manner we cannot accept, and from it the inference is drawn that, in my opinion, does not logically follow.

For even if we grant the imputation of another's righteousness to us, regardless of its nature, all justification by the law and its works, as understood in Scripture, is forever eliminated. Accepting imputation removes all power from the law to justify, for it can justify no one except on the basis of a righteousness that is originally and inherently their own: "The man who does those things shall live by them." If the righteousness that is imputed serves as the foundation of our justification and is made ours through that imputation, then that justification is of grace, not of the law.

Moreover, I am not aware of anyone who claims that God considers us to have personally done what Christ did. Such a notion would imply — falsely — that God judges us in our own persons as having performed acts we never did. What Christ did for us and in our stead is imputed and communicated to us as we become one mystical person with Him through faith, and it is on this basis that we are justified. This completely undermines all justification by the law or its works, even though the law is established, fulfilled, and accomplished so that we may be justified.

Furthermore, no one, when considering the imputation of Christ's righteousness as it should be understood, can claim to merit their own salvation. Satisfaction and merit are attributes of Christ's righteousness that belong inherently to His own person and cannot be transferred to another. Therefore, when it is imputed to individual believers, it does not carry the properties that belong solely to its existence in the person of the Son of God. This has been addressed previously, along with much of what is necessary to reiterate here.

I have noted these objections because the responses to them help explain the truth further. I will now support that explanation with arguments and testimonies from Scripture.

11. Our Own Righteousness Cannot Justify

There is a justification of convinced sinners upon their belief. On this basis their sins are pardoned, their persons accepted by God, and they are granted a right to the heavenly inheritance. This state is immediately conferred upon them when they put their faith in Jesus Christ. It is a state of actual peace with God. I take these points for granted at present, as they form the foundation of everything I will argue in this discussion.

I mention this because some deny any real, actual justification of sinners upon their belief in this life. They argue that justification is merely a general, conditional sentence declared in the gospel whose execution is postponed until the day of judgment. They say that while people are in this world, since the entire condition is not fulfilled, they cannot partake in it or be actually and absolutely justified. Consequently, they conclude there is no real state of assured rest and peace with God through Jesus Christ for anyone in this life. I will not dispute this point now, since it seems to undermine the entire gospel, the grace of our Lord Jesus Christ, and all the comfort of believers; I hope we are not yet called to contend over it.

Our inquiry is how convinced sinners obtain the remission of sins, acceptance with God, and a right to eternal life upon their belief. If this can only be achieved through the imputation of Christ's righteousness, then they are justified in God's sight solely by that means. This assertion rests on the premise that some righteousness is required for the justification of any person. When God justifies someone, He declares them acquitted of all charges and regards them as righteous in His sight; this must be based on a righteousness that allows for such acquittal, for God's judgment is according to truth.

We have sufficiently demonstrated this in the legal procedure pictured in Scripture concerning the justification of a believing sinner. If there is no righteousness by which we may be justified except that of Christ imputed to us, then we must be justified by it or not at all. If any other righteousness exists, it must be our own — inherent in us and produced by us. The two kinds of righteousness — our own and Christ's — divide the entire nature of righteousness with respect to the justification we seek.

I will first prove that there is no inherent righteousness — no righteousness of our own — by which we may be justified before God. I will do this first by adducing explicit testimonies from Scripture and then by considering the matter itself. I should state up front that I will not treat our own righteousness in isolation but only in relation to the satisfaction and merit of Christ.

Many will concede that our inherent righteousness is insufficient to justify us before God. Some, however, may argue that it acquires value from the merit of Christ and is therefore accepted as worthy of eternal life. We will acknowledge any worth that can reasonably be attributed to this righteousness because of its connection to Christ's merit, and then show why that is not enough to establish it as a basis for justification.

People from different backgrounds assign different roles to our own righteousness in the matter of justification, and there is no single consensus among them. I will therefore attempt to address the range of those views in the arguments that follow.

My aim is to show that our own righteousness cannot play such a role in justification before God as to diminish Christ's righteousness as the sole ground of our acceptance.

To support this, we will present several scriptural testimonies. Psalm 130:3-4 says, "If You, Lord, should mark iniquities, O Lord, who could stand? But there is forgiveness with You, That You may be feared." This passage asks how a person may be justified before God—how they may stand in His presence and be accepted by Him. Psalm 1:5 declares, "Therefore the ungodly shall not stand in the judgment," which means they will not be acquitted at their trial.

At first glance one might think to plead one's own obedience as the basis for justification, since that is what the law requires and what conscience seems to demand. But the psalmist makes it clear that no one can successfully plead justification on the basis of their own obedience, because even the best obedience of the best people contains iniquities against the Lord their God.

If men are brought to trial before God to determine whether they will be justified or condemned, those iniquities must be taken into account. Therefore no one can "stand" or be "justified" on the footing of their own works. The wisest and safest course, then, is to abandon that plea and not rely on our own obedience, lest our sins be discovered and taken into account. No one can offer a valid reason on their own behalf to prevent this; if they are considered, even the best of men will be condemned, as the psalmist indicates.

Two things are required for a sinner to stand in judgment:

1. That their iniquities are not observed; for if they are, they are lost forever.

2. That a righteousness is produced and pleaded which can withstand the trial; for justification must rest on a justifying righteousness.

Regarding the first requirement, the psalmist tells us it must be by pardon or forgiveness. Psalm 130:4 says, "But there is forgiveness with You, That You may be feared," and that is our only relief against the condemning sentence of the law concerning our iniquities. This forgiveness comes through the blood of Christ, for Ephesians 1:7 says, "In Him we have redemption through His blood, the forgiveness of sins," which shows the source of our pardon.

The second requirement cannot be met by our own obedience because of our iniquities. Therefore the psalmist directs us to Psalm 71:16: "I will go in the strength of the Lord God; I will make mention of Your righteousness, of Yours only." The righteousness of God, not our own, is the only plea we should present in this case.

If no person can stand trial before God on the basis of their own obedience—because their personal iniquities would be taken into account—and if our only plea in such a case is the righteousness of God alone, then there is no personal, inherent righteousness in any believer by which they may be justified. That is the point that must be proven.

This is further confirmed by the same psalmist in Psalm 143:2: "Do not enter into judgment with Your servant, For in Your sight no one living is righteous." This testimony merits special attention because it goes back to the law (see Exodus 34:7) and is reiterated in the gospel, being cited by the apostle for the same purpose in Romans 3:20 and Galatians 2:16.

The individual who insists on this plea before God identifies himself as His servant: "Do not enter into judgment with Your servant." This indicates he is someone who loves God, fears Him, and offers sincere obedience. He is not a hypocrite, nor an unbeliever, nor an unregenerate person who has performed only legal works—those required by the law and done solely in the strength of the law. Such works are universally acknowledged to be excluded from justification, and many suppose they are the only ones that should be excluded.

David, however, was not only converted and a true believer, but filled with the Spirit of God and aided by special grace in his obedience. He bore the testimony of sincerity: he was "a man after My own heart." He had this witness in his own conscience about his integrity, uprightness, and personal righteousness. He affirms them frequently, appeals to God concerning their truth, and uses them as grounds for judgment between himself and his adversaries. Thus we have the example of a sincere and eminent believer who excelled in inherent, personal righteousness.

This person, in such circumstances, testifies both to God and in his own conscience about the sincerity and even the eminence of his obedience. He considers how he may "stand before God" and "be justified in His sight." Why, then, does he not plead his own merits—claiming that, if not "ex condigno," at least "ex congruo," he deserves to be acquitted and justified? He leaves that plea to those who would come after him, who would justify themselves and despise others.

But even if he lacked such confidence in the merit of his works as some now possess, why does he not boldly enter into judgment with God and test whether he should be justified by pleading that he has fulfilled the conditions of the new covenant—the everlasting covenant God made with him, ordered in all things, and sure? Given the procurement of that covenant and the terms established by Christ (assuming the virtue of that purchase extends to the Old Testament), this was all that would have been required of him.

Is it not strange that he seems to see no necessity for personal holiness and righteousness, especially when he should have been relying on them most? At the very least, he might have pleaded his faith as his own duty and work, to be imputed to him for righteousness. However, whatever the reason, he rejects all these pleas and completely shrinks from a trial based on them. "…he who hears My word and believes in Him who sent Me has everlasting life, and shall not come into judgment," (John 5:24) — he trusts the promise that the believer "shall not come into judgment."

If this holy person renounces all considerations of his personal, inherent righteousness in every form and will not insist upon it under any pretense or in any place as a basis for his justification before God, we can safely conclude there is no such righteousness in anyone by which they may be justified.

If people would abandon the shadows and cloaks under which they conceal themselves in argument—if they would relinquish the pretenses and distinctions that lead them to deceive themselves and others, and plainly state what plea they dare make in the presence of God based on their own righteousness and obedience for justification— they would make their true beliefs clearer.

There is, I admit, one who speaks with some confidence on this matter: Vasquez the Jesuit, in 1, 2, disp. 204, cap. 4: "Inherent righteousness so renders the soul just and holy, and consequently a daughter of God, that by this very fact it makes her worthy of eternal glory; indeed, God Himself cannot make such a just person unworthy of eternal blessedness." Is it not tragic that David should reveal such ignorance regarding the value of his inherent righteousness and exhibit such timidity concerning his trial before God, while Vasquez claims God

Himself could not order it otherwise than that such a person was, and must be, worthy of eternal blessedness?

The reason the psalmist says he will not put the matter to the test — whether he should be acquitted or justified based on his own obedience — is this general principle: "For in Your sight no one living is righteous." This must be understood either absolutely or with respect to some specific means or cause of justification.

If it is taken absolutely, then the work of justification would cease entirely and there would be no such thing as justification before God. That would contradict the whole Scripture and undermine the gospel. Therefore, the declaration must be understood as referring to our own obedience and works.

He does not pray absolutely that God "Do not enter into judgment with Your servant," for that would mean relinquishing God's governance of the world. Rather, he asks that God not enter into judgment with him on the basis of his own duties and obedience. If these duties and this obedience met, in any sense, what is required of us as righteousness for justification, there would be no reason for him to shrink from a trial based on them.

Yet, since the Holy Spirit positively affirms that "no one living is righteous in Your sight" by or based on his own works or obedience, it astonishes me that some interpret the apostle James as if he were asserting the exact opposite — that we are justified in the sight of God by our own works — when he actually does not say that.

Therefore, this is an eternal rule of truth: by or based on his own obedience, no man living can be justified in the sight of God. One might argue: "If God enters into judgment with anyone based on their own obedience according to the law, then indeed none can be justified before Him; but if God judges according to the gospel and the terms of the new covenant, men may be justified based on their own duties, works, and obedience."

That objection will be considered below.

In response:

1. The negative assertion is general and unlimited—that "no one living is righteous" (based on his own works or obedience) "in Your sight." To try to limit it to this or that method of judgment is not to distinguish but to contradict the Holy Spirit.

2. The judgment intended concerns justification alone, as the words make clear. But there is no judgment of our works or obedience concerning righteousness and justification except by the proper rule and measure of them, which is the law. If our works will not endure the trial by the law, they will not endure any trial regarding righteousness and justification in the sight of God.

3. On this assumption, the prayer and plea of the psalmist run as follows: "O Lord, do not enter into judgment with Your servant based on the law; rather, enter into judgment with me regarding my own works and obedience according to the rule of the gospel." He gives this reason: "For in Your sight no one living is righteous," which is clearly far from his intention.

4. The judgment of God for justification according to the gospel does not proceed from our works of obedience, but from the righteousness of Christ and our interest in that righteousness by faith. This is too evident to be modestly denied.

Despite this exception, we argue: if the most holy of God's servants, after a course of sincere, fruitful obedience—testified to by God Himself and witnessed in their own consciences—while having the greatest evidence of their sincerity and that they are indeed the servants of God, renounce all thoughts of a righteousness by which they might be justified before God, then there is no such righteousness in anyone. It is the righteousness of Christ alone, imputed to us, on which we are justified. That they do so, and ought to do so, is plainly affirmed by the general rule laid down here: in the sight of God, no man living shall be justified.

I have no doubt that many learned individuals, after all their arguments for the role of personal righteousness and works in our justification before God, ultimately adopt the method of the psalmist. They cry, as the prophet Daniel does in the name of the church, "We do not present our supplications before You because of our righteous deeds, but because of Your great mercies" (Daniel 9:18). Therefore Job, after a lengthy and earnest defense of his faith, integrity, and personal righteousness—wherein he justified himself against the accusations of Satan and men—when called to plead his case before God and to declare on what grounds he expected to be justified, renounces all his previous pleas and turns to the same plea as the psalmist (Job 40:4; 42:6).

It is true that in particular cases, and for specific purposes in God's providence, a person may plead their own integrity and obedience before God. This was the case with Hezekiah when he prayed for the extension of his life, as seen in Isaiah 38:3: "Remember now, O Lord, I pray, how I have walked before You in truth and with a loyal heart, and have done what is good in Your sight." This can be done with respect to temporal deliverance or any other specific end that concerns the glory of God, as was greatly the case in the sparing of Hezekiah's life at that time. Having zealously and diligently reformed religion and restored the true worship of God, cutting him off in the midst of his days would have led the idolatrous multitude to view him as dying under a sign of divine displeasure. However, no one has ever made this plea before God for the absolute justification of their person. Similarly,

Nehemiah, in the significant contest regarding the worship of God and the service of his house, pleads the remembrance of his actions before God in justification against his adversaries, but ultimately resolves his personal acceptance with God into pardoning mercy: "and spare me according to the greatness of Your mercy!" (Nehemiah 13:22).

Another testimony that supports this purpose is found in the prophet Isaiah, who speaks in the name of the church in Isaiah 64:6: "We are all like an unclean thing, and all our righteousnesses are like filthy rags." While the prophet makes a profound confession of the sins of the people, he also identifies himself with them and asserts their special interest as those whom God has adopted — declaring that God was their Father and they were His people (Isaiah 63:16; 64:8-9). The righteousness of all who are children of God is of the same kind, even if they may differ in degrees; while some may be more righteous than others, it is described in such a way that we cannot justly expect justification in the sight of God based on it. However, since the nature of our inherent righteousness pertains to the second way of confirming our current argument, I will not further elaborate on this testimony here.

Many other testimonies I will omit — namely, those in which the saints of God, or the church, humbly acknowledge and confess their own sins, turning to the mercy and grace of God alone as dispensed through the mediation and blood of Christ. Also omitted are those in which God promises to pardon and blot out our iniquities for His own sake, for His name's sake — to bless the people not for any good in them, nor for their righteousness or works, which He excludes from having any influence on His grace toward them. Furthermore, there are passages in which God expresses His delight in those who hope in His mercy, trusting in His name, turning to Him as their only refuge, and pronouncing accursed those who trust in anything else or glory in themselves. Such testimonies contain singular promises for those who turn to God as fatherless, hopeless, and lost in themselves.

There are numerous testimonies that support this purpose, and they clearly show that even the best of God's saints do not possess a righteousness of their own on which they can be justified before God in any sense. In the cited passages they renounce any such righteousness of their own—including all that is within them and all that they have done or can do—and they turn to grace and mercy alone. As established, God exercises grace in the justification of anyone with respect to a righteousness that He declares makes them righteous and accepted before Him. This righteousness is not inherent in us but is imputed to us.

The essence of our inquiry into justification lies here. All other discussions about qualifications, conditions, causes, or any interest in our own works and obedience regarding justification before God are merely the speculations of the comfortable. The conscience of a convicted sinner, standing before God, reduces everything to this one point: will he trust in his own personal, inherent righteousness, or will he, in a complete renunciation of it, turn to the grace of God and the righteousness of Christ alone? In other matters he is not concerned. Regardless of how others describe his own righteousness—whether they call it meritorious or merely evangelical, non-legal, or a fulfillment of the new covenant's condition—it will be difficult for him to find confidence in it regarding justification before God without being misled in the end.

The second part of the current argument focuses on the nature of personal, inherent righteousness—what it is, what it consists of, and its role in our justification. It is important to note that we acknowledge an inherent righteousness in all believers, as previously stated: "For the fruit of the Spirit is in all goodness, righteousness, and truth" (Ephesians 5:9). "And having been set free from sin, you became slaves of righteousness" (Romans 6:18). It is our duty to "pursue righteousness, godliness, faith, love, patience, gentleness" (1 Timothy

6:11). Although righteousness is often understood as a specific grace or duty distinct from other graces and duties, we recognize that it can also refer to the entirety of our obedience before God. The term is used in Scripture where our own righteousness is contrasted with the righteousness of God.

This righteousness can be either habitual or actual. There is a habitual righteousness inherent in believers, as they have "and that you put on the new man which was created according to God, in true righteousness and holiness" (Ephesians 4:24); they are "For we are His workmanship, created in Christ Jesus for good works" (Ephesians 2:10). Actual righteousness consists of the good works to which we are created, or the fruits of righteousness that bring glory to God through Jesus Christ.

Regarding this righteousness, note the following:

1. Scripture says people are considered just or righteous by it, but it nowhere says anyone is justified by it before God.

2. It is not ascribed to, or found in, anyone except those who are actually justified in the prior order of nature.

This doctrine is held consistently across the Reformed churches and by its theologians. It is a gross misrepresentation to claim otherwise of those who hold to the imputation of Christ's righteousness for our justification before God. Bellarmine asserts that no Protestant writers acknowledge inherent righteousness except Bucer and Chemnitius. In fact, none of them deny the concept itself or its necessity. Some allowance may be made for the way they sometimes expressed themselves, since they always carefully distinguished between inherent holiness and the righteousness by which we are justified.

Yet one critic says that even if we affirmed it a hundred times, he would scarcely believe us. That is harsh. Though he speaks of one person, the charge applies equally to all who uphold the imputation of Christ's righteousness, which he denies. This group comprises the majority of Protestant theologians, and he portrays them as either so foolish as not to understand their own words or so dishonest as to say one thing and believe another.

He offers several reasons to support his criticism. First, he argues that inherent righteousness can only be said to be ours because it makes us righteous—that is, because it is the condition of our justification required by the new covenant. If this is denied, he says, then all inherent righteousness is denied.

But how is that proven? What if someone maintains that every believer is inherently righteous, yet this inherent righteousness is not the condition of their justification but a consequence of it? How can the opposite be established?

Scripture does affirm that there is such inherent righteousness in all believers while also declaring that we are justified before God by faith without works. Therefore, to assert that inherent righteousness is the condition of our justification and so precedes it contradicts the apostle's statement: "But to him who does not work but believes on Him who justifies the ungodly, his faith is accounted for righteousness" (Romans 4:5).

Furthermore, it is not a condition of the covenant itself—the thing upon which the entire grace of the covenant depends. As habitual righteousness, in which the primary sense of being called righteous is taken, it is a grace given within the covenant and therefore not a condition of it (Jeremiah 31:33; 32:39; Ezekiel 36:25–27). If, however, one means by it merely the actual exercise of what is required of all included in the covenant to achieve its full ends, we agree; but that does not make it the condition of our justification.

It is also argued that all righteousness belongs to a law and a rule by which it is judged—so that the righteous person is he who has done what that law requires. First, this is not how Scripture speaks of our justification before God, which is the specific point under consideration. We do not present a personal righteousness of our own that conforms to the law by which we are judged; to claim that is to contradict the gospel and to undermine the grace of God in Jesus Christ.

Second, it is admitted that all righteousness pertains to some law as its rule, including the moral law, which is the sole, eternal, and unchangeable standard of righteousness. If a supposed righteousness does not essentially conform to that law, it is not true righteousness. Yet it does conform: insofar as it is habitual, it consists in the renewal of God's image, in which that law is written on our hearts; and all actual duties arising from it are, in substance, what that law requires.

But in how it is communicated to us and performed by us—through faith in God by Jesus Christ and love for Him, the source of all grace and mercy—it belongs to the gospel. What follows from this? It is true that the one who does what the law requires is just. This is certain; for "For not the hearers of the law are just in the sight of God, but the doers of the law will be justified" (Romans 2:13). "For Moses writes about the righteousness which is of the law, 'The man who does those things shall live by them'" (Romans 10:5).

Yet, although the righteousness we discuss is required by the law—indeed, it is nothing more than the law written in our hearts, by which we walk in God's ways and keep His statutes or commandments—it does not correspond to the law in such a way that any person can be justified by it. One might argue that if this supposed righteousness does not align with the law and rule by which we are judged, then it is not true righteousness. I agree: it is not perfect righteousness. It fails to meet the standard and the law to the degree required for justification or for safe judgment on its basis. However, insofar as it does conform to the law, it is a kind of righteousness—imperfect, to be sure—and therefore an imperfect righteousness. Even so, it still merits the designation "righteous" for those who possess it, both absolutely and comparatively.

It is said that this is "the law of grace or the gospel from which we are called righteous with this righteousness." But the claim that the gospel denominates us righteous on the basis of any righteousness that is not required by the moral law cannot be proven. The law of grace, the gospel, does not demand or prescribe such a righteousness as the ground of our justification before God. What it requires of all who are to be justified is faith in Christ Jesus—acceptance of Him as presented in its promises. It likewise requires "repentance from dead works" of all who believe, together with the fruits of faith: conversion to God, works of righteousness that glorify God through Jesus Christ, and perseverance in these until the end. All of this may properly be called our evangelical righteousness, since it is our obedience to God according to the gospel.

Yet the graces and duties that compose this evangelical righteousness do not, any more than our natural conformity to the moral law, perfectly fulfill the commands of the gospel. To suggest that the gospel relaxes the law's demand for holiness, treats as non-sin what the law declares sin, or approves a lower degree of love for God than the law requires, is a blasphemous notion.

The claim that the gospel requires all these things completely and equally as the condition of our justification before God—thus antecedent to justification—has not been proven and never will be. Some conclude, "this is our righteousness according to the evangelical law which demands it; by this we are made righteous — meaning, not guilty of failing to meet the condition required in that law." Such assertions may seem plain to their proponents, but to us they are intricate and confusing.

I therefore utterly reject the view that our faith, obedience, and righteousness — when considered as ours and as produced by us — though accepted by God through Jesus Christ according to the grace revealed in the gospel, perfectly fulfill the gospel's commands in matter, manner, and degree. For that reason I maintain it is impossible for them to be the cause or the condition of our justification before God.

In discussing these points, the same author adds that "our flawed and imperfect righteousness is accepted for salvation as if it were entirely absolute and perfect; for Christ has merited this through His most perfect righteousness." But our present concern is justification, not salvation, and Scripture clearly and repeatedly distinguishes the relation of works of obedience or righteousness to salvation from their relation to justification.

If our weak and imperfect righteousness is regarded and accepted as entirely perfect before God, that could mean one of two things. Either God perceives it as perfect and so declares us just and justified on that basis; or God perceives it as incomplete and imperfect, yet still declares us perfectly righteous in His sight through this imperfect righteousness. I believe neither alternative can be reasonably accepted.

Some will then argue that neither of those alternatives holds; rather, "Christ has obtained, through His complete and most perfect righteousness and obedience, that our weak and imperfect righteousness should be accepted as entirely perfect." If that were the case, some might conclude it is better not to rest on our weak, flawed, and imperfect righteousness at all, but to rely directly for justification on the most perfect righteousness of Christ — a posture Scripture surely commends.

They may think that a righteousness that cannot justify itself, one that must depend on grace and pardon through Christ's merits, will never be able to justify them. But what follows from the claim that our imperfect righteousness is accepted for justification on Christ's merit? It seems to lead to one of two conclusions: either Christ has procured that God should regard as perfect what is actually imperfect and thus declare us perfectly righteous when we are not; or He has procured that God should recognize the righteousness as still imperfect, yet declare us perfectly righteous through that imperfect righteousness.

These are the clear routes that those take who cannot deny that some righteousness is required for our justification or that we may be pronounced righteous before God according to His judgment. Yet, having denied the imputation of Christ's righteousness to us, they leave us with no other righteousness for that purpose than one so weak and imperfect that no one can justify it in conscience, nor can anyone, without a delusion of pride, consider themselves perfectly righteous by it.

In response to the claim that "he is blind who does not see that our righteousness is subordinate to the righteousness of Christ," I must respectfully disagree, despite the severity of this criticism. It seems to me that the righteousness of Christ is represented as subordinate to our own righteousness in that statement, rather than the reverse. The ultimate goal is our acceptance with God as righteous. But according to this view, it is our own righteousness on which we are immediately accepted with God as righteous. Only Christ has earned, through His righteousness, that our righteousness may be accepted in this way; thus, for the purposes of our justification before God, it is subordinate to His.

Returning from this digression to our argument: the personal, inherent righteousness that we acknowledge in believers, according to Scripture, is not the righteousness by which we are justified before God. It is not perfect and does not fully satisfy any rule of obedience given to us. Therefore it cannot serve as our righteousness before God for justification. Consequently, we must either be justified by the righteousness of Christ imputed to us, or be justified without regard to any righteousness at all — otherwise we cannot be justified.

There are three forms of imperfection that accompany it:

Regarding its principle, as it habitually resides in us.

There is a contrary principle of sin that coexists with it in the same subject while we are in this world. Contrary qualities can exist in the same subject, provided neither is in the highest degree. This is the case here, as stated in Galatians 5:17: "For the flesh lusts against the Spirit, and the Spirit against the flesh; and these are contrary to one another, so that you do not do the things that you wish."

None of the faculties of our souls are perfectly renewed while we are in this world. As Scripture says in 2 Corinthians 4:16, "the inward man is being renewed day by day," and in 2 Corinthians 7:1 it urges, "let us cleanse ourselves from all filthiness of the flesh and spirit." This includes everything Scripture mentions and what believers experience: the remnants of indwelling sin, the darkness of our minds, and our limited understanding. These things cause us to wander from the path (Hebrews 5:2), because of the deceitfulness of the heart and the disorder of our affections.

I cannot comprehend how anyone could think to plead their own righteousness before God or believe they could be justified by it, given the imperfection of its habitual principle. Such ideas arise from ignorance of God and ourselves, or from a lack of proper consideration of both.

Furthermore, I do not see how a multitude of distinctions can safely introduce it into any consideration of our justification before God. Anyone who can, to any degree, examine their own heart and soul through spiritual insight will find that "God, be merciful to me a sinner!" is a better plea than any they could derive from their own worth. "What is man, that he could be pure? And he who is born of a woman, that he could be righteous?" (Job 15:14-16; 4:18, 19). Gregory states in Job 9, Book 9, Chapter 14, "As we have often said, all human righteousness is proven to be unrighteousness if judged distinctly." Bernard speaks similarly, almost in the same words, in Sermon 1, Feast of All Saints: "What can all our righteousness be before God? Will it not be regarded, according to the prophet, as 'a menstruous rag'? And if judged strictly, all our righteousness will be found to be unrighteousness, and lacking."

A person cannot be justified in any sense by that righteousness which, upon examination, will appear to be more akin to unrighteousness.

It is imperfect concerning every act and duty, whether internal or external. There is iniquity clinging to our holy things, and "all our righteousnesses are like filthy rags" (Isaiah 64:6). It has been frequently and rightly noted that if a man, even the best of men, were left to choose the best of his works that he has ever performed and enter into judgment with God based solely on this notion—that he has fulfilled and met the condition required of him for acceptance with God—it would be his wisest course (at least according to Bellarmine) to renounce it and turn to grace and mercy alone.

It is imperfect because actual sins remain. Therefore our Savior taught us to pray continually, "And forgive us our sins." He also warns, "If we say that we have no sin, we deceive ourselves," and teaches that "For we all stumble in many things." What confidence can be placed in this righteousness, which those who advocate it here admit is weak, flawed, and imperfect?

I have only touched on these matters; they might be explored more fully and are certainly important to our present argument. But enough has been said to show that, although this righteousness of believers may in other respects be likened to the fruit of the vine that gladdens God and man, with respect to our justification before God it is like the wood of the vine—no pin can be taken from it to support any part of this argument.

Two things are argued in favor of this righteousness and its role in our justification:

1. It is claimed to be absolutely complete and perfect. Some assert they are perfect and sinless in this life, needing no further mortification of sin or growth in grace. Indeed, that is the only rational basis for assigning our justification before God to such a righteousness. If anyone were truly sinless, what would prevent their being justified before God except that they had once been a sinner? That line of reasoning undermines the whole case. This notion, however, is so contrary to Scripture and to the experience of all who truly fear the Lord and know what it is to walk humbly before Him that I will not dwell on its refutation here.

2. It is argued that although this righteousness does not perfectly fulfill the moral law, it nevertheless meets the condition of the new covenant and fully satisfies the law of grace.

This view entirely removes the concept of sin and the need for pardon, just as the notion of sinless perfection does, which we have already rejected. If our obedience meets the only law and standard by which it is to be judged, then there is no sin in us and no need for pardon. No further requirement would exist for anyone to be kept absolutely free from sin other than their actual conformity to that standard. On that assumption there is, therefore, neither sin nor any need of pardon. To say that both sin and the need for pardon still exist with respect to God's moral law is to acknowledge that law as the true standard of our obedience—yet this righteousness does not fulfill that standard. Hence no one can be justified by it in the sight of God.

Although this righteousness is accepted in justified persons by the grace of our Lord Jesus Christ, we must examine its underlying principles and the acts and duties it comprises as prescribed by the gospel. Those acts and duties do not, taken together or separately, fulfill the commands of the gospel any more than they fulfill the commands of the law. Therefore they cannot constitute a righteousness that perfectly conforms to the gospel's requirements. It is impious to suppose that the gospel, in requiring duties such as the love of God, makes any concession as to the matter, manner, or degree of perfection required compared with the law. Does the gospel require a lesser or less perfect love of God than the law required? God forbid. The same holds for the inward disposition of our natures and for every other duty. Thus, while this righteousness is accepted in justified persons (as God respected Abel and his offering), with respect to the commands of the gospel both it and all its duties remain imperfect, just as they would be if judged only by the law of creation.

I do not understand what some intend. On the one hand they say our Lord Jesus Christ has enlarged and exalted the spiritual sense of the moral law, even adding precepts that call for a more exact obedience than before. On the other hand they suggest He has relaxed or removed the law's obligation, so that a person, by their own adaptation of it to the gospel, will be judged by God as having fulfilled all the obedience required—even though they have never observed any of its precepts according to their original meaning and binding force. That must follow if this imperfect righteousness is to be taken as the fulfillment of the standard of our obedience on which we are to be justified before God.

This opinion creates an irreconcilable conflict between law and gospel that no distinctions can resolve. According to it, God declares a person perfectly righteous, justified, and blessed on the basis of a righteousness that is imperfect, while the law pronounces a curse on anyone who does not continue in all things required by it exactly as required. Yet proponents say this righteousness should be treated only as the condition of the new covenant, by which we obtain remission of sins through Christ's satisfaction, and in which our justification consists.

Some indeed hold this view, though not all, not the majority, and certainly not the most learned disputants in the controversy. In defending what we believe to be the truth, we cannot treat every private opinion that opposes it as equally authoritative.

That justification consists solely in the pardon of sin is so contrary to the meaning of the word, its consistent use in Scripture, the common understanding of it among people, and the awareness of individuals in their own consciences — who recognize their obligation to duty and cite testimonies from Scripture — that I am somewhat astonished it can even be suggested. This point will, however, be addressed further elsewhere.

If this righteousness is the fulfillment of the condition of the new covenant upon which we are justified, it must necessarily align with some rule or law of righteousness and therefore be perfect. It is not perfect; hence it cannot serve as the righteousness by which we are justified.

The assertion that this righteousness is the condition of our justification before God, or of our interest in the righteousness of Christ through which we are justified, is unsupported and will remain so.

I will briefly present two or three considerations that exclude this personal righteousness from the role some assign it in our justification, and then conclude this argument.

First, that righteousness which neither fulfills the law of God nor accomplishes God's purpose in our justification through the gospel is not the basis on which we are justified. Such is the inherent righteousness of believers, even of the best among them.

1. It has been shown that this righteousness does not fulfill the law of God because it is imperfect. No reasonable person would claim that it perfectly satisfies the law of our creation. As long as the relationship remains between God as Creator and Rewarder and us as creatures capable of obedience and receiving rewards, that law cannot be annulled. Therefore, that which does not fulfill this law cannot justify us; God will not abolish the law so that its transgressors may be justified. As the apostle states, "Do we then make void the law through faith? Certainly not! On the contrary, we establish the law" (Romans 3:31).

2. Furthermore, being justified by this righteousness does not fulfill God's purpose in our justification through the gospel. The aim of the gospel is to remove every ground for boasting in ourselves and to leave no occasion for it, so that everything may be to the praise of His grace through Christ (Romans 3:27; 1 Corinthians 1:29-31). We have shown how faith alone brings glory to God in this matter. Yet plainly, no one has, or can have, any greater reason to boast in themselves regarding their justification than if they were justified on the basis of their own performance of the condition, namely their personal righteousness.

No one has ever been justified by it in their own conscience, much less can they be justified by it in the sight of God; "for God is greater than our heart and knows all things." There is no person so righteous or holy in the whole world, nor has there ever been, whose own conscience would not accuse them in many respects of falling short of the obedience required—whether in substance, manner, kind, or degree of perfection; for there is no person who lives and does not sin. Absolutely, "Nemo absolvitur se judice." If anyone were to be put on trial concerning whether they can be justified in their own conscience by their own righteousness, they would be found guilty in their own judgment. Whoever does not conclude from this that there must be another righteousness by which they must be justified—one that is not originally or inherently their own—will struggle to find peace with God. It may be argued that "men can be justified in their consciences if they believe they have fulfilled the condition of the new covenant," which is all that is claimed regarding this righteousness. I have no doubt that people can have a comforting assurance of their own sincerity in obedience and satisfaction in its acceptance by God. However, this comfort comes when they view it as the fruit of faith by which they are justified, and not as the condition of their justification. If they frame their understanding as, "This is my righteousness which I present to God so that I may be justified," they will likely find it very difficult to attain that righteousness, if I am not mistaken.

None of the holy men of old, whose faith and experiences are recorded in Scripture, ever appealed to their own personal righteousness in any sense—neither as to the merit of their works nor as to their complete performance of what was required of them as the condition of the covenant—to obtain their justification before God. This has been considered previously.

12. God's Requirement of Perfect Obedience

Our second argument will focus on the nature of the obedience or righteousness that God requires for us to be accepted and approved by Him. This is a broad subject. To address it adequately here, I will condense what is relevant to our present discussion into several key observations.

God, being a perfect and free agent, directs all His actions toward mankind — including His dealings, constitutions, and laws — according to His sovereign will and pleasure. No other reason can account for the origin of the entire system of these laws. Scripture attests to this, as seen in Psalm 115:3; 135:6; Proverbs 16:4; Ephesians 1:9, 11; and Revelation 4:11. The existence and natural circumstances of all creatures are effects of God's free counsel and pleasure, and everything related to them must ultimately be traced back to this.

Given the free acts of God's will and their execution, an order is established among things that outwardly derive from Him, together with their mutual relations. Some things may become necessary in this relative state, even if they were not absolutely necessary by nature. The order of all things and their interrelations depend on God's free constitution just as much as their existence does.

Thus, it was a free and sovereign act of God's will to create man — a being intelligent, rational, and capable of moral obedience, with the potential for rewards and punishments. However, once man was created he could not be governed except by a moral law or rule that influences his rational faculties toward obedience and guides him in that obedience. He could not be governed by mere physical influence, as is the case with irrational creatures. To suggest otherwise would be to deny or undermine the essential faculties and powers with which he was created. Therefore, it was necessary that a law or rule of obedience be prescribed to him as the instrument of God's governance.

This necessary law arose directly and inevitably from the constitution of our nature in relation to God. Considering the nature, existence, and attributes of God alongside the being and nature of man, and his necessary relation to God, the law in question is simply the rule governing that relationship. That relationship cannot exist or be maintained without it.

Consequently, this law is eternal and indispensable, allowing for no variation other than that which corresponds to the relationship between God and man, which necessarily arises from their distinct natures and properties.

The essence of this law is that man must adhere to God absolutely, universally, unchangeably, and without interruption — in trust, love, and fear — recognizing Him as the ultimate good and the primary author of his existence and all present and future benefits. Man is to yield obedience to God, respecting His infinite wisdom, righteousness, and almighty power to protect, reward, and punish in all things known to be His will, whether revealed by the light of his own mind or by special revelation.

It is clear that the establishment of this law requires nothing more than that God be God and man be man, together with the necessary relationship that follows. Therefore, this law eternally and unchangeably obliges all men to obey God, requiring both the obedience it demands and the manner in which it requires it. The substance of what it requires and the manner of its performance — in measures and degrees — are equally necessary and unalterable on the principles already established. God cannot deny Himself, nor can the essence of man change in any way that would affect this law, whatever circumstances may arise. Although God could add arbitrary commands that do not necessarily spring from the relationship between Him and us, such commands would still be rooted in the principle that God must be absolutely trusted and obeyed in all things.

"Known to God from eternity are all His works." In establishing this order, God made it possible and foresaw that man would rebel against the prescriptive power of the law, thereby disturbing the order under which he was placed. This rebellion necessitated the establishment of punishment for man's transgression of the law, which was not an arbitrary act but rather a necessary consequence of divine righteousness.

Given the creation of man, the law was necessary because of the divine properties of God's nature. If man were to transgress the law, the constitution of punishment for his sin was a necessary outcome of divine righteousness. This penalty would not be arbitrary; it is as necessary as the law itself. Therefore, the constitution of this penalty cannot be changed, altered, or abrogated any more than the law itself, without altering the relationship between God and man.

This is the law that our Lord Jesus Christ came "not to destroy but to fulfill," making Him "the end of the law for righteousness to everyone who believes." He did not abolish this law, nor could He do so without destroying the relationship between God and man that arises necessarily from their distinct natures and properties. Since this relationship cannot be destroyed, Christ came for the opposite purpose — to repair and restore it where it had been weakened.

Thus, this law — which requires sinless, perfect obedience and imposes the penalty of death on all transgressors — must remain in force forever in this world. All that is required for this to be true is simply that God is God and man is man. Furthermore, it will be demonstrated that:

There is no indication in Scripture of any alteration or abrogation of this law. Nothing it designates as a duty can be exempted, nor can anything it identifies as sin be declared innocent, whether in matter or in degree. Likewise, nothing the law classifies as sin can be relieved from the punishment it prescribes. "For the wages of sin is death." If any scriptural evidence can be produced to support either claim — that anything is not sin according to this law, or that any sin is exempt from the punishment it merits — it will be duly considered. Therefore this law remains universally applicable to all mankind. The only relief in this situation is to "Behold! The Lamb of God."

In response to this, some argue that when the law was first given to Adam it served as the rule and instrument of a covenant between God and man — a covenant of works requiring perfect obedience. They further contend that, once sin entered, it ceased to function as a covenant for anyone. Even if a man could meet the perfect righteousness the law requires, they say he still would not be justified or receive benefit from the covenant.

This argument implies that the law has become ineffective as a covenant because we can no longer perform it, and thus that it has ceased to be a covenant in its very nature. These points, however, are not directly relevant to our present discussion and remain unproven.

1. Our focus is not on the federal or contractual aspect of the law, but on its moral nature. As a law, it continues to obligate all mankind to

perfect obedience under its original penalty. Consequently, unless its commands are fulfilled, the penalty will attach to every transgressor. Those who admit the law still stands as a rule of obedience concede what we assert: it requires no obedience other than the sinless, perfect obedience it originally demanded, and it forbids no sin except under the original penalty of death for disobedience.

2. It is true that a sinner, even if he later yields perfect obedience to God as the law requires, cannot claim the covenant's benefits. He is already a sinner and therefore under the law's curse; no one can be under that curse and at the same time claim the promise. But to suggest that a person, once freed from the curse caused by sin, could not rightfully claim the promise of life upon fulfilling the law's requirement of perfect, sinless obedience is to deny God's truth and dishonor His justice. Jesus Christ Himself was justified by this law, and it remains immutable that "The man who does those things shall live by them."

3. It is acknowledged that mankind did not continue to observe this law in the role it played as the rule of the covenant. The law was not the covenant itself but the rule governing it; that rule was superadded to the covenant's existence. The covenant also contained elements not directly arising from the necessary relationship between God and man. Thus, through sin and demerit, mankind may be said to have broken that covenant and, with respect to personal benefit, to have annulled its claim.

It is also true that God never formally and absolutely renewed or reissued this law as a covenant. There was no need to do so, except perhaps for declarative purposes, as at Sinai. The law's authority flows from eternal right and truth, and it must remain fully in force forever. It is only broken as a covenant in the sense that all mankind, having transgressed its commands, has forfeited any interest in its promise and the possibility of obtaining that interest. Yet, in respect to its power to obligate all men to obedience and to the unchangeable truth of its promises and threats, it remains unchanged from the beginning.

If we remove this law, there is left no standard of righteousness for mankind and no clear boundaries between good and evil. The foundational principles on which God established the earth would be left to drift, like the island of Delos in the sea. Some maintain that the rule of good and evil for humanity is not this law in its original form but the light of nature and the dictates of reason. If by that they mean the original light created with our nature, together with the first intimations of right and wrong given by reason, then they are effectively affirming that this law remains the unchanging rule of obedience for all mankind.

However, if they mean the remaining fragment of natural light in each individual after the fall, compounded by traditions, customs, prejudices, and various lusts, their position is fundamentally defective. It yields no definitive boundaries of good and evil. What one person calls good may, on that ground, be called evil by another — and vice versa. Such a rationale could be used to excuse every idolatrous practice that has ever existed.

Conscience bears witness to this truth. No person can persuade or bribe their conscience to ignore any good or evil required or forbidden by this law, whatever their personal stake. Conscience will accuse or excuse, condemn or free, according to the judgment of this law, whatever one might attempt otherwise.

In summary, it is acknowledged that God, by virtue of His supreme authority over all, may in certain instances alter the course or order of things so that the precepts of divine law do not operate with their usual effect. This was evident in His command to Abraham to sacrifice his son and in His direction to the Israelites to plunder the Egyptians. But, assuming the continuance of the order that this law preserves, the intrinsic nature of the good and evil commanded and forbidden in it is not open to divine alteration, as even the scholastics generally agree.

From what we have discussed, two conclusions inevitably follow:

1. All humanity has fallen under the penalty threatened for transgressing this law because of sin. That penalty — eternal death — cannot be compatible with acceptance before God or the enjoyment of blessedness. Therefore it is utterly impossible for any individual descended from Adam to be justified in God's sight, accepted by Him, or blessed by Him unless this penalty is either endured and suffered by them personally or borne on their behalf. The dikaiōma tou Theou in this context is not to be abolished but to be established.

2. To obtain acceptance with God, justification before Him, and blessedness from Him, the righteousness required by this eternal law must be fulfilled in us in such a way that, in God's judgment — rooted in truth — we may be regarded as having fulfilled it and treated accordingly. If we fail in this, the law's sanction is not arbitrary; the penalty must be enforced because of the righteousness of God as the supreme Governor of all.

Regarding the first point, our disagreement is solely with the Socinians, who deny the necessity of Christ's satisfaction. I have treated that matter at length elsewhere and do not expect an answer here. Concerning the latter point, we must ask how we might comply with the rule and meet the righteousness of this unalterable law, from which we cannot exempt ourselves. We maintain that the obedience and righteousness of Christ, imputed to us — His obedience as the surety of the new covenant, granted to us and made ours through God's gracious constitution, sovereign appointment, and gift — is the ground on which we are judged and reckoned to have fulfilled the law's righteousness. "by one Man's obedience many will be made righteous" (Romans 5:19). "that the righteous requirement of the law might be fulfilled in us"

(Romans 8:4). Therefore, if there is no other means by which the law's righteousness can be fulfilled in us—without which we cannot be justified and would inevitably fall under the penalty for transgressing it—then the righteousness of Christ imputed to us is the only righteousness by which we are justified in God's sight. Since the first statement is true, the latter must also be true.

Given the existence of this law, its original obligation to obedience, and its sanctions and threats, there are only three ways in which we can be justified before God, having sinned and being unable to perform the required obedience ourselves. Each way involves a sovereign act of God in relation to this law.

1. The first is the abrogation of the law, so that it no longer obliges us either to obedience or to punishment. We have shown this to be impossible, and those who rely on it deceive themselves.

2. The second is the transfer of its obligation to a surety or common undertaker for the purpose of justification. This is the position we advocate, for it contains the essence of the gospel and centers on the person and grace of that surety. In this view, all things aim to exalt the glory of God in the holy attributes of His nature while at the same time fulfilling and establishing the law itself (Matthew 5:17; Romans 3:31; 8:4; 10:3, 4).

3. The third way involves an act of God regarding the law and another regarding us, by which the nature of the righteousness required by the law is altered. We will examine this as the only alternative to our present argument.

It is claimed, therefore, that through our own personal obedience we fulfill the righteousness of the law to the extent it requires. But no rational person can believe that we can—or that anyone in our fallen condition ever has—rendered the perfect, sinless obedience to God that the law of creation demands. Two assumptions underlie this claim. First, that our obedience, however imperfect, may be accepted by God as if it were sinless and perfect. Second, that while some deny the imputation of Christ's righteousness to us as it truly is, others insist our own righteousness is imputed to us as if it were something it is not. These two points concern, respectively, the law and our obedience.

Concerning the law itself, its abrogation is not at issue. It might seem easiest to say that the law of creation is entirely abrogated by the gospel — both its obligation to obedience and its penalties — and that no law remains in force except one that requires merely sincere obedience, without any absolute rule or measure for duties or their manner of performance. But that view is not tenable.

Those who hold this position do not claim the law has been abrogated so that it loses its force and efficacy toward us. That is impossible and cannot be justified. Humanity has broken this law, and we all continue to break it, especially in regard to its primary purpose: to establish our subjection to God and our dependence on Him according to its demands. Yet it is foolish to think the failings of those to whom a righteous law is rightly given can nullify or invalidate the law itself.

A good and just law can cease to bind only when the relationship it governs ends. As the apostle states, "But if the husband dies, she is released from the law of her husband" (Romans 7:2). The relationship between God and us, established at our creation, cannot come to such an end.

A law cannot be abrogated except by the enactment of a new law by the same authority that created it or by one of equal authority — either by expressly revoking the old law or by establishing provisions that are inconsistent with and contradict its observance. This is the way the law of Mosaic institutions was abrogated and rendered void. No positive statute was passed to repeal it; rather, the gospel introduced a new form of worship that conflicted with the old, thereby stripping the former law of its obligatory force and efficacy.

But God has used neither of those methods to remove the obligation of the original law of obedience—neither as to duty nor as to the rewards for compliance. He enacted no direct law to abrogate it, nor has He provided any new moral law inconsistent with it. On the contrary, the gospel declares that the law is established and fulfilled.

It is true, as already noted, that this law was given as the instrument of a covenant between God and humanity. Because of that, one might insist there is another reason for its existence: God has introduced another covenant that is inconsistent with and contrary to it. But that fact alone does not immediately or ipso facto free all people from the law of the first covenant.

For a law to bind, three things are required: its content must be just and righteous; it must be enacted by one with rightful authority; and it must be sufficiently communicated to those bound by it. Thus, the proclamation of a new law will, ipso facto, abrogate any prior law that contradicts it, freeing everyone who is subject to the new law from the earlier obligation—provided they are properly within the scope of the new enactment.

But a covenant does not operate solely by sovereign authority; it is not a covenant without the consent of those with whom it is made. Therefore, the establishment of the new covenant does not confer any benefit or freedom from the old covenant on anyone who has not actually accepted it, chosen it, and become interested in it. The first covenant with Adam was one we consented to and accepted through him. Consequently, despite our sin, we remain under its obligations—to duty and to punishment—until we are made partakers of the new covenant through faith. It is not enough to say the law's righteousness concerns us no longer simply because the covenant has been superseded.

Nor can it be claimed that the law has received a new interpretation to the effect that it no longer requires sinless and perfect obedience but can be fulfilled on much easier terms. The law was given when we were sinless, with the intention of preserving us in that state. To assert it did not require sinless obedience is absurd; that is not an interpretation but a distortion of its meaning.

Furthermore, the gospel gives no ground for that idea. Our Savior's teaching about the law entirely refutes it. The scribes and Pharisees tried to bend the law to suit men's desires through false interpretations. This was done both publicly and practically: those who press their own commands on others often try to balance that by granting indulgences concerning God's commands. Christ rejects every such accommodation and restores the law to its original glory—the very restoration the Jews expected the Messiah to accomplish.

Nor can one rightly speak of a relaxation of the law. If such a notion has any coherence, it affects the law's whole force: either suspending its obligation (at least temporarily) or allowing some other person, not originally bound, to fulfill its demands in place of those who were. Some argue that the Lord Christ was made under the law for us by such a relaxation of its original obligation; but no proper justification can be offered for that view.

This supposed divine act would reduce the law's binding force with respect to obedience. The law originally required perfect, sinless obedience in every duty and in the manner of performing it. God may still require obedience of us, the claim goes, but not to that absolute standard of completeness and perfection. If the law still demanded that perfection, then either it is fulfilled for us in the righteousness of Christ, or no human being could ever be justified before God.

Thus the view is that the law still obliges us to obedience, but no longer to that which is entirely sinless and perfect. Our obedience may be performed with less intensity of love for God or at a lower degree than originally required; yet, so the theory runs, if it is sincere and covers all the parts of duty, it suffices. This is alleged to be the requirement adapted to the service of the new covenant and the rule of obedience under the law of Christ. In this way, the law's prescriptive aspect, so far as we are concerned, is said to be fulfilled. We will shortly examine whether these assertions are true.

Consequently, it is maintained that God's act concerning our obedience is not an act of judgment by any rule of His own. Rather, it is an acceptilation, or an estimation, whereby He counts and accepts our imperfect obedience as if it were perfect — treating it in place of that which is perfect, though it is not so in reality.

It is further claimed that both effects depend on and result from the obedience, suffering, and merits of Christ. Because of these, our weak and imperfect obedience is accepted as if it were perfect, and the law's power to demand absolute perfection in obedience is nullified. These consequences are said to flow from the righteousness of Christ, which is alleged to be imputed to us on that account and to that extent.

Yet, despite the considerable efforts to present these ideas as true, they are mere fictions and imaginations of men — unsupported by Scripture and at odds with believers' experience. To touch briefly on the latter: every true believer holds two convictions firmly in mind and conscience:

1. There is nothing in their principles, habits, qualities, or actions that attains the perfect compliance the holy law of God requires. Any shortcoming in this regard is sinful and worthy of the curse that attaches to breach of that law. Therefore, they do not regard the law's

obligation as having been removed, weakened, or diminished in any way.

2. They acknowledge that there is no relief from what the law requires or threatens except by the mediation of Jesus Christ alone, who is made righteousness for them by God. Consequently, they do not trust in the acceptance of their own imperfect obedience to satisfy the law, but rely solely on Christ for their acceptance with God.

Both of those doctrines are doctrinally incorrect. Regarding the first:

1. It is unwritten. Scripture gives no indication of any such dispensation regarding the original law of obedience. Much is said of our deliverance from the curse of the law through Christ, but Scripture makes no mention of any reduction in the law's prescriptive authority.

2. It contradicts Scripture, which plainly teaches that the law is not to be abolished but fulfilled; not made void but established; and that its righteousness must be fulfilled in us.

3. It is an unreasonable and impossible supposition. For:

- The law was a representation of God's holiness and righteousness in governing His creatures. No alteration can be made in this respect, for God does not change.

- It would remove any objective standard of righteousness, producing a subjective measure that varies with each individual, and thus as many different standards of righteousness as there are believers.

- It introduces a variation in the fundamental relationship between humanity and God—a relationship that must remain constant if what was once necessary is to continue in force.

- It dishonors the mediation of Christ by suggesting that the main purpose of His work was to permit God to accept for our justification a righteousness far inferior to what the law of creation required. That implication would make Him a minister of sin, as if He procured indulgence not by satisfaction and pardon, which remove guilt from the church, but by altering the nature and demerit of sin itself.

4. It reflects poorly on the goodness of God. If He has adjusted His law so that it may be satisfied by weak and imperfect obedience, accompanied by numerous failures and sins, what defense can be offered, consistent with His goodness, for giving a law that required perfect obedience while knowing that one sin would bring humanity under the penalty of ruin?

All these points, and many others like them, also follow from the second assumption: an acceptilation or imaginary estimation of the imperfect as if it were perfect, and of the sinful as if it were sinless. But God's judgment rests on truth; He will not account as perfect the sort of righteousness that is as filthy rags—especially when He has promised us the garments of salvation and the robe of righteousness.

What necessarily follows from this discussion is that there is no other way for the original, immutable law of God to be established and fulfilled with respect to us except through the imputation of the perfect obedience and righteousness of Christ, who is the end of the law for righteousness to everyone who believes.

13. Christ's Obedience Imputed to Believers

From the preceding general argument, a particular point arises about the imputation of Christ's active obedience or righteousness to us. That obedience is an essential part of the righteousness by which we are justified before God. The argument is as follows:

If it was necessary for the Lord Christ, as our surety, to endure the penalty of the law in our place because we have all sinned, then it was also necessary that, as our surety, He should render obedience to the prescriptive part of the law for us. If the imputation of the one is essential for our justification before God, then the imputation of the other is equally necessary for the same end and purpose.

Why was it necessary, or why would God determine, that the Lord Christ, as the surety of the covenant, should undergo the curse and penalty of the law which we incurred by sin so that we might be justified in His sight? Was it not to secure that the glory and honor of His righteousness—as the author of the law and the supreme Governor of all mankind—would not be violated by the absolute impunity of those who break it?

If it was requisite for the glory of God that the penalty of the law be endured for us, or suffered by our surety in our place because we have

333

sinned, then why is it not equally requisite for the glory of God that the prescriptive part of the law be complied with for us, since obedience to it is required of us?

Just as we are no more able to fulfill the law by obedience than we are able to endure its penalty, so there is no reason to suppose that God is any less concerned, in honor and glory, that the prescriptive power of the law be fulfilled by perfect obedience than that its sanction be vindicated by enduring the penalty.

Therefore, on the same grounds that the Lord Christ's suffering the penalty of the law for us was necessary for our justification before God, and that the satisfaction He made might be imputed to us as if we ourselves had made satisfaction to God — as Bellarmine admits — it was equally necessary, for the glory and honor of the Legislator and supreme Governor ordained by the law, that He should fulfill its prescriptive part by His perfect obedience. That perfect obedience must also be imputed to us for our justification.

On the first point, concerning Christ's satisfaction and the imputation of it to us, our main disagreement is with the Socinians. I have written at length elsewhere to defend this truth, so I will not repeat those arguments here. It is assumed for the present, though I recognize there are differing understandings of Christ's suffering in our place and the imputation of those sufferings to us. For now I only insist that Christ's obedience to the law, and its imputation to us, is just as necessary for our justification before God as His enduring the penalty and the imputation of that suffering. The precise nature of this imputation and what is formally imputed has been addressed in other writings.

The imputation of Christ's obedience as our mediator will be supported later by scriptural testimonies. Here I intend only to vindicate the argument just presented, which will require somewhat more time. No doctrine of justification meets more fierce and varied opposition; yet the truth is strong and will prevail.

The objections commonly raised against the imputation of Christ's obedience to our justification may be reduced to three main points:

1. It is impossible.

2. It is useless.

3. It is pernicious to believe it.

If the arguments supporting these objections were truly as compelling as the accusations are severe, they would inevitably shake the conviction of all reasonable people regarding this doctrine. In practice, however, there is often a wide gap between what is asserted and what is proved; that will be shown here. The claim of impossibility rests on the premise that Christ's obedience to the law was owed to Him personally and performed for Himself, and therefore cannot be regarded as having been done for us or imputed to us.

It is argued to be useless because, they say, all our sins of omission and commission are pardoned in our justification by Christ's death and satisfaction. Thus, we are accounted perfectly righteous, and the imputation of Christ's obedience becomes unnecessary.

Moreover, it is alleged to be pernicious because, so the charge runs, it removes the need for our own personal obedience and thus leads to antinomianism, libertinism, and other evils.

I will address that last accusation in its proper place. Some use it specifically against the imputation of Christ's obedience; others level it against the doctrine of justification as a whole. Even if we conceded that Christ's obedience is not imputed to us for justification, this charge would still cling unless one renounces Christ's entire satisfaction and merit. We are not prepared to pay such a price for peace with the world. I will therefore treat this charge fully when discussing the whole doctrine of justification and all its causes, which we profess and defend.

The first part of the charge—the impossibility of imputing Christ's obedience to us—is pressed most strongly by Socinus in his De Servat., part 3, chapter 5. Since then, little has been advanced that does not borrow from him or that he has not foreseen. He builds on this point to attack the whole doctrine of Christ's merit. His argument runs: if all that Christ did in obedience was owed to Him personally and was the duty He owed to God for Himself, it cannot be meritorious for us or imputed to us. To undermine the doctrine of His satisfaction and its imputation, he likewise contends that Christ offered for Himself in the kind of offering made on the cross. His view is that whatever sacrifice attended Christ's death was for Himself—an act of obedience pleasing to God like a sweet-smelling savor. Any offering for us, he thinks, is merely Christ's presentation of Himself in God's presence in heaven, where He has no further duties to discharge. If Christ's obedience was only for Himself, there would be no ground to claim His merit or its imputation to believers.

What we maintain is that the Lord Christ fulfilled the whole law for us: He did not merely endure the penalty due for our sins but rendered the perfect obedience the law required. I will not enter here into the fine dispute between active and passive obedience. He exercised the highest active obedience even in His sufferings when He offered Himself to God through the eternal Spirit. All His obedience, considered in connection with His person, was joined with suffering as part of His humiliation. Scripture says, "though He was a Son, yet He learned obedience by the things which He suffered." While doing and suffering are distinct categories, we should not restrain scriptural testimony by narrow philosophical distinctions.

It should be stressed that Christ's sufferings, while penal, cannot be fairly called His passive righteousness; righteousness is either an action or a habit, and suffering is neither. No one is made righteous by what he endures, nor do sufferings fulfill the law's commands, which require obedience. Therefore, if any righteousness is required for our justification, Christ's sufferings alone cannot suffice. My point is that Christ's obedience in fulfilling the law's commands must be imputed to us for our justification just as much as His suffering the law's penalty is imputed to us.

It sounds wrong to every Christian ear to assert that "the obedience of our Lord Jesus Christ, as our mediator and surety, was for Himself alone and not for us," or that what He did was not intended to be the end of the law for righteousness to believers, nor a means by which the law's righteousness is fulfilled for us. This is especially striking given the church's confession that He was given and born for us; that for us men and for our salvation He came down from heaven and did and suffered all that was required of Him. Yet some who deny the imputation of Christ's obedience to us for justification concentrate chiefly on its alleged uselessness. In what follows I shall consider only Socinus's arguments on this point, since they represent the principal effort of some today to obscure the truth.

To this end, he discusses in part three, chapter five of De Servat: "Now indeed it is clear that Christ, because He was born a man, and as Paul says, born under the law, was no less subject to the divine law, which is eternal and unchangeable, than other men. Otherwise, Christ could have disregarded the eternal law of God or even broken it at will, which is impious to even consider. Moreover, as was explained earlier, unless Christ Himself was subject to the divine law, as indicated by Paul's words, He could not assist those who are obliged to keep that law and lead them to a firm hope of immortality. Thus, in this respect, Christ, when He was born a man, was no different from other men. Therefore, He could not satisfy the divine law for others any more than any other man, since He Himself was entirely obligated to keep it." I have transcribed his words to show the weapons some young debaters among us use against the truth.

The essence of his argument is that our Lord Jesus Christ was obliged to all the obedience He performed for Himself, and he attempts to prove this by saying, "Because if it were otherwise, He could have neglected the whole law of God and broken it at His pleasure." He fails to consider that if He were not obliged to it for Himself but for us, whose cause He had undertaken, then the obligation to perfect obedience would be the same as if He were originally obliged for Himself. Nevertheless, he concludes, "That what He did could not be for us because it was for Himself; just as what any other man is bound to do for himself cannot be considered as done for another." He does not accept any of the considerations regarding the person of Christ that would make what He did and suffered fundamentally different from what any other man can do or suffer. He further states that "whatever Christ did that was not required by the law in general was done at the special command of God, and thus was for Himself; therefore, it cannot be imputed to us." In doing so, he excludes the church from any benefit from Christ's mediation, except for what consists of His doctrine, example, and the exercise of His power in heaven for our good, which is precisely what he aimed to achieve. However, we will also consider those who use his arguments, even if they do not openly endorse all his conclusions.

To clarify the truth here, note the following points. The obedience we are discussing was the obedience of Christ as our mediator. However, the obedience of Christ, as "the mediator of the covenant," was the obedience of His person. As stated in Acts 20:28, "the church of God which He purchased with His own blood." This obedience was performed in human nature, but it was the person of Christ who carried it out.

Just as in a person some actions stem from the body and some from the soul, yet all are acts of the person, so the acts of Christ in His mediation—regarding their immediate operation—were actions of His distinct natures: some divine and some human. However, in terms of their ultimate efficacy, they were the acts of His whole person, for His power of operation is an attribute of His person.

Therefore, the obedience of Christ, which we assert was for us, was the obedience of the Son of God. However, the Son of God was never absolutely made hupo nomon, meaning "under the law," nor could He be formally obligated by it. Indeed, as the apostle testifies, He was made so in His human nature, wherein He performed this obedience: "born of a woman, born under the law" (Galatians 4:4). He was made under the law only in the sense that He was made of a woman; in His person, He remained "Lord of the Sabbath" (Mark 2:28) and thus of the entire law.

However, the obedience itself was that of a person who could never be absolutely made under the law in His entirety, for the divine nature cannot be subjected to an external work such as the law, nor can it be commanded by it, as it would need to be if it were made hupo nomon. The apostle argues that, "And, so to speak, through Abraham even Levi, who receives tithes, paid tithes," because Levi was in the loins of Abraham when he paid tithes to Melchizedek (Hebrews 7).

But could it not be argued that the Lord Christ was also in the loins of Abraham, just as Levi was? For indeed, as the same apostle states, "For indeed He does not give aid to angels, but He gives aid to the seed of Abraham." It is true that He was so in respect to His human nature. However, as He was typified and represented by Melchizedek in His whole person—"without father, without mother, without genealogy, having neither beginning of days nor end of life"—He was not absolutely in Abraham's loins and was exempt from being tithed by him.

Thus, the obedience we are discussing is not merely the obedience of the human nature in isolation, even though it was performed in and through the human nature. Rather, it is the obedience of the person of the Son of God, even though the human nature was subject to the law (the specifics of which will be explained later). This obedience was not for Himself, nor could it be for Himself, because His entire person was not obligated to it.

It is therefore misguided to compare the obedience of Christ with that of any other man, whose entire person is under the law. While it may not be for himself and others (which we will demonstrate can be the case in some instances), it must be for others and not for Himself. This is a crucial point to maintain. If the obedience that Christ rendered to the law were for Himself, then His whole person, including the divine nature, would be made under the law, which cannot be the case. Although it is acknowledged that, in God's ordination, His humiliation preceded His glorious exaltation, as the Scriptures testify (Philippians 2:9; Luke 24:26; Romans 14:9), His glory was ultimately a direct consequence of the hypostatic union (Hebrews 1:6; Matthew 2:11).

I admit that Socinus evades the strength of this argument by denying the divine person of Christ. However, in this discussion, I take that for granted, having proven it elsewhere beyond what any of his followers can contradict. If we cannot rely on truths he denies, we will hardly have any principles of evangelical truth left to support anything. Nevertheless, I am currently addressing those who agree with him on the matter under discussion but reject his views concerning the person of Christ.

As our Lord Jesus Christ did not owe this obedience for Himself — because no authority or power of the law held over Him — He did not intend it for Himself but for us. Taken with the previous point, this gives strong proof for the truth we defend. If He was not obliged to obey for Himself — His person that yielded it not being under the law — and if He did not intend it for Himself, then it must have been for us; otherwise it would have been useless. He performed all this obedience in our human nature. The assumption of our nature was a voluntary act on His part, directed toward a particular end; and the purpose of assuming our nature was the same as the purpose of all He did in it. He assumed our nature for us, not for Himself, and nothing was added to Him by it. Therefore, in the outcome of His work He aims only to be restored to "that glory which He had with the Father before the world was," by removing the veil placed upon it during His humiliation. That He assumed our nature for us is the foundation of Christian faith, as the apostle indicates in Hebrews 2:14 and Philippians 2:5-8.

Some of the older schoolmen maintained that the Son of God would have been incarnate even if humanity had not sinned; Osiander pressed this view especially, as I have shown elsewhere. But none of them supposed that He would have been made man in such a way as to be under the law and obliged to perform the obedience He actually fulfilled. They expected Him to be a glorious head over all creation. It is a common conviction among Christians — except among those who adapt doctrines to their private opinions — that the obedience Christ rendered to the law on earth, in the state in which He yielded it, was not for Himself but for the church, which was obligated to perfect obedience yet unable to achieve it. This understanding is a central article of faith for most Christians, and to deny it would undermine the grace and love of both the Father and the Son in His mediation.

I deny the claim that "this obedience was necessary as a qualification of His person, so that He might be fit to be a mediator for us; therefore, it was for Himself." The Lord Christ was fully fitted for the whole work of mediation by the ineffable union of human nature with the divine. That union raised the human nature in dignity, honor, and worth above anything that could otherwise follow. By this union He became, in His whole person, the object of all divine worship and honor; for "But when

He again brings the firstborn into the world, He says: 'Let all the angels of God worship Him.'" Moreover, what is an effect of the Mediator's person, as constituted such, is not a qualification necessary to constitute it. In short, what He did as Mediator did not contribute to making Him fit for that role. All the obedience He yielded to the law falls into this category; as such, "for thus it is fitting for us to fulfill all righteousness."

Therefore, since He was neither made man nor descended from the posterity of Abraham for Himself, but for the church — specifically to become the surety of the covenant and representative of the whole — His obedience as a man to the law in general, and as a son of Abraham to the law of Moses, was for us and not for Himself. It was designed and performed with us in view. Without the church it would have been of no use to Him. He was born for us, given for us; He lived for us, died for us; obeyed for us, and suffered for us — so that "so also by one Man's obedience many will be made righteous." This is the grace of our Lord Jesus Christ, and this is the faith of the catholic church. What He did for us is imputed to us; that imputation is inherent in the very notion of His doing it for us. I advise caution against undermining the foundations of Christian faith by distinctions and evasions fashioned to defend private opinions. It is easier, as the proverb says, to wrest the club from Hercules than to persuade true believers that what the Lord Christ did in obedience to God, according to the law, He did not intend in His love and grace to do for them. He needed no obedience for Himself; He did not assume that position to yield obedience for Himself, but for us. Therefore, He fulfilled the law in obedience to God for our sake. The obligation on Him to obey was originally no less for us, no less necessary for us, no more for Himself, and no more necessary for Him than His obligation, as surety of the covenant, to suffer the penalty of the law.

Putting aside the consideration of Christ's grace and love and the agreement between the Father and the Son regarding His undertaking for us — which plainly show that all He did toward those ends was for us and not for Himself—I maintain that, even apart from these things, the human nature of Christ, by virtue of its union with the person of the Son of God, had a right to and could have been immediately admitted into the highest glory without any prior obedience to the law. From the very first moment of that union, the whole person of Christ, with our nature included, was the object of divine worship by angels and men. That worship itself is the highest exaltation of that nature.

It is true that there was a particular glory Christ was to partake of because of His prior obedience and suffering, as described in Philippians 2:8-9. The actual possession of that glory was ordained by God to follow His obedience and suffering, and this was for our sake, not for His. Yet, in regard to the inherent right and capacity of the human nature, all the glory it could possess was due to it from the moment of its union with the divine. In that union it was exalted above what any creature could attain by mere creation.

The notion that the foundation of Christ's divine glory was established by His obedience is a Socinian fiction. His obedience was the means by which He actually came into possession of that aspect of glory which consists in His mediatorial authority and power over all. The true foundation of all His glory was laid in the union of His person, and that is why He prays that the Father would glorify Him with the glory which He had with the Father before the world was.

I concede that the Lord Christ was a "viator" while in this world, not an absolute "possessor." Yet this condition was not necessary for Him personally; He took it upon Himself by special dispensation for our sake. Therefore, the obedience He performed in that condition was for us, not for Himself.

It is acknowledged that the human nature of Christ was made "born under the law," as the apostle affirms, "born of a woman, born under the law." This made obedience necessary for Him while He was a viator. However, this was by special dispensation, as indicated by the phrase "made under the law," namely, in that He was born of a woman—through divine condescension, as expressed in Philippians 2:6–8. Thus, the obedience He yielded was for us, not for Himself.

This is clear because He was made under the law not only to owe obedience to its precepts but also to be subject to its curse. It cannot be said that He was made so for Himself; He was made so for us. We owed obedience to the law and were subject to its curse—or, as the phrase runs, "hupodikoi tō Theō." Obedience was required of us, and it was as necessary for us to enter into life as it was for us to answer for the curse if we were to escape eternal death. Christ, as our surety, was made under the law for us, making Him liable to the obedience the law demanded and to the penalty it threatened. Who would claim that He underwent the penalty of the law for us but yielded obedience for Himself alone? Such a view would disturb the entire harmony of His mediatorial work.

Judah, the son of Jacob, volunteered to be a bondsman in place of his brother Benjamin so that Benjamin could go free, as stated in Genesis 44:33. There is no doubt Joseph could have accepted that stipulation. Had he done so, the service and bondage Judah undertook would have been necessary for him and just for him to bear. However, Judah acted not for himself but for his brother Benjamin, and his service would have been imputed to Benjamin in Benjamin's freedom.

Similarly, when the apostle Paul wrote to Philemon about Onesimus, he said, "If he has wronged you or owes you anything, put that on my account" (Philemon 18). Paul implies that Philemon might have a double claim against Onesimus: one for wrong and another for loss or debt, which are distinct legal actions. Paul obliges himself to answer for both, stating, "I, Paul, write this with my own hand." Thus, he was obliged to make satisfaction to Philemon, yet he was doing it for Onesimus, not for himself.

Therefore, whatever obedience was due from the Lord Christ in His human nature—whether as a man or as an Israelite—was not required for Himself. It was a voluntary condescension and stipulation taken on for our sake. In every respect, it was for us, not for Himself.

The Lord Christ, in His obedience, acted not as a private individual but as a public person. He obeyed as the surety of the covenant and as the mediator between God and man. This status is not reasonably disputable; He cannot be considered apart from that capacity.

What a public person does as a representative of others, regardless of any personal interest, is done for those others, not for himself. If others were not involved, the action would lack its representative significance. It is contradictory to act as a public representative yet do so solely for oneself. A public person may handle matters that concern only himself, but when he acts in his representative capacity, he necessarily acts for others.

Thus, when Socinus and his followers suggest that Christ offered for Himself, they effectively make Him a mediator for Himself, which is both foolish and impious. Likewise, to assert that His mediatorial obedience was for Himself and not for others is nearly as impious.

It is acknowledged that the Lord Christ, having a human nature—which is a creature—must be subject to the law of creation. That relation follows from the fact of a creator and a creature. Every rational creature is eternally bound, by the nature of God and its relation to Him, to love, obey, depend upon, and submit to God, making Him its ultimate end, blessedness, and reward.

The law of creation does not pertain only to this present life but also to the future state of heaven and eternity. The human nature of Christ is subject to this law even in heaven and glory, so long as it remains a creature and not God—that is, so long as it has its own finite being.

No one suggests there is a transfusion of divine properties into Christ's human nature to the point that it becomes self-subsisting and absolutely immense; that would destroy its creaturely nature. Nevertheless, it is clear He was not "under the law" in the sense the apostle intends when speaking of the law's application to His human nature only while He was in this world.

This also answers Socinus's objection that, if Christ were not obliged to obedience for Himself, He might neglect the law. Such an idea is absurd regarding that "holy thing" which was hypostatically united to the Son of God; that union made deviation from the divine will impossible. The eternal, indispensable law of love, adherence, and dependence upon God—under which Christ's human nature was and is as a creature—secures against any such supposition.

There is another aspect of the law of God to consider—namely, how it is imposed on creatures by special dispensation: for a specific time and purpose and with considerations, rules, and orders that do not essentially belong to the law itself. This describes the nature of the written law of God, to which the Lord Christ was made subject—not necessarily as a creature in the ordinary sense, but by a special dispensation.

The law, in this sense, is presented to us not absolutely and eternally, but while we are in this world, with the specific purpose that through obedience we may obtain the reward of eternal life. It is evident that the obligation of the law in this context ceases once we attain that reward. It no longer formally obliges us with the command, "do this and you will live," when the promised life is enjoyed.

In this sense, the Lord Christ was not made subject to the law for Himself, nor did He yield obedience for Himself; He was not obliged to it by virtue of His created condition. From the very moment of the union of His natures, being "holy, harmless, undefiled, separate from sinners," He could have been established in glory despite the law to which He was made subject. The one who is the object of all divine worship does not need new obedience to procure a state of blessedness.

If He had been subject to the law merely by virtue of being a creature, He would have been so eternally, which is not the case. Things that depend solely on the natures of God and the creature are eternal and immutable. Thus, since the law in this sense was given to us not absolutely but with respect to a future state and reward, the Lord Christ voluntarily subjected Himself to it for our sake. His obedience to it was for us, not for Himself.

These points, together with what I have previously written on the subject—which has met no substantial opposition but only trivial objections—are sufficient to answer the first part of the charge about the impossibility of imputing Christ's obedience to us. That supposed impossibility is no greater than that of imputing Adam's disobedience to us, which the apostle says made us all sinners.

II. The second part of the objection against the imputation of Christ's obedience to us is that it is unnecessary for those who are to be justified. Since they receive the pardon of all their sins in justification, they are thereby righteous and have a right or title to life and blessedness. A person who is pardoned and not considered guilty of any sin of omission or commission lacks nothing required for justification. They are not unrighteous; and to be not unrighteous is equated here with being righteous—just as being not dead is the same as being alive.

There is no middle state between death and life. Therefore, those who have all their sins forgiven possess the blessedness of justification, and there is neither need nor use for any further imputation of righteousness to them. Various other arguments of a similar nature are raised to support this point; all of these will either be addressed in the forthcoming discourse or answered elsewhere.

This issue is of greater importance and is more clearly articulated in Scripture than to be reduced to such subtleties, which are more philosophical than theological. Thus, this objection might be dismissed with the simple response that a well-established truth should not be questioned or abandoned because of every entangling sophism, however insoluble it may seem. Still, as we will see, there is no real difficulty in these arguments that cannot be readily discussed.

Since the matter raised in these arguments is used by several learned individuals who agree with us on the core doctrine of justification—namely, that it is by faith alone, without works, through the imputation of the merit and satisfaction of Christ—I will briefly clarify the misunderstandings that underlie these objections.

The objection presupposes that one who is pardoned for sins of omission and commission is regarded as having done all that is required of them and having committed nothing forbidden. Without that assumption, mere pardon of sin cannot make, constitute, or designate anyone as righteous. But this is far from the truth; no such notion is inherent in the nature of pardon.

In the pardon of sin, neither God nor man judges that the one who has sinned did not sin, which would have to happen if the pardoned individual were to be seen as having fulfilled all righteousness. If a person is tried for wrongdoing and, after being legally convicted, is discharged by sovereign pardon, it is true that, in the eyes of the law, they are considered innocent with respect to the punishment due. However, no one believes that they are made righteous by this, nor that they are regarded as having done what they actually did and for which they were convicted.

Consider the case of Joab and Abiathar the priest: both were guilty of the same crime. Solomon ordered Joab to be executed for his crime, but he pardoned Abiathar. Did that make Abiathar righteous? Solomon himself declares otherwise; he calls him unrighteous and guilty and only remits the punishment for his fault (1 Kings 2:26). Thus, the pardon of sin frees the guilty person from liability to anger, wrath, or punishment due to their sin, but it does not imply that they should be considered or adjudged as having done no evil and as having fulfilled all righteousness.

Some argue that pardon grants a righteousness of innocence but not of obedience. Yet it cannot provide a righteousness of innocence in the absolute sense that Adam possessed — Adam had done no evil. Pardon only removes guilt as it relates to punishment, according to the law. This mistaken assumption is the clear error that underpins the whole objection.

The same can be said about the assumption that not being unrighteous, which a person is after receiving a pardon for sin, is equivalent to being righteous. If not being unrighteous is understood negatively, it aligns with being just or righteous, since it would imply the individual has fulfilled all duties required for righteousness.

However, taken purely as a negative, it does not imply that. At best it suggests a person has not yet acted against the standard of righteousness. That state can occur even when someone has not performed any duties necessary to be counted righteous, simply because the opportunities to do so have not arisen. This was the case with Adam in his state of innocence, which represents the highest state achievable through complete pardon of sin.

This argument rests on the assumption that the law, in the case of sin, does not require both punishment and obedience to be satisfied, fulfilled, or complied with. If the law does require both, then the pardon of sin — which only frees us from the penalty — does not remove the necessity of fulfilling the law's demands for obedience.

I contend this is a clear misunderstanding, one that does not "establish the law, but makes it void." I will show why. The law has two parts or powers:

1. Its prescriptive part, which commands and requires obedience, with a promise of life attached: "do this and you will live."

2. The sanction that binds the sinner to punishment in the event of disobedience: "In the day that you eat of it you shall surely die."

Every law, properly speaking, operates on these principles of obedience and disobedience. Its authority to command and to punish is inseparable from its nature.

The law we are discussing was first given to humanity in a state of innocence; thus its initial force was solely active: it obligated obedience. An innocent person could not be subject to its sanction, which imposes punishment only in the case of disobedience. Therefore, the law did not bind our first parents to both obedience and punishment at the same time, since the obligation to punishment could be enforced only upon actual transgression.

The law served as a moral cause and a motive for obedience and for humanity's preservation from sin. It was stated to Adam, "in the day that you eat of it you shall surely die." The neglect of that command and of its guiding influence opened the door to sin. But it is contradictory to suggest that an innocent person was under an actual obligation to punishment from the law's sanction. Before any transgression, the law bound them only to obedience, as all penal laws do.

But upon committing sin—this applies to everyone guilty of sin—humanity comes under an actual obligation to punishment. This is as indisputable as the prior obligation to obedience. The question then arises: does the law's initial intention and obligation to require obedience cease to affect the sinner, or does it continue to bind him to both obedience and punishment, both powers remaining operative toward him? To this I reply:

1. Had the punishment threatened been immediately enforced to the fullest, there would be no question; humanity would have died immediately, both temporally and eternally, and been cast out of the state in which they could relate to the law's prescriptive power. A person who is finally executed has fulfilled the law to the point that they owe no further obedience to it.

However, 2. God, in His wisdom and patience, has ordered things otherwise. Humanity remains a traveler on the way to its final end, not yet fixed in an eternal and unchangeable state where neither promise nor threat, reward nor punishment, could properly be proposed.

In this condition, humanity falls under two considerations:

1. As a guilty person, they are obligated to the full punishment that the law threatens. This is not disputed.

2. As a human being, a rational creature of God, they have not yet reached their eternal end.

In this condition, the law remains the only means of maintaining the relation between God and mankind. Therefore, under this consideration it must still oblige obedience, unless we assert that by sin mankind has absolved itself from God's government. Thus the law continues to uphold God's rule while mankind is traveling toward its final end; every act of disobedience and every transgression of its commands further binds them under the obligation to punishment.

This cannot be otherwise. No living person, not even the worst, can escape the judgment that they are obliged to obey God's law, according to the understanding they have of it by natural light or other means. A wicked servant punished for his crime, if the punishment leaves him still in his state of servitude, is not freed from his duty under the law. His obligation respecting the crime for which he was punished is not dissolved until the punishment is capital and thus ends his state. Therefore, since pardon of sin frees only from the obligation to punishment, obedience to what the law requires remains necessary for our justification.

This strengthens the argument we defend: as sinners we are subject both to the command and to the curse of the law. Both must be addressed, or we cannot be justified. Just as the Lord Christ could not satisfy the curse of the law by His perfect obedience — "you shall surely die" — neither could He fulfill the command of the law — "do this and you will live" — by suffering alone. Suffering in itself is not obedience, although there can be obedience in suffering, as seen in Christ's obedience in His suffering. Therefore, while we assert that Christ's death is imputed to us for our justification, we deny that it is imputed to us for our righteousness. The imputation of Christ's sufferings obtains remission or pardon of our sins and delivers us from the curse of the law which He bore; yet we are not accounted just or righteous without the obedience the law requires. Grotius expresses this well: "When we say that Christ has procured for us both impunity and reward, the former is attributed to satisfaction, the latter to the merit of Christ's perfect obedience on our behalf."

The objection just mentioned also assumes that the pardon of sin grants a right to eternal blessedness and enjoyment of God; for justification gives this right, and those who hold this view maintain no other righteousness is required for it beyond the pardon of sin. It is generally granted that justification gives a right to adoption, acceptance with God, and a heavenly inheritance, as has already been shown. The pardon of sin depends solely on the death and sufferings of Christ: "In Him we have redemption through His blood, the forgiveness of sins, according to the riches of His grace." But suffering as punishment does not confer a right or title; it only satisfies a requirement and does not merit reward. It is never said, "Suffer this, and live," but rather, "do this and you will live."

I admit these things are inseparably joined in God's ordinance, appointment, and covenant. Whoever has his sins pardoned is accepted by God and has a right to eternal blessedness. They are inseparable, though not identical. The apostle shows their inseparable relation in Romans 4:6–8: just as David also describes the blessedness of the man to whom God imputes righteousness apart from works: "Blessed are those whose lawless deeds are forgiven, And whose sins are covered; Blessed is the man to whom the Lord shall not impute sin." It is the imputation of righteousness that gives the right to blessedness; yet the pardon of sin is inseparable from it and follows from it, and both stand opposed to justification by works or by any internal righteousness of our own.

It is one thing to be freed from the liability of eternal death, and another to possess the right and title to blessed, eternal life. It is one thing to be redeemed from under the law—that is, from its curse; another to receive the adoption of sons. One thing to be freed from the curse, and another to have the blessing of Abraham come upon us, as the apostle distinguishes in Galatians 3:13–14 and 4:4–5. Our Lord also marks this distinction in Acts 26:18: "to open their eyes, in order to turn them from darkness to light, and from the power of Satan to God, that they may receive forgiveness of sins and an inheritance among those who are sanctified by faith in Me." The pardon of sins received by faith in Christ is the dismissal of sin from being used against us for condemnation; hence, "There is therefore now no condemnation to those who are in Christ Jesus." Yet it does not itself confer the right and title to glory or the heavenly inheritance. Can all the great effects of present grace and future blessedness be assumed to follow from mere pardon of sin? Can we be pardoned without also being made sons, heirs of God, and joint heirs with Christ?

The pardon of sin is, in God's view, a free and gracious act toward the sinner — "forgiveness of sins through the riches of His grace." But with respect to Christ's satisfaction, it is an act of judgment: God absolves and acquits the sinner in view of that satisfaction. Still, pardon granted in a legal framework, whatever its basis, does not of itself confer any right or title to favor, benefit, or privilege; it only delivers. There is a difference between being acquitted before a sovereign — by clemency or other considerations — and being made his son by adoption and heir of his kingdom.

Scripture presents these things as distinct and dependent on different causes. The vision of Joshua the high priest illustrates this in Zechariah 3:4-5: "Then He answered and spoke to those who stood before Him, saying, 'Take away the filthy garments from him.' And to him He said, 'See, I have removed your iniquity from you, and I will clothe you with change of garments.' And I said, 'Let them put a clean turban on his head.' So they put a clean turban on his head and clothed him with garments." It is commonly held that this passage represents a sinner's justification before God. The removal of filthy garments signifies the passing away of iniquity. When a man's filthy garments are taken away, he is no longer defiled by them; yet he is not yet clothed. That subsequent grace and favor is the act of clothing him with new garments. The nature of that raiment is described in Isaiah 61:10: "For He has clothed me with the garments of salvation; He has covered me with the robe of righteousness," which the apostle alludes to in Philippians 3:9. Thus the removal of filthy garments and the clothing with new raiment—pardon of sin and the robe of righteousness—are distinct: by the former we are freed from condemnation; by the latter we obtain the right to salvation. This distinction is similarly set forth in Ezekiel 16:6–12.

I have already cited this passage in the discussion of communion with God, which Mr. Hotchkis attempts to answer in his usual way. Setting aside his derogatory remarks and unsupported assertions, he claims that the change of raiment spoken of by the prophet refers to our own personal righteousness, though he grants the passage represents our justification before God. He appeals to the verse in Isaiah 61:10, where the change of raiment is called "the garments of salvation and the robe of righteousness," and argues that our righteousness before God is our personal righteousness, which alone is at issue.

To counter these claims, I will refer to the same prophet, which he may consider at his leisure and eventually acknowledge. Isaiah 64:6 states, "But we are all like an unclean thing, And all our righteousnesses are like filthy rags;" He who can transform filthy rags into garments of salvation and robes of righteousness possesses a skill in creating spiritual attire that I am not familiar with. I will not address the remaining points in the chapter where this response is given, as they merely reflect his usual practice of misrepresenting my words to support his reproach against myself and others.

Therefore, there is no validity in comparing these matters to natural life and death, which are directly opposed: "He who is not dead is alive, and he who is alive is not dead," since there is no distinct state between life and death. These concepts are of different natures, so the comparison fails as an argument. While this contrast may hold in natural matters, moral and political contexts differ, and justification must properly be represented as a forensic matter.

If it were the case that there is no difference between being acquitted of a crime before a judge and having a right to a kingdom, then it would follow that there is no intermediate state between being pardoned and having a right to the heavenly inheritance.

But this is a foolish notion.

It is true that the right to eternal life follows from freedom from the guilt of eternal death: "that they may receive forgiveness of sins and an inheritance among those who are sanctified." However, this does not follow necessarily from the nature of the things themselves, but from the free constitution of God. Believers receive the pardon of sin, and with it in God's arrangement they receive an immediate right and title to His favor, adoption as sons, and eternal life. Yet there is another state possible in the nature of things which God might have actualized, had He pleased.

Who does not see that there could be a condition in which one is neither under the guilt of condemnation nor yet has an immediate right to glory as an inheritance? God could have pardoned all past sins and placed individuals in a state of seeking righteousness for the future by the works of the law, allowing them to live — thus resembling Adam's original state. He has not chosen to do so. While He could have, it is plain that the arrangement by which persons are placed in a state of right to life and salvation does not depend on the pardon of sin alone but has another cause: the imputation of Christ's righteousness to us, because He fulfilled the law on our behalf.

Indeed, most of our adversaries in this debate hold this view. They say that, besides the remission of sin — some asserting it absolutely, without reference to Christ's merit or satisfaction — others relate it to those merits. But they all insist that a righteousness of works is required for our justification. They maintain that this is our own partial, imperfect righteousness, imputed to us as if it were perfect; in other words, accounted for what it is not, rather than the righteousness of Christ imputed to us for what it truly is.

From what has been discussed, it is evident that our justification before God requires not only that we be freed from the condemning sentence of the law, which we obtain through the pardon of sin, but also that "that the righteous requirement of the law might be fulfilled in us," or that we possess a righteousness that meets the obedience the law demands. Our acceptance with God, through the riches of His grace, and our title to the heavenly inheritance depend on this. We do not possess such righteousness in ourselves, nor can we attain it, as has been shown. Therefore the perfect obedience and righteousness of Christ must be imputed to us; otherwise we can never be justified in the sight of God.

The objections raised by the Socinians and their followers carry no weight against the truth here. They ask, "The righteousness of Christ can only be imputed to one person, if to any; for how can the same righteousness of one become the righteousness of many, even all who believe? Furthermore, He did not perform all the duties required of us in all our relations, since He was never placed in those particular situations."

These arguments are both foolish and impious, for they subvert the whole gospel. All depends on God's ordination. Scripture teaches that "for if by the one man's offense many died," yet "much more the grace of God and the gift by the grace of the one Man, Jesus Christ, abounded to many." Likewise, "as through one man's offense judgment came to all men, resulting in condemnation, even so through one Man's righteous act the free gift came to all men, resulting in justification of life;" and "so also by one Man's obedience many will be made righteous," as the apostle argues in Romans 5.

"God did by sending His own Son in the likeness of sinful flesh, on account of sin: He condemned sin in the flesh, that the righteous requirement of the law might be fulfilled in us," as stated in Romans 8:3-4. He is "the end of the law" (the ultimate purpose of it) "for righteousness to everyone who believes," as stated in Romans 10:4. This is the appointment of God's wisdom, righteousness, and grace: that the entire righteousness and obedience of Christ should be accepted as our complete righteousness before Him, imputed to us by His grace, and made ours through faith. Consequently, this applies to all who believe.

If the actual sin of Adam is imputed to all of us, who derive our nature from him, for condemnation—despite his not sinning in our specific circumstances—why should it be strange that the actual obedience of Christ is imputed to those who derive a spiritual nature from Him for justification? Moreover, both the satisfaction and obedience of Christ, in relation to His person, were, in some sense, infinite—possessing infinite value—and thus cannot be considered in parts, as if one part were imputed to one person and another part to another. Rather, the whole is imputed to every believer. If the Israelites could claim that David was "worth ten thousand of us now" (2 Samuel 18:3), we may rightly affirm that the Lord Christ, and all that He did and suffered, is worth more than all of us combined, and all that we can do and suffer.

There are also several other misconceptions contributing to the charge against the imputation of Christ's righteousness to us, which we have now examined. I refer to His righteousness because the apostle uses the terms dikaiōma and hupakoē—"righteousness" and "obedience"—as synonymous in Romans 5:18-19.

These misconceptions include: the belief that remission of sin and justification are the same, or that justification consists solely in the remission of sin; the notion that faith itself, as our act and duty, is imputed to us for righteousness since it is the condition of the covenant; and the idea that we possess a personal, inherent righteousness that serves as our righteousness before God for justification—whether as a condition, a disposition toward it, or as having some merit that deserves the grace of justification. All these are merely different expressions of the same concept, reflecting varied understandings of individuals regarding the matter. However, all these misconceptions have been addressed and refuted in our previous discussions.

To conclude this argument and our defense of it, I acknowledge that our blessedness and eternal life are often attributed to the death of Christ in Scripture. First, this is so primarily: the death of Christ is the principal cause of everything, and without it no imputation of obedience could justify us. The penalty of the law had to be borne without fail.

Second, it is so in a secondary sense: the death of Christ is inseparably connected to other obedience mentioned in Scripture, though it is not the exclusive cause named everywhere. As Bernard states, "Christus in vita passivam habuit actionem; in morte passionem activam sustinuit; dum salutem operaretur in medio terræ." Thus the resurrection is also attributed as a demonstration and evidence. Still, the death of Christ, in relation to His obedience, is nowhere claimed as the sole cause of eternal life, which includes the immense weight of glory that accompanies it.

Thus far, we have discussed and defended the imputation of Christ's active obedience to us, deriving the truth of it from the obligation of the law of creation. I will now briefly confirm it with additional reasons and testimonies.

1. What Christ, the mediator and surety of the covenant, did in obedience to God in fulfilling His office, He did for us; and that is imputed to us. This has been previously established and is too evident to be denied. He was "For unto us a Child is born, Unto us a Son is given;" (Isaiah 9:6); for "For what the law could not do in that it was

weak through the flesh, God did by sending His own Son in the likeness of sinful flesh, on account of sin: He condemned sin in the flesh, that the righteous requirement of the law might be fulfilled in us" (Romans 8:3-4).

All that is said about the grace, love, and purpose of God in sending or giving His Son, or about the love, grace, and condescension of the Son in coming and undertaking the work of redemption, or about the office itself of a mediator or surety, supports this assertion. Indeed, it is the fundamental principle of the gospel and the faith of all who truly believe.

As for those who deny the divine person and satisfaction of Christ, thereby undermining the entire work of His mediation, we will not consider them at this time. Therefore, we must inquire into what He did. The Lord Christ, our mediator and surety, was, in His human nature, made "born under the law" (Galatians 4:4). We have previously established that He was not made so for Himself by the necessity of His condition; it was for us.

As one made under the law, He yielded obedience to it; this was for us and is imputed to us. The Socinians' objection that only the judicial law is intended is too trivial to warrant further discussion, since He was made under the law whose curse we are delivered from. If we are delivered only from the curse of the law of Moses, which they argue contains neither promises nor threats of eternal matters, we remain in our sins, under the curse of the moral law, despite all He has done for us.

It is also argued, with more semblance of reason, that He was made under the law only concerning its curse. However, the text clearly states that Christ was made under the law as we are. He was "to redeem those who were under the law, that we might receive the adoption as sons." If He was not made so as we are, there is no consequence from His being made under it for our redemption from it.

We were under the law not only to be subject to its curse but also to be obliged to all the obedience it required, as has been demonstrated. If the Lord Christ has redeemed us only from the curse of the law by undergoing it, while leaving us to fulfill its obligation to obedience, then we are not truly freed or delivered.

The expression "under the law" primarily signifies being under the obligation to obey it. Only secondarily does it refer to the curse.

Galatians 4:21 states, "Tell me, you who desire to be under the law, do you not hear the law?" They did not desire to be under the curse of the law, but under its obligation to obedience, which is the primary sense of that expression. Therefore, since the Lord Christ was made under the law for us, He yielded perfect obedience to it on our behalf; this obedience is imputed to us. The fact that what He did was done for us rests entirely on imputation.

As He was made under the law, so He actually fulfilled it through His obedience to it. He testifies concerning Himself, "Do not think that I came to destroy the Law or the Prophets. I did not come to destroy but to fulfill" (Matthew 5:17). These words of our Lord Jesus Christ, as recorded by the evangelist, are continually objected against by the Jews, who claim they contradict what Christians assert—that He has destroyed and taken away the law. Maimonides, in his treatise De Fundamentis Legis, makes many blasphemous remarks about the Lord Christ, labeling Him a false prophet in this regard.

However, the reconciliation is clear and straightforward. Two types of law were given to the church: the moral law and the ceremonial law. The moral law, as we have proven, is of eternal obligation. The ceremonial law was given only for a time.

The apostle demonstrates from the Old Testament that the ceremonial law was to be taken away and abolished—especially in his Epistle to the Hebrews. Yet it was not to be removed without its fulfillment. That fulfillment occurred when it ceased to exist. Therefore, our Lord Christ did not dissolve or destroy that law except by fulfilling it; thus He brought it to an end, as is declared in Ephesians 2:14-16.

But the law that obligates all men always to obedience to God—this law—He did not come to destroy. This is evident from the term katalusai. That term is ascribed to the Mosaic law, as seen in Hebrews 9:26 (and used in the same sense in Matthew 24:2; 26:61; 27:40; Mark 13:2; 14:58; 15:29; Luke 21:6; Acts 5:38-39; 6:14; Romans 14:20; 2 Corinthians 5:1; Galatians 2:18, mostly with an accusative case). The apostle denies that Christ did this, stating, "Do we then make void the law through faith? Certainly not! On the contrary, we establish the law." (Romans 3:31)

To "establish the law" means to confirm its obligation to obedience. For the moral law this obligation is maintained by faith alone; for the ceremonial law the obligation to obedience is rendered ineffective. This is the law our Lord affirms He came "not to destroy." He expressly declares this in His subsequent discourse, showing both the law's continuing power to obligate us and providing an exposition of it.

The term plērōsai (to fulfill) in Scripture is synonymous with emplēsai (to fill) in other writings; that is, it signifies yielding full, perfect obedience to the commands of the law and so fulfilling them entirely. Plērōsai nomon does not mean to make the law perfect—the law has always been nomos teleios, the "perfect law" (James 1:25); rather, it means to render perfect obedience to it.

This is the same obedience our Savior refers to when He speaks of plērōsai pasan dikaiosunēn—"to fulfill all righteousness"—in Matthew

3:15. In that passage He means obeying all of God's commands and institutions. The apostle uses the same expression in Romans 13:8, saying, "for he who loves another has fulfilled the law."

It is a futile objection to claim that Christ fulfilled the law solely through His teachings and interpretations. The opposition between plērōsai (to fulfill) and katalusai (to destroy) does not allow for such an interpretation. Our Savior Himself clarifies this "fulfilling of the law" by indicating that it involves doing the commands of the law (Matthew 5:19). Therefore, as our mediator and surety, Christ fulfilled the law by yielding perfect obedience to it, and this obedience is imputed to us.

This is clearly affirmed by the apostle in Romans 5:18-19: "Therefore, as through one man's offense judgment came to all men to condemnation, even so through one Man's righteous act the free gift came to all men, resulting in justification of life. For as by one man's disobedience many were made sinners, so also by one Man's obedience many will be made righteous."

The full argument and vindication of this testimony will be addressed in its proper context regarding the imputation of Christ's righteousness to our justification in general. Here, I will only note that the apostle explicitly states that "so also by one Man's obedience many will be made righteous" or justified, which can only occur through the imputation of that obedience to us.

I have encountered no serious attempt to refute this clear testimony, except for the assertion that the obedience of Christ refers only to His death and sufferings, wherein He was obedient to God, as the apostle notes: He was "obedient to the point of death, even the death of the cross" (Philippians 2:8). However, this argument lacks any substantial basis.

First, it is acknowledged that there is a close connection between Christ's obedience and His sufferings. Although they may be distinguished, they cannot be separated. He suffered throughout His entire life of obedience, from the womb to the cross, and He obeyed in all His sufferings until His last moment. Yet they are distinct realities, as we have proven; "yet He learned obedience by the things which He suffered" (Hebrews 5:8).

Second, in this passage (Romans 5), "hupakoē" (obedience) in verse 19 and "dikaiōma" (righteousness) in verse 18 are synonymous. "By the righteousness of one" and "by the obedience of one" refer to the same thing. But suffering, by itself, is not "dikaiōma"; if it were, then anyone who suffers what they deserve would be righteous and thus justified — even the devil himself.

Third, the righteousness and obedience here are contrasted with "tō paraptōmati" (the offense) of one. The offense was an actual transgression of the law; thus "paraptōma" signifies a fall from, or within, the course of obedience. Therefore, "dikaiōma" must refer to actual obedience to the commands of the law, or else the force of the apostle's reasoning and contrast would be lost.

Fourth, specifically, this obedience is contrasted with the disobedience of Adam — "one man's disobedience" versus "one Man's obedience." The disobedience of Adam was an actual transgression of the law; therefore, the obedience of Christ intended here was His active obedience to the law, which is what we advocate. I will not pursue this argument further at this time, as its strength in confirming the truth we contend for will be included in the following discussions.

14. Justification and the Two Covenants

What we argue in the third place is the difference between the two covenants. By the two covenants I mean those that were absolutely given to the whole church and were intended to bring it to "eis teleiotēta," a complete and perfect state. This includes the covenant of works, or the law of our creation, which was given to us with promises and threats, or rewards and punishments, attached to it; and the covenant of grace, revealed and proposed in the first promise.

As for the covenant of Sinai and the New Testament, which was confirmed in the death of Christ, along with all the spiritual privileges that arise from it, these do not pertain to our current argument.

The whole nature of the covenant of works was this: that upon our personal obedience, according to the law and its requirements, we should be accepted by God and rewarded by Him. This is the essence of the covenant; and any covenant that operates on these terms, or has this nature, regardless of any variations or additions, remains the same covenant and is not another.

Just as in the renewal of the promise, wherein the essence of the covenant of grace was contained, God often made other additions to it (as with Abraham and David), it remained the same covenant in substance and not another. Similarly, any variations or additions made to the dispensation of the first covenant, as long as the rule "Do this, and live" is retained, still constitute the same covenant in essence.

Thus, two things belong to this covenant:

First, all transactions were conducted directly between God and man. There was no mediator; no one undertook anything on either God's or man's behalf. Since everything depended on each person's obedience, there was no need for a mediator.

Second, only perfect, sinless obedience would be accepted by God or preserve the covenant in its original state. There was no provision for the pardon of sin or any allowance for defects in personal obedience.

Therefore, once this covenant was established between God and man, no new covenant could be made unless its essential form was of a different nature. In other words, our personal obedience could not be the rule and cause of our acceptance and justification before God. As long as that remains true, the covenant is still the same, regardless of how its administration may be reformed or adjusted to fit our current condition.

Any grace introduced into it could not exclude all works from being the cause of our justification. If a new covenant is made, such grace must be provided that is entirely inconsistent with any works of ours concerning the original purposes of the covenant, as the apostle declares in Romans 11:6.

Thus, the covenant of grace, if it is to be a new, real, absolute covenant and not merely a reformation of the old or an adjustment to our present condition, must differ in essence, substance, and nature from the first covenant of works. This cannot be true if we are to be justified before God on the basis of our personal obedience, which is the essence of the first covenant. If the righteousness by which we are justified is our own personal righteousness, then we remain under the first covenant and have no other.

However, matters in the new covenant are quite different.

First, it is based on grace, which entirely excludes works. Thus our own works are not the means of justification before God, as already noted.

Second, it includes a mediator and surety. This rests on the understanding that what we cannot accomplish—what the law of the first covenant required but could not enable us to perform—must be fulfilled for us by the mediator and surety.

Even if this is not explicitly stated in the very definition of a mediator and surety, it is inherent in the role of one who voluntarily intervenes. Such a mediator acknowledges that those for whom he acts are utterly incapable of fulfilling what was required of them. This understanding is fundamental to the truth of Scripture.

A core tenet of the Christian faith is that the Lord Christ was given to us and born for us. He came as a mediator to accomplish for us what we could not do ourselves, not merely to suffer the consequences of our actions.

In this context, instead of relying on our own righteousness, we receive "the righteousness of God." Rather than being righteous in ourselves before God, He is "THE LORD OUR RIGHTEOUSNESS."

Only a righteousness of a different kind and nature—one that leads to justification before God—could establish a new covenant. Therefore, the righteousness by which we are justified must be the righteousness of Christ imputed to us; otherwise we remain under the law and the covenant of works.

One might argue that our personal obedience is not claimed to be the righteousness by which we are justified before God, as it was under the covenant of works. But that misses the point. The issue is not merely the manner or means of justification, but its very essence.

If personal obedience is involved in any way, no matter the qualifications, we remain under that covenant. If justification depends on works in any form, it cannot be by grace.

Some assert that the differences between the covenants are sufficient to mark them as distinctly separate. For example:

1. "The perfect, sinless obedience was required in the first covenant; but in the new covenant, imperfect obedience, accompanied by many sins and failings, is accepted." This is merely an assertion and does not touch the core issue. No righteousness can be accepted for justification before God unless it is perfect.

2. "Grace is the original fountain and cause of all our acceptance before God in the new covenant." That was also true under the old covenant. The creation of man in original righteousness was an act of divine grace and kindness; the reward of eternal life in God's presence was granted solely by sovereign grace. Yet what then counted as works was not grace, and the same distinction applies now.

3. "There would then have been merit in works, which is now excluded." If by merit one means an equality or proportion between works and reward under the principle of commutative justice, no such merit existed under the first covenant. In no other relevant sense is it now rejected by those who oppose the imputation of Christ's righteousness.

4. "All is now resolved into the merit of Christ, based solely on which our own personal righteousness is accepted before God for our justification." The real question is not on what basis or for what reason it is accepted, but whether it is accepted at all—because acceptance of our own righteousness in that way would be constitutive of a covenant of works.

15. No Works Contribute to Justification

We now present our fourth argument, founded on the explicit exclusion of all works, of whatever kind, from our justification before God. This is the heart of our claim: no acts or works of our own serve as causes or conditions for justification. Instead, justification is rooted entirely in the free grace of God through Jesus Christ, who is the mediator and surety of the covenant.

The Scripture speaks directly to this matter. Romans 3:28 states, "Therefore we conclude that a man is justified by faith apart from the deeds of the law." Romans 4:5 says, "But to him who does not work but believes on Him who justifies the ungodly, his faith is accounted for righteousness." Romans 11:6 adds, "And if by grace, then it is no longer of works." Galatians 2:16 affirms, "Knowing that a man is not justified by the works of the law but by faith in Jesus Christ, even we have believed in Christ Jesus, that we might be justified by faith in Christ and not by the works of the law; for by the works of the law no flesh shall be justified." Ephesians 2:8-9 states, "For by grace you have been saved through faith, and that not of yourselves; it is the gift of God, not of works, lest anyone should boast." Titus 3:5 declares, "Not by works of righteousness which we have done, but according to His mercy He saved us."

These testimonies are clear and directly support everything we argue. I am convinced that no unbiased person, whose mind is not clouded by preconceived notions or by distinctions absent from the cited texts, can reasonably conclude otherwise. The law, in every sense, and all kinds of works that sinners or believers perform are excluded from our justification before God.

If this is true, then we must rely solely on the righteousness of Christ, or the discussion ends. The apostle draws this very conclusion from one of the cited texts, Galatians 2:19-21, where he says, "For I through the law died to the law that I might live to God. I have been crucified with Christ; it is no longer I who live, but Christ lives in me; and the life which I now live in the flesh I live by faith in the Son of God, who loved me and gave Himself for me. I do not set aside the grace of God; for if righteousness comes through the law, then Christ died in vain."

Our opponents are deeply divided among themselves and cannot reach any consistent understanding of the apostle's assertions. What is plain to all—especially the opposition set up between the law and works on one hand, and faith, grace, and Christ on the other, which the apostle treats as incompatible in the matter of our justification—they refuse to accept. They cannot do so without undermining their own positions.

Therefore we will examine their various conjectures and show their inconsistencies, supporting our present argument. Some claim that only the ceremonial law and its works are intended, or that the law given to Moses on Sinai—the covenant later abolished—is what is meant. That was once a common schoolmen's opinion, but it has now been largely discredited.

The recent argument that Paul excludes justification from the works of the law only insofar as he means perfectly sinless obedience—not because no one can render that perfect obedience, but because the law itself cannot justify anyone by observance—is merely a revival of that outdated notion.

This view is largely irrelevant to, and contradicts, the apostle's intent, and even Bellarmine rejects it. The apostle speaks of the law whose doers will be justified (Romans 2:13), yet proponents of this view would treat it as a law that cannot justify anyone who observes it.

The law he refers to is the one that provides knowledge of sin. He explains that we cannot be justified by its works because "by the law is the knowledge of sin" (Romans 3:20). He clarifies which law supplies this knowledge by saying, "For I would not have known covetousness unless the law had said, 'You shall not covet'" (Romans 7:7), a reference specifically to the moral law.

This law is the one that stops every mouth and makes the whole world guilty before God (Romans 3:19). It is the law whose requirements were written in the hearts of men at their creation (Romans 2:14-15). This law declares that "The man who does those things shall live by them" (Galatians 3:12; Romans 10:5) and brings everyone under the curse for sin (Galatians 3:10).

This law is established by faith and is not made void (Romans 3:31). The ceremonial law does not fulfill this role, nor does the covenant of Sinai. The righteousness of this law is "to be fulfilled in us" (Romans 8:4).

The example the apostle gives of justification apart from the works of the law—Abraham's justification—occurred centuries before the ceremonial law was given. I do not deny, however, that the ceremonial law and its works are excluded from the apostle's meaning. When that law was given, its observances were a particular instance of the obedience required under the first table of the Decalogue. Therefore, excluding its works from our justification also excludes all other works, since those ceremonial observances were a kind of moral obedience owed to God.

But to insist that only that law could never justify anyone by observance, even if perfectly observed, is a mistaken and self-contradictory notion. Augustine explicitly rejects such a claim in On the Spirit and the Letter, chapter 8. He warns, "Let no one suppose that the apostle said here that no one is justified by the law that contains many figurative precepts in the old sacraments, including the circumcision of the flesh. He immediately adds what he calls the law, saying, 'for by the law is the knowledge of sin.'"

He says the same thing elsewhere in a letter: not only those works of the law that belong to the old sacraments—circumcision of the flesh, the carnal Sabbath, abstaining from certain foods, animal sacrifices, new moons, unleavened bread, and similar observances—are not the ground of justification for Christians under the new covenant; but also that command of the law, "You shall not covet," which no Christian doubts is part of the moral law, does not justify a person except through faith in Jesus Christ and by the grace of God through our Lord Jesus Christ.

Some maintain the opposite view: that Paul excludes only the perfect works demanded by the law of innocence. This is essentially the position of the Socinians. Socinus writes: "Paul speaks of works and perfect works in this statement; therefore, he added 'apart from the deeds of the law' to indicate that he is referring to the works required by the law, and thus to the perpetual and perfect obedience to divine commandments as the law requires. Since no one can render such obedience as the law demands, the apostle asserts that we are justified by faith—by trust and by the obedience each person can render, striving daily to do as much as possible, even though he cannot perfectly fulfill the whole law as he ought."

However, several objections may be made to this view:

1. Here they concede precisely what we contend: the apostle intends the moral, indispensable law of God, and by the works of this law no one is justified. He excludes all such works from justification, for he speaks of justification "apart from the deeds of the law." The works of this law, if performed according to it, would justify those who do them, as he states in Romans 2:13; and Scripture elsewhere declares that "The man who does those things shall live by them." But because no sinner can ever fulfill the law perfectly, all such works are thereby excluded from our justification.

2. It is an absurd fiction to suggest that the apostle's argument is merely that perfect works cannot justify, while imperfect works will. That turns his argument on its head.

3. Even if we grant that the intended law is the moral law given at creation, the apostle gives no hint that justification is by some imperfect obedience we can render. There is nothing in his words or design to suggest that imperfect works, which fail to meet the law's demands, are the basis of justification.

4. Their evasion—that Paul only opposes justification by works to a certain kind of faith which they identify with our imperfect obedience—is futile. When the apostle excludes justification by the law and its works, he does not propose our own faith and obedience as the substitute. Instead he adds the remedy: "being justified freely by His grace through the redemption that is in Christ Jesus, whom God set forth as a propitiation by His blood."

Recently some among us, following predecessors, assert that the works the apostle excludes are only outward works done without an inward principle of faith, fear, or love. They argue that merely servile works—

performed out of fear of the law's threats — are what cannot justify. This opinion is not only mistaken but impious.

1. The apostle excludes even the works of Abraham, which were not mere outward, servile performances, as these detractors imagine.

2. The works excluded are those required by the law, which is holy and just and good. A law that requires only outward works, devoid of internal love for God, is neither holy, just, nor good.

3. The law condemns all works that are separated from the internal principles of faith, fear, and love. It requires that, in all our obedience, we love the Lord your God with all your heart. The apostle states that we are not justified by the works that the law condemns, nor by those that the law commands.

4. It greatly honors God that He — who alone can know the hearts of men and therefore regards them in all duties of obedience — should be represented as giving a law that requires only outward, servile works. If the law were intended to require more, those would not be the only works excluded.

Some claim, in general, that it is the Jewish law that is intended, thinking this will resolve the entire difficulty. However, if by the Jewish law they mean only the ceremonial law or the law as given by Moses, we have already demonstrated the futility of that claim. If they refer to the entire law or rule of obedience given to the church of Israel under the Old Testament, they express a significant portion of the truth, perhaps more than they intended.

Some assert that it is works performed with a notion of merit — which makes the reward a matter of debt rather than grace — that the apostle excludes. However, no such distinction appears in the text or context.

1. The apostle excludes all works of the law, meaning those that the law requires of us in obedience, regardless of their nature.

2. The law does not require works with a notion of merit.

3. The works of the law originally included no merit, for merit arises from the proportion of one thing to another in the balance of justice; this is the sense in which those who argue for an interest of works in justification are mistaken.

4. The merit that the apostle excludes is that which is inseparable from works, so it cannot be excluded unless the works themselves are excluded. Two things contribute to their merit:

- First, a comparative boasting, which is not absolute in the sight of God, but that which gives one person a preference over another in obtaining justification; this is something grace does not allow, as stated in chapter 4, verse 2.

- Second, if the reward is conditioned on works, it is not purely of grace; it becomes a matter of debt. This debt does not arise from an internal condignity (which would not have existed under the law of creation), but from some congruity in relation to the promise of God, as seen in verse 4.

In these two respects, merit is inseparable from works. Therefore the Holy Spirit, to exclude it completely, excludes all works from which it is inseparable.

5. The apostle does not merely exclude the merit of works; he excludes all works. He reasons that to admit works would necessarily introduce the kind of merit described, which is inconsistent with grace. Some who are accused of asserting merit when they speak of our works in justification protest that the charge is unfair. Yet those among them

who best understand themselves and the controversy are not averse to some form of merit, since they know it is inseparable from works.

Some maintain that the apostle excludes only works done before believing—works performed by our own will and natural ability without the aid of grace. They hold that the works required by the law are those we perform solely under the law's direction and command. But the law of faith requires works that are enabled by grace, and those are not excluded. This is the position adopted by many learned and judicious members of the Roman Church today.

Those among us who argue for a role of works in our justification often deploy various distinctions to clarify their view and to distance themselves from the opinions of the Papists. Yet they still deny the concept of merit in the sense held by the Roman Church—a stance also renounced by all Socinians. Consequently, they rely on the prior argument that the apostle excludes merit and that only meritorious works are excluded. But the apostle's clear point is that works are excluded because any merit that opposes grace is inseparable from their acceptance.

However, the Roman Church finds it difficult to abandon the notion of merit entirely. So they must identify a class of works they are willing to exclude as non-meritorious. These are the works already described—those they claim are done before believing and without the aid of grace—and they assert that all works of the law fall into this category.

They pursue this argument with more modesty and sobriety than some among us who would confine the discussion to external acts and observances. They acknowledge that certain internal acts—such as attrition and sorrow for sin—also belong to this excluded category. Nevertheless, they insist that it is the works of the law that are excluded.

This whole argument, together with the sophistries that support it, has been thoroughly examined and refuted by Protestant writers of every stripe against Bellarmine and others. It is therefore unnecessary to repeat those refutations or add to them here. The falsehood of their claims will be sufficiently exposed in what we shall shortly demonstrate regarding the law and the works the apostle refers to.

Nevertheless, we can briefly outline the key points that demonstrate the truth of the matter:

1. The apostle excludes all works without distinction or exception. We should not make distinctions where the law makes none.

2. All works of the law are excluded. Therefore, all works performed after believing—even those done with the aid of grace—are likewise excluded, since they are required by the law (see Psalm 119:35; Romans 7:22). Works not required by the law are no less abominable to God than transgressions of the law.

3. The apostle expressly excludes from justification the works of believers performed after conversion with the aid of grace. This exclusion even covers Abraham's post-conversion works, though he was a believer for many years and excelled in good works to the praise of God. The apostle therefore sets aside his own works after conversion (Galatians 2:16; 1 Corinthians 4:4; Philippians 3:9) as well as the works of all other believers (Ephesians 2:9-10).

4. All works that could give occasion for boasting are excluded (Romans 4:2; 3:27; Ephesians 2:9; 1 Corinthians 1:29-31). This exclusion is primarily directed at the good works of regenerate persons rather than at any deeds of unbelievers.

5. The law demands faith and love in all our works. Consequently, if every work of the law is excluded, then even the best works of believers are excluded.

6. All works that oppose grace's free operation in our justification are excluded; this applies to every kind of work (Romans 11:6).

7. In Galatians the apostle rejects as necessary for justification the very works the false teachers insisted upon. They pressed the necessity of believers' works—works already performed by those converted to God—and the apostle excludes those requirements.

8. The apostle excludes good works from justification. There can be no claim of justification by works that are not truly good or that lack the essential qualities that make works good. All works done by unbelievers, without the aid of grace, are not good and are not accepted by God, for they lack what is fundamentally necessary. It would be absurd to suppose the apostle argues about excluding such works from justification, since no reasonable person would count them worthy of inclusion.

9. No one can be justified by the law because no one can render perfect obedience to it; according to the law only perfect obedience can justify (Romans 2:13; 10:5). Therefore every work that falls short of absolute perfection is excluded, and the best works of believers are not perfect, as has already been shown.

10. If any place is allowed for the works of believers performed with the aid of grace in our justification, it must be either as co-causes of justification or as indispensably subservient to whatever causes justification. Yet it is not asserted that they are co-causes, nor can it be maintained that they are necessarily subservient.

They are not subservient to the efficient cause, which is solely the grace and favor of God (Romans 3:24-25; 4:16; Ephesians 2:8-9). They are not subservient to the meritorious cause, which is Christ alone (Acts 13:38; 26:18; 1 Corinthians 1:30; 2 Corinthians 5:18-21). They are not subservient to the material cause, which is the righteousness of Christ alone (Romans 10:3-4). Nor are they subservient to faith, wherever faith is placed, for faith alone is mentioned as the means by which Christ's righteousness is reckoned to us, with no suggestion that works share in that role. Indeed, in the matter of justification, works and faith are set in opposition to one another (Romans 3:28). Many other arguments to the same effect could be offered.

Some contend that the apostle excludes all works from our initial justification but not from our ongoing or continued justification. We have already examined those distinctions and found them to be without foundation.

It is therefore evident that such individuals put themselves in an uncertain, precarious position. They can find nothing solid to rely on, nor any semblance of truth to support their denial of the apostle's clear and frequently repeated assertion.

In light of this, I will further examine what the apostle means by "the law" and by "the works" he discusses. Whatever these are in relation to our justification, they stand entirely and universally opposed to grace, to faith, to the righteousness of God, and to the blood of Christ. They are fundamentally inconsistent with those realities, and the apostle's intention to demonstrate that inconsistency cannot reasonably be denied or questioned.

In general, it is plain that by "the law" and "the works" the apostle intends what the Jews understood by those terms: the Jews meant the whole obedience required by the law. This cannot be disputed; without that assumption nothing said about them can be proved against the

Jews, nor can the apostle's addresses make sense. If the apostle and his opponents meant different things by "the law" and "works," then no just conclusions can be drawn from his arguments. Therefore he proceeds on the basis that the meanings of those terms are well known and agreed upon between him and his readers.

The Jews understood "the law" to mean what the Old Testament Scriptures meant by that term. They were not censured for having any false notion of the law, nor did they regard as law anything not recognized as such in Scripture. The oral law, as developed later, had not yet come into being, though the Pharisees were beginning to formulate it.

"The law" in the Old Testament refers directly to the law given at Mount Sinai, and there is no distinct mention of it prior to that event. It is commonly called "the law" in an absolute sense, and more frequently "the law of God," "the law of the Lord," or "the law of Moses," on account of Moses' role in delivering it: "Remember the Law of Moses, My servant, Which I commanded him," (Malachi 4:4). This is what the Jews meant by "the law."

The law given at Horeb may be divided into three parts:

1. The Ten Commandments — Deuteronomy 4:13, "the Ten Commandments;" also found in chapter 10:4. This part of the law was given first. It serves as the foundation of the whole and contains the perfect obedience required of humanity by the law of creation. The church received it with the highest attestations of its indispensable obligation to obedience and its sanction of punishment.

2. The Statutes — which the Septuagint renders "dikaiōmata," meaning rites or statutes. The Latin term derived from this, "justificationes," has caused serious misunderstanding among many ancient and modern theologians. We commonly call this the ceremonial law. The apostle

specifically refers to this portion as "the law of commandments contained in ordinances" (Ephesians 2:15), and it consists of a multitude of arbitrary commands.

3. The Judicial Law — this division completes the Old Testament legislation. In many passages the general term "the law" denotes only the Ten Commandments (עֲשֶׂרֶת הַדְּבָרִים). See Malachi 4:4 for this usage.

These parts of the law given at Sinai are collectively called "the law" (וּבֹרָה), meaning the instruction God provided to the covenant community as the rule of obedience He prescribed. This is the consistent use of the term in Scripture when taken absolutely. It does not refer solely to the statute delivered at Horeb, but embraces all Old Testament revelations that expound and confirm that law — its rules, motives, directions, and means of enforcing obedience.

Therefore, — "the law," — is the complete rule of obedience that God provided to the church in the Old Testament, together with all the power that accompanied it through God's ordinances. This includes every promise and warning meant to motivate the obedience God required. This is what God and the church called "the law" in the Old Testament, and it is the same term used by the Jews with whom our apostle interacted.

What we call "the moral law" serves as the foundation of the whole system. The parts we identify as "the judicial and ceremonial law" were specific instances of the obedience required of the church in the Old Testament, especially in the unique governance and the divine worship necessary at that time.

The Scripture testifies to two things concerning this law:

1. It was a perfect and complete rule of all internal spiritual and moral obedience required by God from the church: "The law of the Lord is

perfect, converting the soul; The testimony of the Lord is sure, making wise the simple;" (Psalm 19:7).

2. It encompassed all external duties of obedience, regarding matter and manner, time and season, so that the church could walk "To the law and to the testimony!" (Isaiah 8:20).

Although the original duties of the moral part of the law are often given priority over the specific instances of obedience in outward worship, the entire law has always been the comprehensive rule of all obedience — internal and external — that God required from the church and accepted from those who believed.

This law, this rule of obedience, was ordained by God as the instrument of His governance over the church. Because it was adapted to the covenant made with Abraham, its introduction at Sinai did not annul that covenant. It was accompanied by a power and efficacy that enabled obedience.

The law itself, as merely preceptive and commanding, did not provide any power or ability for those under it to yield obedience — just as the mere commands of the gospel do not. Moreover, under the Old Testament it weighed on the minds and consciences of people by the manner of its initial delivery and the severity of its sanctions, producing fear and bondage. It was also joined with burdensome rules of outward worship, making it a heavy yoke for the people.

However, as God's doctrine, teaching, and instruction in all acceptable obedience to Himself, and being adapted to the covenant of Abraham, it was accompanied by an administration of effective grace that procured and promoted obedience within the church. The law should not be viewed apart from the aids to obedience that God provided under the Old Testament; their effects are therefore attributed to the law itself. See Psalms 1, 19, and 119.

This understanding of "the law," as perceived by the apostle and those he engaged with, leads to the next inquiry: What did they mean by "works" or "works of the law"? It is clear they intended to denote the universal, sincere obedience of the church to God according to this law.

The law of God acknowledges no other works; in fact, it explicitly condemns all works that contain any defect rendering them unacceptable to God. Thus, despite all the commands God positively gave for the strict observance of sacrifices, offerings, and similar practices, when the people performed them without faith and love, He expressly stated that He "commanded them not" to be observed in that manner.

In these works, therefore, lay their personal righteousness, as they walked "walking in all the commandments and ordinances of the Lord blameless" (Luke 1:6), serving God "night and day" (Acts 26:7). They regarded this as their own righteousness, their righteousness according to the law, as it indeed was (Philippians 3:6, 9).

Although the Pharisees greatly corrupted the doctrine of the law and imposed false interpretations on various precepts, there is no indication that the church of those days understood "the works of the law" as merely ceremonial duties, external works, or works performed with a notion of merit, or without an internal principle of faith and love to God.

All this is clearly articulated in the affirmation made by the scribe regarding the essence and purpose of the law, as well as the nature of the obedience it requires, which was articulated at his request by our blessed Savior.

In Mark 12:28-33, "Then one of the scribes came, and having heard them reasoning together, perceiving that He had answered them well, asked Him, 'Which is the first commandment of all?'" (or as it is in Matthew 22:36, "Teacher, which is the great commandment in the law?") "Jesus answered him, 'The first of all the commandments is: "Hear, O Israel: The Lord our God, the Lord is one. And you shall love the Lord your God with all your heart, with all your soul, with all your mind, and with all your strength." This is the first commandment. And the second, like it, is this: "You shall love your neighbor as yourself." There is no other commandment greater than these.'"

The scribe replied, "So the scribe said to Him, 'Well said, Teacher, You have spoken the truth; for there is one God, and there is no other but He. And to love Him with all the heart, with all the understanding, with all the soul, and with all the strength, and to love one's neighbor as oneself, is more than all the whole burnt offerings and sacrifices.'"

This is so explicitly stated by Moses as the sum of the law — namely, faith and love as the principle of all our obedience (Deuteronomy 6:4, 5) — that it is astonishing what could lead any learned, sober person to adopt any other interpretation, such as limiting it to ceremonial or external works, or those that may be performed without faith or love.

This is the law concerning which the apostle argues, and this is the obedience that constitutes the works of it. Beyond this, in the realm of obedience, God has never required nor will require anything more from anyone in this world. Therefore, the law and its works, which the apostle excludes from justification, are those by which we are obliged to believe in God as the one true God and to love Him with all our hearts and souls, and our neighbors as ourselves. Any works that can be performed by individuals, whether regenerate or unregenerate, in the strength of grace or without it, that are acceptable to God, can be categorized under these principles.

The apostle himself declares that it is the law and its works, in the sense we have expressed, that he excludes from our justification. The law he refers to is "the law of righteousness" (Romans 9:31) — the law whose righteousness is to be "fulfilled in us" (Romans 8:4), so that we may be accepted by God and freed from condemnation.

This law is the basis of our own personal righteousness, whether we consider it before conversion (Romans 10:3) or after it (Philippians 3:9). It is the law which, if a man observes, "the man who does those things shall live by them" and be justified before God (Romans 2:13; Galatians 3:12; Romans 10:5). This law is "holy and just and good," revealing and condemning all sin (Romans 7:7, 9).

From what has been said, two things clearly support our present argument:

The law meant by the apostle, when he denies that anyone can be justified by the works of the law, is the full rule and guide for our obedience to God. It embraces the whole framework and spiritual constitution of our souls, together with all acts of obedience or duties that He requires of us.

The works of this law — which the apostle frequently and plainly excludes from justification and opposes to the grace of God and the blood of Christ — include all duties of obedience. These are both internal and supernatural, as well as external and ritual, regardless of how we are enabled to perform them.

With these things excluded, we are justified before God solely on account of the righteousness of Christ imputed to us.

The real difference among us today about the doctrine of justification before God is, so far as I can discern, the same difference that existed between the apostle and the Jews — and nothing more.

Religious controversies often seem new when they are only varied or clothed in new terms and expressions. This is true of the dispute concerning nature and grace; in its essential character it is the same today as it was between the apostle Paul and the Pharisees, and later between Augustine and Pelagius.

Yet the question has passed through so many forms and terminologies that it is scarcely recognizable. Many will condemn Pelagius and the doctrine he taught in his own words, while at the same time embracing and approving the very thoughts he intended.

Every change in philosophical learning gives the impression that the controversies themselves have changed. But if we strip away the layers of philosophical expressions, distinctions, metaphysical notions, and futile terms of art that ancient schoolmen and later disputants have applied, we shall find that the disagreement about grace and nature among us is fundamentally the same as it was in the past, as even the Socinians acknowledge.

Thus, when the apostle treats our justification before God he uses terms that both express the matter itself and were well understood by those he addressed. The Holy Spirit, in revealing these truths, had consecrated those terms for their proper use.

On the one hand, he expressly excludes the law, our own works, and our own righteousness from any role in justification. On the other hand, and in direct opposition to them, he attributes justification entirely to the righteousness of God — righteousness imputed to us; the obedience of Christ; Christ made righteousness for us; the blood of Christ as a propitiation; faith; receiving Christ; and the atonement.

Every awakened conscience, guided by even a small degree of spiritual illumination, clearly understands these matters and what is intended by them.

However, the introduction of foreign learning — with its philosophical terms and notions — has altered the whole matter and given it a new appearance. This has produced a blending of concepts that the apostle directly opposes as contrary and inconsistent.

Consequently, all our discussions about preparations, dispositions, conditions, and merits — "de congruo et condigno" — together with a plethora of distinctions, risk becoming so convoluted that, unless we set limits to inventing and creating these terms (an easy task that presses upon us daily), we may soon be unable to discern the intended meanings or to understand one another correctly.

As someone has said about lies, arbitrary distinctions must be continually re-covered, or they will leak through. The best course is to strip away all these coverings. Then we will quickly see that the real difference about the justification of a sinner before God is the same as it was in the days of the apostle Paul — between him and the Jews.

All the arguments people now advance about causality in our justification before God — under names like preparations, conditions, dispositions, merit, or first and second justification — are as effectively excluded by the apostle as if he had explicitly named each one. These pleadings are framed according to our own conceptions and the language of current learning, and they defend personal righteousness, which the Jews maintained against the apostle.

A true understanding of what he means by the law, its works, and righteousness would settle this controversy — if people had not become so skilled in the art of endless wrangling.

16. Justification by Faith Alone

The truth we uphold consists of two parts:

1. The righteousness of God imputed to us for the justification of life is the righteousness of Christ. Through His obedience we are made righteous.

2. Faith alone is required on our part to lay hold of that righteousness, enabling us to accept God's offer and receive it for our use and benefit.

Although this faith is the root principle of all obedience — since anything that does not show itself in works is not of the same nature — it is nevertheless by this faith that we are justified. Its act and duty are such that no other grace, duty, or work can be joined with it or have any bearing on justification.

Both of these points are clearly supported by Scripture's descriptions of the nature of faith and of believing for the justification of life.

I recognize that many expressions used to describe the nature and work of faith here are metaphorical, or at least are commonly regarded as such. Nevertheless, these are the expressions the Holy Spirit, in His infinite wisdom, chose for the instruction and edification of the church.

I must say that those who fail to see how effectively these expressions communicate the light of knowledge to believers' minds—and the sense of the spiritual experiences intended—have not given them proper consideration. Whatever our skill, we do not always recognize which expressions are metaphorical. Often what appears to be metaphor is actually the most appropriate description.

Therefore, it is safest to adhere to the Holy Spirit's expressions and to avoid interpretations that contradict them.

Consequently, the faith by which we are justified is often described in the New Testament as receiving. I treated this earlier in our general inquiry into its role in justification, so I will not elaborate on it here.

Two observations can be made regarding this concept:

1. It is expressed in relation to the entire object of faith, or all that contributes to our justification. We are said to receive Christ Himself: "But as many as received Him, to them He gave the right to become children of God, to those who believe in His name:" (John 1:12); "As you therefore have received Christ Jesus the Lord, so walk in Him," (Colossians 2:6). In contrast, unbelief is described as not receiving Him (John 1:11; 3:11; 12:48; 14:17). This reception of Christ includes acknowledging Him as "The Lord our Righteousness," for God has made Him righteousness for us.

Because no grace or duty can cooperate with faith in this respect—this reception of Christ is not of their nature nor included in their exercise—any other righteousness is excluded from our justification. We are "justified by faith." Faith alone receives Christ, and what it receives is the cause of our justification, by which we become children of God.

We also "received the reconciliation" made by the blood of Christ (Romans 5:11), for "whom God set forth as a propitiation by His blood, through faith" (Romans 3:25). This reception of the atonement includes the soul's approval of the way of salvation through the blood of Christ, as well as the appropriation of that atonement for our own souls. Through this, we receive the forgiveness of sins: "that they may receive forgiveness of sins and an inheritance among those who are sanctified by faith in Me" (Acts 26:18).

In receiving Christ, we receive the atonement; and in the atonement, we receive the forgiveness of sins. Moreover, the grace of God and righteousness itself—both the efficient and the material cause of our justification—are received as well, specifically "abundance of grace and of the gift of righteousness" (Romans 5:17).

Thus, faith—regarding all the causes of justification—is expressed as receiving. It also receives the promise, the instrumental cause on God's part (Acts 2:41; Hebrews 9:15).

The nature of faith, and its action concerning all the causes of justification, consists in receiving. This means the object of faith must be offered, presented, and given to us as something that is not our own but becomes our own through this giving and receiving. This is evident in the general nature of receiving.

As noted, no other grace or duty can concur with it. Therefore the righteousness by which we are justified cannot be our own prior to this reception, nor can it ever be inherent in us.

If the work of faith in our justification is the receiving of what is freely granted, given, communicated, and imputed to us—that is, of Christ, the atonement, the gift of righteousness, and the forgiveness of sins—then our other graces, obedience, duties, and works have no influence on our justification. They are neither the receiving nor the thing received, and thus they are not causes or conditions of justification.

Faith is also expressed as looking: "Look to Me, and be saved," (Isaiah 45:22); "a man will look to his Maker, And his eyes will have respect for the Holy One of Israel" (Isaiah 17:7); "then they will look on Me whom they pierced" (Zechariah 12:10). See also Psalm 123:2.

The nature of this faith is illustrated in John 3:14-15: "And as Moses lifted up the serpent in the wilderness, even so must the Son of Man be lifted up, that whoever believes in Him should not perish but have eternal life." He was to be lifted up on the cross in His death (John 8:28; 12:32). The story is recorded in Numbers 21:8-9.

It is generally accepted that the stinging of the people by fiery serpents and the resulting death were types of the guilt of sin and the sentence of the fiery law. These events occurred as types (1 Corinthians 10:11). When anyone was bitten, if they sought other remedies, they died. Only those who looked to the brazen serpent that was lifted up were healed and lived, for this was the ordinance of God—the only appointed way of healing. Their healing was a type of the pardon of sin and everlasting life.

Thus, the act of looking is how the nature of faith is expressed. Our Savior clearly explains it: "even so must the Son of Man be lifted up, that whoever believes in Him"—that is, just as the Israelites looked at the serpent in the wilderness—"should not perish."

Although some have ridiculed this expression of the great mystery of the gospel as presented by Christ, it remains profoundly instructive. It teaches us about the nature of faith, justification, and salvation through Christ as clearly as any passage in Scripture.

If faith by which we are justified is a looking unto Christ—acknowledging our guilt and lost condition, and seeking all help, relief, deliverance, righteousness, and life solely in Him—then it excludes all other graces and duties, for we do not look to them and they are not what we seek. This is how the nature and exercise of faith is expressed by the Holy Spirit, and those who believe understand His intent.

Regardless of any claims that this is merely a metaphor, faith is the act of the soul by which those who are hopeless, helpless, and lost in themselves seek all help and relief in Christ alone. If it does not do this, it lacks truth. This also sufficiently demonstrates the nature of our justification by Christ.

Faith is frequently expressed as coming to Christ: "Come to Me, all you who labor" (Matthew 11:28). See also John 6:35, 37, 45, 65; 7:37. Coming to Christ for life and salvation means believing in Him for justification. No other grace or duty constitutes coming to Christ; therefore, they have no place in justification.

Anyone who has been convinced of sin, who is weary from its burden, and who genuinely desires to escape the coming wrath, upon hearing Christ's invitation in the gospel to come to Him for help and rest, will tell you that this coming to Christ involves a complete renunciation of all personal duties and righteousness. It requires placing all trust and confidence in Christ alone and His righteousness for the pardon of sin, acceptance with God, and a right to the heavenly inheritance.

Some may argue that this is not true belief but mere canting; let us leave that judgment to the church of God.

Faith is also expressed as fleeing for refuge: "who have fled for refuge to lay hold of the hope set before us" (Hebrews 6:18). See also Proverbs 18:10. Some have defined faith as perfugium animæ, the flight of the soul to Christ for deliverance from sin and misery.

This definition sheds much light on the intended meaning. It assumes that the believer is first convinced of their lost condition and understands that if they remain in it, they will perish eternally. They recognize that they have nothing of their own to deliver them from this state and must turn to something else for relief.

To this end, they consider Christ as presented to them in the promise of the gospel. They judge this path to be holy and safe for their deliverance and acceptance with God, since it bears the marks of all divine excellencies. Consequently, they flee to it for refuge, acting with diligence and urgency so that they do not perish in their present condition. They place their entire trust and reliance on it.

The entire nature of our justification by Christ is better expressed through this concept than through a hundred philosophical arguments about it.

The terms and notions used to express faith in the Old Testament include leaning on the Lord (Micah 3:11) or leaning on her beloved (Song of Solomon 8:5); rolling or casting our burdens on the Lord (Psalm 22:8; 37:5) — expressions that some have profanely derided; resting in the Lord (2 Chronicles 14:11; Psalm 37:7); cleaving to the Lord (Deuteronomy 4:4; Acts 11:23); as well as trusting, hoping, and waiting in numerous passages.

It is noteworthy that those who acted in faith as described by these expressions consistently declare themselves to be lost, hopeless, helpless, desolate, poor, and orphaned, placing all their hope and expectation solely on the Lord.

From these observations, I conclude that the faith by which we believe for the justification of life, or which is required of us as a duty to be justified, is an act of the whole soul. It involves convinced sinners completely going out of themselves to rest upon God in Christ for mercy, pardon, life, righteousness, and salvation, with a heartfelt acquiescence therein. This encapsulates the entirety of the truth being advocated.

17. Biblical Testimony

We now turn to the explicit testimonies from Scripture that affirm the doctrine of justification by the imputation of Christ's righteousness. It is essential to consider those passages where the justification of sinners is directly addressed. From these Scriptures we must derive our understanding, and our faith must be anchored in their authority, which takes precedence over all human arguments and objections. These passages illuminate believers' minds far more than the most intricate philosophical debates.

It is scandalous that among some Protestants entire books have been written on justification without citing a single Scripture, or else citing it only to evade its force. Although the Apostle Paul thoroughly articulated and defended the doctrine of evangelical justification, many writers fail to ground their views in his writings. Instead, they often criticize his clarity, suggesting his words encourage dangerous misunderstandings, and counter his teachings by recourse to their own flawed principles while seldom acknowledging his insights. It is as if we think ourselves wiser than he, or than the Spirit who inspired him.

Nothing could be more contrary to the essence of the Christian faith than neglecting the humble pursuit of understanding the mystery of

God's grace as revealed in Scripture. Whatever paths people choose in their religious professions, the foundation of God remains steadfast.

For the testimonies I will present, I ask the reader to note:

1. These are only a few of many passages that could be cited for the same purpose.

2. I will omit those testimonies that have been or will be mentioned on specific occasions, particularly those from the Old Testament.

3. In my exposition of these testimonies I will diligently adhere to two main principles:

a. The analogy of faith—that is, the clear intention and purpose of God's revelation in Scripture. This revelation aims to exalt the freedom and richness of His grace, the glory and excellence of Christ and His mediation, and to show the lost and desperate condition of humanity because of sin. It likewise serves to reduce any reliance on ourselves for life, righteousness, and salvation—a truth evident to anyone whose senses are trained in the Scriptures.

b. The experiences of believers, together with the condition of those who seek justification through Jesus Christ.

In other matters, I intend to employ the best available aids and rules for interpreting Scripture, without neglect.

There is significant weight placed on the name of the Lord Jesus Christ, the Son of God, as promised and given to us — specifically, "THE LORD OUR RIGHTEOUSNESS." (Jeremiah 23:6) Just as the name Jehovah signifies His divine nature, the title of our righteousness indicates that we are made righteous solely through Him.

He is foreshadowed by Melchizedek, who is first called the "king of righteousness" and then the "king of peace" (Hebrews 7:2); for it is through His righteousness alone that we have peace with God. Some Socinians attempt to evade this testimony by claiming that righteousness in the Old Testament sometimes refers to kindness and mercy, suggesting that this may apply here. However, most acknowledge that it refers to God's righteousness in delivering and vindicating His people. As Brenius succinctly states, "He is called so because the Lord will execute judgment and justice for Israel through Him."

Yet these are evasions from those who care little whether their claims align with the analogy of faith or the clear words of Scripture. Bellarmine, more cautious in his responses, offers various reasons why Christ is called "THE LORD OUR RIGHTEOUSNESS." He acknowledges that Christ may be termed our righteousness because He is the efficient cause of our righteousness, just as God is described as our "strength and salvation."

Moreover, he states, "Christ is said to be our righteousness, as He is our wisdom, redemption, and peace; because He has redeemed us, grants us wisdom and righteousness, and reconciles us to God." Other similar reasons are provided by others. However, not fully trusting these interpretations, he adds, "Christ is called our righteousness because He has made satisfaction to the Father for us, and He communicates that satisfaction to us when He justifies us, so that it can be said to be our satisfaction and righteousness."

He further states, "In this sense, it would not be absurd for someone to say that Christ's righteousness and merits are imputed to us, as if we ourselves had satisfied God."

In this context, we affirm that Christ is "THE LORD OUR RIGHTEOUSNESS." There is nothing of significance in the entire doctrine of justification that we uphold which is not acknowledged by the cardinal, and he does so using terms that some among us find objectionable.

Thus, I will delve deeper into this testimony, which has elicited such a notable confession of truth from a formidable opponent. "Behold, the days are coming," says the Lord, "That I will raise to David a Branch of righteousness; ... Now this is His name by which He will be called: THE LORD OUR RIGHTEOUSNESS." (Jeremiah 23:5-6)

It is widely accepted among Christians that this is a remarkable renewal of the first promise regarding the incarnation of the Son of God and our salvation through Him. This promise was first given when we lost our original righteousness and were seen only as those who had sinned and fallen short of the glory of God. In this state, a righteousness was absolutely necessary for us to be accepted by God; without a perfect and complete righteousness, we could never be accepted.

In this context, it is promised that He shall be our "righteousness," or as the Apostle expresses it, "the end of the law for righteousness to everyone who believes." (Romans 10:4) There can be no doubt that He fulfills this role. The inquiry remains: how does He do so?

Most sober and modest of our adversaries assert that He is the efficient cause of our righteousness, meaning our personal, inherent righteousness. However, this righteousness can be viewed in two ways:

1. In itself, as an effect of God's grace, it is good and holy, even though it is not perfect and complete.

2. As it is ours— inherent in us— it is accompanied by the remaining impurities of our nature.

In this regard, the prophet affirms that "we are all like an unclean thing, And all our righteousnesses are like filthy rags;" (Isaiah 64:6).

The term כָּל־צִדְקֹתֵינוּ encompasses our entire personal, inherent righteousness; therefore, the Lord Christ cannot be called יְהוָה צִדְקֵנוּ — "The Lord our Righteousness," since all of it is as filthy rags.

Thus, it must be a different kind of righteousness from which this title is derived, and on account of which this name is given to Him. Therefore He is our righteousness, because all our righteousnesses are found in Him.

The church, which confesses all her own righteousnesses to be as filthy rags, declares, "In the Lord there is righteousness and strength" (Isaiah 45:24), which the Apostle interprets as referring to Christ (Romans 14:11).

"Only in the Lord are my righteousnesses," which the Apostle expresses in Philippians 3:8–9: "that I may gain Christ and be found in Him, not having my own righteousness which is from the law, but that which is through faith in Christ, the righteousness which is from God by faith;" (Philippians 3:8–9) (in this case, as filthy rags).

Hence, it is stated, "In the Lord all the descendants of Israel shall be justified" (Isaiah 45:25), because He is, in His being, actions, and what He has done for us, our righteousness. Our righteousness is entirely in Him, which excludes our personal, inherent righteousness from any role in our justification and attributes it wholly to the righteousness of Christ.

Thus, the psalmist's emphatic declaration, "I will go in the strength of the Lord God; I will make mention of Your righteousness, of Yours only" (Psalm 71:16), affirms that, in holiness and obedience, all our spiritual strength comes from Him alone. The repetition of the possessive pronoun excludes any confidence or trust in anything but the righteousness of God alone.

The Apostle affirms that this is the purpose of God in making Christ our righteousness — "that no flesh should glory in His presence; but he who glories, let him glory in the Lord" (1 Corinthians 1:29, 31).

It is by faith alone that we acknowledge, in our justification, the righteousness of God, which excludes all boasting (Romans 3:27).

Moreover, beyond what will be further discussed from specific testimonies, Scripture clearly declares that He is "The Lord our Righteousness," saying "to make an end of sins, to make reconciliation for iniquity, to bring in everlasting righteousness" (Daniel 9:24).

Through these actions our justification is completed: the satisfaction made for sin, the pardon of sin in our reconciliation to God, and the provision of everlasting righteousness. Therefore He is rightly called "The Lord our Righteousness."

Given that we lost our original righteousness and have none of our own remaining, we stand in need of a perfect and complete righteousness to secure our acceptance with God. Such a righteousness must leave no occasion for boasting in ourselves. The Lord Christ, being given and made unto us "The Lord our Righteousness," in whom we possess all our righteousness (our own righteousnesses are like filthy rags in God's sight), accomplishes this by making an end of sin, reconciling us for iniquity, and bringing in everlasting righteousness.

It is solely through His righteousness that we are justified in the sight of God and can boast. This expresses the heart of our position, and Scripture presents it in a way that gives believers truer spiritual light and understanding than the philosophical distinctions and expressions that claim to be proper and exact.

18. Gospel Testimonies on Justification

The reasons why the doctrine of justification through the imputation of Christ's righteousness is more fully developed in the later writings of the New Testament than in the evangelists' accounts have been previously discussed. Still, their writings sufficiently affirm this doctrine regarding the state of the church before Christ's death and resurrection.

I will consider a few of the many testimonies from their writings that support this purpose. First, the primary aim of our blessed Savior's sermon, particularly the portion recorded in Matthew 5, is to reveal the true nature of righteousness before God. The scribes and Pharisees, from whom He sought to liberate the consciences of His listeners, placed all righteousness before God in the works of the law or in personal obedience to it. They taught the people this doctrine and justified themselves by it, as He charges them in Luke 16:15, "You are those who justify yourselves before men, but God knows your hearts. For what is highly esteemed among men is an abomination in the sight of God."

In this sermon He makes it clear that all those under their leadership sought to "establish their own righteousness, but as it were, by the works of the law" (Romans 9:32; 10:3). Yet they were convinced in their own consciences that they could not attain the law's righteousness or the perfect obedience it required. Nevertheless, they would not abandon their proud delusion of justification by their own righteousness. As is common among people in similar circumstances, they sought other means to ease their convictions. To this end they corrupted the whole law with false interpretations, reducing its true demands to what they boasted they could fulfill.

Our Savior illustrates this principle and the practice of the whole society in a parable (Luke 18:11-12), and in the case of the young man who said he had kept all these things from his youth (Matthew 19:20).

To eradicate this harmful error from the church, our Lord Jesus Christ offers many examples showing the true spiritual meaning and intention of the law. He reveals what righteousness the law requires and the conditions under which a person may be justified by it. Among various declarations, He makes two points especially clear:

1. The law, in its precepts and prohibitions, pertains to the regulation of the heart, including all its initial impulses and actions. He asserts that the innermost thoughts of the heart and the first stirrings of desire, even if not consented to or acted upon in outward sinful deeds, are directly forbidden by the law. This is evident in His holy exposition of the seventh commandment (Matthew 5:27-30).

2. He declares that the penalty for even the slightest sin is hell, as He states that unjust anger is forbidden by the sixth commandment. If people would examine themselves by these standards and others provided by our Savior, it might deter them from boasting in their own righteousness and justification.

However, just as it was then, it is still the case today. Most who advocate for justification by works attempt to distort the meaning of the law to fit their practices. The reader may find a notable demonstration of this in a recent excellent treatise titled "The Practical Divinity of the Papists Discovered to be Destructive of Christianity and Men's Souls."

The spirituality of the law, along with the severity of its consequences, extends even to the smallest and most imperceptible movements of sin in the heart. These are not recognized or properly considered by those who argue for justification by works in any form. Therefore, the main purpose of our Savior's sermon is to declare the nature of the obedience that God requires through the law and to prepare the minds of His disciples to seek after another righteousness, which, in its cause and means, had not yet been fully revealed. Many of them, having been prepared by John's ministry, were already hungry and thirsty for it.

He sufficiently indicates what this righteousness consists of by affirming, "I did not come to destroy but to fulfill" (Matthew 5:17). What He came for, He was sent for; for as He was sent not for Himself, "He was born to us, given unto us." His purpose was to fulfill the law so that its righteousness might be fulfilled in us.

If we cannot fulfill the law in the proper sense of its commands (which is not to be abolished but established, as our Savior declares), if we cannot escape the curse and penalty of transgressing it, and if He came to fulfill it for us (all of which He has declared), then His righteousness—specifically, that which He accomplished in fulfilling the law—is the righteousness by which we are justified before God.

Here, two types of righteousness are presented to us: one is the righteousness achieved through Christ's fulfillment of the law, and the other is our own perfect obedience to the law, as He has defined it.

There is no middle ground between these two. It is left to the consciences of convicted sinners to decide which of these they will trust in, and guiding them in this decision is the primary aim we should have in declaring this doctrine.

I will bypass all those passages where the foundations of this doctrine are securely laid, as they do not explicitly mention it; however, they do necessarily imply it in their proper interpretation. Such passages include those where the Lord Christ is said to die for us or in our stead, to lay down His life as a ransom for us or in our stead, and similar statements. I will not dwell on these, as I do not wish to deviate from the current argument.

The representation made by our Savior regarding the means by which individuals are justified before God, illustrated in the parable of the Pharisee and the publican, serves as a guide for all who share the same intention. In Luke 18:9-14, He states: "Also He spoke this parable to some who trusted in themselves that they were righteous, and despised others: 'Two men went up into the temple to pray, one a Pharisee and the other a tax collector. The Pharisee stood and prayed thus with himself, "God, I thank You that I am not like other men—extortioners, unjust, adulterers, or even as this tax collector. I fast twice a week; I give tithes of all that I possess." And the tax collector, standing afar off, would not so much as raise his eyes to heaven, but beat his breast, saying, "God, be merciful to me, a sinner!" I tell you, this man went down to his house justified rather than the other; for everyone who exalts himself will be humbled, and he who humbles himself will be exalted.'"

The intent of our Savior in this parable is to illustrate the path to justification before God. This is evident from the description of the individuals He reflects upon in verse 9. They were those who "trusted in themselves that they were righteous," believing they possessed a personal righteousness before God.

Furthermore, the general principle He uses to confirm His judgment regarding these individuals is found in verse 14: "Everyone who exalts himself will be humbled, and he who humbles himself will be exalted." This principle applies to the Pharisee and his prayer. It shows clearly that claiming our own works as the basis for justification before God is a form of self-exaltation that God despises. In contrast, the publican's acknowledgment of his sinfulness is the only preparation on our part for acceptance with Him through faith.

Thus both individuals are depicted as seeking justification. Our Savior states the outcome of their appeal to God: one was justified, while the other was not.

The plea of the Pharisee consists of two parts:

1. He claims that he has fulfilled the conditions necessary for justification. He does not appeal to any merit, either of congruity or condignity. Instead, he points to the two aspects of God's covenant with the church—one relating to the moral law and the other to the ceremonial law—and cites examples from both to demonstrate his obedience. He also notes that he fasts twice a week, which suggests that those who seek righteousness and justification by works often feel compelled to do something extraordinary, beyond what the law requires. This tendency produced the pharisaical austerities later seen in the Papacy. His actions are not to be dismissed simply because he was a hypocrite and a boaster; for all who seek justification by works commonly display similar tendencies. Yet these actions do not justify him—his self-exaltation and reliance on his own righteousness are the real problem.

2. He attributes all that he has done to God: "God, I thank You." Though he performed these acts, he acknowledges the assistance of God's grace in them. He sees himself as significantly different from others but does

not credit himself for his actions. All the righteousness and holiness he claims are attributed to the goodness of God. Therefore, he neither claims merit in his works nor asserts that he performed them without divine help. He simply says that, by the grace of God, he has fulfilled the covenant's conditions and expects to be justified. God judges the intentions behind people's prayers by what they trust for their justification. If some remain true to their principles, this is the prayer they ought to make, mutatis mutandis.

If it is argued that the Pharisee is criticized for "trusted in themselves" and "despised others," which led to his rejection, I respond:

1. This criticism does not concern merely the individual's frame of mind but the nature and consequences of the belief in justification by works. Justification by works inherently fosters contempt for others; as Scripture puts it, "For if Abraham were justified by works, he has something to boast about," though not before God.

2. The persons he despised were those who placed their complete trust in grace and mercy, like the publican. We may hope that others of the same mindset do not fall into the same trap.

The problem with this man is that he was not justified; nor will anyone ever be justified on the basis of his own personal righteousness. Our Savior tells us that when we have done all—that is, when our consciences testify to the integrity of our obedience—we should not plead it for our justification. Instead, we should honestly acknowledge, as our duty requires, that we are douloi achreioi—"unprofitable servants" (Luke 17:10). As the apostle says, "I know nothing against myself, yet I am not justified by this" (1 Corinthians 4:4).

He who is a doulos achreios and has nothing to trust in but his service will be cast out from the presence of God (Matthew 25:30). Therefore, to confess ourselves as douloi achreioi, even on the basis of our best obedience, is to admit that, after all, we deserve to be cast out from God's presence.

In contrast, the state and prayer of the publican, who likewise sought justification before God, are described. The outward actions are presented as signs of his inner condition: "And the tax collector, standing afar off," and "would not so much as raise his eyes to heaven;" he "beat his breast." These actions portray a man who is despondent, even despairing in himself.

Such is the nature and effect of conviction of sin, which we have already argued is necessary for justification. He experiences displeasure, sorrow, a sense of danger, and fear of God's wrath. In short, he declares himself guilty before God, his mouth stopped as to any apology or excuse. His prayer is a sincere cry of his soul to sovereign grace and mercy for deliverance from the state in which the guilt of sin has placed him.

The use of the word hilaskomai points to propitiation. His whole address contains:

1. Self-condemnation and abhorrence.

2. Displeasure and sorrow for sin.

3. A complete renunciation of all his own works as any condition for his justification.

4. An acknowledgment of his sin, guilt, and misery.

This is all that is required on our part for justification before God, except for the faith by which we apply ourselves to Him for deliverance.

Some make a weak attempt to prove that justification consists solely in the remission of sins because, in the publican's prayer for mercy and pardon, he is said to be "justified." However, this argument is weak because:

1. The whole nature of justification is not declared here; only what is required on our part is mentioned. The reference to Christ's mediation has not yet been expressly brought to light, as shown before.

2. Although the publican approaches God with a deep sense of guilt, he does not pray merely for the bare pardon of sin. He prays for the full sovereign mercy or grace that God has provided for sinners.

3. The term "justification" must have the same meaning when applied to the Pharisee as when applied to the publican. If it means that the publican was pardoned, it must mean the same for the Pharisee — and he was not pardoned. But the Pharisee did not come seeking pardon; he came to be justified, and he made no mention of his sin or any awareness of it.

Therefore, although the pardon of sin is included in justification, to justify here refers to a righteousness by which a man is declared just and righteous. In the publican's case that righteousness is rooted in the sovereign cause — God's mercy.

A few testimonies may be added from the other evangelist, where they abound: "As many as received Him, to them He gave the right to become children of God, to those who believe in His name:" (John 1:12). Faith is expressed by receiving Christ; to receive Him and to believe in His name are the same.

To receive Him means to accept Him as God has set Him forth to be a propitiation for sin, the great ordinance by which God provides the recovery and salvation of lost sinners. Therefore, this notion of faith includes:

1. The acknowledgement that Christ is proposed and offered to us for some end or purpose.

2. That this proposal is made to us in the promise of the gospel. Thus, when we are said to receive Christ, we are also said to receive the promise.

3. The end for which the Lord Christ is offered to us in the promise of the gospel — which is the same as that for which He was proposed in the first promise — namely, the recovery and salvation of lost sinners.

4. That in the offer of His person there is also an offer of all the fruits of His mediation, the way and means of our deliverance from sin and our acceptance with God.

5. Nothing is required on our part for an interest in the proposed end except receiving Him, that is, believing in His name.

6. By this we are entitled to the heavenly inheritance. We have the right to become sons of God, in which our adoption is declared and justification is included.

What it means to receive Christ, and what that receiving consists of, was previously explained in the discussion of the faith by which we are justified.

From this we argue that nothing more is required to obtain a right and title to the heavenly inheritance than faith alone in the name of Christ — receiving Christ as God's ordinance for justification and salvation. This gives us the original right and our acceptance with God, which is our justification, though more is required for the actual acquisition and possession of the inheritance.

It is sometimes said that other graces and works are not excluded even though the phrase "faith alone" is used. But everything that is not a receiving of Christ is excluded; it is virtually excluded because it is not of the same nature as what is required.

When we speak of the part by which we see, we do not deny that other members belong to the body; we only exclude the eye from the act of seeing. Likewise, if faith is what is required as the receiving of Christ, then every grace and duty that is not this receiving is excluded with respect to the end of justification.

John 3:14-18 states: "And as Moses lifted up the serpent in the wilderness, even so must the Son of Man be lifted up, that whoever believes in Him should not perish but have eternal life. For God so loved the world that He gave His only begotten Son, that whoever believes in Him should not perish but have everlasting life. For God did not send His Son into the world to condemn the world, but that the world through Him might be saved. He who believes in Him is not condemned; but he who does not believe is condemned already, because he has not believed in the name of the only begotten Son of God."

I will note only a few things from these words; they convey a clearer understanding of this mystery to believers' minds than many long discourses by learned men:

1. Our Savior is discussing the justification of people and their right to eternal life based on it. This is clear in verse 18: "He who believes in Him is not condemned; but he who does not believe is condemned already."

2. The means by which we attain this state, on our part, is believing only; this is positively asserted three times with no addition.

3. The nature of this faith is declared:

(1) By its object, which is Christ Himself, the Son of God: "whoever believes in Him," which is frequently repeated.

(2) The specific consideration in which He is the object of faith for justification is as He is the ordinance of God, given, sent, and proposed from the love and grace of the Father: "God so loved the world that He gave His only begotten Son;" "that God has sent His only begotten Son into the world."

(3) The specific act included in the type, which illustrates God's design in Him, is akin to looking at the bronze serpent set on a pole in the wilderness by those who had been bitten by fiery serpents. Our faith in Christ for justification corresponds to this. It includes trusting in Him alone for deliverance and relief.

This is the way. These are the only causes and means of the justification of condemned sinners, and they form the substance of all that we plead for.

It may be said that all this does not prove the imputation of the righteousness of Christ to us, which is the principal inquiry; but if nothing is required on our part for justification except faith acted upon Christ as the ordinance of God for our recovery and salvation, that is the entirety of what we argue for.

Justification by the remission of sins alone, without a righteousness that grants acceptance with God and a right to the heavenly inheritance, is foreign to Scripture and to the common understanding of justification among men. What this righteousness must be, assuming that faith alone is required on our part for participation in it, is sufficiently declared in the words where Christ Himself is often asserted as the object of our faith for that purpose.

Without adding more specific testimonies, which are numerous and support the same purpose in this evangelist, the summary of the doctrine he declares is: "That the Lord Jesus Christ was 'Behold! The Lamb of God who takes away the sin of the world!' — that is, by the offering of Himself, wherein He answered and fulfilled all the typical sacrifices of the law. To this end He sanctified Himself, that those who believe might be sanctified or perfected forever by His own offering of Himself.

In the gospel, He is presented as lifted up and crucified for us, bearing our sins in His own body on the tree. By faith in Him, we have adoption, justification, freedom from judgment and condemnation, and a right and title to eternal life. Those who do not believe are already condemned because they do not believe in the Son of God; and, as He expresses elsewhere, they 'have made Him a liar' by not believing His testimony, namely, that 'God has given us eternal life, and this life is in His Son.'

He does not mention any other means, cause, or condition for justification on our part but faith alone, although He provides many precepts for believers regarding love and keeping the commands of Christ. This faith is the receiving of Christ in the sense just declared, and this is the essence of the Christian faith in this matter. We often obscure rather than clarify it by debating anything in our justification other than the grace and love of God, the person and mediation of Christ, and faith in them.

19. Paul's Doctrine of Justification

The manner and means of our justification before God, along with all its causes, are clearly articulated by the Apostle in the Epistle to the Romans, chapters 3, 4, and 5. He also addresses objections, making his discourse the primary source for understanding this doctrine.

The recent claims by some that the doctrine of justification by faith without works is found only in St. Paul's writings and that these writings are obscure and complex are both false and damaging to the Christian faith. We will not give these claims any consideration here. He wrote as one "moved by the Holy Spirit." The truths he delivered are sacred and demand our faith and obedience. The manner in which he presented them was deemed most suitable by the Holy Spirit for the edification of the church.

As he confidently stated, if the gospel he preached — though considered foolishness by some — was hidden from those who could not understand its mystery, it was "veiled to those who are perishing." Similarly, if what he conveys regarding our justification before God seems obscure or difficult to us, that obscurity reflects our prejudices, corrupt affections, or limited understanding rather than any flaw in his manner of revelation.

Therefore, rejecting all such misguided insinuations and acknowledging our own weaknesses, we will humbly seek to understand the blessed revelation of this great mystery of a sinner's justification before God as declared in those chapters of his glorious Epistle to the Romans. I will do so as briefly as possible, avoiding repetition of what has already been said or anticipating future discussions.

The first thing he does is demonstrate that all people are under sin and guilty before God. This conclusion is drawn from his earlier discourse, particularly from chapters 1:18 and 3:19, 23. This raises the question: how can any of them be justified before God? Since justification is a declaration based on the consideration of righteousness, his primary inquiry is to identify what that righteousness is—the basis on which a person may be justified.

He explicitly states that it is not the righteousness of the law or the works associated with it. What he means by this has been partially explained and will be further clarified in our discussion. In general, he asserts that the righteousness by which we are justified is the righteousness of God, in contrast to any righteousness of our own, as seen in Romans 1:17 and 3:21-22.

He describes this righteousness of God with three characteristics:

1. It is chōris nomou, or "apart from the law" (verse 21); it is entirely separate from the law and cannot be attained through it or any of its works. This righteousness is not based on our obedience to the law, nor can it be obtained through it. No expression could more clearly separate and exclude the works of obedience to the law from any relevance to this righteousness of God. Therefore, anything that we might perform in obedience to the law is excluded from any claim to this righteousness of God or the means of acquiring it.

2. Yet, it "is being witnessed by the Law and the Prophets" (verse 21).

The Apostle, by distinguishing the books of the Old Testament into "the Law and the Prophets," indicates that by "the law" he refers to the books of Moses. In these texts, testimony is given to this righteousness of God in several ways:

1. By declaring the reasons for its necessity for our justification. This is illustrated by the account of our apostasy from God, the loss of His image, and the ensuing state of sin. Through this, all hope of acceptance with God based on our personal righteousness is eliminated.

2. When sin entered the world, our own righteousness was removed, so another righteousness—approved by God and called "the righteousness of God"—was required. Without that righteousness, all possibility of love and favor between God and humanity would cease forever.

In the way of recovery from this state, the first promise of the blessed Seed generally declares how this righteousness of God would be accomplished and introduced. For He alone was "To make an end of sins, To bring in everlasting righteousness" (Daniel 9:24, NKJV); that righteousness of God would serve as the means of justification for the church in all ages and under all dispensations.

By excluding every other means of righteousness through the threatenings of the law and the curse accompanying its transgression, Scripture made it clear that a particular righteousness must be provided for our justification before God—one able to remove and satisfy that curse.

The only way and means by which this righteousness of God would be achieved were prefigured throughout the sacrifices, especially in the great annual rite on the Day of Atonement. There the sins of the people were laid upon the head of the sacrifice and thus carried away.

3. He describes the means by which we partake of it: faith alone. "even the righteousness of God, through faith in Jesus Christ, to all and on all who believe. For there is no difference;" (Romans 3:22, NKJV). Faith in Christ Jesus is the sole means by which this righteousness of God is conferred on us, granted only to those who possess that faith, without distinction. Although "faith" can be understood in various senses, in this context the faith of Christ Jesus—referred to as faith in Me (Acts 26:18, NKJV)—can only mean receiving and trusting in Him as the appointed means of righteousness and salvation.

This description of the righteousness of God revealed in the gospel—the apostle's assertion that it alone is the means and cause of our justification, and that it is communicated to us only through the faith of Christ Jesus—fully confirms the truth we defend. If the righteousness by which we must be justified before God is not our own but God's, and if it comes to us only by the faith of Jesus Christ (Philippians 3:9, NKJV), then our personal, inherent righteousness or obedience has no bearing on our justification before God. This argument is unassailable, so long as we maintain proper reverence for the authority of God's Word.

Chapter 3:24-26 explained, and the true meaning of the words clarified — The causes of justification enumerated — Apostolic inference from the consideration of them. Having fully established that no living person possesses any righteousness of their own by which they may be justified, but are all confined under the guilt of sin, and having declared that a righteousness of God is now fully revealed in the gospel, by which alone we may be justified—since "for all have sinned and fall short of the glory of God," he proceeds to declare the nature of our justification before God in all its causes, as stated in Romans 3:24-26: "being justified freely by His grace through the redemption that is in

Christ Jesus, whom God set forth as a propitiation by His blood, through faith, to demonstrate His righteousness, because in His forbearance God had passed over the sins that were previously committed, to demonstrate at the present time His righteousness, that He might be just and the justifier of the one who has faith in Jesus." (NKJV)

Here we might reasonably expect some place to be assigned to our personal obedience in justification. If one supposed (though it cannot be reasonably argued) that the apostle excluded only the works of the law in their absolute perfection, or only works performed in our own strength without grace, or only meritorious works, it would still be expected that, when he declared fully the nature and means of our justification, he would recognize our personal righteousness somewhere — whether as a primary cause, a secondary cause, a continuation, or at least mentioned under some gracious qualification so it would not seem entirely excluded.

It is clear the apostle had no such intention, nor was he concerned about any objections that might be raised against his doctrine as though it undermined the necessity of obedience. Considering his design and context, the argument from his complete silence about our personal righteousness in justification is unanswerable. And this is not all; as we proceed, we will see that he explicitly and directly excludes it.

All unbiased readers must agree that no words are more explicit and emphatic in assigning the whole of our justification to the free grace of God through the blood and mediation of Christ — where faith alone gives us an interest — than those the apostle uses here. I confess I do not know how to state the matter more clearly or forcefully. If we could all accept the apostle's answer about how, by what means, on what grounds, and by what causes we are justified before God — namely, that "we are justified freely by His grace through the redemption that is in

Christ Jesus, whom God set forth as a propitiation by His blood, through faith," — there could be an end to this controversy.

However, the principal passages of this testimony must be considered distinctly. First, the principal efficient cause is expressed with particular emphasis, or the "causa proēgoumenē;" Dikaioumenoi dōrean tē autou chariti — "being justified freely by His grace." God is the principal efficient cause of our justification, and His grace is the only moving cause thereof. I shall not dwell on the objections from those of the Roman church who claim that by tē chariti autou (which their translation renders "per gratiam Dei") the internal, inherent grace of God is intended, which they make the formal cause of justification. They have nothing to support this claim but that which undermines it, namely, that it is added to dōrean, "freely," which would be unnecessary if it signified the free grace or favor of God. Both expressions, "gratis per gratiam," "freely by grace," are used together to emphasize this assertion, wherein the entirety of our justification is attributed to the free grace of God.

As far as they can be distinguished, one denotes the principle from which our justification proceeds—namely, grace—and the other denotes the manner of its operation—it works freely. Moreover, the grace of God in this context consistently signifies His goodness, love, and favor, as has been undeniably proven by many. See Romans 5:15; Ephesians 2:4, 8, 9; 2 Timothy 1:9; Titus 3:4, 5.

"Being justified dōrean (as the LXX renders the Hebrew particle חִנָּם), — 'without price,' without merit, without cause; — and sometimes it is used to mean 'without end;' that is, what is done in vain, as dōrean is used by the apostle in Galatians 2:21; — without price or reward, Genesis 29:15; Exodus 21:2; 2 Samuel 24:24; — without cause, merit, or any means of procurement, 1 Samuel 19:5; Psalm 69:4; in this sense it is rendered by dōrean in John 15:25. The purpose of the word is to exclude all consideration of anything in us that could be the cause or condition of our justification. Charis, 'favor,' when considered absolutely, may have regard to something in the one to whom it is shown. For it is said that Joseph found grace or favor, charin, in the eyes of Potiphar, Genesis 39:4; but he did not find it dōrean, without any consideration or cause; for he "his master saw that the Lord was with him, and that the Lord made all he did to prosper in his hand," verse 3.

However, no words can be found that free our justification before God from all regard to anything in ourselves, except what is expressly added as the means of its participation on our part, through faith in His blood, more emphatically than those used by the apostle: Dōrean tē autou chariti — "freely by His grace." And with those who do not accept this as excluding all works or obedience of our own, all conditions, preparations, and merit, I shall despair of ever expressing my thoughts on the matter intelligibly to them.

Having asserted this righteousness of God as the cause and means of our justification before Him, in opposition to all righteousness of our own, and declared the cause of its communication to us on the part of God to be mere free, sovereign grace, the means on our part whereby, according to the ordination of God, we receive, or are truly made partakers of, that righteousness of God on which we are justified, is by faith: Dia tēs pisteōs en autou haimati — that is, through faith. Nothing else is proposed; nothing else is required for this purpose.

It is argued that there is no indication that it is by faith alone, or that faith is asserted to be the means of our justification exclusively to other graces or works. However, there is such an exclusion directly included in the description given of that faith whereby we are justified, with respect to its special object — "by His blood, through faith;" for faith that looks to the blood of Christ as that through which propitiation was made for sin — wherein the apostle affirms that we are justified through faith — does not allow for association with any other graces or duties. Neither do they have any part in the nature of fixing on the blood of

Christ for justification before God; therefore, they are all directly excluded here. Those who think otherwise may attempt to introduce them into this context without corrupting it or perverting its sense.

Moreover, the other evasion will not provide our adversaries the least relief—namely, that by faith, not the single grace of faith is intended, but the whole obedience required in the new covenant, faith and works together. For as all works, as our works, are excluded in the declaration of the causes of our justification on the part of God (Dōrean tē autou chariti — "freely by His grace"), by virtue of that great rule, Romans 11:6, "And if by grace, then it is no longer of works; otherwise grace is no longer grace." So the determination of the object of faith in its act or duty, whereon we are justified—namely, the blood of Christ—is absolutely exclusive of all works from an interest in that duty; for whatever looks to the blood of Christ for justification is faith, and nothing else. As for calling it a single act or duty, I refer the reader to our preceding discourse regarding the nature of justifying faith.

The apostle infers three things from the declaration he has made regarding the nature and causes of our justification before God, all of which further illustrate the meaning and sense of his words:

That boasting is excluded: "Where is boasting then? It is excluded." (Romans 3:27). It is evident from this and from what he affirms concerning Abraham in Romans 4:2, that a significant part of the controversy he had about justification was whether it allowed for any kauchēsis or kauchēma in those who were justified.

It is known that the Jews placed all their hopes in those things they believed they could boast about—namely, their privileges and their righteousness. However, from the declaration made regarding the nature and causes of justification, the apostle concludes that all boasting is utterly shut out—exekleisthē.

In our language, boasting is considered a vice and is never used in a positive sense. However, kauchēsis and kauchēma, the terms used by the apostle, are ek tōn mesōn—of indifferent significance. As they are applied, they may denote a virtue as well as a vice, as seen in Hebrews 3:6.

However, in every situation and place there is something unique about those to whom certain things are attributed. Whenever something is ascribed to one person and not to another—particularly regarding a good outcome—there exists a foundation for boasting. The apostle asserts that, in the matter of our justification, all such boasting is completely excluded.

Wherever there is any consideration of a condition or qualification in one person over another—especially if it pertains to works—there is a basis for boasting, as he states in Romans 4:2. From comparing that verse with this context, it becomes clear that whenever our own works influence our justification, a ground for boasting is created. In evangelical justification, however, no such boasting is permitted. Therefore, there is no place for works in our justification before God; for if there were, it would be impossible to avoid some form of boasting, whether before God or man.

He draws a general conclusion: "Therefore we conclude that a man is justified by faith apart from the deeds of the law," as stated in Romans 3:28. The meaning of "the law" and "the works of the law" in the apostle's discourse regarding our justification has been previously explained. If we are justified freely through faith in the blood of Christ, that faith—specifically directed to Christ's propitiation—cannot share its role with any other grace or duty.

Being justified in such a way that all boasting is excluded—boasting that would arise from any differing graces or works in ourselves—means that all works of the law are excluded. It is certain that we are justified by faith alone in Christ. Not only are all works excluded, but the apostle's method of discourse effectively shuts the door to their return; no amount of human reasoning can reintroduce them into our justification before God.

He asserts from this that we "Do we then make void the law through faith? Certainly not! On the contrary, we establish the law," as stated in Romans 3:31. The manner in which this is accomplished, and how it can only be done in this way, has been explained above.

This encapsulates the resolution the apostle provides to the significant question of how a guilty, convinced sinner may be justified in the sight of God: "The sovereign grace of God, the mediation of Christ, and faith in the blood of Christ are all that is required." Regardless of other notions people may hold about justification, it is unwise to rely on any other solution for this case and inquiry; we are not wiser than the Holy Spirit.

In Chapter 4, the apostle's purpose in this discourse is set out. An analysis of his discussion — particularly focusing on verses 4 and 5 — is provided, along with a vindication of their true meaning.

The works that are excluded from Abraham's justification are examined. It is clarified who is meant by "does not work," and in what sense the ungodly are justified. All men are ungodly prior to their justification. Faith alone is the means of justification on our part.

It is emphasized that faith itself, considered by itself, is not the righteousness imputed to us. This point is supported by several arguments in Romans, particularly in chapter 4. At the beginning of that chapter the apostle confirms what he had doctrinally declared by presenting a significant example: the justification of Abraham, the father of the faithful. His justification serves as a pattern for ours, as he explicitly states in verses 22-24. A few observations will be made regarding this example as we proceed to the fifth verse, where our discussion will be anchored.

He denies that Abraham was justified by works, as stated in verse 2.

1. These works were not those of the Jewish law, which some claim are the only works excluded from our justification in this context. These were the works Abraham performed hundreds of years before the law was given at Sinai; therefore, they refer to his moral obedience to God.

2. The works must be understood as those that Abraham possessed at the time he is said to be justified in the testimony provided for that purpose. The works that Abraham had then were works of righteousness, performed in faith and love toward God — works of new obedience guided and aided by the Spirit of God, which are required in the covenant of grace.

These are the works that are excluded from Abraham's justification. These points are clear, explicit, and evident, and cannot be evaded by any distinctions or arguments. All of Abraham's evangelical works are expressly excluded from his justification before God.

He proves through Scripture that Abraham was justified solely by the means he previously declared — namely, by grace through faith in Christ Jesus, as stated in verse 3. "Abraham believed God, and it was accounted to him for righteousness." He was justified by faith in the manner described (for there is no other justification by faith), in contrast to all his own works and personal righteousness.

From the same testimony, he explains how he became a partaker of the righteousness by which he was justified before God, which was through imputation: it was counted or imputed to him for righteousness. The nature of imputation has been previously discussed.

He asserts and proves the special nature of this imputation—namely, that it is of grace, without regard to works—in verse 4, using what is contrary to this idea: "Now to him who works, the wages are not counted as grace but as debt;" where works are taken into account, there is no room for the kind of imputation by which Abraham was justified. It was a gracious imputation, and that is not based on what is our own beforehand, but on what is made our own through that imputation. What is our own cannot be imputed to us in a way of grace; it can only be considered ours in a way of debt. What belongs to us, along with all its effects, is due to us.

Therefore, those who argue that faith itself is imputed to us to lend some support to an imputation of grace claim that it is imputed not for what it is, for then it would be counted as debt, but for what it is not. Socinus states, "When faith is imputed to us for righteousness, it is imputed because faith itself is neither righteousness nor truly contains it," (De Servat., part iv, cap. 2). This kind of imputation, being merely a false notion, has been disproven previously. All works are inconsistent with the imputation by which Abraham was justified.

Some say, "All works that are meritorious, performed with an opinion of merit, which make the reward a matter of debt, are excluded; but other works are not." This distinction is not derived from the apostle; for according to him, if merit and meritorious actions are defined by the reward being counted as debt, then all works in justification fall into that category. Without distinction or limitation, he states that "to him who works, the wages are not counted as grace but as debt;" he does not exclude some kinds of works or works in some sense because they would make the reward a matter of debt; rather, he affirms that all would do so, thereby excluding gracious imputation.

In the fifth verse, the essence of the apostle's doctrine, which he has argued for and proven, is expressed: "But to him who does not work but believes on Him who justifies the ungodly, his faith is accounted for righteousness." It is universally acknowledged that the conclusion of the verse, "his faith is accounted for righteousness," expresses the justification of the person in question. He is justified, and the means of this justification is that his faith is counted or imputed. Therefore, the preceding words clarify the subject of justification and its qualification, or the description of the person to be justified, along with all that is required on his part.

First, it is stated that he is ho mē ergazomenos — "who does not work." It is not required for his justification that he refrain from working or performing any duties of obedience to God in any form, as that is considered working; for every person in the world is always obligated to fulfill all duties of obedience, according to the light and knowledge of God's will, which is provided to him. However, the expression should be limited by the subject matter being discussed: he "who does not work" refers specifically to justification. This does not pertain to the intention of the person but rather to the nature of the matter at hand. To say that he who does not work is justified through believing means that his works, whatever they may be, have no influence on his justification, nor does God consider them when justifying him. Therefore, only he who does not work is the subject of justification — the person to be justified; that is, God does not take into account anyone's works or duties of obedience in his justification, since we are justified dōrean tē autou chariti — "freely by His grace."

When God explicitly states that He justifies him who does not work, and that He does so freely by His grace, I cannot comprehend what role our works or duties of obedience could possibly have in our justification. Why should we concern ourselves with inventing what consideration they may have in our justification before God when He Himself affirms that they have none at all? The words are not open to any evasive interpretation. He who does not work is indeed he who does not work, regardless of what others may say or how long they may distinguish. It is a boldness not to be justified for anyone to oppose such clear divine testimonies, no matter how they may be cloaked in philosophical notions and arguments, which are merely thorns and briars that the word of God will pass through and consume.

Furthermore, the apostle adds in his description of the subject of justification that God "justifies the ungodly." This expression has provoked much anger among many, and some seem to be quite displeased with the apostle himself for it. If anyone else dares to say that God justifies the ungodly, they are personally criticized as someone whose doctrine undermines the necessity of godliness, holiness, obedience, or good works; "for what need is there for any of them if God justifies the ungodly?" Nevertheless, this is a periphrasis of God, that He is ho dikaiōn ton asebē—"He who justifies the ungodly." This is His prerogative and characteristic; as such, He will be believed in and worshipped, which adds weight and emphasis to the expression. We must not disregard this testimony of the Holy Spirit, regardless of how angry men may become.

"But the difference lies in the interpretation of the words." If that is the case, it may be accepted without mutual offense, even if we misunderstand their proper meaning. However, it must be acknowledged that God "justifies the ungodly." Some say, "That refers to those who were formerly ungodly, not those who remain ungodly when they are justified." This is indeed true. All who are justified were previously ungodly; and all who are justified are at the same time made godly.

The question is whether they are regarded as godly or ungodly at any moment prior to their justification. If they are seen as godly, then the apostle's words—that God justifies the ungodly—would not be true, for the contrary proposition would hold: God justifies none but the godly. These propositions—"God justifies the ungodly" and "God justifies none but the godly"—are contradictory; here we have expressly kataphasis and apophasis antikeimenai, which is antiphasis.

Although, in the justification of a sinner, he is made godly—endowed with that faith which purifies the heart and serves as the vital principle of all obedience, and with the conscience cleansed from dead works by the blood of Christ—yet prior to this justification he is ungodly and is regarded as ungodly.

He is one who does not work, and whose duties and obedience contribute nothing to his justification. Since he does not work, all works are excluded from being the causa per quam (the cause by which). And since he is ungodly, they are also excluded from being the causa sine qua non (the necessary cause) of his justification.

The qualification of the subject, or the means by which the person to be justified actually becomes justified, is faith, or believing: "but believes on Him who justifies the ungodly." This means that it is faith alone. It is the faith of one who does not work. And its specific object—God as justifying the ungodly—is exclusive of any works whatsoever.

This is faith alone, and it is necessary to use the word "alone" to express it. Faith is asserted in opposition to all our works: "to him who does not work." Its specific nature is declared in its object—God as "justifies the ungodly"—which means freely by His grace, through the redemption that is in Christ Jesus.

Therefore there is no room for any works to make even the slightest claim toward our justification before God, under any pretext. The nature of justifying faith is also defined here. It is not merely assent to divine revelation. It is not merely a firm assent that leads us to obey Scripture's precepts—though those aspects are included. Rather, it is belief in and trust in Him who justifies the ungodly through the mediation of Christ.

Regarding this person, the apostle affirms that "his faith is accounted for righteousness." This means he is justified in the manner previously declared. However, there is a difference in interpreting these words.

Some say the meaning is that faith, as an act, a grace, a duty, or a work of ours, is imputed. Others argue that it is faith as it apprehends Christ and His righteousness which is properly imputed to us. Thus they claim that faith justifies, or is counted for righteousness, relatively — concerning its object — and they acknowledge a figure of speech in the words. This interpretation is fiercely opposed, as if it denied the explicit words of Scripture, when in fact it is only interpreting this unique expression in light of many others that declare the same thing.

Those who support the first interpretation assert that faith here includes obedience or works, either as the essence of faith or as necessary accompaniments that have the same influence on our justification or are similarly conditions of it. In doing so they also admit a figure of speech in the words, which they vehemently criticize in others.

They thus interpret the entire statement as: "To him who does not work, but believes in Him who justifies the ungodly, his faith and works are counted to him for righteousness." This not only denies what the apostle affirms but also ascribes to him a clear contradiction.

I find it somewhat astonishing that any unbiased person would interpret this solitary expression in a way that contradicts the apostle's intent, the words of the same sentence, and the whole subsequent context. The apostle's main point, which he seeks to confirm, is that we are justified by the righteousness that is of God through faith in the blood of Christ. It will soon be shown that this righteousness cannot be faith itself.

In the text all works are excluded, if any words can sufficiently exclude them. Yet faith, as a singular grace, act, and duty of ours — especially insofar as it includes obedience — is a work. In that latter sense it would embrace all works.

In the ensuing context he proves that Abraham was not justified by works. To say that one is not justified by works and yet is justified by some works — as if faith itself were a work — would mean that if faith is imputed to us for righteousness, we are justified by it as such. Those are contradictory statements.

Therefore I offer a few arguments against this erroneous interpretation of the apostle's words. To believe absolutely — as faith is an act and duty of ours — does not oppose works, for faith is a work, a specific kind of working. However, faith, as we are justified by it, and works, or to work, are opposed: "to him who does not work but believes." See Galatians 2:16; Ephesians 2:8, 9.

It is the righteousness of God that is imputed to us, for we are "become the righteousness of God in Him" (2 Corinthians 5:21); "the righteousness of God, through faith in Jesus Christ, to all and on all who believe" (Romans 3:21, 22). However, faith, when considered absolutely, is not the righteousness of God.

"To whom God imputes righteousness apart from works" (Romans 4:6), but there is no indication of a double imputation — of two types of righteousness, one that is the righteousness of God and another that is not. Faith, when considered absolutely, is not the righteousness of God; for the thing to which the righteousness of God is revealed, by which we believe and receive it, is not itself the righteousness of God. Nothing can be the cause or means of itself.

The righteousness of God is "revealed from faith to faith" (Romans 1:17), and it is "received the reconciliation" by it (Romans 3:22; 5:11).

Faith is not the righteousness of God that comes through faith; rather, the righteousness of God that is imputed to us is "the righteousness which is from God by faith" (Romans 3:22; Philippians 3:9).

What we seek, obtain, and submit to regarding the righteousness of God is not the righteousness itself. That is the role of faith (Romans 9:30–31; 10:3–4).

The righteousness that is imputed to us is not our own prior to that imputation. As it is written, "And be found in Him, not having my own righteousness" (Philippians 3:9). However, faith is something that belongs to a person: "But someone will say, 'You have faith, and I have works.' Show me your faith without your works, and I will show you my faith by my works" (James 2:18).

"to whom God imputes righteousness apart from works:" (Romans 4:6). The righteousness that God imputes to us is the righteousness by which we are justified. It is imputed to us so that we may be justified. Yet we are justified by the obedience and blood of Christ: "so also by one Man's obedience many will be made righteous" (Romans 5:19); "Much more then, having now been justified by His blood, we shall be saved from wrath through Him" (Romans 5:9); "but now, once at the end of the ages, He has appeared to put away sin by the sacrifice of Himself" (Hebrews 9:26); "By His knowledge My righteous Servant shall justify many, For He shall bear their iniquities" (Isaiah 53:11). However, faith is neither the obedience nor the blood of Christ.

As previously stated, faith is our own, and what is our own may be imputed to us. However, the apostle's discussion concerns what is not our own prior to imputation but is made ours through that imputation, as we have demonstrated; for it is of grace. The imputation to us of what is genuinely our own prior to that imputation is not of grace in the sense intended by the apostle. This is because what is imputed is recognized for what it is, and nothing more.

The act of Phinehas was imputed to him for righteousness; God judged it and declared it to be a righteous, rewardable act. Therefore, if our faith and obedience are imputed to us, that imputation is merely God's accounting that we are believers and obedient. As the prophet declares, "The righteousness of the righteous shall be upon himself, and the wickedness of the wicked shall be upon himself" (Ezekiel 18:20). Just as the wickedness of the wicked is upon him or is imputed to him, so the righteousness of the righteous is upon him or imputed to him.

The wickedness of the wicked is upon him when God judges him wicked based on his works; similarly, the righteousness of a man is upon him or imputed to him when God judges his righteousness as it is. Therefore, if faith, when considered absolutely, is imputed to us as it contains or is accompanied by works of obedience, then it is imputed to us either as a perfect righteousness, which it is not, or as an imperfect righteousness, which it is; or the imputation of it is the accounting of something imperfect as if it were perfect. However, none of these can be affirmed:

1. It is not imputed to us as a perfect righteousness, which is the righteousness required by the law, for it does not fulfill that requirement. Episcopius admits in his disputation (dispute 45, sections 7-8) that the righteousness imputed to us must be "most absolute and most perfect." He defines the imputation of righteousness to us as "the gracious estimation of the divine mind, by which He regards the believer in His Son as if he were perfectly just and had always complied with His law and will." No one would claim that faith is such a most absolute and most perfect righteousness that it fulfills the righteousness of the law in us, as is achieved by the righteousness imputed to us.

2. It is not imputed to us for what it is—an imperfect righteousness. First, this would provide no advantage to us, for we cannot be justified before God by an imperfect righteousness. This is evident in the prayer of the psalmist: "Do not enter into judgment with Your servant, for in Your sight no man living shall be justified" (Psalm 143:2). Secondly, the imputation of anything to us that was ours prior to that imputation, for what it is and no more, contradicts the imputation described by the apostle, as has been proven.

This imputation being argued for cannot be a declaration of something imperfect as if it were a perfect righteousness, for God's judgment is based on truth. If it is not judged to be perfect, it cannot be accepted as such. To accept anything as something other than what we judge it to be is to be deceived.

Lastly, if faith, as a work, is imputed to us, it must be as a work that is accomplished through faith; for no other work is accepted by God. Therefore, that faith through which it is accomplished must also be imputed to us, since it is both faith and a good work. Consequently, there must be another faith from which it originates, leading to an infinite regression.

There are many other points in the subsequent explanation of Abraham's justification, the nature of his faith, and his righteousness before God, along with their application to all who believe, which could justly be argued in support of this truth alongside the passages we have discussed. However, if every testimony given by the Holy Spirit regarding this truth were cited, there would be no end to the writing. One more observation I will make to conclude our discussion on this chapter.

Romans 4:6-8. The apostle continues his argument to prove the freedom of our justification by faith, without regard to works, through the imputation of righteousness—particularly regarding the forgiveness of sins, which is essential to it. He does this by referencing the psalmist, who highlights the blessedness of a man in the remission of sins. His aim is not to redefine justification, which he has already done, but to demonstrate its freedom from any association with works in this essential aspect.

"Even as David also describes the blessedness of the man to whom God imputes righteousness apart from works" (which is the sole point he intends to prove with this testimony), "saying, Blessed is he whose transgression is forgiven." He illustrates their blessedness by this. Not that their entire blessedness consists in that alone, but that it contributes to it—especially where no regard can possibly be given to any works.

He rightly describes a man's blessedness by noting that the imputation of righteousness and the non-imputation of sin (which the apostle mentions separately) are inseparable. Both are essential to our complete justification, as has been demonstrated.

Since the remission of sin is the first and primary part of justification, and is always accompanied by the imputation of righteousness, a man's blessedness can be well described by it. Indeed, since all spiritual blessings are found together in Christ (Ephesians 1:3), a man's blessedness may be described by any one of them.

However, the imputation of righteousness and the remission of sin are not the same, just as righteousness imputed and sin remitted are not the same. The apostle does not present them as identical; he mentions them distinctly, and both are equally necessary for our complete justification, as has been proven.

Romans 5:12–21. Boasting is excluded in ourselves but may be asserted in God. The design and summary of the apostle's argument, and the objection raised by Socinus, are addressed. The apostle compares the two Adams and those who derive from them.

He explains how sin entered the world and what that sin entails. He also defines death—what it comprises and what it signifies.

The meaning of the words "inasmuch" or "because all sinned" is clarified and vindicated. The various contrasts the apostle uses in this discourse are primarily between sin or the fall and the free gift; between the disobedience of one and the obedience of another; and between judgment on one hand and justification unto life on the other.

The entire context is explained, and the argument for justification through the imputation of the righteousness of Christ is fully confirmed.

"Therefore, just as through one man sin entered the world, and death through sin, and thus death spread to all men, because all sinned — (for until the law sin was in the world, but sin is not imputed when there is no law. Nevertheless death reigned from Adam to Moses, even over those who had not sinned according to the likeness of the transgression of Adam, who is a type of Him who was to come. But the free gift is not like the offense. For if by the one man's offense many died, much more the grace of God and the gift by the grace of the one Man, Jesus Christ, abounded to many. Moreover the gift of righteousness abounded to many through one Man, Jesus Christ. For as by one man's disobedience many were made sinners, so also by one Man's obedience many will be made righteous.) Therefore, as through one man's offense judgment came to all men, resulting in condemnation, even so through one Man's righteous act the free gift came to all men, resulting in justification of life. For as by one man's disobedience many were made sinners, so also by one Man's obedience many will be made righteous. Moreover the law entered that the offense might abound. But where sin abounded, grace abounded much more, so that as sin reigned in death, even so grace might reign through righteousness to eternal life through Jesus Christ our Lord."

The apostle, in chapter 3, verse 27, affirms that in the matter of justification all boasting (kauchēsis) is excluded. However, in the preceding verse he allows for a boasting or kauchēma: "And not only that, but we also rejoice in God." He excludes boasting in ourselves because there is nothing in us that can procure or promote our justification. He permits us to boast in God because of the excellence of the means of justification that He has graciously provided.

The kauchēma, or boasting in God, permitted here has a specific reference to what the apostle intends to discuss further. "And not only that" includes what he has primarily treated before regarding our justification—particularly as it relates to the pardon of sin.

Although he mentions the imputation of righteousness, his primary emphasis is our justification through the pardon of sin and our freedom from condemnation, which excludes all boasting in ourselves.

However, he aims to go further and show what our glorying in God, founded on a right and title freely given to us for eternal life, depends upon. This is the imputation of the righteousness and obedience of Christ for the justification of life—the reign of grace through righteousness unto eternal life.

Many have complained about the obscurity of the apostle's discourse in this passage, citing various ellipses, antapodota, hyperbata, and other figures of speech that are either present or supposed. Yet I believe that anyone familiar with the fundamentals of the Christian faith and the nature and guilt of our original apostasy, reading this passage without prejudice, will see the apostle's intention.

He intends to show that just as the sin of Adam was imputed to all men for condemnation, so the righteousness or obedience of Christ is imputed to all who believe for justification unto life. Theodoret summarizes this well in Dial. III: "See how the things of Christ are compared with those of Adam, as sickness with medicine, as a wound with a plaster, as sin with righteousness, as a curse with a blessing, as condemnation with remission, as transgression with obedience, as death with life, as hell with the kingdom, Christ with Adam, man with man."

The differences among interpreters about the exposition of these words concern the use of certain particles and prepositions, and the dependence of one passage on another. None of these matters, however, affects the truth being argued. The apostle's clear intention and explicit propositions stand; if people would accept them, this controversy could be resolved.

Socinus admits that this passage of Scripture affords, as he says, the greatest occasion for our view; for he cannot deny that at least a strong appearance of what we hold is contained in the apostle's words. Accordingly, he labors to distort and misrepresent them. Many of his tactics have been taken up by later annotators, but he himself offers nothing substantial beyond what he borrows from Origen and from Pelagius's commentary on this epistle, as preserved by Jerome and earlier cited by Erasmus.

His argument is that Adam's actual transgression is not imputed to his descendants, nor is a corrupt nature transmitted to them. He allows that Adam incurred the penalty of death, and that those who derive their nature from him in that state are made subject to death. But he denies that our internal corruption or inclination to sin is derived from Adam; instead he says it arises from habits formed by many successive acts of our own. Likewise, he denies that Christ's obedience or righteousness is imputed to us. Rather, when we become His children by our obedience to Him—He having gained eternal life for Himself by His obedience—we participate in its benefits. This is the gist of his long treatment in De Servatore, Book IV, chapter 6. But it neither explains the apostle's words nor accords with them, as the following examination will show.

I do not aim to expound the apostle's entire discourse here. I will comment only on those passages that plainly reveal the manner in which we are justified before God.

A comparison is drawn between the first Adam, through whom sin entered the world, and the second Adam, through whom it is removed. This is a contrast of opposites: there is likeness in some respects and dissimilarity in others, and both aspects serve to illustrate the truth.

The general proposition is contained in verse 12: "Therefore, just as through one man sin entered the world, and death through sin, and thus death spread to all men, because all sinned—" The entrance of sin and punishment into the world occurred through one man and through one sin, as the apostle later clarifies. Those consequences were not confined to that one individual but extended to all.

The apostle reverses the order of cause and effect for emphasis. First he names the cause and then the effect: "just as through one man sin entered the world, and death through sin." When he applies it to all men, he first states the effect and then the cause: "and thus death spread to all men, because all sinned."

At the first entrance of sin, death passed upon all; that is, all became liable and subject to it as the punishment due for sin. All who have ever existed, now exist, or will exist were not personally present at that first act; yet, when sin first entered, they were all made subject to death or rendered liable to punishment. This occurred by divine constitution on the ground of their federal relation to the one man who sinned. They become in their own persons subject to the sentence of death at their first natural existence, being born as children of wrath.

It is therefore plain what sin the apostle means—the actual sin of Adam, the single transgression of that one common representative. Although the corruption and depravity of our nature necessarily follow in every individual born through natural descent, it is solely the guilt of Adam's actual sin that made them all liable to death when sin first entered the world. Thus death entered by sin—the guilt of that sin, rendering all universally liable to it.

Death comprises the whole punishment due for sin; there is no need to dispute that. "For the wages of sin is death," and nothing else. Whatever penalty God has appointed or threatened for sin is included in death: "for in the day that you eat of it you shall surely die." Therefore the apostle grounds his comparison on the fact that, through Adam's actual sin, all men are rendered liable to death—that is, the guilt of that sin is imputed to them.

To impute sin to a person is to render that person justly liable to the punishment due for sin; to refuse to impute sin frees a person from liability to punishment. This exposes the error of the Pelagian view, which holds that death passed to all merely by natural descent from the one who deserved it, without any imputation of his guilt. That position contradicts the apostle's plain statement, which makes the guilt of sin, not mere natural propagation, the ground of death.

Having mentioned sin and death—sin being the sole cause and guilt, and death the consequent punishment—he explains how all men became universally liable to that punishment: "because all sinned—" (Romans 5:12). This phrase points back to the one man who sinned, in whom all sinned, as the outcome shows: "For as in Adam all die," (1 Corinthians 15:22); or, as he puts it here, "and thus death spread to all men."

This interpretation is reinforced by the use of the preposition epi in place of en, a variation not uncommon in Scripture. See the references to Matthew 15:5; Romans 4:18; 5:2; Philippians 1:3; Hebrews 9:17. Esteemed Greek writers use similar constructions. For example, Hesiod says, "The measure in all things is best." Likewise, "It is in you" may be rendered by "Eph' humin estin," and "It lies in me" by "Touto ep' emoi keitai." Augustine argues for this reading against the Pelagians and rejects their alternative interpretation. I will not dispute the reading of the words here.

Our adversaries try to persuade others that the strength of our argument for imputing Adam's sin to his descendants rests solely on reading "eph' hō" as "in whom." We may concede that it can be better rendered by Latin phrases such as "eo quod," "propterea," or "quatenus," meaning "inasmuch as" or "because." Still, we must insist that this reading explains why "death passed on all men," insofar as "all sinned—" referring to the sin through which death first entered the world.

It is true that, under the original constitution of the law, death is due for every sin whenever it is committed. But the present question is how death passed at once on all men. How did they become liable to it when it first entered the world through Adam's actual sin? That liability cannot be due to their own actual sin, because the apostle later affirms that death passed even on those who had not sinned actually in the way Adam did.

If the apostle meant the actual sins of men, imitating Adam, then men would have been liable to death before they had sinned. Yet death, at its first entrance into the world, passed on all men when only Adam had actually sinned. To claim that men were liable to death—the penalty for sin—when they had not sinned is an obvious contradiction. Though God, by His sovereign power, could inflict death on an innocent creature, an innocent creature cannot be guilty of death; to be guilty of death is to have sinned.

Thus the expression "because all sinned—" conveys the desert and guilt of death at the moment when sin and death first entered the world. The only sin intended here is Adam's sin and our connection to it: "For we were all in that one man." That connection can exist only through the imputation of Adam's guilt to us. Since Adam's act is not inherently or subjectively ours, we cannot be affected by its consequence except by imputing its guilt to us. By imputation we mean the communication of what is not inherently in us.

This point is the foundation of the whole comparison, and I have elaborated it because the apostle treats it as the basis for everything he later infers. Some have argued that he omits the corresponding clause for Christ; that is, he states the proposition about Adam but does not explicitly state what corresponds to it in Christ. Origen even suggested the apostle remained silent to prevent any misapplication that might encourage sloth and negligence.

He states, "just as through one man sin entered the world, and death through sin," so the expected conclusion would be, "So through one righteousness entered the world, and life through righteousness."

The apostle recognizes that this would complete the comparison, but he did not state it—apparently to prevent people from abusing it as a license to negligence or presuming that what must be done has already been done. Yet that view contradicts and undermines much of what he later asserts in his exposition. He did not conceal any truth for such reasons.

He makes the implied contrast plain in verse 19, and there he shows how foolish and wicked it is for anyone to suppose this gives them license to indulge in sin.

Some admit the apostle withholds the explicit expression of what belongs to Christ in contrast to what he affirms about Adam and his sin until verse 19. But in fact the contrast is sufficiently implied at the end of verse 14, where he says that Adam was "a type of Him who was to come."

The way righteousness and life are introduced and communicated to men corresponds to the way Adam introduced sin and death, which affected the whole world. Just as Adam affected his natural descendants with sin and death, so the Lord Christ, the second Adam, affects His spiritual descendants with righteousness and life.

Thus we argue: If Adam's actual sin was imputed to all his descendants so that it was regarded as their own sin and led to their condemnation, then the actual obedience of Christ, the second Adam, is imputed to all His spiritual offspring (that is, all believers) for justification. I will not press this argument further, since its foundation will be addressed later.

I will skip the next two verses, which contain an objection and its answer, since they do not concern us directly.

In verses 15 and 16 the apostle continues to clarify his comparison by highlighting the differences between the two subjects: "But the free gift is not like the offense. For if by the one man's offense many died, much more the grace of God and the gift by the grace of the one Man, Jesus Christ, abounded to many."

The contrast is drawn between paraptōma on one side and charisma on the other. This dissimilarity does not concern only their opposite effects of death and life, but the degrees of their effectiveness relative to those effects. Paraptōma refers to the offense, the fall, the sin, or the transgression—specifically "by one man's disobedience," as mentioned in verse 19. Thus Adam's first sin is commonly called "the fall" — the paraptōma.

In contrast, charisma denotes the gift or free gift, the benefit God grants freely. This is further clarified as "the grace of God and the gift by the grace of the one Man, Jesus Christ." Although the term here will specifically denote Christ's righteousness in the following verse, it broadly includes all the causes of our justification in opposition to Adam's fall and the entrance of sin through it.

The consequence of tou paraptōmatos — "of the offense," or the fall — is that "many died." Here "many" does not mean a limited group; it indicates that the effect of that one offense was not restricted to a single individual. If we ask who is included in "many," the apostle makes clear that it means all men universally, that is, all of Adam's descendants. By that one offense, since they all sinned, death spread to all men; they were rendered liable to death as the punishment due for that one offense.

Thus it is misguided to take the words of verse 12, "because all sinned — ", as referring to any sin other than Adam's first sin, since it is presented as the reason why death passed upon them. It is explicitly stated that death spread to all men because of that one offense.

The effectiveness of tou charismatos — "of the free gift" — is expressed as something that abounded much more. Beyond the assertion itself, the apostle argues for the fairness of our justification by grace through Christ's obedience by comparing it with the condemnation that resulted from Adam's sin. If it was just for all men to be subjected to condemnation because of Adam's sin, it is all the more just that those who believe should be justified by Christ's obedience through God's grace and the gift by grace through Jesus Christ.

The apostle later explains how the gift by grace abounded to many, surpassing the fall's effectiveness in bringing condemnation. Through this gift we are freed from condemnation far more than we were made liable to it by Adam's fall and sin. This justification comes solely by the grace of God and the gift by grace through Jesus Christ, as affirmed in verse 16. He supplies another distinction between the two subjects, illustrating the previously stated dissimilarity: "And the gift is not like that which came through the one who sinned. For the judgment which came from one offense resulted in condemnation, but the free gift which came from many offenses resulted in justification."

By "one who sinned," or di' henos hamartēsantos, is equivalent to di' henos paraptōmatos, meaning "by one sin," the single offense of that man. The term krima is translated "judgment." Most interpreters render it as "reatus," "guilt," or "crimen," derived from it. Similarly, מִשְׁפָּת, meaning "judgment," is used in Hebrew for guilt, as seen in Jeremiah 26:11, which states, "This man deserves to die! For he has prophesied against this city, as you have heard with your ears."

First, there was paraptōma—the sin, the fall—tou henos hamartēsantos, the one man's actual sin. From that followed krima, or "reatus," the guilt that ensued for all. Through that one sin, guilt came upon all. The consequence of this guilt is katakrima, or "condemnation"—that is, guilt leading to condemnation. This guilt came ex henos, from one person, from one sin.

This is the order of things regarding Adam:

1. Paraptōma, the one sin;

2. Krima — the guilt that ensued for all;

3. Katakrima — the condemnation that the guilt deserved.

The opposites in the second Adam are:

1. Charisma — the free gift of God;

2. Dōrēma — the gift of grace itself, or the righteousness of Christ;

3. Dikaiōma, or dikaiōsis zōēs — meaning "justification of life."

Although the apostle distinguishes these concepts to illustrate his comparison and opposition, his intention in all of them is to highlight the righteousness and obedience of Christ, as he explains in verses 18 and 19. In terms of our justification, he refers to it as:

1. Charisma — concerning the free, gratuitous grant of it by the grace of God;

2. Dōrea tēs charitos, and 3. Dōrēma — regarding us who receive it; it is a free gift to us;

4. Dikaiōma — in relation to its effect of making us righteous.

Therefore, by the sin of Adam imputed to them, guilt came upon all men leading to condemnation. We must inquire how the free gift differs: "But the free gift is not like the offense." This is evident in two ways:

1. Condemnation came upon all through one offense. However, being under the guilt of that one offense, we in effect incur the guilt of countless others. If the free gift had only addressed that one offense, it would not have been sufficient for our deliverance. Hence, it is said to be "from many offenses," meaning it encompasses all our sins and trespasses.

2. Adam and all his descendants were initially in a state of acceptance with God, positioned to obtain eternal life and blessedness, where God Himself would have been their reward. Through sin's entrance, they lost God's favor and incurred the guilt of death or condemnation, which are synonymous. Yet they did not forfeit an immediate right and title to eternal life; they had not yet attained that right, nor could they obtain it without fulfilling the required course of obedience. Thus, what came upon all through the one offense was the loss of God's favor in their present state and the judgment or guilt of death and condemnation. An immediate right to eternal life, however, was not taken away by that one sin.

The free gift operates differently: through it we are freed not only from one sin but from all our sins. Additionally, through it we gain a right and title to eternal life, for "grace might reign through righteousness to eternal life," as stated in verse 21.

This truth is further explained and confirmed in verse 17: "For if by the one man's offense death reigned through the one, much more those who receive abundance of grace and of the gift of righteousness will reign in life through the One, Jesus Christ." The apostle's intent has been sufficiently revealed in our observations on the previous verses.

It is noteworthy how the apostle employs a variety of expressions to describe God's grace in the justification of believers: Dikaiōma, dōrēma, charis, charisma, perisseia charitos, dōrea tēs dikaiosunēs. Nothing is omitted that might express the freedom, sufficiency, and efficacy of grace for this purpose. Although some of these terms may seem synonymous and used interchangeably, each carries a unique aspect and together they illustrate the full scope of grace's work.

Dikaiōma appears to refer to dikaiologēma, the foundation of a case in trial—the matter pleaded upon which the accused is to be acquitted and justified; this is the righteousness of Christ, "through one Man."

Dōrēma, or a free donation, excludes all merit and conditions on our part; it is that by which we are freed from condemnation and obtain the right to justification of life. Charis signifies the free grace and favor of God, the original or efficient cause of our justification, as declared in chapter 3, verse 24. Charisma has been previously explained. Perisseia charitos — "the abundance of grace" — is included to assure believers of the certainty of the effect; it shows that nothing is lacking for our justification. Dōrea tēs dikaiosunēs expresses the free grant of that righteousness which is imputed to us for our justification of life, later referred to as "one Man's obedience."

Regardless of how wise and learned men may be, we should all learn to think and speak of these divine mysteries from this blessed apostle, who understood them better than we and wrote under divine inspiration.

It is astonishing how some people transgress the boundaries the apostle has drawn around the grace of God and the obedience of Christ in our justification, seeking to introduce their own works of obedience and find a place for them there. Paul's intent, and that of some who discuss our justification before God, seems directly opposed. His whole discourse centers on the grace of God, and on the death, blood, and obedience of Christ, as if he could never more fully declare them without excluding any mention of our works or duties, or any implication that they belong to this matter.

In contrast, their arguments center on their own works and duties, and they have devised as many terms to describe them as the Holy Spirit has used to express and declare the grace of God. Instead of the words of wisdom previously mentioned, which the Holy Spirit has taught and with which he fills his discourse, theirs are filled with conditions, preparatory dispositions, merits, causes, and various embellishments for our own works. For my part, I would rather learn from him and align my understanding and expressions of gospel mysteries, especially regarding our justification, with his, who cannot mislead me, than rely on any other guidance, no matter how appealing its pretenses may be.

It is clear from this verse that nothing more is required of anyone for justification than to receive the "abundance of grace and of the gift of righteousness." This is the description the apostle provides of those who are justified regarding what is required of them.

This excludes all works of righteousness that we perform, since none of them grant us the abundance of grace and of the gift of righteousness. It also excludes the imputation of faith itself for our justification, because faith is an act and duty of our own. Faith is the means by which we receive the gift of righteousness through which we are justified.

It cannot be denied that we are justified by the gift of righteousness — the righteousness given to us — for it grants us the right and title to life. However, our faith is not this gift; the one who receives and that which is received are not the same.

Where there is perisseia charitos and charis huperperisseuousa — "abundance of grace," "grace abounded much more" — exercised in our justification, nothing more is required. How can it be said to abound, indeed to superabound, not only in freeing us from condemnation but also in granting us a title to life, if it must be supplemented by our own works and duties? The intended meanings fill these expressions, though to some they may sound like mere empty noise.

There is a gift of righteousness required for our justification, which all must receive who are to be justified. All who receive it are justified; for those who receive it shall "reign in life through the One, Jesus Christ."

Thus, it follows that:

The righteousness by which we are justified before God cannot be our own, nothing inherent in us, nor something performed by us. It is that which is freely given, and this donation is by imputation: "just as David also describes the blessedness of the man to whom God imputes righteousness apart from works," as stated in chapter 4, verse 6. By faith we receive what is given and imputed; otherwise we contribute nothing to our participation in it. This is what it means to be justified in the apostle's sense.

It is a righteousness that grants a right and title to eternal life; for those who receive it will "reign in life through the One, Jesus Christ." Therefore, it cannot consist solely of the pardon of sin; for:

1. The pardon of sin cannot reasonably be called "the gift of righteousness." Pardon and righteousness are distinct concepts.

2. Pardon of sin does not confer a right and title to eternal life. It is true that one whose sins are pardoned will inherit eternal life; however, this is not merely by virtue of that pardon, but through the imputation of righteousness that inseparably accompanies it and serves as its foundation.

The description provided here of our justification by grace stands in contrast to the condemnation we incurred through the sin of Adam. It highlights the superiority of grace over the first sin. Grace not only grants forgiveness for many sins, but it also conveys to us a right to eternal life.

This is summarized in the statement: "those who receive abundance of grace and of the gift of righteousness," which gives us the right to life through Jesus Christ. Thus, to be justified means to receive the imputation of Christ's righteousness by faith alone.

The conclusion of what has been demonstrated in the comparison discussed is clearly expressed and further confirmed in chapter 5, verses 18 and 19.

Verse 18: "Therefore, as through one man's offense judgment came to all men, resulting in condemnation, even so through one Man's righteous act the free gift came to all men, resulting in justification of life." This is how we read the words.

"through one man's offense": the Greek manuscripts vary here. Some read Tō heni paraptōmati, which Beza follows, and our translation notes in the margin as "By one offense"; most read Di' henos paraptōmatos, meaning "By the offense of one." Both convey the same idea. The offense referred to is that of one person—Adam; and the righteousness referred to is that of one person—Jesus Christ.

The introduction of this assertion with ara oun, a marker of syllogistic inference, indicates that what is being asserted here is the core of the truth being argued. The comparison continues with hōs, signalling that these matters are to be understood in a similar manner.

What is affirmed on one side is Di' henos paraptōmatos eis pantas anthrōpous eis katakrima, meaning "through one man's offense judgment came to all men, resulting in condemnation." This indicates judgment, as we reiterate krima from the previous verse. However, krima eis katakrima refers specifically to guilt. Through the sin of one, all men became guilty and were subject to condemnation.

The guilt of this sin is imputed to all men; otherwise it could not come upon them as condemnation, nor could they be made liable to death and judgment on its account. It has been established that, in the apostle's discussion, the entirety of the punishment due for sin is intended by death and condemnation. This, therefore, is clear from that perspective.

In response to this, the dikaiōma of one, regarding the cause of justification, is contrasted with the paraptōma of the other, which pertains to the cause of condemnation: Di' henos dikaiōmatos, meaning "through one Man's righteous act." This refers to the righteousness that is applicable for justification; dikaiōma is a righteousness claimed for that purpose.

Our translators render that "the free gift came to all men," echoing charisma from the previous verse, just as they had done with krima on the other side. The Syriac reading, given for comparison, would read essentially the same sense as the NKJV: "Therefore, as through one man's offense judgment came to all men, resulting in condemnation, even so through one Man's righteous act the free gift came to all men, resulting in justification of life." The sense of the words is clear without the need for any supplementary words in the text.

In the original the sequence is not katakrima eis pantas anthrōpous, but eis pantas anthrōpous eis katakrima, and thus something from his earlier words must be supplied to align with the apostle's intention. This refers to charisma, "gratiosa donatio," or the free grant of righteousness; or dōrēma, "the free gift" of righteousness for justification. The righteousness of one, Christ Jesus, is freely granted to all believers for the justification of life; for the "all men" mentioned here are defined and limited to those who "receive abundance of grace and of the gift of righteousness," as stated in verse 17.

Some insist, mistakenly, that this passage grants righteousness and life to all men, even though the majority never partake of it. Nothing could be more contrary to the apostle's intent. People are not made guilty of condemnation by Adam's sin through some divine arrangement that leaves room for exemption. Each person, as soon as they exist and by virtue of being a descendant of the first Adam, is personally liable to condemnation, and the wrath of God rests upon them.

On the other hand, only those who, through faith in the Lord Christ, the second Adam, actually partake in the justification of life are intended. The debate here is not about the universality of redemption through Christ's death. Those who assert universal provision do not claim the free gift of justification automatically extends to all; they know it does not. There is a provision of righteousness and life for believers, but that provision is the focus of this passage.

What is declared here is the certain justification of believers and the means by which it is achieved. The analogy under discussion does not allow for any other interpretation. The "all" referred to are those who derive their existence from Adam by natural propagation. If a person did not do so, they would not be implicated in Adam's sin or fall, as was the case with the man Christ Jesus.

Conversely, those on the other side are only those who receive spiritual life from Christ. If a person does not receive that life, they have no part in the righteousness of the "one" for justification unto life.

Our argument from these words is this: just as through one man's offense judgment came to all men, resulting in condemnation—the offense of the first Adam imputed to them—so the righteousness of the one, which leads to justification of life for believers, is the righteousness of Christ imputed to them. What could be stated more clearly or more evidently confirmed by the apostle?

This is expressed even more clearly in verse 19: "For as by one man's disobedience many were made sinners, so also by one Man's obedience many will be made righteous."

Cyrillus Alexandrinus explains this well in his work on John, book 11, chapter 25: "Just as through the transgression of the first man we were subjected to death as the first fruits of our kind, so through the obedience and righteousness of Christ, who subjected Himself to the law though He was the author of the law, the blessing and life that come through the Spirit penetrated our entire nature."

Leo, in his twelfth letter to Juvenal, states: "In order to restore the life of all, He took on the cause of all. Just as through the sin of one all became sinners, so through the innocence of one all would become innocent; thus righteousness would flow to humanity where human nature was assumed."

What he previously referred to as paraptōma and dikaiōma, he now expresses as parakoē and hupakoē—"disobedience" and "obedience." The parakoē of Adam, his disobedience, was the actual transgression of God's law. The apostle says "many were made sinners," meaning they became sinners in such a way that they were subject to death and condemnation. They could not be liable to death unless they were first made sinners or guilty. They could not be guilty unless they were considered to have sinned in Adam, and so the guilt of his sin was imputed to them. Therefore he affirms that Adam's actual sin was the sin of all men, making them sinners and subject to death and condemnation.

What he opposes to this is hē hupakoē—the obedience of one, referring to Jesus Christ. This obedience was the actual compliance He demonstrated with the whole law of God. Just as Adam's disobedience was his transgression of the whole law, Christ's obedience was His fulfilment of the whole law. The contrast requires this parallel.

Through this, many are made righteous. How? By the imputation of that obedience to them. Just as men are made sinners through the imputation of Adam's disobedience, so they are made righteous through the imputation of Christ's obedience. This grants us the right and title to eternal life, as the apostle states in verse 21: "so that as sin reigned in death, even so grace might reign through righteousness to eternal life through Jesus Christ our Lord."

This righteousness is none other than the "obedience of one" — that is, of Christ — as mentioned in verse 19. It is said to "come" upon us, meaning it is imputed to us; for "Blessed is the man to whom God imputes righteousness." Through this we not only escape the death and condemnation we were liable to because of Adam's sin, but we also receive pardon for many offenses — that is, all our personal sins — and a right to eternal life by God's grace, for we are "justified freely by His grace through the redemption that is in Christ Jesus."

The apostle clearly and fully presents these matters, and it is our duty to align our understanding with his words and sense as closely as possible. What is offered in opposition is full of exceptions, evasions, and complicated disputes that draw us away from the straightforward teaching of Scripture. Consequently, the conscience of a convinced sinner struggles to find rest and assurance and is left unsure what to believe for justification.

Piscator, in his comments on this chapter and elsewhere, argues strongly against the imputation of Christ's obedience for our justification. But his argument rests on a clear misunderstanding and a false assumption, and it contradicts the plain words of the text. It is true, as he observes and shows, that our redemption, reconciliation, pardon of sin, and justification are often ascribed specifically to the death and blood of Christ.

The reasons for this have been partially mentioned before, and a further explanation will follow. But it does not follow that the obedience of Christ in fulfilling the whole law, being made under it for us, is therefore excluded from any role in our justification or that it is not imputed to us. Against this he argues: "the just for the unjust," as stated in 1 Peter 3:18 — "For Christ also suffered once for sins, the just for the unjust, that He might bring us to God." He continues: "If we were made righteous by His life, there would have been no reason for Him to die for us, because the justice of God does not allow punishing the righteous. But He punished us in Christ, or, which is the same, He punished Christ for us and in our place, after He had lived a holy life, as is certain from Scripture. Therefore we are not made righteous by the holy life of Christ. Furthermore, Christ died to acquire that righteousness for us," as noted in 2 Corinthians 5:21. "Thus, He had not acquired it before His death."

However, this whole argument rests on a plain mistake. It assumes a temporal order in which Christ's obedience — His righteousness in fulfilling the law — is first imputed to us, and only afterward the righteousness of His death is imputed. From that assumed sequence it concludes the earlier imputation would be useless. But no such temporal order or divine arrangement is proposed for our justification.

It is true that Christ's life and His obedience to the law preceded His sufferings and the curse He bore. That order was necessary according to the law of nature. But it does not follow that the same order must be followed in the imputation or application of those acts to us. How these acts are applied is a matter of divine wisdom and grace, governed not by the natural sequence of Christ's obedience and suffering but by the moral purposes to which God assigns them.

I do not maintain that there are separate acts of imputation for Christ's obedience — one for the justification of life — and for His suffering — one for the pardon of our sins and deliverance from condemnation. By God's ordinance we receive both by Christ's whole mediation, so that Christ may be all in all. Still, with respect to how God brings sinners to justification, the application of Christ's death for the pardon of sin and deliverance from condemnation is prior in the order of nature and in the exercise of faith to the application of His obedience as the ground and title of eternal life.

A person seeking justification stands under sin and wrath and is liable to death and condemnation. This is what a convinced sinner first recognizes and what he most urgently seeks to be delivered from: "What must I do to be saved?" This need is first met by the doctrine and promise of the gospel, which serve as the rule and instrument of its application. Deliverance comes through the death of Christ. Without that, no actual righteousness imputed to him—not even Christ's own obedience—can relieve him, for he knows he has sinned and thus fallen short of the glory of God, placing him under the condemnatory sentence of the law.

Until he receives deliverance from that state, it is pointless to propose what would grant him a right to eternal life. Once deliverance is established, he is also rightly concerned with what gives him the title to reign in life through righteousness. Conscience cares as much about being freed from condemnation as about the order of justification. This order is expressed in the declaration of the fruit and effects of Christ's mediation, as seen in Daniel 9:24: "To make reconciliation for iniquity, To bring in everlasting righteousness."

There is no force in the objection that Christ's obedience actually preceded His suffering; the method of application is not dictated by that sequence. The condition of sinners who need justification and the nature of their justification require a different approach, ordained by God. Because Christ's obedience and sufferings were inseparable from beginning to end—both belonging to His state of humiliation—they cannot be separated in any effect, except in notion or imagination. He suffered in all His obedience and obeyed in all His sufferings, as stated in Hebrews 5:8. Neither part of our justification—freedom from condemnation and the right to eternal life—can stand without the other according to God's ordinance. Therefore the whole effect is to be ascribed to the whole mediation of Christ, insofar as He acted on our behalf, fulfilling the whole law with respect both to the penalty required of sinners and to the righteousness required for life as an eternal reward. For many reasons, Scripture most commonly attributes our justification to Christ's death and shedding of blood.

1. The grace and love of God — the primary and efficient cause of our justification — are most clearly and conspicuously displayed in Christ's death. Scripture often sets this forth as the highest instance and undeniable demonstration of divine love and grace. This is the principal consideration in our justification, for the ultimate purpose of God in this matter is the display of these attributes.

He assigns our acceptance to grace: "to the praise of the glory of His grace, by which He made us accepted in the Beloved," as stated in Ephesians 1:6. Since this grace is the source and sole cause of Christ's obedience and its imputation to us, as well as of the pardon and righteousness that follow, Scripture consistently presents it as the primary object of faith in justification, in direct opposition to our own works. All of God's design in this is that "grace may reign through righteousness unto eternal life." Because this grace is most manifest in Christ's death, our justification is often specifically ascribed to that death.

The love of Christ and His grace are especially exalted in our justification: "that all should honor the Son just as they honor the Father." This theme is frequently expressed for this purpose in passages such as 2 Corinthians 8:9; Galatians 2:20; Philippians 2:6–7; and Revelation 1:5–6. These attributes are displayed most prominently in His death, and to that death the effects and fruits of them are often ascribed. It is common to attribute an effect to the most significant among several contributing causes, especially when the causes cannot be conceived as truly separable.

This is the clearest testimony that what the Lord Christ did and suffered was for us, not for Himself. If we ignored this, His obedience to the law might be thought to have been solely for His own sake, making Him resemble the Socinians' idea of a Savior who does everything with us from God but nothing with God for us. Yet His suffering the curse of the law — though He was not merely an innocent man but the Son of God — plainly shows that what He did and suffered was for our sake. Therefore it is no surprise that our faith in justification is chiefly directed toward His death and bloodshed.

All of Christ's obedience was directed toward the sacrifice of Himself that was to follow. It found its fulfillment there, and its effectiveness for our justification depended on that sacrifice. Just as no imputation of actual obedience could justify sinners from the condemnation imposed on them through Adam's sin, so the efficacy of Christ's obedience for our justification depended on the suffering that was to come when His soul was made an offering for sin.

As noted above, reconciliation and the pardon of sin by the blood of Christ primarily relieve us from the condition into which Adam's sin cast us: the loss of God's favor and our liability to death. That is what a lost, convinced sinner whom Christ calls primarily seeks. Hence, justification is often presented as the fruit of Christ's death and bloodshed — these are the immediate grounds of our reconciliation and pardon. But none of this implies that the obedience of the one Man, Christ Jesus, is not imputed to us, so that grace may reign through righteousness unto eternal life.

The same truth is fully asserted and confirmed in Romans 8:1–4. That passage has recently been examined and vindicated in a learned exposition by Dr. Jacomb (see especially part I, on verse 4, p. 587ff.), so there is little of significance to add. His answers to the common and serious objections against the imputation of Christ's righteousness ought to satisfy any unprejudiced and impartial reader. For that reason I will pass over this testimony, not wishing to repeat points that have already been thoroughly defended.

Romans 10:3-4 is explained and emphasized for the same purpose: "For they" (the Jews, who had a zeal for God but not according to knowledge), "being ignorant of God's righteousness, and seeking to establish their own righteousness, have not submitted to the righteousness of God. For Christ is the end of the law for righteousness to everyone who believes."

The apostle begins his discussion in Romans 9:30 with a proposition that may seem strange and not easily understood. He introduces it with the question, "What shall we say then?" This question serves to clarify whether there is any "unrighteousness with God?" as mentioned in verse 14, or to inquire, "What shall we say about these things?"

He asserts that the Gentiles, who did not pursue righteousness, have attained it—specifically, the righteousness that comes from faith. In contrast, Israel, which diligently sought the law of righteousness, failed to achieve it; they did not attain righteousness before God.

Nothing appears more contrary to reason than the facts related. The Gentiles, who lived in sin and indulgence without striving to obtain righteousness before God, nonetheless attained it through the preaching of the gospel. Conversely, Israel, which earnestly pursued righteousness by the works of the law and obedience to God, fell short and did not attain it.

All preparations, dispositions, and merits relating to righteousness and justification are excluded from the Gentiles. They did not pursue righteousness in any way. Instead, they attain righteousness solely through faith in Him who justifies the ungodly, thus receiving the righteousness of faith. Attaining righteousness by faith and attaining the righteousness which is of faith are the same.

Therefore, all actions that could be regarded as pursuing righteousness—our duties and works—are excluded from influencing our justification. This demonstrates the sovereignty and freedom of God's grace: we are justified freely by His grace, and all boasting is excluded. Whatever men may claim or debate, those who attain righteousness and justification before God do so not by their own efforts, but through the gracious imputation of another's righteousness to them.

One may argue that although the Gentiles did not pursue righteousness during their time of heathenism, they began to seek it once the gospel was revealed, and so they attained it. But that contradicts the apostle's plain assertion: they did not attain righteousness by their own efforts; he affirms the opposite.

Furthermore, this argument undermines the distinction he makes between the Gentiles and Israel, where one group pursued righteousness while the other did not. In this context, to follow after righteousness means to pursue a righteousness of our own, as indicated in Romans 10:3, where it speaks of "seeking to establish their own righteousness." This pursuit is not a means to attain righteousness. Rather, it serves as the most effective barrier to achieving it.

If those who possess no righteousness of their own—who are so far from it that they never even attempted to attain it—can still receive the righteousness by which they are justified before God through faith, they do so by the imputation of Christ's righteousness to them. If there is any other way to explain this, it must be presented.

On the other side of this discussion regarding Israel, some must hear what they may not wish to accept.

Three points are made regarding them:

1. Their attempt.

2. Their success.

3. The reason for it.

Their attempt or endeavor was this: they followed after the law of righteousness. The Greek word diōkō, which expresses their endeavor, signifies earnestness, diligence, and sincerity. The apostle uses this term to declare what his own endeavor was and what ours should be in the duties and practice of gospel obedience, as seen in Philippians 3:12.

They were not negligent in this matter, but they served God day and night. They were not hypocritical either; the apostle bears them witness that "they have a zeal for God" (Romans 10:2). What they sought after was the law of righteousness, which prescribes a perfect personal righteousness before God. The Scripture states, "The man who does those things shall live by them" (Romans 10:5).

Therefore, the apostle refers to the ceremonial law only as it branches from the moral law by God's will, and as obedience to it pertains to that. When he speaks of it separately, he calls it the law of commandments contained in ordinances, but he never calls it the law of righteousness, which is fulfilled in us (Romans 8:4). Thus, their pursuit of this law of righteousness was their diligence in performing all duties of obedience according to the directions and precepts of the moral law.

The outcome of this attempt is that they "has not attained to the law of righteousness" (Romans 9:31). This means they did not achieve a righteousness before God through it. Although the law's purpose was to provide a righteousness before God by which a person might live, they could never attain it.

An explanation is given for their failure to attain what they earnestly sought. This was due to two mistakes: first, concerning the means of attaining it; second, concerning the righteousness itself that was to be sought. The first mistake is explained in Romans 9:32: "Because they did not seek it by faith, but as it were by the works of the law."

Faith and works are the only two means by which righteousness may be attained, and they are opposed and inconsistent. Therefore no one can seek after righteousness by both. They cannot be mixed into a single means of attaining righteousness. They oppose one another as grace and works; what is of one is not of the other (Romans 11:6). Any attempt to combine them in this matter ends in failure.

The reason is that the righteousness which faith seeks, or which is attainable by faith, is given to us and imputed to us, and faith merely receives it. It receives "abundance of grace and of the gift of righteousness." In contrast, the righteousness attainable by works is our own— inherent in us, produced by us, and not imputed to us. It consists solely of the works themselves, considered in relation to the law of God.

If righteousness before God is to be obtained solely by faith, and in contradiction to all works—so that if a man does them according to the law, "The man who does those things shall live by them"—then it is by faith alone that we are justified before God. Nothing else on our part is required for this. The nature of this righteousness must be evident.

Moreover, if faith and works are contrary and inconsistent when viewed as means of attaining righteousness or justification before God, then it is impossible for us to be justified before God by both in the same sense, way, and manner.

Therefore, when the apostle James states that a man is justified by works, and not by faith only, he cannot be referring to our justification before God, where it is impossible for both to concur. Not only would this render them inconsistent in that context, but it would also introduce various forms of righteousness into justification, each destructive of the other. This was the first mistake of the Jews that led to their failure—they sought not after righteousness by faith, but, as it were, by the works of the law.

Their second mistake concerned the very righteousness by which a person might be justified before God. They believed this to be their own righteousness (Romans 10:3). They viewed their personal righteousness—consisting of their duties of obedience—as the only basis for justification before God. Consequently they endeavored to establish this, just as the Pharisee did (Luke 18:11-12). This mistake, their intention to establish their own righteousness, was the primary reason they rejected the righteousness of God—a failing that persists in many today.

Whatever is done in us or performed by us as obedience to God is our own righteousness. Even when done in faith and by God's grace, it remains subjectively ours. As far as it is a righteousness, it is ours. But all righteousness that is our own is distinct from the righteousness by which we are justified before God. The most earnest effort to establish our own righteousness—making it the basis of justification—will inevitably lead us to reject submission to and acceptance of the only means by which we can be justified.

This misguided approach ruined the Jews and will lead to the ruin of all who follow their example in seeking justification. Yet it is not easy for people to choose another path or to be dissuaded from this one. The apostle hints at this in his statement, "have not submitted to the righteousness of God." That righteousness is such that the proud human mind is entirely unwilling to bow to it. But it can be attained only through a submission of mind that involves a complete renunciation of any righteousness of our own. Those who mock others for claiming that those pursuing moral righteousness are not on a right path to receive the grace of God by Jesus Christ are, in effect, ridiculing the doctrine of the apostle—the doctrine of the Holy Spirit himself.

Therefore, the apostle's clear purpose is to show that faith and the righteousness it brings are inconsistent with our own righteousness by works when it comes to justification before God. Mixing our own works into the pursuit of righteousness as a means of justification diverts us entirely from accepting or submitting to the righteousness of God. The righteousness that comes by faith is not ours; it is God's righteousness, which He imputes to us. By contrast, the righteousness of works is our own, produced by what is done in and by us.

Works have neither the capacity nor the humility to obtain or receive a righteousness that is not our own and must be imputed to us. In that sense they are opposed to such righteousness, for they would undermine their legal standing as our righteousness. Likewise, faith cannot be an inherent righteousness in itself nor be regarded as such when imputed to us. Its primary role is to fix all trust, confidence, and expectation of the soul for righteousness and acceptance with God upon another.

Here lies the ruin of the Jews: they thought it a safer, more probable, and indeed a more righteous and holy course to seek their own righteousness by strict obedience to God's law than to accept that they could be accepted by faith in another. No argument will persuade them otherwise. If they cannot present a righteousness of their own before God, they fear the law has not been fulfilled and that they will be condemned.

To meet this last form of unbelief, the apostle insists the law must reach its appointed end and be fully accomplished; otherwise we have no standing as righteous before God. He then explains how this is achieved and where it is to be found: "Christ is the end of the law for righteousness to everyone who believes" (Romans 10:4). We need not be troubled by various speculative interpretations about how Christ is the end of the law. The apostle plainly affirms that He is the end of the law specifically for righteousness to all who believe.

The point at issue is a righteousness for justification before God—the same righteousness the law requires. God asks of us only the righteousness prescribed in the law. The law is the rule of righteousness; its original design was to make us righteous before God. Other uses of the law, such as exposing sin and pronouncing condemnation, are secondary to that design. The Jews sought the righteousness the law demands by their own performance of its duties. Yet, despite their best efforts, they could never attain the law's required righteousness or reach its goal; and failure to fulfil it brings eternal ruin.

Therefore the apostle declares that this requirement is met in another way: the righteousness the law demands is fulfilled, and its goal—righteousness before God—is attained through Christ. What the law required, He accomplished; and that righteousness is accounted to everyone who believes.

Here the apostle treats the whole question of the righteousness needed for justification before God, especially how the demands of the law are satisfied. What we could not produce—what the law could not accomplish in us because of our weakness in the flesh—Christ has accomplished on our behalf. Thus, He is "the end of the law for righteousness to everyone who believes."

The law demands righteousness from us; achieving that righteousness is its ultimate end and is necessary for justification before God. That end cannot be attained by any works or by any righteousness of our own. The Lord Christ fulfils this for us. How He accomplishes it can only be known through the imputation of His obedience and righteousness in fulfilling the law—an inner mystery I cannot fully explain, and which I do not think the apostle attempts to explain either.

The way we attain the law's end, which we cannot reach by trying to establish our own righteousness, is by faith alone, for "Christ is the end of the law for righteousness to everyone who believes." To mix anything with faith here contradicts the nature of both faith and works regarding their fitness and humility to obtain righteousness. Such mixture conflicts directly with the apostle's expressed intent.

Let others occupy themselves with distinctions I do not understand (and perhaps should be ashamed to confess this, though I am persuaded they understand them not either), or with objections and fancied consequences that I set little store by. For my part, I shall forever desire to fix and find rest for my soul in this truth: "Christ is the end of the law for righteousness to everyone who believes."

I believe that everyone who truly understands what God's law requires, recognizes how essential it is to obey, and sees how utterly insufficient their own efforts are to meet its demands, will, when the time for controversy is past, turn to the same refuge and find rest.

1 Corinthians 1:30. Christ, who is made righteousness for us by God — The response of Bellarmine to this testimony is dismissed — The argument of Socinus is disproved — The true meaning of the words is established. The next passage I will consider in the letters of this apostle is 1 Corinthians 1:30: "But of Him you are in Christ Jesus, who became for us wisdom from God—and righteousness and sanctification and redemption;"

The apostle's purpose in these words is to show that whatever we lack to please God, to live for Him, and to enjoy Him, we have in and through Jesus Christ. God grants this purely by His free and sovereign grace, as verses 26-29 declare. We receive all these benefits through our union with Him: ex autou — "from," "of," or "by Him." By His grace He is the principal and effective cause of what we receive.

The result is that we are in Christ Jesus — that is, grafted into Him or united with Him as members of His mystical body, which is the consistent meaning of that expression in Scripture. The way we partake of these benefits is made clear: who became for us. It is ordained by God that He Himself shall be made or become all these things for us: Hos egenēthē hēmin apo Theou, where apo indicates the effective cause, just as ex did before.

But how is Christ made unto us by God, or what act of God is intended? Socinus claims it is "a general act of God's providence, which results in Christ being said to be all this for us." However, it is a specific ordinance and institution of God's sovereign grace and wisdom, designating Christ to be all this for us, with actual imputation attached, and nothing else is intended.

Therefore, whatever interest we have in Christ and whatever benefits we receive from Him depend entirely on God's sovereign grace and not on anything within ourselves. Since we have no righteousness of our own, God has appointed Christ to be our "righteousness," and He is made so for us; this can only mean that His righteousness is imputed to us.

This is to ensure that all boasting in ourselves is utterly excluded, and that "he who glories, let him glory in the Lord," as stated in verses 29-31. There is a type of righteousness, or a way of being righteous, that allows for some boasting, as seen in Romans 4:2, and does not exclude boasting, as in chapter 3:27. This can only occur when our righteousness is inherent in us; for, regardless of how it is procured, purchased, or wrought in us, it is still our own, as far as anything can be our own while we are creatures.

Thus, this kind of righteousness is excluded here. The Lord Christ is made righteousness for us by God in such a way that all boasting and glorying on our part is shut out — indeed, He is made so for this very purpose. This can only be through the imputation of His righteousness to us, for that exalts the grace of God and the honor of His person and mediation, while completely removing any occasion for glorying in ourselves.

We seek no more from this testimony than to affirm that, while we are in ourselves devoid of all righteousness in the sight of God, Christ is, through a gracious act of divine imputation, made of God to be our righteousness, so that all our glorying should be in the grace of God and the righteousness of Christ Himself.

Bellarmine offers three responses to this testimony; the first two are similar, and in the third, pressed by truth, he confesses and concedes everything we argue for. First, he claims, "That Christ is said to be our righteousness because He is the efficient cause of it, just as God is said to be our strength; thus, there is a metonymy of the effect for the cause." I agree that the Lord Christ, by His Spirit, is the efficient cause of our personal, inherent righteousness. By His grace it is accomplished and wrought in us; He renews our natures into the image of God, and without Him we can do nothing. Hence, our habitual and actual righteousness comes from Him.

However, this personal righteousness is our sanctification and nothing else. The same inward habit of inherent grace, together with its suitable operations, is sometimes called our sanctification and sometimes our righteousness; but it is not divided into two things, as if we had both a sanctification and a separate righteousness.

His being made righteousness for us in this context is entirely distinct from His being made sanctification for us. The latter denotes the inherent righteousness wrought in us by the Spirit and the grace of Christ. The operation of personal righteousness in us—our sanctification—and the imputation of His righteousness to us—by which we are declared righteous before God—are consistent with one another; indeed, one cannot exist without the other.

He argues, "Christ is said to be made righteousness for us, just as He is made redemption. He is our redemption because He has redeemed us. Therefore, He is said to be made righteousness for us because through Him we become righteous," or, as another puts it, "because through Him alone we are justified." This resembles the previous argument, suggesting a metonymy of the effect for the cause in such expressions. Yet I cannot see what cause they intend when they say, "By Him alone we are justified."

Still, Bellarmine is approaching the truth. Just as Christ is said to be made redemption for us because we are redeemed by His blood and freed from sin, death, and hell by the ransom He paid, so He is said to be made righteousness for us because, through His righteousness granted to us by God, we are justified. In this sense God's making Him our righteousness, our becoming the righteousness of God in Him, and the imputation of His righteousness to us are all the same.

His third response, as already noted, concedes everything we contend for. It is the same answer he gives to Jeremiah 23:6, which he links to this passage, treating them as identical in sense and weight and thus yielding his whole case to them, as he does in Book II, Chapter 10.

Socinus begins his reply to this testimony with astonishment that anyone would use it in this controversy, insisting it is irrelevant. His feigned contempt for his opponents' arguments is his chief tactic in these replies and evasions. I regret that many who oppose the imputation of Christ's righteousness have followed his example, and that this testimony — which placed Bellarmine in so difficult a position — has recently been dismissed on Socinus's objections alone.

His objections, however, are so weak that one must wonder how any learned person could be misled by them. He simply argues, "If Christ is said to be made righteousness for us because His righteousness is imputed to us, then He must be said to be made wisdom for us because His wisdom is also imputed, and the same goes for His sanctification; which no one would accept. Indeed, He must be redeemed for us, and His redemption must be imputed to us."

There is no force in this argument; it rests on the false assumption that Christ must be made all these things to us in the same way. But these things are of such different natures that they cannot coherently be made to us in an identical manner. For example, He is made sanctification for us in that we are sanctified by His Spirit and grace. He cannot, however, be said to be made redemption for us in that manner. If one says He is made righteousness for us because He works inherent righteousness in us through His Spirit and grace, then that is plainly the same as saying He is made sanctification for us.

Moreover, Socinus does not maintain that Christ is made all these things to us in the same way; he does not specify any particular manner. Instead, he obscures the matter with vague language, claiming Christ becomes these things to us in the providence of God. If you press him to say how Christ is made sanctification for us, he will answer that it is by His doctrine and example, with some general assistance from the Spirit that God permits.

But this is not how Christ is made redemption for us. Redemption is an external act; it is not something wrought within us. Christ can be made redemption for us only by the imputation of what He accomplished for our redemption — by reckoning His redemptive work on our behalf —

not by saying He was redeemed for us, as he childishly argues, but by recognizing that He did what was necessary for our redemption.

Thus, Christ is made of God righteousness for us in the manner that the nature of the matter requires. Some say, "It is because through Him we are justified." However, the text does not say that through Him we are justified, but that He is made righteousness for us by God. That is not our justification itself, but the ground, cause, and reason for our justification. Righteousness is one thing, and justification another. Therefore we must inquire how we come to possess that righteousness by which we are justified. The same apostle plainly states it is by imputation: "just as David also describes the blessedness of the man to whom God imputes righteousness apart from works:" (Romans 4:6)

It follows, then, that Christ being made righteousness for us by God can only mean that His righteousness is imputed to us. This text undeniably confirms that.

2 Corinthians 5:21. In what sense Christ knew no sin — emphasis in that expression — how He was made sin for us — by the imputation of sin to Him — mistakes of some regarding this expression — understanding of the ancients — Bellarmine's objections to this testimony answered, along with other arguments of his to the same effect.

The truth being argued is even more emphatically expressed: "For He made Him who knew no sin to be sin for us, that we might become the righteousness of God in Him." Augustine's paraphrase on these words captures their meaning: "He Himself became sin so that we might become righteousness—not our righteousness, but God's; not in us, but in Him," (Enchiridion to Laurent, Chapter 4). The words of Chrysostom on this passage, which serve the same purpose, have been cited before at length.

To illustrate the greatness of God's grace in our reconciliation through Christ, the phrase "who knew no sin" is employed. He understood sin in terms of its nature and experienced its effects in what He endured and suffered; yet He did not know it in the sense of committing it or bearing its guilt. Therefore, "He knew no sin" amounts to the same thing as "who committed no sin, nor was guile found in His mouth," (1 Peter 2:22); or as that He was "who is holy, harmless, undefiled, separate from sinners," (Hebrews 7:26).

There is, however, an emphatic force in the expression that must not be overlooked. As Chrysostom observes, the apostle uses an auxesis — he does not merely say "the one who did not sin," but "the one who knew no sin." Many learned writers after him have noted this. Those who wish to grasp the fullness of God's grace in this matter will be impressed by that emphatic wording, which the Holy Spirit chose to convey for this purpose; therefore the point should not be dismissed.

"For He made Him who knew no sin to be sin for us;" — that is, say many interpreters, a sacrifice for sin. "Just as He was offered for sins, it is not without reason that He is called sin, because the animal offered for sins in the law is also called sin," as Ambrose observes here. Thus the sin and trespass offerings are frequently expressed by חַטָּאת and אָשָׁם — "the sin" and "trespass," or "guilt."

I will not contest that interpretation, for it aligns with the truth. Yet there is another, more precise meaning of the word: hamartia can signify hamartōlos — "sin" used to mean a "sinner" (that is, passively, not actively; not by inhesion, but by imputation). The phrase and the force of the antithesis seem to require this sense. Estius himself approves another explanation, drawn from the Greek fathers, including Chrysostom: sin is emphatically interpreted as a great sinner; as if the apostle were saying He was treated for our sake as though He were sin itself, as though He were a notoriously wicked man, so that in Him our iniquities might be placed.

If that is the interpretation adopted by the Greek scholars, then Luther was not the first to assert that Christ was made the greatest sinner — namely, by imputation. Nevertheless, I will accept the earlier interpretation so long as the true notion of a sin-offering or expiatory sacrifice is acknowledged. That sacrifice did not consist in a transfusion of inherent sin from the person into the offering, but in the transfer of the guilt of the sinner to it, as is fully explained in Leviticus 16:20-21.

I concede this meaning of the word to avoid contention. Some maintain that hamartia sometimes signifies sin and a sacrifice for sin; this, however, cannot be accepted without qualification. חָטָא in Kal means "to err, to sin, to transgress the law of God." In Piel it can mean the opposite — "to cleanse from sin" or "to make expiation for sin." Thus חַטָּאת is most frequently used in the first conjugation to signify "sin," "transgression," and "guilt," but sometimes with the second, when it denotes "a sacrifice for sin," to make expiation.

Thus the LXX. renders it variously: sometimes by hilasmos (Ezekiel 44:27) and sometimes by exilasmos (Exodus 30:10; Ezekiel 43:22), meaning "propitiation" or "propitiatory sacrifice." At other times it uses hagnisma and hagnismos (Numbers 19:19), meaning "purification" or "cleansing." Yet hamartia by itself does not, in any reputable author or in Scripture generally, signify a sacrifice for sin — unless one would allow that sense in this single exceptional instance.

The LXX. consistently translates חַטָּאת as hamartia when the word signifies sin. When it denotes an offering for sin and they wish to retain that idea, they use peri hamartias — an elliptical expression they coined for something the bare word hamartia did not itself mean (see Leviticus 4:3, 14, 32, 35; 5:6-11; 6:30; 8:2). They never omit the preposition unless they actually name the sacrifice, as in moschos tēs hamartias. The same practice appears in the New Testament. Twice the apostle, when referring to the sin-offering, employs the phrase peri hamartias

(Romans 8:3; Hebrews 10:6); he never uses hamartia alone for that purpose.

If hamartia has that meaning here, it does so in this passage alone. Some have tried to equate it with the Latin piaculum, but that is a misunderstanding. The primary meaning of hamartia is admitted to be "sin," and to assume it is then misused to mean a sacrifice for sin is a stretch. Piaculum properly denotes a sacrifice or anything by which sin is expiated or satisfaction is made. Very rarely it is misapplied to mean such a sin or crime as deserves public expiation and cannot otherwise be pardoned; as Virgil puts it, "He deferred the piacula committed to a late death."

We will not quarrel over words when we can agree about the sense intended.

The only question is how God made Him to be sin. The apostle's expression is best rendered by the New Testament: "For He made Him who knew no sin to be sin for us," which expresses an act of God. Isaiah likewise speaks of this work, saying, "And the Lord has laid on Him the iniquity of us all" (Isaiah 53:6). This was accomplished by the imputation of our sins to Him, just as the sins of the people were laid upon the head of the scapegoat, so that the sins were no longer theirs but His, and He was to carry them away.

Whether we take "sin" in the sense of a sacrifice for sin or in the sense of a sinner by imputation, the imputation of guilt must be understood as preceding the punishment. In every sin-offering there was first an imposition of sin upon the animal to be offered, before it suffered and died. Hence the person bringing the offering was required to put his hand on the head of the burnt offering (Leviticus 1:4). That act signified the transfer of guilt, as Leviticus 16:21 explicitly teaches. Thus, if God made Christ a sin-offering for us, it was by imputing our guilt to Him before His suffering.

No offering for sin could be made without a typical transfer of guilt to it. For example, when an offering was made for the expiation of guilt in the case of an unsolved murder, the elders of the nearest city did not offer a sacrifice because there was no guilt to confess over it or to lay upon the victim. Rather, when they brought the heifer down to the valley, they were to break the heifer's neck there, and the priests would come near; then all the elders were to wash their hands over the heifer. They thus testified their own innocence and prayed for atonement on behalf of the people (Deuteronomy 21:1-8). A sacrifice for sin without the imputation of guilt is therefore impossible.

If we take the word in the second sense — namely, as denoting a sinner by imputation and in God's reckoning — that too presupposes the imputation of guilt. Suffering alone does not make one a sinner. No one argues that Christ was made sin merely by receiving punishment divorced from imputation. Rather, the sense is that sin was imputed to Him as the ground of punishment; that is, the guilt of sin was imputed to Him. The guilt of sin is its relation to punishment — the obligation to punishment that follows from it.

It is impossible, on justice, that someone should be punished for sin without guilt being imputed to them. If punishment could be inflicted apart from imputation, it would be unjust; it would be wrong to punish anyone for sins that are not theirs. If the sin is not theirs by nature, it can only be theirs by imputation. A person may suffer on account of another's sin without it being their own; but to be punished justly requires that the guilt be reckoned to them. If that were otherwise, where would the justice lie in punishing one for what does not belong to them?

Moreover, the acts of imputing sin and of inflicting punishment are distinct, and the imputation always precedes the punishment. Therefore, the imputation concerns the guilt of sin alone. Accordingly, the Lord Christ was made sin for us by the imputation of our sins' guilt to Him.

It is argued that if "the guilt of sin were imputed to Christ, He would be excluded from all possibility of merit, as He would have suffered only what was due to Him, thus undermining the entire work of Christ's satisfaction. This must be the case if God, in judgment, reckoned Him guilty and a sinner." However, these expressions are ambiguous. If the claim is that God reckoned Him guilty and a sinner in His own person, that is not true. Rather, God laid all our sins on Him and did not spare Him in judgment with respect to what was due for those sins.

Thus, He did not suffer what was due to Him on His own account but what was due because of our sin. To deny this is impious. If it were not so, He died in vain and we remain in our sins. His satisfaction consists in this fact, and it could not exist apart from it. This in no way diminishes His merit. Given the infinite dignity of His person and His voluntary acceptance of our sin to atone for it—which did not change His essential state—His obedience in this matter was supremely meritorious.

In consequence, we are made "the righteousness of God in Him." That was the purpose of His being made sin for us. By whom are we made so? It is by God Himself; for "It is God who justifies" (Romans 8:33); it is God who "imputes righteousness" (Romans 4:6). Therefore, the act of God in our justification is what is intended here.

To be made the righteousness of God means to be justified before God. The expression uses the abstract for the concrete, just as was said earlier about Christ being made sin for us. To be made the righteousness of God is to be justified, and to be made so in Him—just as He was made sin for us—is to be justified by the imputation of His righteousness to us, even as our sin was imputed to Him.

No one can propose any other way that He was made sin—certainly not, above all, by God—except by God's laying all our iniquities upon Him, that is, by imputing our sin to Him. How, then, are we made the righteousness of God in Him? "By the infusion of a habit of grace," say the Papists generally. If that were so, then by the rule of antithesis He must be made sin for us by the infusion of a habit of sin—a blasphemous notion.

"By His meriting, procuring, and purchasing righteousness for us," say others. In that sense we might be made righteous by Him; but we cannot be made righteous in Him in that way. To be righteous in Him is to be righteous with His righteousness, because we are one mystical person with Him. Therefore, to be made the righteousness of God in Christ—just as He was made sin for us—can only mean to be made righteous by the imputation of His righteousness to us, as we are in Him or united to Him. All other interpretations are superficial and strained, and they divert the mind from the plain, first meaning of the words.

Bellarmine objects to this interpretation. His first argument against the imputation of Christ's righteousness appears in Book II, Chapter 7 of De Justificatione: "Fifthly, it is refuted because if the righteousness of Christ is truly imputed to us so that we are considered just by it, as if it were intrinsically our own formal righteousness, then we should be regarded and considered as just as Christ Himself; therefore, we ought to be called and regarded as redeemers and saviors of the world, which is utterly absurd."

A thorough answer to this argument has been given so often by Protestant theologians that I would not have mentioned it, except that some among ourselves are pleased to borrow it from him and make use of it. They say, "If the righteousness of Christ is imputed to us so that it becomes ours, then we are as righteous as Christ Himself, because we are righteous with His righteousness."

1. These statements are plainly affirmed in Scripture. On the one hand it is said, "we are all like an unclean thing, And all our righteousnesses are like filthy rags" (Isaiah 64:6); on the other hand it declares, "Surely in the Lord I have righteousness and strength. In the Lord all the descendants of Israel Shall be justified, and shall glory" (Isaiah 45:24–25).

Thus, while we acknowledge our sinful state, we are still "the righteousness of God in Christ." These two ideas are consistent despite any objections that human reason may raise. They must be accepted unless one follows Socinus's rule of interpretation—which says that when Scripture affirms something that seems contrary to our reason, we should not accept it but instead force the meaning to conform to our reasoning.

2. Despite the imputation of Christ's righteousness to us, and our being made righteous by it, we remain sinners in ourselves (the Lord knows how greatly so, even the best among us). Thus we cannot be said to be as righteous as Christ; we are made righteous in Him, even while remaining sinners in ourselves.

3. To claim that we are as righteous as Christ is to equate Christ's personal righteousness with our personal righteousness, as if they were the same kind of thing. That is foolish and impious. Despite any personal righteousness we may have, we are still sinful; Christ knew no sin. If the comparison is between Christ's inherent, personal righteousness and the righteousness imputed to us—two different concepts—then it is irrelevant. Christ was actively righteous; we are made righteous only passively. When our sin was imputed to Him, He did not become a sinner in the way we are, inherently and subjectively;

He bore our guilt by imputation only. Just as He was made sin yet knew no sin, so we are made righteous yet remain sinful in ourselves.

4. The righteousness that was personally Christ's was the righteousness of the Son of God, possessing infinite perfection and worth. It is imputed to us only in respect of our personal need — given to our souls as they require and partake of it. It is not offered or applied in the same manner or measure as it exists in Him. Therefore, there is no sound basis for comparing them as though they were identical.

5. As for Bellarmine's addition — that from this doctrine we should be said to be redeemers and saviors of the world — the absurdity lies with him; the consequence does not follow. He explicitly states in Book I, De Purgator., Chapter 14, that "a man may be rightly called his own redeemer and savior," which he attempts to prove from Daniel 4. Some in his church assert that saints may improperly be called redeemers of others. We do not need to debate those points here. From the imputation of Christ's righteousness it follows only that those to whom it is imputed are redeemed and saved, not that they are redeemers and saviors.

It is also necessary to address the vanity of his seventh argument in the same case, for some among ourselves have borrowed it. This argument runs: "If by the imputation of the righteousness of Christ to us we may be truly called righteous and the sons of God, then Christ, by the imputation of our unrighteousness, may be said to be a sinner and a child of the devil."

1. What Scripture affirms regarding the imputation of our sins to Christ is that "For He made Him who knew no sin to be sin for us, that we might become the righteousness of God in Him." The Greek interpreters — Chrysostom, Theophylact, Œcumenius, and many others — render this as meaning "a sinner." But they all understand that such a designation is derived solely from imputation: He had sin

imputed to Him and bore the penalty due to it, just as we have righteousness imputed to us and enjoy its benefits.

2. The imputation of sin to Christ did not involve any pollution or inward defilement being transferred to Him—an impossibility. Therefore no true designation can arise from it that would imply any real connection to sin. To think otherwise is impious and dishonoring to the Son of God. His being made sin by the imputation of guilt is, rather, His honor and glory.

3. The sins of fornicators, idolaters, adulterers, and the like—such as the Corinthians were before their conversion—were theirs inherently and actively, and thus they were rightly called by those names. But to say that He who knew no sin voluntarily took on the guilt of those sins—and in doing so acted in the highest righteousness and obedience to God—so that He should be called an idolater or adulterer, is foolish. The designation "sinner" applied to one from inherent, active sin is a reproach. Yet even the designation that arises by imputation—where no personal guilt or defilement was experienced by Him to whom it is imputed, and where the act was the highest obedience for the greatest glory of God—is itself not a dishonor but is the means of His glory.

4. The imputation of sin to Christ took place before any real union between Him and sinners, and He took their sin upon Himself according to His own will and for His own purposes. By contrast, the imputation of His righteousness to believers follows from their union with Him, whereby it becomes theirs in a unique way. There is, therefore, no parity of reason for treating Him as a sinner as there is for treating believers as righteous.

5. We admit that, concerning the imputation of sin to Christ, it is said that "For He made Him who knew no sin to be sin for us," which He could not be except through that imputation—and He was so only by an act whose effects were transient, limited to the time in which He

bore the punishment due for it. By contrast, in the imputation of His righteousness to us we are "made the righteousness of God," receiving an everlasting righteousness that remains ours forever.

6. To be a child of the devil through sin is to do the works of the devil (John 8:44). However, the Lord Christ, in taking our sins upon Himself — when those sins were imputed to Him — performed the work of God in the highest act of holy obedience. In doing so He demonstrated Himself to be the Son of God and destroyed the works of the devil. Thus it is both foolish and impious to suppose that any absolute change of state or relation in Him resulted from this.

The interpretation that "the righteousness of God" here refers to our own faith and obedience in accordance with the gospel is so far removed from the intent of the passage and the meaning of the words that I will not examine it in detail. The righteousness of God is revealed to faith and received by faith; it is not, therefore, faith itself.

The force of the antithesis is entirely distorted by this notion. Where is the connection in saying that He was made sin by the imputation of our sin to Him, and that we are made righteous by the imputation of our own faith and obedience to ourselves? Just as Christ had no involvement in sin except insofar as God made Him sin — sin was never inherently in Him — so this righteousness is not inherently in us but only imputed to us.

Moreover, the act of God in making us righteous is His justification of us. This is not accomplished by the infusion of a habit of faith and obedience, as we have shown. I do not know what act of God is meant by those who claim that the righteousness of God which makes us righteous is our own righteousness. It cannot be the constitution of the gospel law, for that does not make anyone righteous. The persons of believers are the object of this divine act, and they are regarded as they are considered in Christ.

Galatians 2:16 states, "Knowing that a man is not justified by the works of the law but by faith in Jesus Christ, even we have believed in Christ Jesus, that we might be justified by faith in Christ and not by the works of the law; for by the works of the law no flesh shall be justified."

The entire epistle of the same apostle to the Galatians is intended to vindicate the doctrine of justification by Christ apart from the works of the law, and to explain the way this blessing is to be maintained. The essence of his argument is summed up in his words to the apostle Peter concerning his failure, as recorded in this chapter.

What he asserts here is so well known and so fundamental a principle of truth among believers that their conviction of it was the basis for their turning from Judaism to the gospel and for their faith in Jesus Christ.

In these words the apostle addresses the important question of how a person is justified before God. The subject is stated generally: "A man" — that is, any man, whether Jew or Gentile; believer or unbeliever; the apostle himself and those to whom he wrote — the Galatians, who had also believed and professed the gospel for some time.

The answer given to this question is both negative and positive, asserted with the highest assurance and presented as the common faith of all Christians, except those who had been led astray by deceivers. He maintains that justification is not, and cannot be, "by the works of the law." What the apostle means by "the law" in these discussions has been explained previously. Sometimes the law of Moses is specifically intended — not absolutely, but as it relates to those who were clinging to a law-righteousness and would not submit themselves to the righteousness of God. To suppose that the moral law and its duties are excluded from this discussion is a weak assumption; such an exclusion would also deny the duty of the ceremonial law, since its observance, while it was in force, was a requirement of the moral law.

By "the works of the law" he means the actions and duties that God's law requires, performed in the manner the law prescribes—namely, in faith and out of love for God above all, as has been shown. To claim that the apostle only excludes works that are absolutely perfect, which no one has done or could do since the entrance of sin, misunderstands his argument. That point is not what he is addressing in his discourse.

Furthermore, he does not mean to exclude only those works regarded as meritorious. He excludes all works so that there may be no place for merit in our justification, as has already been shown. The Galatians to whom he writes were not seeking justification by any works other than those they performed as believers. Therefore, every kind of work is excluded from any role in our justification.

The apostle insists so strongly on excluding works from our justification that he warns it undermines the whole gospel. As he states in verse 21, "For if righteousness comes through the law, then Christ died in vain." That is indeed a perilous position to take.

It is not only some kinds of works, or some ways of doing them, or some particular interest in our justification that are excluded. Rather, all works—whatever their nature and however they are performed—are excluded from consideration as contributing to our justification as our own works or duties of obedience.

The Galatians, whom the apostle rebukes, wanted works of the law or duties of obedience to be counted alongside faith in Christ Jesus in a believer's justification. There is no reason to think they intended to reject faith in Christ and attribute justification solely to works—that would be a foolish misunderstanding. By contrast, the apostle plainly attributes our justification solely to faith in Christ.

"not by the works of the law but by faith in Jesus Christ" means by faith alone. The particles "ean mē" should not be read as introducing an exception but as adversative. Protestant theologians have convincingly shown this, and even some within the Roman church, who have approached the controversy modestly, acknowledge it. The words of Estius deserve notice: "Nisi per fidem Jesu Christi; sententiam reddit obscuram particula nisi" (the Vulgar Latin translates "ean mē" as "but" or "but only"). If taken as it sounds to Latin ears, it would imply an exception to what precedes, as if a person were not justified by the works of the law unless faith in Christ accompanied those works.

But that interpretation splits justification, assigning part of it to the works of the law and part to faith in Christ. That contradicts the apostle's clear and absolute statement. Such an interpretation must therefore be rejected as contrary to the apostolic intent and purpose.

Indeed, it is clear that the word "nisi" is often used in Scripture in an adversative sense, meaning essentially "but only."

It seems unlikely we will settle this dispute in this life when people refuse to accept such clear determinations given by the Holy Spirit himself.

The interpretation that men cannot be justified by works they cannot perform — works that would have to be absolutely perfect — but can be justified by works they can and do perform, even if done not in their own strength but by the help of grace, is not consistent with the mind of the Holy Spirit. That view is incompatible with the apostle's teaching and must be set aside.

Faith in Christ Jesus, which the apostle sets over against all works, necessarily includes all the works he excludes, with respect to the purpose for which they are excluded.

Ephesians 2:8-10 provides the evidence for this testimony. The apostle's purpose from the chapter's outset is plain. He sets forth, step by step, the grace of God and affirms that grace alone is the cause of deliverance from a life of sin.

Several points deserve attention about the causes of spiritual deliverance. The apostle magnifies grace, and the argument and proof he draws from it are powerful. He sums up the case in the general statement, "by grace you have been saved."

What does it mean to be saved? It is akin to being justified, though not identical. The causes of our justification are stated both positively and negatively. The whole matter rests on the grace of God through Christ, and our participation in it comes through faith alone.

Works are excluded — but what works? Not the works of Moses' law, not works that come before believing, but the works of true believers. This exclusion opposes both the grace of God and the faith that is within us.

The force of the argument is weighty. Works are excluded to prevent boasting on our part. If works contributed to justification, boasting would naturally follow, and that is precisely what the apostle seeks to guard against.

This point answers a common objection: If we are not justified by works, what purpose do they serve? The answer is found in Ephesians 2:8-10: "For by grace you have been saved through faith, and that not of yourselves; it is the gift of God, not of works, lest anyone should boast. For we are His workmanship, created in Christ Jesus for good works, which God prepared beforehand that we should walk in them."

It is unlikely that the Holy Spirit would, from the start, have anticipated and precluded every possible human evasive tactic designed later to pervert the doctrine of justification and yet not have expressed the truth plainly enough to prevent them. If we pause and consider the passage without bias, the apostle's meaning becomes clear.

It cannot be denied that the apostle's intent, from the beginning of the chapter through the end of verse 11, is to set forth how lost and condemned sinners are rescued and translated into a state of acceptance with God and eternal salvation.

Accordingly, he first fully depicts their natural condition, emphasizing their subjection to God's wrath. That was the apostle's method: he regularly prefaced the declaration of God's grace with a sober account of our sin, misery, and ruin. Others may dislike this approach, but its validity stands unchanged.

To that end he tells the Ephesians that they "were dead in trespasses and sins," showing how sin had the power of death over their souls and governed their spiritual life and actions. He also observes that they lived and walked in sin, and thus were "children of wrath," or subject to eternal condemnation (verses 1–3).

What such individuals can do toward their own deliverance is described in many ways, none of which I can accept; the apostle's whole design is to prove that they can do nothing. He points to another cause, or causes, of their deliverance that stand in direct opposition to anything we might do: "But God, who is rich in mercy," (verse 4).

This adversative statement rejects any effort on our part and confines the whole work to God. Had people accepted this divine revelation, the church would have been spared many of the perverse opinions and disputes that have plagued it. Yet many are unwilling to give up the idea that they have some part in securing their own happiness.

We can note two points in the apostle's assignment of the causes of our deliverance from sin and acceptance with God. First, he attributes the whole work to grace, love, and mercy. Second, he excludes any consideration of our contributions, as we will see in verses 5 and 8.

He magnifies this grace in a striking way.

First, he names it by every title that signifies it — mercy, love, grace, and kindness. In this context he wants our attention fixed wholly on grace.

Second, he ascribes to that divine mercy and grace such qualities and descriptions as to make it the sole cause of our deliverance through Jesus Christ, and thus singularly worthy of adoration: "rich in mercy," "great love with which He loved us," "the exceeding riches of His grace in His kindness" (verses 4–7).

It is hard to deny that the apostle aims to move the minds and hearts of believers deeply, so they recognize the grace and love of God in Christ as the only cause of their justification before God. I believe no words can fully express the thoughts that this portrayal of grace should awaken.

Whether people consider it their duty to be like-minded and to agree with the apostle's design — who seldom speaks of God's grace without showing its full efficacy — is not difficult to judge.

Some may object, "These are good words, indeed, but they are only general; there is no argument in this adoration of the grace of God in the work of our salvation."

That may seem true to many. But frankly, I find more argument in this single consideration — the ascription here made to the grace of God —

than in a hundred sophistries that do not agree with Scripture or with the experience of believers.

Anyone who properly understands the grace of God as presented here, and who recognizes that the Holy Spirit intended to render it glorious and solely trustworthy, will not readily be persuaded to seek added support from their own works and obedience, as some suggest.

Yet we can go further into his words.

The case the apostle presents—the inquiry he addresses and the truth he teaches the Ephesians, and through them the whole church—is this: how may a lost, condemned sinner be accepted by God and thus be saved?

This is the only question at issue in this controversy. We will not go beyond it, whether invited or provoked. On this point his position and determination is, "By grace you have been saved."

He first mentions this among the benefits we receive through Christ (v. 5). Not satisfied with that, he asserts it again in verse 8, using the same words. He apparently foresaw how slow people would be to accept a truth that strips them of every ground for boasting in themselves.

We must inquire what he means by our being saved.

It would not diminish but rather strengthen the truth we advocate if "being saved" referred to eternal salvation. However, that cannot be the meaning here, except insofar as that salvation is included among the effects experienced in this life.

I do not believe the expression "By grace you have been saved" refers only to our justification, though that is certainly a principal aspect. Conversion to God and sanctification are included as well, as verses 5 and 6 show, and they are no less the result of sovereign grace than our justification itself.

The apostle is speaking of what the Ephesians—now believers—partook of in this life. The whole context makes that clear. After describing their condition at the chapter's beginning, which they shared with all Adam's descendants (vv. 1-3), he then sets out their distinct condition in contrast to the Jews: they were Gentiles, idolaters, and atheists (vv. 11-12).

Their present deliverance through Jesus Christ from that miserable state—both the condition they shared with all mankind and the additional misery that uniquely afflicted them—is what he means by their being "saved."

The primary focus in describing this state is that they were liable to the wrath of God, guilty before Him, and subject to His judgment. This point is made in verse 3 and follows the same method and grounds the apostle consistently uses in declaring the doctrine of justification (Romans 3:19-24; Titus 3:3-5).

From this state, they found deliverance through faith in Christ Jesus, for to all who received Him, to them He gave the right to become children of God (John 1:12). "He who believes in Him is not condemned;" meaning he is saved in the sense the apostle intends here (John 3:18). "He who believes in the Son has everlasting life;" (is saved), while "he who does not believe the Son shall not see life, but the wrath of God abides on him." (verse 36)

In this sense, the terms saved and salvation are frequently used in Scripture. Moreover, the apostle gives a full description of the salvation he has in view from Ephesians 2:13 through the end of the chapter, leaving no doubt.

It involves being "made near by the blood of Christ" (verse 13), having "peace" with God through His death (verses 14 and 15), experiencing "reconciliation" through the blood of the cross (verse 16), and having "access to God," along with all spiritual privileges that depend on it (verses 18–20), and so forth.

Therefore, the apostle's inquiry and his conclusion concern the causes of our justification before God. He presents them both positively and negatively.

Positively:

1. The supreme moving cause on God's part is His free, sovereign grace and love, which He illustrates by the attributes and properties mentioned earlier.

2. The meritorious, procuring cause is Jesus Christ in His mediatorial work, as ordained by God to make this grace effective for His glory (verses 7, 13, 16).

3. The only means or instrumental cause on our part is faith: "By grace you have been saved through faith" (verse 8). To ensure he does not diminish the grace of God by asserting the necessity and use of faith, he adds the clarification, "and that not of yourselves; it is the gift of God." The impartation of this faith to us is as much an act of grace as the justification we receive through it. Thus, the entire work is secured to the grace of God through Christ, which we receive by faith alone.

However, not content with this, he also describes the work negatively, excluding what others might claim has relevance in the matter. He distinctly states three things:

1. What he excludes.

2. The reason for this exclusion.

3. The confirmation of that reason, addressing an objection that might arise:

What he excludes is works: "not of works" (verse 9). He clarifies what types of works he refers to, at least primarily. Some argue that he means the works of the law, specifically the law of Moses. But what relevance did these have for the Ephesians, that the apostle should inform them that they were not justified by those works? They were never under that law, never sought righteousness through it, nor had any regard for it, except that they were delivered from it.

Perhaps he only means works done in the strength of our own natural abilities, without the aid of grace, and before believing. But what were the works of these Ephesians before believing? He explains this both before and after. For, "dead in trespasses and sins," they "walked according to the course of this world, fulfilling the desires of the flesh and of the mind" (verses 1–3).

It is clear that these works have no influence on our justification, and equally clear that the apostle had no reason to exclude them, as if anyone could claim advantage from them in the matter of deliverance from them. Therefore, the works excluded by the apostle are those performed by the Ephesians as believers, made alive with Christ; even the "works which God prepared beforehand that we should walk in them" (verse 10).

He excludes these works not only in opposition to grace but also in opposition to faith: "through faith; not of works." Thus, he not only rejects their merit as inconsistent with grace but also their co-interest with faith in the work of justification before God.

If we are saved by grace through faith in Christ, excluding all works of obedience, then such works cannot be any part of our righteousness for justification. Therefore, we must have another righteousness or perish forever.

I know many arguments are presented, and distinctions are made, to retain some role for works in our justification before God. However, it will not be difficult for anyone to determine whether it is safer to rely on these arguments or on this clear, explicit divine testimony when they consider the matter for themselves.

The apostle provides a reason for this exclusion of works: "not of works, lest anyone should boast." God has ordained the order and method of our justification by Christ in this way so that no one might have grounds, reason, or occasion to glory or boast in themselves.

This is expressed in 1 Corinthians 1:21, 30, 31; Romans 3:27. The intention of God is to exclude all boasting on our part, which consists in attributing something to ourselves that is not present in others regarding justification. Works alone can provide any occasion for such boasting: "For if Abraham was justified by works, he has something to boast about" (Romans 4:2).

This boasting is excluded solely by the "law of faith" (Romans 3:27), for the nature and purpose of faith is to find righteousness in another. All works are prone to incite boasting in the minds of men if applied to justification; and where there is any such boasting, the purpose of God in His work of grace towards us is frustrated.

What I emphasize from this is that there are no boundaries fixed in Scripture regarding the role of works in justification that would exclude boasting. The Papists claim that works are meritorious, at least for what they call our second justification. Some argue that this should not be accepted, as it includes boasting. Merit and boasting are inseparable.

Others claim that works are merely "causa sine qua non," the condition of justification; or that they represent our evangelical righteousness before God, on which we are justified; or that they are a subordinate righteousness through which we gain an interest in the righteousness of Christ; or that they are included in the condition of the new covenant by which we are justified; or that they are part of faith, being its form or essence in some way.

Men express themselves in a great variety of ways on this point. However, as long as our works are asserted in relation to our justification, how can anyone be sure they do not allow for boasting, or that they truly reflect the meaning of the words, "not of works, lest anyone should boast"?

There is some form of self-attribution in this matter, and that is boasting. If anyone claims to know what they are doing and insists they do not boast in what they attribute to works, I cannot accept that as a general rule. The Papists insist they are far from boasting, yet I remain convinced that boasting and merit are inseparable.

The question is not what people think they are doing, but what judgment Scripture places on their actions. If it is said that what is in us is also a gift of God's grace, and this is acknowledged, thereby excluding all boasting in ourselves, I would point out that the Pharisee thought the same—and yet he was a conspicuous boaster.

Let us suppose works are wrought in us in whatever way people wish; but if they are also wrought by us and are therefore "the works of righteousness which we have done," I fear that including them in our justification entails boasting, in light of the apostle's assertion, "not of works, lest anyone should boast."

Because this is a critical issue, unless men can provide direct, clear, indisputable boundaries for including our works in justification that do not allow boasting, it is safest to exclude them entirely. In doing so, I see no danger of misunderstanding the Spirit's words: "not of works, lest anyone should boast." If we are foolishly led into such boasting, we will forfeit the benefits we might otherwise expect from God's grace.

The apostle gives another reason why it cannot be of works, addressing an objection that might arise from what he stated in Ephesians 2:10: "For we are His workmanship, created in Christ Jesus for good works, which God prepared beforehand that we should walk in them."

The force of his reasoning — signaled by the causal conjunction — runs like this: all good works, especially the evangelical works he discusses, are the effects of God's grace in those who are in Christ Jesus. In that sense, we are truly justified in relation to them.

However, his primary aim is to answer an anticipated objection: "If good works are excluded from our justification before God, then what use are they? We may live as we please, utterly neglect them, and still be justified."

That very objection is still strongly argued by some today against the same doctrine. We often hear the claim that "if our justification before God is not based on works, or if works are not required beforehand, then there is no need for them; men may safely live in complete neglect of obedience to God."

It astonishes me that they do not see which side they take in making this objection — namely, the side of those who opposed the apostle's doctrine of grace. That matter must be dealt with elsewhere.

For now I will say no more: if the apostle's answer does not satisfy them, and if the grounds and reasons he gives for the necessity and use of good works are not judged sufficient to put those works in their proper place and order, I do not feel obliged to offer further satisfaction.

Philippians 3:8-9. Key arguments from this passage—its purpose and context; righteousness as the ground of acceptance with God; the twofold righteousness the apostle considers; how these two kinds of righteousness are opposed with respect to the end aimed at; and the question: which did he embrace—his own righteousness or God's righteousness? The apostle answers this with great fervor. I will note the reasons for his strong language, the point at which he renounced Judaism, the Jewish opposition to this doctrine, how important and yet how unpopular the doctrine is, and his personal sense of sin and grace. I will also note some distinctive expressions he uses about Christ and about all that belongs to us, and the choice posed between clinging to our own righteousness or to that of Christ—rival and incompatible, as regards justification. I will set out arguments drawn from the passage and handle objections to its testimony. I will show that our inherent personal righteousness is the same under law and gospel, that the idea that external righteousness alone is demanded by the law is impious, that only works done before faith are rejected, and that the apparent objection is answered.

"Yet indeed I also count all things loss for the excellence of the knowledge of Christ Jesus my Lord, for whom I have suffered the loss of all things, and count them as rubbish, that I may gain Christ and be found in Him, not having my own righteousness, which is from the law, but that which is through faith in Christ, the righteousness which is from God by faith;"

This is the last testimony I will discuss. Although it is highly important, I will be brief because another has recently defended it, and I see no reasonable reply to that defense. What one other person has attempted since carries no weight; he is completely mistaken in this matter.

The points I wish to draw from this testimony are these: from the opening of the chapter and in these verses the apostle's aim is to state the ground on which we are accepted by God and have cause to rejoice. He sets this out in general as our interest in and participation in Christ through faith, opposed to all the legal privileges and advantages in which the Jews he criticizes boasted and rejoiced: "rejoice in Christ Jesus, and have no confidence in the flesh" (Philippians 3:3).

He assumes that for the acceptance before God, which should be our cause for rejoicing, some righteousness is necessary; whatever that righteousness is, it alone underlies our acceptance. To establish this, he declares that there are two kinds of righteousness that may be claimed and relied upon for that purpose.

1. "my own righteousness, which is from the law."

2. "that which is through faith in Christ, the righteousness which is from God by faith."

He affirms that these two are opposed and incompatible as regards the purpose of our justification and our acceptance with God: "not having my own righteousness, which is from the law, but that which is through faith in Christ," He acknowledges no intermediate righteousness between them.

By placing himself as an example, he emphatically declares — which is unusual in his writings — the righteousness in which he trusted. Several considerations moved his holy mind to press the one righteousness, that which is from God by faith, and to diminish the other, his own righteousness.

1. This was the turning point at which he and others abandoned their Judaism and embraced the gospel. Therefore this had to be secured as the principal instance in which the greatest controversy in the world was debated. He expresses this in Galatians 2:15-16: "We who are Jews by nature, and not sinners of the Gentiles, knowing that a man is not justified by the works of the law but by faith in Jesus Christ, even we have believed in Christ Jesus, that we might be justified by faith in Christ and not by the works of the law."

2. Consequently, there was strong opposition to this doctrine from the Jews everywhere. In many places the minds of multitudes were turned away from the truth — a common tendency in such controversies — and were perverted from the simplicity of the gospel. This deeply affected his holy soul, and he refers to it in most of his epistles.

3. The weight of the doctrine itself, together with people's natural reluctance to embrace it — because it cuts to the root of spiritual pride, self-importance, and self-satisfaction — led many to seek endless subterfuges. They tried to avoid its efficacy and to preserve some claim to merit, resisting a full surrender to the sovereign grace of Christ.

4. He had himself been a great sinner in his days of ignorance, violently opposing Christ and the gospel. He was deeply conscious both of his former guilt and of the excellence of God's grace and of Christ's righteousness by which he was delivered. One must have some experience of what he felt about sin and grace to understand fully his expressions about them.

Thus, in many other places in his writings — but especially in this one — he treats these matters with greater earnestness and intensity than usual.

1. Regarding Christ, whom he seeks to exalt, he mentions not only knowledge of Him but also "the excellence of the knowledge of Christ

Jesus my Lord," emphasizing every word. His repeated expressions—"I also count all things loss;" "that I may gain Christ;" "be found in Him;" "that I may know Him"—all show the working of his affections, guided by faith and truth, toward complete reliance on Christ alone, as all and in all. Some of this frame of mind is necessary for those who would accept his doctrine; those entirely unfamiliar with it will never embrace the other.

2. In speaking of all other things that are our own, which are not Christ—whether privileges or duties, however good, useful, or excellent they may be—he compares them to Christ and His righteousness. With equal fervor he dismisses them, calling them "skubala," or "dog's meat," to be left for those he calls "dogs"—the evil workers of the concision, or the wicked Jews who stubbornly adhered to the righteousness of the law (Philippians 3:2). This account of the apostle's earnestness and the warmth of his expressions is important for understanding his overall design.

Given this context, the question arises: what should any person who desires acceptance with God, or a righteousness by which they may be justified before Him, do? They must choose one of the proposed ways. They can either agree with the apostle in rejecting all their own righteousness and relying on the righteousness of God, which is through faith in Christ Jesus alone, or they can seek exceptions to the apostle's conclusion or make distinctions that allow their own works to play a role in justification. Each person must make this choice for themselves.

In the meantime, we argue: If our own righteousness and the righteousness which is of God by faith—namely, the righteousness God imputes apart from works (Romans 4:6), or the abundance of grace and of the gift of righteousness which we receive (Romans 5:17)—are opposed and inconsistent in the work of justification before God, then we are justified by faith alone through the imputation of Christ's righteousness to us.

The conclusion is clear, because it removes all other means, causes, and conditions as inconsistent with it. But the antecedent is explicitly the apostle's: not having my own righteousness, but that which is through faith in Christ. Furthermore, that by which we are "found in Christ" is that by which we are justified before God; to be found in Christ signifies the state of the person who is to be justified before God, as opposed to being found in ourselves. The judgment of God is based on these different states. For those who are found in themselves, we know what their portion will be. But in Christ, we are found by faith alone.

Various evasions are employed by some to escape the force of this testimony. It is commonly claimed that no reasonable person could suppose the apostle did not wish to be found in gospel righteousness, or that by his own righteousness he meant that his own works alone could entitle him to the benefits of Christ's righteousness. "Nollem dictum."

The criticism is too harsh to be applied universally to Protestant writers who have interpreted this passage of the apostle, and to others — except for a few recent ones swayed by the heat of the controversy.

If the gospel righteousness intended is his own personal righteousness and obedience, it is careless to assert that he desired to be found in it. To be found in what we possess means we will be judged by it. To be found in our own evangelical righteousness before God is to enter into judgment with God about that righteousness — a position none who understand anything of God and themselves will willingly take.

To render his words as, "I do not wish to be found in my own righteousness which is according to the law, but I desire to be found in my own righteousness which is according to the gospel," is improper.

Both would still be his inherent righteousness and therefore the same. This will be disproved shortly.

The claim that our personal gospel righteousness entitles us to the benefits of Christ's righteousness — particularly for our justification before God — is a gratuitous assertion for which no scriptural testimony can be produced. It contradicts many clear testimonies and is inconsistent with the freedom of God's grace in justification as revealed in Scripture.

Moreover, none of the passages that affirm the necessity of obedience and good works in believers — those who are justified — support or imply that our works contribute to our justification. In particular, this assertion directly contradicts the apostle's statement in Titus 3:4-5.

I will refrain from further general elaboration and proceed to consider the specific answers given to this testimony, especially those of Bellarmine, to which I have yet to see any reasonable addition.

Some insist that by his own righteousness, which the apostle rejects, he refers only to his righteousness "ek nomou," or righteousness by the works of the law. But that would be merely an outward, external righteousness — an observance of rites and ceremonies without regard for the inward disposition or obedience of the heart. That notion is impious. The righteousness required by the law is what the law demands, and those who do those works shall live by them; for "but the doers of the law will be justified;" (Romans 2:13).

God has never given any law of obedience to man that did not require him to "You shall love the Lord your God with all your heart, with all your soul, and with all your strength." It is far from true that God required only an external righteousness by the law; He often condemns such externalism as an abomination when it stands alone.

Some argue that the righteousness rejected is simply the righteousness he possessed as a Pharisee. Even if we allow that he could say, "I have lived in all good conscience before God until this day," and that he had regard for both internal and external works of the law, all those works done before faith and conversion must be rejected as contributing to justification.

Works performed in faith and aided by grace — evangelical works — are considered differently. Yet to claim that such works, together with faith, are the conditions for our justification is the very point under dispute.

The apostle opposes evangelical works not only to the grace of God but also to the faith of believers, as shown in the testimony already considered.

He does not make the distinction some assert — that works come in two kinds, one to be excluded from any role in justification while the other is included. He does not mark any such distinction elsewhere in his writings on the same subject. On the contrary, he speaks of the use of all works of obedience in believers, which excludes assuming any such twofold division. He directly rejects his own righteousness — that is, his personal, inherent righteousness — whatever its form or source.

He clearly distinguishes between two states — his Judaism before conversion and his state by faith in Christ Jesus. In the first state, he reflects on its privileges and declares the judgment he formed about them when Christ was revealed to him. He says that he counted them; that is, at his conversion he considered the advantages, gains, and reputation he had from them as nothing, rejecting them all for Christ because their esteem and continued possession as privileges was incompatible with faith in Christ Jesus.

Next, he proceeds to describe his present condition. One might suppose that, having renounced all his legal privileges for Christ, he now, united to Him by faith, retained something of his own to rejoice in—something that could give him acceptance with God (which is precisely what he is arguing about). Otherwise, he would have given up everything for nothing.

Therefore, he—who had no intention of reserving anything to boast about—plainly states his judgment concerning all his present righteousness and the obedience in which he now engages, given the goals he is pursuing.

Philippians 3:8: "Yet indeed I also count all things loss for the excellence of the knowledge of Christ Jesus my Lord," The transition from what he previously affirmed about his Judaic privileges to this verse reflects a superficial reading of the context.

There is a clear auxesis in these words, "Yet indeed I also." He could not express more plainly the elevation of what he had already affirmed when he moves on to other matters or considers himself in a different state: "But, moreover, beyond what I have already asserted."

The change in tense from hēgēmai, which refers to the past, to hēgoumai, which pertains only to the present and not to what he had previously rejected, makes evident his progression into matters of a different nature.

Thus, in addition to rejecting all his former Judaic privileges, he adds his judgment concerning his own current personal righteousness. However, it could be objected that by rejecting everything before and after conversion he had nothing left to rejoice in, nothing to boast about, and nothing to give him acceptance with God. He assures us otherwise—namely, that he found all these things in Christ and in the righteousness of God that comes through faith. Therefore, in these words, "not having my own righteousness, which is from the law," he is not merely referring to the righteousness he had before his conversion; in fact, he does not intend to refer to it at all.

The words of Davenant on this passage of the apostle are, in my judgment, not only sober but also weighty. I shall transcribe them: "Here the apostle teaches what that righteousness is which we must strive for before God, namely, that which is apprehended by faith, and this is imputed to us. He also shows the reason why it is justly ours, namely, because we belong to Christ and are found in Him; because we are incorporated into His body and united with Him in one person, therefore His righteousness is accounted as ours," De Justif. Habit. cap. 38.

Whereas some begin to interpret our being "in Christ" and being "found in Him" as merely referring to our profession of faith in the gospel, the historic faith of the Catholic Church regarding the mystical union of Christ and believers throughout the ages cannot be dismissed with a few empty words and unproven assertions.

The answer, therefore, is full and clear regarding the general objection: namely, that the apostle rejects our legal righteousness, but not our evangelical righteousness.

1. The apostle does not absolutely reject, disclaim, or disown either type of righteousness. Rather, he compares them to Christ and considers their specific purpose in justification before God—that is, a righteousness in His sight.

2. In that sense he rejects all our own righteousness; however, our evangelical righteousness, as argued, remains our own— inherent in us and performed by us.

3. Our legal righteousness and our evangelical righteousness, insofar as inherent righteousness is concerned, are the same. The distinction intends the different ends and uses of the same righteousness. What is evangelical in motive, end, and the specific causes of acceptance with God is legal concerning its original prescription, rule, and measure. If anyone can point to any act, duty, habit, or effect that is not required by the law which commands us to love the LORD our God with all our heart, with all our soul, and with all our mind, and to love our neighbor as ourselves, they shall be heard.

4. The apostle, in this case, rejects all the "works of righteousness which we have done" (Titus 3:5); but our evangelical righteousness consists in the works of righteousness which we do.

5. He disclaims all that is our own. If by "evangelical righteousness" he means our own, then he sets up another in opposition to it—one that is not ours but is imputed to us.

I will also add some other reasons that render this objection useless or show it to be false:

1. Where the apostle does not distinguish or limit what he says, what grounds have we to distinguish or limit his assertions? Sometimes he says simply "not by works"; at other times he says "the works of righteousness which we have done." Those who argue otherwise remark, "That is, not by some sort of works." But by what authority?

2. The works they claim to exclude—the works that constitute our own righteousness and are rejected—are said to be works done without faith and without the aid of grace. But such acts are not good works, nor can they properly be called righteous; for "without faith it is impossible to please Him." What purpose would the apostle have in excluding evil and hypocritical works from justification? Who ever imagined that anyone could be justified by them? There might have

been some case for this interpretation had the apostle said "his own works"; but since he rejects his own righteousness, to limit that rejection to such works that are not righteous at all is utterly absurd.

3. Works done in faith, if applied to our justification, would give even more occasion for boasting than any others, since they would be regarded as better and more praiseworthy.

4. Elsewhere the apostle excludes from justification the works Abraham performed after he had long been a believer, and likewise the works of David when he describes the blessedness of a man whose transgression is forgiven.

5. The question under discussion in his Epistle to the Galatians was explicitly about the works of those who believed. He is not arguing with the Jews — who would readily concede that, if the inheritance is of the law, it is no longer of promise; and that, if righteousness comes through the law, then Christ died in vain. He is addressing believers who would have joined their works with Christ and the gospel for justification.

6. If the apostle's intent was to exclude one kind of works while asserting the necessity of another for the same end, why did he not state this explicitly? It was necessary for him to do so in order to meet the objections against his doctrine — objections he acknowledges and answers on other grounds — yet he gives no indication of such a distinction.

Bellarmine treats this testimony in three places: Book I, Chapter 18; Book I, Chapter 19; and Book V, Chapter 5 of De Justificatione. He offers three replies that summarize the arguments advanced by others on the same subject. He states:

1. "The righteousness that is by the law, contrasted with the righteousness that is by faith, is not the righteousness written in the law or required by the law, but rather a righteousness achieved without the aid of grace and based solely on knowledge of the law."

2. "The righteousness that comes through faith in Christ consists of 'opera nostra justa facta ex fide' — our own righteous works done in faith, which others call our evangelical works."

3. "It is blasphemous to refer to the duties of inherent righteousness as zēmian kai skubala — 'loss and dung.'"

However, he struggles with these assertions; they are full of sophistry.

Regarding the first point:

1. To claim that "the righteousness which is of the law" does not mean the righteousness the law requires is a bold assertion and directly contradicts the apostle in Romans 9:31 and 10:5, where he clearly treats the righteousness which is of the law as the righteousness demanded by the law.

2. The works that he excludes are described in Titus 3:5 as "not by works of righteousness which we have done," and these are precisely the works the law requires.

As for the second point:

1. The essence of this argument is that the apostle would profess, "I desire to be found in Christ, not having my own righteousness, but having my own righteousness." This is self-contradictory, because evangelical inherent righteousness is properly his own.

2. It is concerning that some interpret the apostle's words as meaning he desired to be found in his own righteousness before God for justification. That interpretation contradicts not only the consistent theme of his discussions on this subject but also the testimony of other holy men in Scripture.

3. I believe very few true believers today would agree with the desire to be found in their own personal, evangelical righteousness or in the works they have done when standing before God for justification. We should reflect on our own hearts and on the writings of others about this matter.

3. The righteousness that is of God through faith is not our own obedience or inherent righteousness, but rather its opposite. It is the righteousness that God imputes to us, as stated in Romans 4:6, and is received as a gift, as noted in Romans 5:17.

4. The phrase "that which is through faith in Christ" does not refer to our own inherent righteousness. This is shown by the apostle excluding all his own righteousness when he is found in Christ—that is, whatever he had done as a believer. If there is no contrast in these words between a righteousness that is our own and one that is not, I do not know how to express it.

Regarding the third point:

1. The apostle does not claim that our inherent righteousness is "rubbish"; rather, he states that he "counts" it as such.

2. He does not regard it as such absolutely, which he is far from doing, but only in comparison to Christ.

3. He does not consider it so in itself, but only in relation to his trust in it concerning one specific purpose—namely, our justification before God.

4. The prophet Isaiah, in a similar context, refers to all our righteousness as "filthy rags" in Isaiah 64:6, and the Hebrew term בֶּגֶד עִדִּים conveys as much contempt as the term skubala.

Some argue that all works are excluded as meritorious of grace, life, and salvation, but not as the condition of our justification before God. However:

1. Whatever the apostle excludes, he does so absolutely and without exception, as he sets up something else in opposition to it.

2. There is no basis for such a distinction in this context. For all the apostle requires for our justification is:

a. That we are found in Christ, not in ourselves.

b. That we possess the righteousness of God, not our own.

c. That we become partakers of this righteousness by faith. This is the essence of what we advocate.

20. Imputed Righteousness and Holy Living

The remaining task is to address some general objections to the truth we advocate. Many of those objections have already been raised and answered, including the principal ones now emphasized.

The scriptural evidence cited by those in the Roman Church for justification by works has been thoroughly and repeatedly answered by Protestant theologians. It is unnecessary to revisit those arguments unless new support has arisen, which it has not.

Most of what we deal with now are sophistical arguments that rely on supposed absurd consequences rather than on genuine theological objections. Some who try to find a middle way between the imputation of Christ's righteousness and justification by works waver between the positions, or speak so cautiously that their intentions are hard to discern.

Thus, I will not assert that this or that is any particular person's opinion, even if it seems clear to me. Instead, I will state whether I approve or disapprove of any opinion, regardless of who holds it.

The drift away from the common doctrine of justification by the imputation of Christ's righteousness tends increasingly to end in a direct assertion of justification by works. That position has no resting place until it reaches that conclusion. This tendency shows more clearly in the objections raised against the doctrine than in its defenses. Defenders often avoid extremes but rely on objections that can easily be reduced to the crude supposition of justification by works.

There are two main points generally raised by various groups—Papists, Socinians, and others—that I will address. First: that the doctrine of justification by the imputation of Christ's righteousness makes personal righteousness unnecessary and removes the need for a holy life. Second: that the apostle James, in his epistle, attributes our justification to works, which seems to conflict with the many other scriptural testimonies we uphold.

Regarding the first objection: although those who oppose the truth we uphold come from various and often contradictory perspectives, they all share a fervent commitment to this charge.

It must be acknowledged by all reasonable people that the way the Church of Rome has revived this accusation—originally conceived by others—is a blatant slander. The most learned among them, such as Bellarmine, Vasquez, and Suarez, openly claim that Protestant writers deny all inherent righteousness (with Bellarmine making exceptions for Bucer and Chemnitius). They assert that individuals can be saved even while living in all manner of sin, claiming that all that is required is belief in the forgiveness of their sins. They suggest that as long as individuals believe this, they can indulge in the most sensual vices and still be assured of their salvation.

"Tantum religio potuit suadere malorum!" (Such great evils could religion persuade!) In their misguided zeal to promote their own interests in the religion they profess, some willingly engage in the worst evils, such as false accusations and blatant slander. These assertions have no support from the writings or sermons of those who are unjustly accused. Those who perpetuate such blatant falsehoods should consider whether this approach truly aids in achieving justification by works in the sight of God.

As for myself, I maintain that I am indifferent to the religion of those who can justify such actions. Those among us who utilize this objection either understand the doctrine they oppose or they do not. If they do not understand it, the wise man advises that "He who answers a matter before he hears it, It is folly and shame to him." If they do understand it, it is clear they are not sincere but are instead using deceitful tactics and false pretenses for personal gain, which is disgraceful to religion.

Socinus aggressively pursues this charge against the doctrine of the Reformed churches, making it the foundation for his opposition to the doctrine of Christ's satisfaction, which he ultimately denies. He has written a treatise on this subject, defended by Schlichtingius against Meisnerus.

He employs the same dishonest tactics as others before him, accusing Protestant divines of teaching that God justifies the ungodly — not only while they are ungodly but even if they continue in their ungodliness. He claims they require no inherent righteousness or holiness from anyone, nor could they require it based on their principles, since the imputed righteousness of Christ suffices for them even if they live in sin and do not perform the duties and obedience that please God. Thus, he alleges, they introduce libertinism and antinomianism into the church.

He believes that it is a sufficient refutation of this doctrine to cite that "Neither fornicators, nor idolaters, nor adulterers," etc., "will inherit the kingdom of God."

These are some of the tactics that have made religious controversies scandalous and repugnant — methods no wise or good person would engage in unless compelled by the needs of the church. These claims are openly false and are used with shameful dishonesty to promote a corrupt agenda.

When I encounter individuals engaged in such conduct, I have little concern for what they subsequently say, whether it is true or false. Their guiding principle is what serves their own interests or promotes their agenda, regardless of its righteousness.

As for Socinus, there is no article of faith (the main ones being rejected by him) on which he more confidently condemns us to eternal ruin than on the doctrine of Christ's satisfaction and its imputation to believers.

There remains much darkness in the minds of many, and they are burdened by deep-seated prejudices—especially if they are not guided by the same enlightening Spirit. Some will boldly condemn others to eternal flames for beliefs that, on sound grounds, give those people hope for eternal blessedness, since they love God and live for Him according to those beliefs.

This unfortunate tactic of condemning all who dissent is eagerly seized by a variety of people. It lets them secure their whole faction in the belief of certain salvation, whatever their conduct. If the absence of the faith they profess will certainly condemn people, no matter how upright their lives, many will readily persuade themselves that their own profession will surely save them regardless of their actions— especially because that conclusion flatters their inclinations.

This approach also serves to intimidate simple-minded people into compliance, since they loudly pronounce damnation on those who do not conform. Those most fervent in denouncing others for failing to believe as they do are often the very ones whose lives, if Scripture is to be believed, would disqualify them from salvation.

For my part, I believe that all unregenerate unbelievers who do not obey the gospel will be condemned, whatever their religion, and no others. All who are born again, who truly believe and obey the gospel, will be saved despite the differences among Christians today.

The best way to promote these truths is for each person to embrace them as they attend to their own salvation. If they meet obstruction in a church or denomination, they should leave that church or way so far as it obstructs them. If any profession or visible church requires things that are absolutely destructive or inconsistent with these truths, no salvation can be obtained through it.

In other matters, each person should walk according to the light of their own understanding, for whatever is not from faith is sin.

However, I return from this digression, prompted by the fervor of the individual we are addressing.

The objection, poorly handled though it may be, runs like this: "If God justifies the ungodly solely by His grace through faith in Christ Jesus — without requiring works of obedience as a prerequisite to justification before God, and without including them in the righteousness by which anyone is justified — then such works are unnecessary. Individuals could be justified and saved without them."

It is further claimed that there is no real connection between faith and justification, on the one hand, and the necessity of holiness, righteousness, or obedience, on the other. Rather, it is argued, we are given grace to live as we please — even in all manner of sin — and yet remain assured of salvation. If we are made righteous by the righteousness of another, we have no need for any righteousness of our own.

It would be beneficial if many who use this argument would show their regard for holiness in some other way. To insist on the necessity of holiness while neglecting it oneself is unbecoming.

I will be brief in my response to this objection, since it has already been sufficiently addressed in earlier discussions concerning the nature of the faith by which we are justified and the continuing relevance of the moral law as the rule of obedience for all believers.

An unbiased consideration of what has been presented will clearly show the unfairness of this charge and how the doctrine we defend gives it no support.

Additionally, I must tell the reader that I previously published a comprehensive discourse on the nature and necessity of gospel holiness, along with its foundations and reasons, in line with the doctrine of justification now set forth. I do not find it necessary to add anything further; I am confident that reading it will thoroughly expose the futility of this charge.

In my work, I addressed several points:

1. It is not claimed that all who have professed this doctrine in the past have lived holy and fruitful lives. Many, unfortunately, have lived and died in sin.

2. I do not know whether any among those who currently oppose this doctrine surpass those who, in earlier ages, firmly adhered to it and consistently showed its practical effect in their walk with God.

3. I cannot name anyone from earlier times who was eminent in holiness (and there were many) who did not wholeheartedly agree with the imputation of Christ's righteousness that we defend.

I have no doubt that many who differ in their interpretation of this doctrine may be, and are, genuinely holy — or at least sincerely so — which is as much as anyone can claim.

However, it is inappropriate for some who show little evidence of their diligent pursuit of "holiness, without which no one will see the Lord" to vehemently criticize a doctrine that has historically borne much fruit in holiness.

It does not seem that attempts to introduce a doctrine contrary to the established one have had much success in reforming people's lives. Personal righteousness or holiness has not thrived under such doctrines, as is evident. It will be time enough to seek support for these new ideas by criticizing what has previously yielded better results when they have demonstrated their own merits by their fruits.

It would be wise if this part of the controversy could be resolved among us by following the apostle James's advice in James 2:18: "Show me your faith without your works, and I will show you my faith by my works." Let us all strive for the fruits of our beliefs to determine their usefulness in promoting righteousness and holiness. Faith that does not manifest itself in works — lacking the evidence James calls for — is of no value in this matter.

The same objection was raised against the doctrine of the apostle Paul from the very beginning, which clearly indicates it is the same doctrine now being attacked. He himself mentions this objection more than once; for example, in Romans 3:31 he asks, "Do we then make void the law through faith?" This objection anticipates the charge against his doctrine of free justification for sinners through faith in the blood of Christ. The essence of the charge is that he undermines the law, removes all obligation to obedience, and introduces Antinomianism.

Again, in Romans 6:1 he asks, "What shall we say then? Shall we continue in sin that grace may abound?" Some thought this was the natural consequence of what he had extensively discussed regarding justification. They reasoned that if what he taught about God's grace in our justification is true, there would be no need to relinquish sin, and continuing in it would seem to exalt the grace he praised. He repeats the objection in verse 15: "What then? Shall we sin because we are not under law but under grace?"

In various other places he addresses this same objection, even when he does not explicitly assume it. Therefore, we have no reason to be surprised or overly disturbed by this objection; it is no different from what was insinuated against the apostle's own doctrine, whatever rhetorical exaggerations are used today. Still, it is evident that deeply ingrained prejudices against this aspect of the gospel mystery arose early and later corrupted the church's teaching on the subject. It would not be difficult to identify the main sources of these prejudices, though that is not our present focus; the point has been partially addressed elsewhere.

It is acknowledged that this doctrine, whether considered on its own or in conjunction with other aspects of God's grace through Christ Jesus, is susceptible to abuse by those dominated by darkness and a love of sin. From the very beginning of the faith, some have mistakenly thought that mere assent to the gospel constitutes the faith that saves, letting them live in sin while neglecting all duties of obedience. This tendency is evident in the epistles of John, James, and Jude.

We cannot offer any remedy against this dangerous error while individuals prefer darkness to light because their deeds are evil. It would be foolish to imagine that altering the doctrine would prevent future abuses. If that alteration prevents abuse, it will have done so only by ceasing to be part of the gospel; for what is truly gospel has always been vulnerable to misuse by those described above.

With these general observations in mind, which are sufficient to remove this objection from the thoughts of sober readers, I will only add the consideration of the responses the apostle Paul gives to it, together with a brief application of them to our present purpose.

The objection against the apostle was that he nullified the law, rendered good works unnecessary, and suggested that, on his doctrine, men could live in sin to promote grace. In response, we observe that he never gives the answer some assert is the only solution—namely, that our own personal righteousness, obedience, or works are necessary for our justification before God. To insist that by the phrase "faith without works" he meant faith plus works is an unreasonable assumption. If anyone claims he gave such an answer, let them produce it; so far it has not been shown.

Is it not strange that if this were indeed his doctrine—that our personal righteousness, holiness, and works have any influence on our justification and serve as our righteousness before God—he who emphasizes their necessity more than any other New Testament writer would omit this truth in answering the objection that he made them unnecessary? His doctrine was challenged, as he acknowledged, and it was rejected by many, as seen in Romans 10:3-4 and Galatians 2:18. He knew that corrupt desires and depraved affections would lead many to devise subtle objections; indeed, through the Holy Spirit he foresaw that his teaching would be distorted and misused.

It was crucial for him to address these evils and to present his doctrine so it would not encourage such misunderstandings. Is it not odd that he did not take the opportunity to say that although he rejected the works of the law, he nevertheless required evangelical works as a condition of our justification before God, or as that by which we are justified according to the gospel? If this had been his doctrine and if that answer could easily resolve the difficulty, surely neither his wisdom nor his concern for the church, guided by the Spirit, would have allowed him to omit it.

However, he is so far from making such a plea that when the most unavoidable occasion arose he not only refrained from it but affirmed something that plainly indicates he did not endorse it. In Ephesians 2:9-10 he positively excludes works from our justification: "not of works, lest anyone should boast." One might then ask, "What purpose do works serve? Are they necessary?" Instead of distinguishing legal from evangelical works as grounds for justification, he asserts the necessity of evangelical works on wholly different grounds and motives. These are the works he expressly excludes as grounds of justification.

Therefore, to follow his example — since he was wiser, holier, and more zealous for personal righteousness in the church than any of us — if we are pressed with this objection repeatedly, we should never try to escape it by claiming that we accept these works as conditions or causes of our justification, or as the basis of our righteousness before God, for he did not do so.

We may observe that in answering this objection, whether explicitly or implicitly, he does not rest on the merely common principle of moral duty. Instead, he focuses on the motives and reasons for holiness, obedience, and good works that are peculiar to believers. The question is not whether all mankind is bound to obey God and fulfill moral duties under the moral law, but whether the gospel imposes an obligation upon believers to pursue righteousness, holiness, and good works that effectively influence their hearts and minds toward those ends.

We will frame the question only this way: whether, based on our free justification through the imputation of Christ's righteousness, the gospel supplies grounds, reasons, and motives that make obedience and good works necessary and that actually move believers to them.

As for unbelievers, we have no concern to show that evangelical grounds and motives are suitable or effective for them; in fact, we know the contrary. They tend to despise and pervert these motives, as seen in 1 Corinthians 1:23-24 and 2 Corinthians 4:4. Such persons remain under the law, and we leave them to the authority of God as expressed in the moral law.

However, it is evident that the apostle confines his inquiry to believers, as seen in various passages where he mentions it: Romans 6:2-3 states, "Certainly not! How shall we who died to sin live any longer in it? Or do you not know that as many of us as were baptized into Christ Jesus were baptized into His death?"; and Ephesians 2:10 declares, "For we are His workmanship, created in Christ Jesus for good works." Therefore, we will not argue about the compelling nature of gospel motives and reasons for the duties of holiness in the minds of unbelievers, regardless of the truth in that case. Instead, we will focus on their power, force, and efficacy toward those who truly believe.

The apostle offers many answers to this objection. He sets forth the necessity, the nature, the purposes, and the uses of evangelical righteousness and good works. These answers make up a large part of the gospel's doctrine. I will mention only some key points that support the same truth.

1. He insists on God's ordination: "For we are His workmanship, created in Christ Jesus for good works." (Ephesians 2:10.) God has ordained that those who believe in Christ should live in, walk in, and abound in good works, fulfilling all duties of obedience to Him.

2. To this end, precepts, directions, motives, and encouragements are provided abundantly throughout Scripture. Hence, we assert that good works—which include the gradual renewal of our natures, our growth in grace, and fruitfulness in life—are necessary because of God's ordination, will, and command.

What further debate is needed about the necessity of good works among those who truly understand what it means to believe or who respect God's commands?

"But what force," some may argue, "is in this command or ordination of God, when despite it, if we do not apply ourselves to obedience, we shall be justified by the imputation of Christ's righteousness and may be saved without them?"

First, as noted above, this inquiry concerns believers alone. None of them would find this objection reasonable. It arises from a complete misunderstanding of their state and relationship with God. To suppose that believers are not influenced by God's authority and commands toward duty and obedience—as if those commands were given solely to secure their justification—is to misunderstand both faith and what it is to be a believer. It also ignores the arguments and motives that chiefly affect and compel the minds of such people. This is the comprehensive answer the apostle gives to the objection in Romans 6:2-3.

Secondly, the fallacy of this objection lies in two points:

1. It separates what God has made inseparable—our justification and our sanctification. To suggest that one can exist without the other undermines the whole gospel.

2. It confuses distinct matters—namely, justification and final salvation—where the role of works and obedience differs for each, as explained above.

Thus, the notion that God's commands to duty—regardless of their purpose—are not equally binding on the consciences of believers, as if they were given solely for their justification, is absurd and rejected by all true believers. In fact, these commands influence believers even more than they would if presumed to operate only before true faith is present.

To claim someone can be a true believer or genuinely respond in faith to the gospel commands and yet not be justified at the same time is not merely a theological quibble; it denies the gospel itself. Faith alone empowers and enables gospel commands to move the soul toward obedience. Therefore, these obligations are more compelling for those who are justified than they would be if the commands existed merely to secure justification.

The apostle responds, as we do, "Do we then make the law void through faith? Certainly not! On the contrary, we establish the law." Although the law is upheld chiefly by the obedience and sufferings of Christ (Romans 8:3-4; 10:3-4), faith and the imputation of Christ's righteousness for justification do not render the law void for believers.

Believers remain obligated to "You shall love the Lord your God with all your heart," and to "You shall love your neighbor as yourself," because of this law. They are freed from the law and its demands as it stands in its original form — "Do this and you will live" — with the stark counterpoint, "Cursed is everyone who does not continue in all things which are written in the book of the law, to do them." Anyone under the law's authority for justification and life thereby falls under its curse the moment they commit even one transgression.

However, we are freed to obey the law on gospel motives and for gospel purposes, as the apostle explains in chapter 6. The obligation remains for all believers, and even the slightest transgression is still sin. But does that mean they are subject to everlasting punishment under the law? Or, as some put it, "Will God condemn them for transgressing the law?" I ask again: what do they think about this? And if they assume He will, what do they imagine will happen to themselves?

For my part, I assert, as the apostle states, "There is therefore now no condemnation to those who are in Christ Jesus."

Then they may ask, "What is the necessity of obedience under the law if God will not condemn those who transgress it?" I answer that it would be better if some people understood what they assert in these matters, or at least learned to remain silent for a while.

The law requires obedience in every instance of duty, if it requires obedience at all. In its obligating power it cannot be partially dispensed with so long as the essential distinctions between good and evil remain. If no one can be bound to duty by its commands without facing condemnation for every transgression, then the law either binds no one at all or no one can be saved.

Yet, although we are freed from the curse and condemning power of the law by Him who ended sin and brought in everlasting righteousness, while we are still viators—travellers striving toward God's design to restore His image in us—we are obliged to pursue all the holiness and righteousness the law requires.

The apostle meets this objection by setting out the necessary relationship between faith and the death of Christ, the grace of God, and the nature of sanctification. He also explains the excellence, usefulness, and purpose of gospel holiness according to God's design. He treats all this at length in Romans chapter 6, aiming to show the compatibility of justification by faith alone with the necessity of personal righteousness and holiness.

A thorough discussion of these matters would require a complete exposition of that chapter, where the apostle outlines the principal reasons and motivations for evangelical obedience. I will only state this briefly.

Those who find the reasons and motives expressed therein—consistent with the doctrine of justification by the imputation of Christ's righteousness—not effective for their personal obedience are profoundly ignorant of the gospel, the nature of faith, the character and inclination of the new creation (for, regardless of mockery, "If anyone is in Christ, he is a new creation"), and the compelling efficacy of God's grace and the love of Christ. They also misunderstand God's ordering of the causes and means of our salvation. Therefore I will not engage further in debate on these matters.

I had intended to add several other considerations to this discussion, including:

1. That to prove the necessity of inherent righteousness and holiness, we utilize the arguments presented in Scripture.

2. That we employ all these arguments in the sense and for the purposes for which they are intended, fully aligning with our teachings on justification.

3. That any purported arguments or motives for evangelical holiness that contradict the imputation of Christ's righteousness actually obstruct and undermine it.

4. That the holiness we assert as necessary for the salvation of believers is of a more excellent, sublime, and heavenly nature in its causes, essence, operations, and effects than what is recognized or accepted by most opponents of the doctrine of justification.

5. That the holiness and righteousness advocated by the Socinians and their followers do not exceed the righteousness of the scribes and Pharisees; nor can anyone adhering to their principles surpass them.

However, since this discourse has already extended beyond my initial intention, and because I have previously addressed the doctrine concerning the nature and necessity of evangelical holiness at length, I will refrain from further elaboration here. I rest in the answers the apostle provides to this objection.

21. James on Faith and Works: Consistent With Paul

The apparent difference between the teachings of the apostles Paul and James regarding faith, works, and justification warrants careful consideration. Many seize on certain words and expressions used by James to oppose the doctrine clearly articulated by Paul. Others have satisfactorily answered those objections, so further discussion here is unnecessary.

While I believe there will always be contention over these matters, as we "know in part and we prophesy in part," I must assert that the usual resolution of this apparent difficulty—defending the doctrine of justification by faith through the imputation of Christ's righteousness against any contradiction from St. James, particularly in chapter 2:14 and onward—remains unchallenged.

Thus, I feel compelled to address this topic, as is fitting in a discourse of this nature. I hope to shed light on and vindicate the truth.

It is generally acknowledged that there is no real contradiction between the teachings of these two apostles. If there were, one of their writings would be pseudepigraphal or falsely attributed and therefore uncanonical. The authority of the Epistle of James has been rashly questioned by some, both formerly and now. For these reasons, their words can indeed be reconciled.

Any failure to reconcile them arises from our own mental darkness, the limits of our understanding, and, for many, the sway of prejudice.

It is also commonly accepted that when Scripture seems to contradict itself, preference should be given to passages that treat an issue directly and at length rather than to those that mention it only incidentally or in passing for other purposes.

Passages that only mention a truth in relation to other matters should be interpreted in light of the more comprehensive passages where the inspired author declares that truth for its own sake and to instruct the church.

This is a reasonable and widely accepted rule for interpreting Scripture.

By this rule, it is indisputable that the doctrine of justification before God must be learned primarily from the writings of the apostle Paul. His writings clarify those other passages where the doctrine appears only incidentally.

This is especially true because the doctrine pervades Scripture and is supported by numerous specific testimonies. Paul wrote at length on our justification before God to state it plainly for its own sake and for the instruction of the church.

He explains why he treated the matter so thoroughly and precisely:

1. The importance of the doctrine itself: he maintains that it is foundational to our salvation and the hinge on which the whole gospel turns (Galatians 2:16–21 and 5:4, 5).

2. There was a plausible and dangerous opposition at the time. It was so convincing that many were led away from the truth—as with the Galatians—and others were turned from the gospel because they disliked it, as noted in Romans 10:3, 4.

3. The corrupt tendencies of human nature created a real potential for abusing the doctrine of grace; some had already misused it. Paul therefore addresses this danger and defends the doctrine against misinterpretation and misuse.

Certainly, no one ever needed to teach a doctrine more fully and clearly than Paul did in his circumstances, given the role and responsibility to which he was called.

We have every reason to learn the truth primarily from his declarations and defenses—especially if we believe he was divinely inspired and guided to reveal this truth for the church's instruction.

By contrast, the apostle James treats justification differently. He does not set out to teach the doctrine of justification before God; he intends something else, which we will examine shortly.

James aims to vindicate the doctrine against abuses some had committed—just as others had perverted doctrines of God's grace into licentiousness.

Therefore, we should chiefly learn about justification from Paul's writings, and interpret other passages in light of what he has clearly taught.

Some today argue otherwise. They insist Paul should be interpreted through James rather than vice versa. To support this, they claim Paul's writings are obscure, cite ancient scholars who supposedly noted difficulties, and point to errors that allegedly arose from them—

problems they say are scandalous to the Christian faith. They contend that because James wrote later, he must interpret Paul's statements, and that Paul's words should be read in light of James.

In response, I will first defend St. Paul's writings, which are now often harshly criticized—an effect, I think, of the subtle rise of atheism. Such a full defence belongs elsewhere, but I cannot see how anyone with even slight familiarity with ancient texts can cite a mistaken passage in Irenaeus, a hasty remark from Origen, or similar comments to undermine the clarity of Paul's writings. It is easy to answer such claims with testimonies from many distinguished church writers of various ages.

For example, Chrysostom, in forty different places, explains why some fail to understand Paul's writings, which are, in themselves, so gloriously clear and evident. For their satisfaction I refer them to the preface of his exposition of Paul's epistles, where further guidance may be found in due course. Still, Paul does not require the testimony of men or of the whole church; our safety and security ought to be built upon the doctrine he taught.

Meanwhile, it may be worthwhile—though the stubbornness of human minds often brings sorrow—to consider how those who share a common agenda agree in their interpretations of his writings. Some claim that, if not all then most, of his epistles were written against the Gnostics and designed to refute their errors. Others argue the opposite: that the Gnostics derived their errors from his writings. Such boldness in handling divine matters is frequently driven by a desire to serve present interests.

Secondly, this was not the judgment of the ancient church for three or four hundred years. Though Paul's epistles were always regarded as the church's principal treasure and the great guide and rule of the Christian faith, the epistle of James was scarcely accepted as canonical by many and was doubted by most, as both Eusebius and Jerome testify.

Thirdly, the purpose of the apostle James is not to explain Paul's meaning in his epistles, as some claim. Rather, James aims to defend the gospel against those who misuse their liberty as a cover for maliciousness, turning the grace of our God into lewdness and continuing in sin under the pretense that grace may abound for that purpose.

Fourthly, as we have said, the apostle Paul defends his doctrine against the objections and abuses that people made of it or to which they twisted it. There is no other doctrine in his epistles than what he preached universally—the foundation of the Christian religion, especially among the Gentiles.

Having established these points, I will briefly demonstrate that there is no contradiction between what these two apostles declare about our justification and its causes.

I will do this by:

1. Presenting some general considerations on the nature and intent of both their discourses.

2. Providing a specific explanation of the context in the epistle of St. James.

Under the first point, I will show:

1. That they do not have the same scope, purpose, or end in their discourses; they do not address the same question, nor do they state the same case, nor do they resolve the same inquiry. Therefore, since

they are not speaking "ad idem," or to the same thing, they do not contradict one another.

2. That faith is a term with various meanings in Scripture, and, as we have shown, it denotes different kinds. Therefore they are not discussing the same faith or the same kind of faith. There can be no contradiction between what one attributes to it and what the other denies, since they are not speaking of the same thing.

3. That they do not speak of justification in the same sense, nor with respect to the same ends.

4. That, concerning works, both refer to the same thing: the works of obedience to the moral law.

Regarding Paul's scope and purpose, the question he addresses, the case he presents, and the conclusions he draws are plain in all his writings, especially in his epistles to the Romans and Galatians. His primary aim is to explain how a guilty, convinced sinner can, through faith in the blood of Christ, have all his sins pardoned, be accepted by God, and obtain the right to heavenly inheritance—that is, to be acquitted and justified in God's sight.

This doctrine is central to the gospel, which was entrusted to him for revelation and proclamation to the Gentiles. As we have noted, he had special reason to stress it because of opposition from the Jews and Judaizing Christians, who ascribed this privilege to the law and to our own obedience under it.

This is the case he presents and the question he resolves in all his discussions on justification. In treating it, he explains its nature and causes and defends it against all objections.

For instance, persons with corrupt minds who wish to indulge their lusts—since people naturally desire what God has made eternally inconsistent, namely to live in sin here and yet attain blessedness hereafter—might conclude that if Paul's declaration is true (that we are justified freely by the grace of God through the imputation of a righteousness not our own), then nothing more is required of us: no renunciation of sin, no attention to the duties of righteousness and holiness.

He counters such impious suggestions and shows their inconsistency with the doctrine he teaches. However, he does not do so by implying or conceding that our own works of obedience or righteousness are necessary to, or have any causal influence on, our justification before God.

If this claim had any truth, and if that supposition were not fundamentally inconsistent with and destructive of his doctrine, he would not have omitted the argument, as we have shown. To suppose that someone else needed to explain and defend his doctrine against the very objections he answers—by using an argument he himself would not use but rejects—is both foolish and impious.

On the other hand, the apostle James had no such scope or purpose, nor any occasion for what he wrote on this matter. He does not ask, nor suggest we ask, how a guilty, convinced sinner—whose mouth is silenced of any plea or excuse—may be justified in God's sight; that is, how he may receive the pardon of sins and the gift of righteousness unto life.

To resolve this question by appealing to our own works would undermine the entire gospel. Instead, he addresses a different matter. As noted above, many in those days professed the Christian religion or faith in the gospel and assumed that, since they were already justified, nothing more was required for their salvation. They thought they had reached a state that suited all the interests of the flesh, so they lived in sin and neglected the duties of obedience while still expecting to be eternally saved.

Some think this harmful idea came from erroneous opinions then spreading, as the apostle Paul warned would happen (2 Timothy 4:1-4). It is commonly believed that Simon Magus and his followers had already corrupted many with their abominations. Among these errors was the pernicious notion that faith licensed sin or erased all distinction between good and evil for those who professed it. Later teachers such as Basilides, Valentinus, and other Gnostics expanded this idea.

Alternatively, the corruption of people's hearts and lives might itself have driven them to seek a justification that would excuse their sins. I believe the latter was the case.

Among professed Christians there were those — much like today — who assumed that simply professing a faith or religion, whatever its character, would save them even if they lived in gross wickedness and remained utterly barren of good works or duties of obedience.

There is no other reason for what he writes in the epistle; he does not mention deceivers, as John does explicitly and frequently at a later time.

Against this sort of person, or for exposing their conviction, he aims to accomplish two things:

1. To prove, in general, the necessity of works for all who profess the gospel or faith in Christ.

2. To show the futility and folly of their pretended justification — that they claimed to be justified and saved by a faith so barren of good works that it served only as a pretext to excuse their sins.

All his arguments serve those two purposes and no other. He demonstrates that the faith which is wholly barren and unfruitful in obedience—and by which people pretended to justify themselves in sin—is not the faith by which we are justified and saved, but a dead carcass, useless and of no benefit.

He closes the point in the chapter's final verse. He does not instruct anyone how to be justified before God. Rather, he convinces some that they are not justified by relying on such a dead faith, and he sets forth the only way someone can truly show and prove that they are justified.

His purpose is so plain that nothing could make it clearer. Those who fail to recognize this in their reading of the context miss the apostle's entire point.

Therefore, since the apostles' primary objectives differ so greatly, there is no contradiction in their statements even when their words appear to conflict. They do not speak "ad idem," nor do they address the same matters "eodem respectu." James is not asking how a guilty, convinced sinner—condemned by the law—may be justified before God; Paul addresses nothing else.

We must apply each author's expressions to his own purpose and scope. If we do not, we violate sound rules of interpretation and make it impossible to understand either correctly. Consequently, there is neither real disagreement nor even the appearance of one between them.

They are not speaking of the same kind of faith. Thus there can be no contradiction between what one attributes to faith and what the other denies, since they mean different things. It is like one person saying that fire will burn while another denies it; there is no contradiction if one means real fire and the other something merely painted, and both speak accordingly.

We have already shown that two kinds of faith are spoken of when people are said to believe and to profess the gospel. What belongs to one kind does not belong to the other. No one, I suppose, will deny that by "faith," in the matter of our justification, St. Paul means genuine faith properly so called: the "faith of God's elect," "precious faith" — "much more precious than gold" — the faith that purifies the heart and the faith "working through love," the faith by which Christ dwells in us and by which we abide in Him and live to God; in short, a living, saving faith is what he intends.

All these and countless other spiritual effects he ascribes to that faith which he insists is the sole means of our justification before God. But of the faith James speaks of he assigns none of these marks. Indeed, his only argument to show that people cannot be saved by that faith is that those qualities are not found in it.

What James intends he calls a dead faith, a lifeless carcass, the faith of demons, a mere verbal profession—no more genuinely what it pretends to be than it would be true charity to send away a naked and hungry person with only words of comfort and no food or clothing. He rightly denies justification in any sense to such a faith, however loudly it is boasted of, while the same denials do not properly attach to the faith Paul describes.

Bellarmine advances several arguments to prove that the faith James intends is justifying faith in itself; but all these arguments are weak and contemptible, grounded on his assumption that true justifying faith is merely a real assent to Catholic doctrine or divine revelation (De Justificat. lib. i. cap. 15).

His first argument runs: "James calls it 'faith' absolutely, whereby always in Scripture true faith is intended."

Response:

James refers to it as a dead faith, the faith of demons, and casts all manner of reproach upon it. He would not have done so regarding any genuine evangelical duty or grace.

Every faith that is merely a real assent to the truth is neither living, justifying, nor saving, as has been proven.

Those described as believing absolutely, or as believing in that bare, absolute sense, never had that faith which is true and saving (John 2:23; Acts 8:13).

Secondly, he argues: "In the same place and chapter, he discusses the faith of Abraham and affirms that it worked with his works (James 2:22, 23); but this vain shadow of faith does not do so; therefore, it was true faith, and that which is most properly called so, that the apostle intends."

This claim is indeed ridiculous. The apostle does not present the faith of Abraham as an example of that faith he treats with such severity. Rather, he holds Abraham up as an example directly contrary to it, to prove that the other faith he criticizes is of no use. Abraham's faith produced good works; the other had none.

Thirdly, he cites verse 24, "You see then that a man is justified by works, and not by faith only." He concludes that the faith James speaks of justifies with works, but a false faith, a shadow of faith, does not do so; therefore, it must be the true, saving faith of which the apostle speaks.

He is utterly mistaken. The apostle does not divide justification between works and faith; rather, as he intends it, he ascribes justification entirely to works in opposition to that faith he discusses. The contrast is clear: works versus faith, as he uses the terms. A dead faith—a faith without works, the faith of demons—is excluded from having any influence on justification.

Fourthly, he adds: "The apostle compares this faith without works to a rich man who gives nothing to the poor (James 2:16) and to a body without a spirit (James 2:26); therefore, just as the knowledge by which a rich man knows the needs of the poor is true and real, so is faith without works also considered true faith by St. James."

These points only undermine the case they are meant to support, aided by a bit of sophistry. The apostle compares this faith to the charity of a man who gives nothing to the poor, pointing instead to his knowledge of their poverty. His knowledge may be true; and the truer and more certain it is, the more false and feigned is the charity he pretends with the words, "Depart in peace, be warmed and filled,"—such is the faith the apostle speaks of.

Although a dead body is a true body in its matter or substance—a carcass—it is not an essential part of a living man. A carcass is not of the same nature or kind as the body of a living person. We assert no other difference between the faith the apostle speaks of and that which is justifying than what exists between a dead, breathless carcass and a living, animated body, fitted and prepared for all vital acts.

Therefore, it is beyond all contradiction—if we do not choose to be contentious—that when the apostle James speaks against faith with respect to our justification, he means only a dead, barren, lifeless faith. This is the sort of faith often pretended by ungodly men to excuse themselves in sin. The faith Paul teaches has no connection to this.

Consideration of the present condition of professed faith in the world will guide us to the best interpretation of this passage.

They do not speak of justification in the same sense or for the same purpose. The apostle Paul addresses our absolute justification before God—the justification of our persons, our acceptance with Him, and the right to the heavenly inheritance. This is the sole focus of his discourse. He explains all the causes of it, including everything on God's part and everything on our part that contributes to it.

He does not discuss the evidence, knowledge, sense, fruit, or manifestation of justification in our own consciences, in the church, or to others who profess the faith. Those matters are treated elsewhere where the context requires. The justification he discusses is a single act, accomplished at once before God. It changes the person's relative state and may be evidenced in various ways for the glory of God and the consolation of true believers.

The apostle James does not address our absolute justification at all. His entire inquiry is about the nature of the faith by which we are justified and the only way it can be shown to be the right kind—faith on which a person may safely rely. Therefore, he discusses justification only in terms of its evidence and manifestation; he had no occasion to do otherwise.

The examples he uses make this clear. The first is Abraham (James 2:21-23). He says that by Abraham being justified by works, "the Scripture was fulfilled which says, 'Abraham believed God, and it was accounted to him for righteousness.'" If his intention were to prove that we are justified before God by works and not by faith, the testimony he cites would contradict that claim. Paul uses the same testimony to show that Abraham was justified by faith apart from works, as the words plainly indicate.

No one can explain how the proposition "Abraham was justified by works"—if it intends absolute justification before God—fulfills the Scripture "Abraham believed God, and it was accounted to him for righteousness," especially given the opposition made here and elsewhere between faith and works in this matter.

Moreover, James asserts that Abraham was justified by works at the moment he offered his son on the altar. We admit this too, but we ask in what sense he was justified. It was about thirty years after it was testified concerning him that "he believed God, and it was accounted to him for righteousness." When righteousness was accounted to him, he was justified; he was not justified twice in the same sense, in the same manner, or by the same kind of justification.

How, then, was he justified by works when he offered his son on the altar? The sensible understanding is that his action evidenced and declared him justified before God and before men. Anyone who thinks otherwise does not grasp the matter, since he had been genuinely justified long before—this is unquestioned and acknowledged by all.

He was justified in the sight of God in the manner declared (Genesis 22:12). His conduct provided a strong testimony to the sincerity of his faith and trust in God, manifesting the truth of the Scripture, "He believed God, and it was accounted to him for righteousness."

In quoting this testimony, the apostle openly acknowledges that he was truly accounted righteous, had righteousness imputed to him, and was justified before God (the reasons and causes of which he does not consider) long before the justification he attributes to his works. This latter justification can only be understood as the evidencing, proving, and manifestation of his faith and justification.

In summary, the Scripture that states, "Abraham believed God, and it was accounted to him for righteousness," was fulfilled when he was justified by works upon offering his son on the altar. This could have been by the imputation of righteousness to him, by a real efficiency or working of righteousness in him, by the manifestation and evidence of his prior justification, or by some other way that must be found.

First, it is clear from the text that it was not by imputation, since righteousness had been imputed to him long before. This is the basis on which the apostle proves that righteousness is imputed without works.

Secondly, it is evident that he was not justified by a real efficiency — a habitual righteousness wrought in him — or by any means that made him inherently righteous when he had been previously unrighteous. He was righteous in that sense long before and had abounded in works of righteousness to the praise of God.

Therefore, what remains is that he was justified by the work mentioned in the sense that it evidenced and manifested his faith and justification.

His other example is of Rahab, concerning whom he asserts that she was "justified by works when she received the messengers and sent them out another way." However, she received the spies "By faith," as the Holy Spirit testifies (Hebrews 11:31); therefore, she had true faith before their arrival. If this is so, she was genuinely justified; for it is destructive to the foundation of the gospel to claim that someone can be a true believer and yet not be justified.

In this state, she received the messengers and made a full declaration of her faith (Joshua 2:9-11). After her belief and justification, and after her confession of faith, she risked her life by concealing and sending them away. In this way, she justified the sincerity of her faith and confession; and in that sense alone is she said to be "justified by works."

In no other sense does the apostle James mention justification in this passage, which he does only incidentally.

Regarding "works," mentioned by both apostles, the same works are intended, and there is no disagreement whatsoever about them. The apostle James refers to works as duties of obedience to God according to the law, as is evident from the entire first part of the chapter, which sets the stage for the discussion of faith and works. The same understanding is also present in the writings of the apostle Paul, as we have previously demonstrated.

As for the necessity of these works in all believers, both for other purposes and as evidence of their faith and justification, it is emphasized equally by both apostles, as has been stated.

With these general points established, we can note specific details from the apostle James' discourse that clearly demonstrate there is no contradiction with what the apostle Paul teaches about our justification by faith and the imputation of righteousness apart from works, nor with the doctrine we have learned and declared from him.

1. He does not join faith and works together in our justification. Rather, he opposes them to one another, affirming faith and rejecting works as the basis of justification.

2. He does not distinguish between a first and a second justification, or between the beginning and the continuation of justification. He speaks of one justification only: our initial, personal justification before God. We are not dealing with any other justification here.

3. In the sense he intends and with respect to the faith he discusses, he attributes justification entirely to works, setting works over against faith.

4. He does not inquire how a sinner is justified before God. Rather, he asks how those who profess the gospel can prove or demonstrate that they are justified, so they do not deceive themselves by relying on a lifeless and barren faith.

All these points will be further supported by a brief consideration of the context itself, with which I shall conclude this discourse.

At the beginning of the chapter (up to verse 14) he reproves his readers for many sins committed against the law, which is the standard for judging both their sins and their obedience. He warns them about these sins and shows the danger in which they stand. In verse 14 he reveals the root and primary cause: a vain assumption and deceptive presumption that the faith required by the gospel is nothing more than a bare assent to its doctrine. This belief leads them to think they are released from all obligations to moral obedience or good works, and that they can live in whatever sins their desires incline them without jeopardizing their eternal state (James 4:1-4; 5:1-6).

The state of such individuals, which frames the entire issue he addresses and guides the interpretation of his subsequent arguments, is articulated in verse 14: "What does it profit, my brethren, if someone says he has faith but does not have works? Can faith save him?"

Suppose a man, one of those guilty of the sins mentioned in the preceding verses, claims or boasts that he has faith, that he professes the gospel, that he has left either Judaism or paganism to embrace the gospel, and therefore believes that, despite lacking good works and living in sin, he is accepted by God and will be saved.

Will this faith indeed save him? This is the question posed. Whereas the gospel clearly states, "Believe on the Lord Jesus Christ, and you will be saved," the inquiry is whether that faith, which may coexist with indulgence in sin and neglect of obedience, is the same faith to which the promise of life and salvation is attached.

From this the inquiry continues: How can any man—especially one who claims to have faith—prove and demonstrate that he possesses the kind of faith that will secure his salvation? The apostle denies that such faith can exist apart from works, and he denies that anyone can show true faith except by works of obedience. His entire subsequent discourse is devoted to that demonstration.

He never proposes the means or causes of the justification of a convinced sinner before God, nor did he have occasion to do so. Thus, when his words are applied with that intention they are openly misconstrued.

The faith the apostle speaks of is utterly ineffective for obtaining its intended end—salvation. He illustrates this by comparing it to love or charity, as in verses 15-16: "If a brother or sister is naked and destitute of daily food, and one of you says to them, 'Depart in peace, be warmed and filled,' but you do not give them the things which are needed for the body, what does it profit?" Such conduct is not the grace of the gospel required of us; anyone who treats the poor this way does not have the love of God dwelling in him (1 John 3:17). Whatever name or pretense it bears, it is not love; it lacks every effect of love and is neither useful nor beneficial. Therefore the apostle concludes in verse 17, "Thus also faith by itself, if it does not have works, is dead." His aim is not to deny justification by faith alone before God, but to show that faith existing alone, without works, is dead, useless, and unprofitable.

After giving this initial proof, he restates the matter hypothetically to make the demonstration fuller. In verse 18 he says, "But someone will say, 'You have faith, and I have works.' Show me your faith without your works, and I will show you my faith by my works." It is clear he is again addressing his main question on the assumption that a dead, useless faith exists, which he has already established. The remaining issue is how true faith—the faith that accords with the gospel—can be shown or evidenced, so that the folly of those trusting any other kind of faith may be exposed. The phrase "Show me your faith" implies: demonstrate your faith to be genuine by the only available means—works.

Thus, although he says, "You have faith," meaning "You profess and boast that you possess the faith that can save you," and "I have works," he does not say, "Show me your faith by your works, and I will show you my works by my faith," as the reverse would suggest. Instead he declares, "I will show you my faith by my works," because the whole discussion is about proving faith, not about proving works.

Faith that cannot be evidenced by works—fruitless faith that amounts to mere assent to divine truth—is not the faith that justifies or saves. The apostle reinforces this by pointing out that such faith is no different from that which the devils possess. No one can reasonably expect to be saved by a faith common to both himself and the devils, who exceed men even in belief. As he says in verse 19, "You believe that there is one God. You do well. Even the demons believe—and tremble!" The belief in one God is here taken as the principal, fundamental truth; from this acknowledgment an assent to divine revelation follows. This is the second argument showing that empty, barren faith is dead and useless.

Having given this second confirmation, he repeats his point in keeping with his final proof: "But do you want to know, O foolish man, that faith without works is dead?"

In these words we may observe several points:

First, he addresses the person he seeks to convince, calling him a "foolish man." This is not a universal charge, since all men are in some sense vain; rather it is directed at one who is particularly deluded in his fleshly mind — someone cherishing vain hopes of salvation by an empty profession of the gospel without any evidence of obedience.

Second, his purpose toward this foolish man is to bring him to a conviction of the erroneous and harmful belief he has embraced: "Do you want to know, O foolish man?"

Third, the sole point he seeks to convince him of is that "faith without works is dead also." This means that faith devoid of works — barren and unfruitful — is dead and useless. This is the only assertion he intends to prove by his subsequent examples and arguments; they have no other purpose. To twist his words to suggest a different intention, when they clearly align with his stated purpose, is to misinterpret them.

To support this, he cites the example of Abraham in verse 21: "Was not Abraham our father justified by works when he offered Isaac his son on the altar?" Several points must be noted to clarify the apostle's intent here:

1. It is certain that Abraham was justified many years before the work he mentions was performed. Long before this, it was testified concerning him, "And he believed in the Lord, and He accounted it to him for righteousness." The imputation of righteousness upon believing is the justification we are concerned with and will defend.

2. It is evident that in the account of the story repeated by the apostle, there is no mention of Abraham being justified before God by that or any other work.

3. However, it is clear that in the context of the story, Abraham was declared justified through an open demonstration of his faith and fear of God, which were sincere and evident in God's sight. God expresses this by using human emotions, as seen in Genesis 22:12: "for now I

know that you fear God, since you have not withheld your son, your only son, from Me."

That this is the justification the apostle intends cannot be denied without a desire for conflict. This declaration serves as a manifestation of the truth and sincerity of his faith by which he was justified before God.

Thus, the apostle undeniably proves his point with this example: "faith without works is dead also."

4. It is equally clear that the apostle has not previously discussed our justification before God and the means of it, so it is absurd to think he introduces that topic here to prove what he has previously asserted, since it does not support that claim at all.

5. The safest rule for interpreting the apostle's meaning, apart from the scope and intent of his current discourse, is to consider the context of the passages and the factual circumstances he refers to. These are clearly as follows: Abraham had long been a justified believer. There were approximately thirty years between the testimony given to him in Genesis 15 and the account of his son's sacrifice in Genesis 22. During that time he walked with God and lived a life of holy, fruitful obedience. Yet God chose to test his faith with a new and significant trial.

In the covenant of grace, God often tests the faith of believers in ways He deems appropriate. This serves to demonstrate how precious faith is (as the trial of faith shows it to be "much more precious than gold that perishes," 1 Peter 1:7) and is intended to glorify God—giving glory to God, which is the nature of faith (Romans 4:20).

This is the situation the apostle presents: How can one determine whether the faith professed by individuals is genuine, precious, and of the right kind that is linked to the gospel promise of salvation?

Secondly, this trial was conducted through works—specifically by an act of obedience prescribed to Abraham for that purpose. Abraham was to be presented as a model for all who would believe afterward. God provided a distinct means for testing his faith—an act of obedience so far removed from the moral law that it appeared contrary to it.

If Abraham is presented as a model of justification by works in God's sight, it must be by works that God had not required in the moral law, but rather by those that seemed to contradict it.

No one can reasonably claim justification by works merely by pointing out that Abraham was justified when he offered his only son to God. Someone could easily reply that no such work was ever required of them.

Thirdly, when Abraham complied with God's command as a test, God Himself—speaking in human terms—declared the sincerity of his faith and his justification on the basis of that obedience, that is, of His gracious acceptance of him.

This encompasses the apostle's whole purpose. It contains all he intends to prove and nothing more.

It is clear that we are not justified by our works before God, since the apostle cites a work performed by a believer many years after he had already been justified before God.

However, it is undeniably proven that "faith without works is dead also," since justifying faith, as demonstrated in Abraham's case, is faith alone that produces works of obedience. It is through such faith that a person is evidenced, declared, and pronounced justified or accepted by God. Abraham was not first justified then; he was not pronounced justified at that time as a new act; rather, he was declared justified, and that declaration was based on his works. This encapsulates the entirety of what the apostle aims to prove.

Therefore, there is no apparent contradiction between this apostle and Paul, who explicitly asserts that Abraham was not justified before God by works. James simply says that by the works Abraham performed after being justified he was manifested and declared to be so. The apostle clarifies his intent in the next verse, where he summarizes what he has proven with this example: "Do you see that faith was working together with his works, and by works faith was made perfect?" (verse 22).

He emphasizes two points to convince the individual he is addressing:

1. That true faith operates through works. Abraham's faith was effective in obedience.

2. That faith was made perfect by works; this means it was evidenced as such. The term "perfect" (teleios) does not denote internal, formal perfection in Scripture, but rather the external completion or manifestation of something. Faith was complete in respect to its intended effect when Abraham was first justified, and it was now manifested as such.

The apostle concludes, "This I have demonstrated through the example of Abraham—namely, that it is works of obedience alone that can show a person to be justified, or to possess that faith by which they may be justified." He further supports what he has affirmed in verse 23: "And the Scripture was fulfilled which says, 'Abraham believed God, and it was accounted to him for righteousness.' And he was called the friend of God."

The apostle affirms two things here:

1. The Scripture mentioned was fulfilled. This fulfillment pertains to the justification by works that he attributes to Abraham. How this Scripture was fulfilled — whether with respect to the time it was spoken or the thing itself — can only be explained by saying that what it asserted was evidenced and declared. What Scripture had affirmed about Abraham long before was then demonstrated to be true by the works produced by his faith; thus that Scripture was accomplished. Otherwise, if we take into account the distinction he makes between faith and works, the opposition he places between them, and the interpretation given by the apostle Paul, nothing could be more contradictory to his purpose than to quote this testimony if he intended to prove our justification before God by works. Therefore this Scripture was not, nor can it be, fulfilled by Abraham's justification by works in any other way than that he was manifested to be justified through them.

2. He adds that, as a result, he was called "Abraham My friend." This is affirmed in Isaiah 41:8 and also in 2 Chronicles 20:7. That title bears the same significance as his being justified by works: he was not called this merely as a justified person, but as one who had received unique privileges from God and responded by living a holy life before Him. Thus his being called "Abraham My friend" was God's approval of his faith and obedience, which is the justification by works that the apostle asserts.

Based on this, he draws a double conclusion (I will not reiterate the instance of Rahab, as it is of the same nature and has been addressed before):

1. Regarding his current argument, in verse 24.

2. Concerning the entirety of his design, in verse 26.

The first conclusion is, "You see then that a man is justified by works, and not by faith only." He addresses those he aims to convince of the futility of supposing they are justified by a dead faith—a lifeless shell of faith, mere assent to the truth of the gospel, a profession consistent with all kinds of impiety and entirely devoid of good fruits. He emphasizes that they can see what kind of faith is required for justification and salvation. Abraham was declared righteous, justified, by the faith that worked through his actions, and not by the kind of faith they claim to possess. A man is justified by works, as Abraham was when he offered his son to God—what he truly was by faith long before, as Scripture testifies, was then evidenced and declared through his actions. Therefore let no one suppose that by the faith they boast of anyone can be justified, since what justified Abraham was that which was evidenced by its fruits.

He presents that significant conclusion — which he has demonstrated throughout his argument and initially set out to confirm — in verse 26: "For as the body without the spirit is dead, so faith without works is dead also." A lifeless body and faith without works are equally dead for the purposes of both natural and spiritual life. This was the point the apostle aimed to make from the beginning — to expose the emptiness of a fruitless profession of faith — and he has supplied ample reason and testimony to prove it.

www.ingramcontent.com/pod-product-compliance
Lightning Source LLC
Chambersburg PA
CBHW031052080526
44587CB00011B/659